Quick Start Training for IBM z/OS Application Developers, Volume 2

VSAM, IMS DB, Intermediate DB2

Robert Wingate

ISBN 13: 978-1717284594

Disclaimer

The contents of this book are based upon the author's understanding of and experience with the following IBM products: VSAM, IMS and DB2. Every attempt has been made to provide correct information. However, the author and publisher do not guarantee the accuracy of every detail, nor do they assume responsibility for information included in or omitted from it. All of the information in this book should be used at your own risk.

Copyright

The contents of this book may not be copied in whole, or in part, without the explicit written permission of the author. The contents are intended for personal use only. Secondary distribution for gain is not allowed. Any alteration of the contents is absolutely forbidden.

Copyright, 2018 by Robert Wingate

ISBN-13: 978-1717284594

ISBN-10: 1717284590

DB2, DB2 UDB, UDB, and MVS are all registered trademarks of the IBM Corporation.

Dedicated to Jim Stuart, whose passion, skills, optimism and selfless leadership was an inspiration to me early in my computer services career at EDS.

Contents

Introduction 11
   Welcome 11
   Assumptions: 11
   Approach to Learning 11
Chapter One: Virtual Storage Access Method (VSAM) 15
   Introduction 15
   Types of VSAM Files 16
      Key Sequence Data Set (KSDS) 16
      Entry Sequence Data Set (ESDS) 16
      Relative Record Data Set (RRDS) 16
   Creating VSAM Files 16
   Loading and Unloading VSAM Files 18
   VSAM Updates with File Manager 20
   Application Programming with VSAM 27
      COBOL Program to Read Records (COBVS1) 27
      PLI Program to Read Records (PLIVS1) 29
      COBOL Program to Add Records (COBVS2) 31
      PLI Program to Add Records (PLIVS2) 33
      COBOL Program to Update Records (COBVS3) 35
      PLI Program to Update Records (PLIVS3) 37
      COBOL Program to Delete Records (COBVS4) 40
      PLI Program to Delete Records (PLIVS4) 42
      COBOL Program to Retrieve Records Sequentially (COBVS5) 45
      PLI Program to Retrieve Records Sequentially (PLIVS5) 47
   Creating and Accessing Alternate Indexes 49
      COBOL Program to Read Alternate Index (COBVS6) 52
      PLI Program to Read Alternate Index (PLIVS6) 56
   Other VSAM JCL 59
      JCL to CREATE ESDS 59
      JCL to CREATE RRDS 59
      JCL to LIST DATASET INFORMATION 60
   VSAM File Status Codes 62
   Chapter One Questions 64
Chapter Two: Information Management System (IMS) 67
   Designing and Creating IMS Databases 67
      Sample System Specification 67
      Database Descriptor (DBD) 70
      Program Specification Block   (PSB) 74

- IMS Application Programming Basics 75
  - The IMS Program Interface 75
  - Loading an IMS Database 80
  - Reading a Segment (GU) 92
  - Reading a Database Sequentially (GN) 98
  - Updating a Segment (GHU/REPL) 106
  - Deleting a Segment (GHU/DLET) 113
  - Inserting Child Segments 119
  - Reading Child Segments Sequentially (GNP) 130
  - Inserting Child Segments Down the Hierarchy (3 levels) 141
  - Read Child Segments Down the Hierarchy (3 levels) 153
- Additional IMS Programming Features 167
  - Retrieve Segments Using Searchable Fields 167
  - Retrieve Segments Using Boolean SSAs 175
  - Command Codes 184
  - Summary of Command Codes 194
  - Committing and Rolling Back Changes 196
  - Performing Checkpoint Restart 214
- IMS Programming Guidelines 234
- Chapter Two Questions 235

Chapter Three: Intermediate DB2 239
- Data Setup 239
- Stored Procedures 242
  - Types of stored procedures 242
  - Examples of Stored Procedures 243
  - Stored Procedure Error Handling 256
  - More Stored Procedure Examples 259
- User Defined Functions 273
  - Types of UDF 273
  - Examples of UDFs 273
- Triggers 287
  - Types of triggers 287
  - Timings of triggers 288
  - Examples of Triggers 288
- Referential Integrity 294
  - Referential Constraints Overview 294
  - Adding a Foreign Key Relationship 295
  - Deleting a Record from the Parent Table 296
- Special Tables 298
  - Temporal and Archive Tables 298

    Business Time Example 299
    Materialized Query Tables 307
    Temporary Tables 309
    Auxiliary Tables 311
XML DATA 320
    Introduction to XML 320
    Basic XML Concepts 320
    DB2 Support for XML 323
    XML Example Operations 323
    Schema Validation for XML 326
    XML Built-In Functions 330
Performance 333
    Creating and Using Explain Data 333
    The EXPLAIN Statement 335
    Visual Explain Using Data Studio 342
    Stage 1 versus Stage 2 Predicates 346
    Basic Query Optimization: 349
    Best Practices 349
    DB2 Trace 350
    Trace Types 350
    Accounting Trace Basics 351
    DB2 Trace Commands 351
Special Project 354
    Project Requirements 354
    Project DDL 355
    Initial Testing 358
    Stored Procedures and Programs for Data Access 363
    Special Project Wrap-up 377
Chapter Three Questions 378
APPENDICES 389
Chapter Questions and Answers 389
    Chapter One: VSAM 389
    Chapter Two: IMS DB 393
    Chapter Three: Intermediate DB2 399
Additional Resources 417
Index 419
Sources 421
Other Titles by Robert Wingate 423
About the Author 429

Introduction

Welcome

Congratulations on your purchase of **Quick Start Training for IBM z/OS Application Developers, Volume 2**. This series will teach you the basic information and skills you need to develop applications on IBM mainframes running z/OS. The instruction, examples and sample programs in this book are a fast track to becoming productive as quickly as possible using VSAM, IMS and DB2. The content is easy to read and digest, well organized and focused on honing real job skills. IBM z/OS Quick Start Training for Application Developers, Volume 2 is a key step in the direction of mastering IBM application development so you'll be ready to join a technical team.

This is not an "everything you'll ever need to know" book. Rather, this text will teach you what you need to know to become **productive quickly** with VSAM, IMS and intermediate DB2. For additional detail, you can download and reference the IBM manuals and Redbooks associated with these products.

Assumptions:

While I do not assume that you know a great deal about IBM mainframe programming, I do assume that you've logged into an IBM mainframe and know your way around. Also I assume that you have a working knowledge of computer programming in some language (for this text, I assume either COBOL or PLI). All in all, I assume you have:

1. A working knowledge of ISPF navigation and basic operations such as creating data sets.

2. A basic understanding of structured programming concepts and experience with either COBOL or PLI.

3. A basic understanding of SQL.

4. Access to a mainframe computer running z/OS with IMS and DB2 (and having COBOL and/or PLI compilers available).

Approach to Learning

I suggest you follow along and do the examples yourself in your own test environment. There's nothing like hands-on experience. Going through the motions will help you learn faster.

If you do not have access to a mainframe system through your job, I can recommend Mathru Technologies. You can rent a mainframe account from them at a very affordable rate, and this includes access to DB2 (at this writing they offer **DB2 version 10**). Their environment supports COBOL and PLI as well. The URL to the Mathru web site is:

http://mathrutech.com/index.html

Besides the instruction and examples, I've included questions at the end of each chapter. I recommend that you answer these and then check yourself against the answers in the back of the book.

Knowledge, experience and practice questions. Will that guarantee that you'll succeed as an IBM z/OS application developer? Of course, nothing is guaranteed in life. But if you put sufficient effort into this well-rounded training plan that includes all three of the above, I believe you have a very good chance of becoming productive as an IBM Application Developer as soon as possible. This is your chance to get a quick start!

Best of luck!

Robert Wingate
IBM Certified Application Developer – DB2 11 for z/OS

Chapter One: Virtual Storage Access Method (VSAM)

Introduction

Virtual Storage Access Method (VSAM) is an IBM DASD (direct access storage device) file storage access method. It has been used for many years, including with the Multiple Virtual Storage (MVS) architecture and now in z/OS. VSAM offers four data set organizations:

- Key Sequenced Data Set (KSDS)
- Entry Sequenced Data Set (ESDS)
- Relative Record Data Set (RRDS)
- Linear Data Set (LDS)

The KSDS, RRDS and ESDS organizations all are record-based. The LDS organization uses a sequence of pages without a predefined record structure.

VSAM records are either fixed or variable length. Records are organized in fixed-size blocks called Control Intervals (CIs). The CI's are organized into larger structures called Control Areas (CAs). Control Interval sizes are measured in bytes — for example 4 kilobytes — while Control Area sizes are measured in disk tracks or cylinders. When a VSAM file is read, a complete Control Interval will be transferred to memory.

The Access Method Services utility program `IDCAMS` is used to define and delete VSAM data sets. In addition, you can write custom programs in COBOL, PLI and Assembler to access VSAM datasets using Data Definition (DD) statements in Job Control Language (JCL), or via dynamic allocation or in online regions such as in Customer Information Control System (CICS).

Types of VSAM Files

Key Sequence Data Set (KSDS)
This organization type is the most commonly used. Each record has one or more key fields and a record can be retrieved (or inserted) by key value. This provides random access to data. Records are of variable length. IMS uses KSDS files (as we'll see in the next chapter).

Entry Sequence Data Set (ESDS)
This organization keeps records in the order in which they were entered. Records must be accessed sequentially. This organization is used by IMS for overflow datasets.

Relative Record Data Set (RRDS)
This organization is based on record retrieval number; record 1, record 2, etc. This provides random access but the program must have a way of knowing which record number it is looking for.

Linear Data Set (LDS)
This organization is a byte-stream data set. It is rarely used by application programs.

We'll focus on KSDS files because they are the most commonly used and the most useful.

A KSDS cluster consists of following two components:

- **Index** – the index component of the KSDS cluster is comprised of the list of key values for the records in the cluster with pointers to the corresponding records in the data component. The index component relates the key of each record to the record's relative location in the data set. When a record is added or deleted, this index is updated.

- **Data** – the data component of the KSDS cluster contains the actual data. Each record in the data component of a KSDS cluster contains a key field with same number of characters and occurs in the same relative position in each record.

Creating VSAM Files
You create VSAM files using the `IDCAMS` utility. Here is the meaning of the keywords in the control statement.

NAME	The cluster name which is then extended one node for the data and index physical files. See example below.
RECSZ	The record length.
TRK	The space allocated for the file. It can be in tracks or cylinders.
FREESPACE	How much free space to leave on each control interval.
KEYS	The length and displacement of the key field.
CISZ	The Control Interval Size specified in bytes
VOLUMES	The DASD volume(s) which will physically store the data.
INDEX	The data set name of the index file.
DATA	The data set name that houses the data records.

Here is sample JCL:

```
//USER01D JOB MSGLEVEL=(1,1),NOTIFY=&SYSUID
//*
//**********************************************
//* DEFINE VSAM KSDS CLUSTER
//**********************************************
//JS010    EXEC PGM=IDCAMS
//SYSUDUMP DD SYSOUT=*
//SYSPRINT DD SYSOUT=*
//SYSOUT   DD SYSOUT=*
//SYSIN    DD *
  DEFINE CLUSTER(NAME(USER01.EMPLOYEE)   -
  RECSZ(80 80)         -
  TRK(2,1)             -
  FREESPACE(5,10)      -
  KEYS(4,0)            -
  CISZ(4096)           -
  VOLUMES(DEVHD1)      -
  INDEXED)             -
  INDEX(NAME(USER01.EMPLOYEE.INDEX))   -
  DATA(NAME(USER01.EMPLOYEE.DATA))
/*
//SYSPRINT DD SYSOUT=*
//SYSUDUMP DD SYSOUT=*
```

This creates a catalog entry with two datasets, one for the record data and one for the index.

```
DSLIST - Data Sets Matching USER01.EMPLOYEE              Row 1 of 11
Command ===>                                             Scroll ===> CSR

Command - Enter "/" to select action       Message          Volume
-------------------------------------------------------------------------
         USER01.EMPLOYEE                                    *VSAM*
         USER01.EMPLOYEE.DATA                               DEVHD1
         USER01.EMPLOYEE.INDEX                              DEVHD1
***************************** End of Data Set list ****************************
```

Loading and Unloading VSAM Files

You can add data to a VSAM KSDS in several ways:

1. Copying data from a flat file

2. Using File Manager

3. Using an application program

We'll show examples of all three. First, let us design a VSAM file. For purposes of this text book, we will be creating and maintaining a simple employee file for a fictitious company. So we'll create objects with that in mind. Here are the columns and data types for our file which we will name EMPLOYEE.

Field Name	Type
EMP_ID	Numeric 4 bytes
EMP_LAST_NAME	Character(30)
EMP_FIRST_NAME	Character(20)
EMP_SERVICE_YEARS	Numeric 2 bytes
EMP_PROMOTION_DATE	Date in format YYYY-MM-DD

Now let's say we have created a simple text file in this format. We can browse it:

```
BROWSE     USER01.EMPLOYEE.LOAD                Line 00000000 Col 001 080
  Command ===>                                            Scroll ===> CSR
----+----1----+----2----+----3----+----4----+----5----+----6----+----7----+----8
******************************* Top of Data ***********************************
3217JOHNSON                   EDWARD             042017-01-01
7459STEWART                   BETTY              072016-07-31
9134FRANKLIN                  BRIANNA            032016-10-01
4720SCHULTZ                   TIM                092017-01-01
6288WILLARD                   JOE                062016-01-01
1122JENKINS                   DEBORAH            052016-09-01
```

We can use this text file to load our VSAM file. Note however that before we load, we need to sort the records into key sequence. Otherwise IDCAMS will give us an error when we try to load. You can edit the file and on the command line issue a SORT 1 4 command (space between 1 and 4) to sort the records.

```
BROWSE     USER01.EMPLOYEE.LOAD                      Line 00000000 Col 001 080
 Command ===>                                             Scroll ===> CSR
----+----1----+----2----+----3----+----4----+----5----+----6----+----7----+----8
******************************** Top of Data *********************************
1122JENKINS                     DEBORAH             052016-09-01
3217JOHNSON                     EDWARD              042017-01-01
4720SCHULTZ                     TIM                 092017-01-01
6288WILLARD                     JOE                 062016-01-01
7459STEWART                     BETTY               072016-07-31
9134FRANKLIN                    BRIANNA             032016-10-01
```

Save the file to apply the changes. Now we are ready. We can use the following IDCAMS JCL to load the VSAM file. The INDATASET is our input file, and the OUTDATASET is the VSAM file. Note that we specify the VSAM file cluster name in this job, not the DATA or INDEX file names.

```
//USER01D JOB 'NAME',MSGLEVEL=(1,1),NOTIFY=&SYSUID
//*
//***************************************************************
//* REPRO/COPY DATA FROM PS TO VSAM KSDS
//***************************************************************
//STEP90   EXEC PGM=IDCAMS                    IDCAMS - REPRO
//SYSPRINT DD SYSOUT=*
//SYSOUT   DD SYSOUT=*
//SYSUDUMP DD SYSOUT=*
//SYSIN    DD *
  REPRO -
  INDATASET (USER01.EMPLOYEE.LOAD) -
  OUTDATASET(USER01.EMPLOYEE)
/*
//*
```

Once loaded, we can view the data using the ISPF **BROWSE** function. If this doesn't work on your system, you'll need to use IBM File Manager or another tool which allows you to browse/edit VSAM files.

```
Browse            USER01.EMPLOYEE.DATA                      Top of 6
Command ===>                                                Scroll PAGE
                        Type DATA        RBA                Format CHAR
                                          Col 1
----+----10---+----2----+----3----+----4----+----5----+----6----+----7----+----
**** Top of data ****
1122JENKINS                        DEBORAH              052016-09-01
3217JOHNSON                        EDWARD               042017-01-01
4720SCHULTZ                        TIM                  092017-01-01
6288WILLARD                        JOE                  062016-01-01
7459STEWART                        BETTY                072016-07-31
9134FRANKLIN                       BRIANNA              032016-10-01
**** End of data ****
```

To edit the data you will need to use a tool such as File Manager. Let's do this next.

VSAM Updates with File Manager

You can perform adds, changes and deletes to data records in File Manager. First, it will be useful if we create a file layout to assist us with viewing and updating data. Let's create a COBOL layout as follows.

```
BROWSE      USER01.COPYLIB(EMPLOYEE) - 01.00         Line 00000000 Col 001 080
Command ===>                                                Scroll ===> CSR
*************************** Top of Data ************************************
****************************************************************
       * COBOL DECLARATION FOR VSAM FILE EMPLOYEE                *
       ****************************************************************
          01  EMPLOYEE.
              05  EMP-ID                 PIC 9(04).
              05  EMP-LAST-NAME          PIC X(30).
              05  EMP-FIRST-NAME         PIC X(20).
              05  EMP-SERVICE-YEARS      PIC 9(02).
              05  EMP-PROMOTION-DATE     PIC X(10).
              05  FILLER                 PIC X(14).
```

Now let's go to File Manager. Select File Manager from your ISPF menu (it may be different on your system). Below is the main FM menu. Select the `EDIT` option.

```
File Manager                      Primary Option Menu
Command ===>

0   Settings        Set processing options              User ID . : USER01
1   View            View data                           System ID : MATE
2   Edit            Edit data                           Appl ID . : FMN
3   Utilities       Perform utility functions           Version . : 11.1.0
4   Tapes           Tape specific functions             Terminal. : 3278
5   Disk/VSAM       Disk track and VSAM CI functions    Screen. . : 2
6   OAM             Work with OAM objects               Date. . . : 2018/03/07
7   Templates       Template and copybook utilities     Time. . . : 02:41
8   HFS             Access Hierarchical File System
9   WebSphere MQ    List, view and edit MQ data
X   Exit            Terminate File Manager
```

Enter your file name, copybook file name, and select the processing option 1.

```
File Manager                      Edit Entry Panel
Command ===>

Input Partitioned, Sequential or VSAM Data Set, or HFS file:
   Data set/path name 'USER01.EMPLOYEE'                                  +
   Member . . . . . .              (Blank or pattern for member list)
   Volume serial . .               (If not cataloged)
   Start position . .                            +
   Record limit . . .              Record sampling
   Inplace edit . . .              (Prevent inserts and deletes)
Copybook or Template:
   Data set name . .  'USER01.COPYLIB(EMPLOYEE)'
   Member . . . . . .              (Blank or pattern for member list)
Processing Options:
  Copybook/template    Start position type   Enter "/" to select option
  1  1. Above           1. Key                  Edit template    Type (1,2,S)
     2. Previous        2. RBA                  Include only selected records
     3. None            3. Record number        Binary mode, reclen 80
     4. Create dynamic  4. Formatted key        Create audit trail
```

Now you will see this screen. Notice the format is `TABL` which shows the data in list format. If you want to change it to show one record at a time, type over the `TABL` with `SNGL` (which means single record).

```
Edit              USER01.EMPLOYEE                                     Top of 6
Command ===>                                                          Scroll PAGE
        Key                        Type KSDS      RBA                 Format TABL
        EMP-ID EMP-LAST-NAME                      EMP-FIRST-NAME      EMP-SERVICE-
        #2     #3                                 #4                            #5
        ZD 1:4 AN 5:30                            AN 35:20            ZD 55:2
        <--->  <---+----1----+----2----+---->     <---+----1----+---->  <->
****** ****    Top of data    ****
000001  1122 JENKINS                              DEBORAH                       5
000002  3217 JOHNSON                              EDWARD                        4
000003  4720 SCHULTZ                              TIM                           9
000004  6288 WILLARD                              JOE                           6
000005  7459 STEWART                              BETTY                         7
000006  9134 FRANKLIN                             BRIANNA                       3
****** ****    End of data    ****
```

Now you can edit each field on the record except the key. You cannot change the key, although you can specify a different key to bring up a different record. Let's bring up employee 6288.

```
Edit              USER01.EMPLOYEE                                     Rec 1 of 6
Command ===>                                                          Scroll PAGE
Key 1122                          Type KSDS      RBA 0                Format SNGL
                                                       Top Line is 1    of 6
Current 01: EMPLOYEE                                                  Length 80
Field                   Data
EMP-ID                     1122
EMP-LAST-NAME           JENKINS
EMP-FIRST-NAME          DEBORAH
EMP-SERVICE-YEARS          5
EMP-PROMOTION-DATE      2016-09-01
FILLER
***   End of record   ***
```

Now we can change this record. Let's modify the years of service by changing it to 8.

```
Edit               USER01.EMPLOYEE                        Rec 4 of 6
Command ===>                                              Scroll PAGE
Key 6288                  Type KSDS      RBA 240          Format SNGL
                                                   Top Line is 1   of 6
Current 01: EMPLOYEE                                      Length 80
Field                Data
EMP-ID               6288
EMP-LAST-NAME        WILLARD
EMP-FIRST-NAME       JOE
EMP-SERVICE-YEARS    6
EMP-PROMOTION-DATE   2016-01-01
FILLER
*** End of record ***
```

Now you can either type SAVE on the command line or simply PF3 to exit from the record. In this case, let's press PF3 to exit the Edit screen. You will be notified that the record was updated by the message on the upper right portion of the screen.

```
File Manager                  Edit Entry Panel        1 record(s) updated
Command ===>
Input Partitioned, Sequential or VSAM Data Set, or HFS file:
   Data set/path name 'USER01.EMPLOYEE'                            +
   Member . . . . . .              (Blank or pattern for member list)
   Volume serial  . .              (If not cataloged)
   Start position . .                                      +
   Record limit . . .              Record sampling
   Inplace edit . . .              (Prevent inserts and deletes)
Copybook or Template:
   Data set name  . . 'USER01.COPYLIB(EMPLOYEE)'
   Member . . . . . .              (Blank or pattern for member list)
Processing Options:
   Copybook/template     Start position type    Enter "/" to select option
1  1. Above             1. Key                    Edit template    Type (1,2,S)
   2. Previous          2. RBA                    Include only selected records
   3. None              3. Record number          Binary mode, reclen 80
   4. Create dynamic    4. Formatted key          Create audit trail
```

Now let's see how we can insert and delete records. Actually it is pretty simple. If you are in table mode, you just use the I(nsert) command to insert a record, or the D(elete) command to delete one. Let's add a record for employee 1111 who is Sandra Smith with 9 years of service and a promotion date of 01/01/2017. To do this, type I on the first line of detail.

```
Edit                USER01.EMPLOYEE                              Rec 1 of 6
Command ===>                                                     Scroll PAGE
     Key 1122                   Type KSDS    RBA 0               Format TABL
        EMP-ID EMP-LAST-NAME               EMP-FIRST-NAME        EMP-SERVICE-
          #2   #3                          #4                              #5
          ZD 1:4 AN 5:30                   AN 35:20              ZD 55:2
          <--->  <---+----1----+----2----+---->  <---+----1----+---->      <->
I00001    1122   JENKINS                   DEBORAH                         5
000002    3217   JOHNSON                   EDWARD                          4
000003    4720   SCHULTZ                   TIM                             9
000004    6288   WILLARD                   JOE                             8
000005    7459   STEWART                   BETTY                           7
000006    9134   FRANKLIN                  BRIANNA                         3
****** ****   End of data      ****
```

Now you can enter the data. You will need to scroll to the right (PF11) to add the correct years of service and promotion date.

```
Edit                USER01.EMPLOYEE                              Rec 1 of 7
Command ===>                                                     Scroll PAGE
     Key 1122                   Type KSDS    RBA 0               Format TABL
        EMP-ID EMP-LAST-NAME               EMP-FIRST-NAME        EMP-SERVICE-
          #2   #3                          #4                              #5
          ZD 1:4 AN 5:30                   AN 35:20              ZD 55:2
          <--->  <---+----1----+----2----+---->  <---+----1----+---->      <->
000001    1122   JENKINS                   DEBORAH                         5
000002    1111   SMITH                     SANDRA                          0
000003    3217   JOHNSON                   EDWARD                          4
000004    4720   SCHULTZ                   TIM                             9
000005    6288   WILLARD                   JOE                             8
000006    7459   STEWART                   BETTY                           7
000007    9134   FRANKLIN                  BRIANNA                         3
****** ****   End of data      ****
```

You could also switch to SNGL mode to make it easier to enter the data on one page.

```
Edit                USER01.EMPLOYEE                              Rec 1 of 7
Command ===>                                                     Scroll PAGE
Key 1111                       Type KSDS    RBA 0                Format SNGL
                                                    Top Line is 1    of 6
Current 01: EMPLOYEE                                             Length 80
Field                   Data
EMP-ID                  1111
EMP-LAST-NAME           SMITH
EMP-FIRST-NAME          SANDRA
EMP-SERVICE-YEARS       9
EMP-PROMOTION-DATE      2017-01-01
FILLER
***   End of record    ***
```

Now type SAVE on the command line.

```
Edit                USER01.EMPLOYEE                          Rec 1 of 7
Command ===>        SAVE                                     Scroll PAGE
Key 1111                      Type KSDS      RBA 0           Format SNGL
                                                  Top Line is 1   of 6
Current 01: EMPLOYEE                                         Length 80
Field                    Data
EMP-ID                   1111
EMP-LAST-NAME            SMITH
EMP-FIRST-NAME           SANDRA
EMP-SERVICE-YEARS        9
EMP-PROMOTION-DATE       2017-01-01
FILLER
***   End of record    ***
```

When you press Enter you can verify the record was saved.

```
Edit                USER01.EMPLOYEE                      1 record(s) updated
Command ===>                                                 Scroll PAGE
Key 1111                      Type KSDS      RBA 0           Format SNGL
                                                  Top Line is 1   of 6
Current 01: EMPLOYEE                                         Length 80
Field                    Data
EMP-ID                   1111
EMP-LAST-NAME            SMITH
EMP-FIRST-NAME           SANDRA
EMP-SERVICE-YEARS        9
EMP-PROMOTION-DATE       2017-01-01
FILLER
***   End of record    ***
```

Finally, to delete a record, just go to TABL mode, find the record you want to delete, and use a D action. Let's delete the record we just added.

```
Edit               USER01.EMPLOYEE                           Rec 1 of 7
Command ===>                                                 Scroll PAGE
         Key 1111              Type KSDS     RBA 0           Format TABL
             EMP-ID EMP-LAST-NAME            EMP-FIRST-NAME  EMP-SERVICE-
             #2 #3                           #4                        #5
             ZD 1:4 AN 5:30                  AN 35:20            ZD 55:2
             <--->  <---+----1----+----2----+----> <---+----1----+----> <->
D00001       1111 SMITH                      SANDRA                     9
000002       1122 JENKINS                    DEBORAH                    5
000003       3217 JOHNSON                    EDWARD                     4
000004       4720 SCHULTZ                    TIM                        9
000005       6288 WILLARD                    JOE                        8
000006       7459 STEWART                    BETTY                      7
000007       9134 FRANKLIN                   BRIANNA                    3
****** ****   End of data    ****
```

When you press Enter, the record will disappear from the list. You can either type SAVE on the command line, or simply exit the file and the delete action will be saved.

```
Edit               USER01.EMPLOYEE                           1 record(s) updated
Command ===>                                                 Scroll PAGE
         Key 1122              Type KSDS     RBA 80          Format TABL
             EMP-ID EMP-LAST-NAME            EMP-FIRST-NAME  EMP-SERVICE-
             #2 #3                           #4                        #5
             ZD 1:4 AN 5:30                  AN 35:20            ZD 55:2
             <--->  <---+----1----+----2----+----> <---+----1----+----> <->
000001       1122 JENKINS                    DEBORAH                    5
000002       3217 JOHNSON                    EDWARD                     4
000003       4720 SCHULTZ                    TIM                        9
000004       6288 WILLARD                    JOE                        8
000005       7459 STEWART                    BETTY                      7
000006       9134 FRANKLIN                   BRIANNA                    3
****** ****   End of data    ****
```

Application Programming with VSAM

COBOL Program to Read Records (COBVS1)

Now it's time to use VSAM in an application program. A program to retrieve a record is not much different from reading a flat file.[1] The main difference is that with VSAM you specify the key value of the record you want to retrieve. Let's name our first program COBVS1.

In our file definition, we must reference the DD name of the VSAM cluster name. We also specify that the file is indexed, and that we will be accessing it in random mode. We specify the EMP_ID as the file key. Finally we specify a variable name that VSAM will use to return the status code from each action on the file. In VSAM we want the file status to be 00 which indicates a successful operation.

Here is our program listing. Take a few minutes to look it over. Notice that we are checking for a file status of zero which means the data operation (in this case a read) was successful.

```
       IDENTIFICATION DIVISION.
       PROGRAM-ID. COBVS1.

      ******************************************************
      *      PROGRAM TO RETRIEVE A RECORD FROM              *
      *      EMPLOYEE VSAM FILE.                            *
      ******************************************************

       ENVIRONMENT DIVISION.
       INPUT-OUTPUT SECTION.

           FILE-CONTROL.
               SELECT EMPLOYEE-VS-FILE    ASSIGN TO EMPVSFIL
               ORGANIZATION IS INDEXED
               ACCESS MODE  IS RANDOM
               RECORD KEY   IS EMP-ID
               FILE STATUS  IS EMP-FILE-STATUS.

       DATA DIVISION.

       FILE SECTION.
       FD EMPLOYEE-VS-FILE.
           01 EMPLOYEE.
               05 EMP-ID              PIC 9(04).
               05 EMP-LAST-NAME       PIC X(30).
               05 EMP-FIRST-NAME      PIC X(20).
```

---

[1] If you are not familiar with the basics of how to read a file in COBOL, you might want to check out volume 1 of this Quick Start Training for z/OS Application Developers series. It covers basic COBOL.

```cobol
            05  EMP-SERVICE-YEARS      PIC 9(02).
            05  EMP-PROMOTION-DATE     PIC X(10).
            05  FILLER                 PIC X(14).

       WORKING-STORAGE SECTION.

           01  WS-FLAGS.
               05  SW-END-OF-FILE-SWITCH   PIC X(1) VALUE 'N'.
                   88  SW-END-OF-FILE               VALUE 'Y'.
                   88  SW-NOT-END-OF-FILE           VALUE 'N'.

           01  EMP-FILE-STATUS.
                   05  EMPFILE-STAT1     PIC X.
                   05  EMPFILE-STAT2     PIC X.


       PROCEDURE DIVISION.

               PERFORM P100-INITIALIZATION.
               PERFORM P200-MAINLINE.
               PERFORM P300-TERMINATION.
               GOBACK.

           P100-INITIALIZATION.

               DISPLAY 'COBVS1 - SAMPLE COBOL PROGRAM: VSAM INPUT'.
               OPEN INPUT  EMPLOYEE-VS-FILE.

               INITIALIZE EMPLOYEE.
               MOVE '3217' TO EMP-ID.

          P200-MAINLINE.

       *    READ THE INPUT FILE TO GET THE REQUESTED RECORD
       *    AND DISPLAY THE DATA VALUES

               READ EMPLOYEE-VS-FILE
               IF  EMP-FILE-STATUS = '00' THEN
       *           DISPLAY THE DATA
                   DISPLAY 'EMPLOYEE DATA IS ' EMPLOYEE
               ELSE
                   DISPLAY 'RECORD WAS NOT FOUND'.

          P300-TERMINATION.

               CLOSE EMPLOYEE-VS-FILE.

               DISPLAY 'COBVS1 - SUCCESSFULLY ENDED'.

       *    END OF SOURCE CODE
```

Compile and link (according to the procedures in your installation), and then run the program. Here is our output:

```
SDSF OUTPUT DISPLAY USER01D  JOB05473  DSID    101 LINE 1       COLUMNS 02- 81
 COMMAND INPUT ===>                                              SCROLL ===> CSR
COBVS1 - SAMPLE COBOL PROGRAM: VSAM INPUT
EMPLOYEE DATA IS 3217JOHNSON                     EDWARD                042017-01
COBVS1 - SUCCESSFULLY ENDED
```

As you can see, we successfully retrieved the record for employee 3217. That's all there is to it. Not much different than reading a flat file, but obviously more powerful because of the random access to the data based on the record key.

PLI Program to Read Records (PLIVS1)

A PLI version of the program is named PLIVS1, and the listing is here. In PLI we define the VSAM file by specifying DIRECT INPUT KEYED and additionally ENV(VSAM). We also intercept certain PLI oncodes to detect record not found, and duplicate record error conditions. In another difference from COBOL, we specify the record key in PLI using the READ statement.

```
READ FILE (EMPVSFIL) INTO (EMPLOYEE) KEY(EMP_ID);
```

Finally, notice that we trap some oncodes that pertains to VSAM, such as record not found, and duplicate record. Here's the program.

```
PLIVS1: PROC OPTIONS(MAIN) REORDER;
/*****************************************************************
* PROGRAM NAME :   PROGRAM TO READ A RECORD FROM A VSAM FILE.    *
*****************************************************************/

/*****************************************************************
/*              F I L E S   U S E D                               *
*****************************************************************/

   DCL EMPVSFIL FILE RECORD DIRECT INPUT KEYED ENV(VSAM);

/*****************************************************************
/*              W O R K I N G   S T O R A G E                     *
*****************************************************************/

   DCL SW_END_OF_FILE         STATIC BIT(01) INIT('0'B);

   DCL 01 EMPLOYEE,
          05 EMP_ID            PIC'9999',
          05 EMP_LAST_NAME     CHAR (30),
          05 EMP_FIRST_NAME    CHAR (20),
          05 EMP_SERVICE_YEARS PIC '99',
```

```
            05 EMP_PROMOTION_DATE   CHAR (10),
            05 FILLER               CHAR (14);

/*********************************************************************
/*                O N   C O N D I T I O N S                          *
*********************************************************************/

   ON ENDFILE (EMPVSFIL) SW_END_OF_FILE = '1'B;

   ON KEY(EMPVSFIL) BEGIN;
      IF ONCODE=51 THEN PUT SKIP LIST ('NOT FOUND ' || EMP_ID);
      IF ONCODE=52 THEN PUT SKIP LIST ('DUPLICATE ' || EMP_ID);
   END;

/*********************************************************************
/*                P R O G R A M   M A I N L I N E                    *
*********************************************************************/

CALL P100_INITIALIZATION;
CALL P200_MAINLINE;
CALL P300_TERMINATION;

P100_INITIALIZATION: PROC;

   PUT SKIP LIST ('PLIVS1: VSAM FILE INPUT');
   OPEN FILE (EMPVSFIL);
   EMPLOYEE = '';

END P100_INITIALIZATION;

P200_MAINLINE: PROC;

   /*  READ THE INPUT FILE, AND WRITE THE RECORD TO OUTPUT */

   EMP_ID = '3217';
   READ FILE (EMPVSFIL) INTO (EMPLOYEE) KEY(EMP_ID);
   PUT SKIP DATA (EMPLOYEE);

END P200_MAINLINE;

P300_TERMINATION: PROC;

   CLOSE FILE(EMPVSFIL);
   PUT SKIP LIST ('PLIVS1 - SUCCESSFULLY ENDED');

END P300_TERMINATION;

END PLIVS1;
```

Here is the output from running the PLI program.

```
PLIVS1: VSAM FILE INPUT
EMPLOYEE.EMP_ID=3217    EMPLOYEE.EMP_LAST_NAME='JOHNSON          '
```

```
EMPLOYEE.EMP_FIRST_NAME='EDWARD            '  EMPLOYEE.EMP_SERVICE_YEARS=04
EMPLOYEE.EMP_PROMOTION_DATE='2017-01-01'      EMPLOYEE.FILLER='493082938     '
PLIVS1 - SUCCESSFULLY ENDED
```

COBOL Program to Add Records (COBVS2)

Now let's do a program `COBVS2` to add a record. Let's add back the record for the employee we previously deleted. This is employee 1111 who is Sandra Smith with 9 years of service and a promotion date of 01/01/2017. Here's how the add program will look.

Notice we have opened the VSAM file for input and output (**I-O**). We simply load the record structure, and then do the `WRITE`. Also we are checking file status after opening, writing and closing the file. A list of VSAM file status codes is provided at the end of this chapter.

```
       IDENTIFICATION DIVISION.
       PROGRAM-ID. COBVS2.

      ******************************************************
      *      PROGRAM TO ADD A RECCORED TO THE              *
      *      EMPLOYEE VSAM FILE.                           *
      ******************************************************

       ENVIRONMENT DIVISION.
       INPUT-OUTPUT SECTION.

           FILE-CONTROL.
               SELECT EMPLOYEE-VS-FILE   ASSIGN TO EMPVSFIL
                  ORGANIZATION IS INDEXED
                  ACCESS MODE  IS RANDOM
                  RECORD KEY   IS EMP-ID
                  FILE STATUS  IS EMP-FILE-STATUS.

       DATA DIVISION.

       FILE SECTION.
       FD EMPLOYEE-VS-FILE.
           01   EMPLOYEE.
               05 EMP-ID                PIC 9(04).
               05 EMP-LAST-NAME         PIC X(30).
               05 EMP-FIRST-NAME        PIC X(20).
               05 EMP-SERVICE-YEARS     PIC 9(02).
               05 EMP-PROMOTION-DATE    PIC X(10).
               05 FILLER                PIC X(14).

       WORKING-STORAGE SECTION.

           01 WS-FLAGS.
               05   SW-END-OF-FILE-SWITCH    PIC X(1) VALUE 'N'.
```

```cobol
              88  SW-END-OF-FILE              VALUE 'Y'.
              88  SW-NOT-END-OF-FILE          VALUE 'N'.

       01  EMP-FILE-STATUS.
              05  EMPFILE-STAT1       PIC X.
              05  EMPFILE-STAT2       PIC X.

   PROCEDURE DIVISION.

       PERFORM P100-INITIALIZATION.
       PERFORM P200-MAINLINE.
       PERFORM P300-TERMINATION.
       GOBACK.

   P100-INITIALIZATION.

       DISPLAY 'COBVS2 - SAMPLE COBOL PROGRAM: VSAM INSERT'.
       OPEN I-O EMPLOYEE-VS-FILE.

       IF  EMP-FILE-STATUS = '00' OR '97' THEN
          NEXT SENTENCE
       ELSE
          DISPLAY 'ERROR ON OPEN - FILE STATUS ' EMP-FILE-STATUS.

       INITIALIZE EMPLOYEE.

   P200-MAINLINE.

   *   SET UP DATA ON THE RECORD STRUCTURE AND
   *   THEN WRITE THE RECORD

       MOVE '1111' TO EMP-ID
       MOVE 'SMITH'       TO    EMP-LAST-NAME
       MOVE 'SANDRA'      TO    EMP-FIRST-NAME
       MOVE '09'          TO    EMP-SERVICE-YEARS
       MOVE '2017-01-01' TO    EMP-PROMOTION-DATE

       WRITE EMPLOYEE

       IF  EMP-FILE-STATUS = '00' THEN
   *       DISPLAY THE DATA
          DISPLAY 'ADD SUCCESSFUL - DATA IS ' EMPLOYEE
       ELSE
          DISPLAY 'ERROR ON INSERT - FILE STATUS ' EMP-FILE-STATUS.

   P300-TERMINATION.

       CLOSE EMPLOYEE-VS-FILE.

       DISPLAY 'COBVS2 - SUCCESSFULLY ENDED'.

   *   END OF SOURCE CODE
```

Now when we compile, link and run the program we get this output.

```
COBVS2 - SAMPLE COBOL PROGRAM: VSAM INSERT
ADD SUCCESSFUL - DATA IS 1111SMITH                      SANDRA              092017-01-01
COBVS2 - SUCCESSFULLY ENDED
```

And we can verify that the record was added by checking File Manager.

```
 View             USER01.EMPLOYEE                               Top of 7
 Command ===>                                                   Scroll PAGE
    Key                    Type KSDS     RBA                    Format TABL
       EMP-ID  EMP-LAST-NAME             EMP-FIRST-NAME         EMP-SERVICE-
         #2   #3                            #4                        #5
         ZD 1:4 AN 5:30                    AN 35:20                  ZD 55:2
         <--->  <---+----1----+----2----+----> <---+----1----+---->    <->
 ****** ****  Top of data  ****
 000001  1111 SMITH                        SANDRA                      9
 000002  1122 JENKINS                      DEBORAH                     5
 000003  3217 JOHNSON                      EDWARD                      4
 000004  4720 SCHULTZ                      TIM                         9
 000005  6288 WILLARD                      JOE                         8
 000006  7459 STEWART                      BETTY                       7
 000007  9134 FRANKLIN                     BRIANNA                     3
 ****** ****  End of data  ****
```

PLI Program to Add Records (PLIVS2)

The PLI version of the program is here. Notice that we define the file for output. Also we've set an **ON KEY** condition to trap a duplicate record condition (oncode 52).

```
PLIVS2: PROC OPTIONS(MAIN) REORDER;
/****************************************************************
* PROGRAM NAME :   PROGRAM TO ADD A RECORD TO A VSAM FILE.      *
****************************************************************/

   DCL ONCODE BUILTIN;

/****************************************************************
/*              F I L E S    U S E D                             *
****************************************************************/

   DCL EMPVSFIL FILE RECORD DIRECT OUTPUT KEYED ENV(VSAM);

/****************************************************************
/*              W O R K I N G    S T O R A G E                   *
****************************************************************/

   DCL SW_END_OF_FILE         STATIC BIT(01) INIT('0'B);

   DCL SW__IO_ERROR           STATIC BIT(01) INIT('0'B);

   DCL 01  EMPLOYEE,
```

```pli
                05 EMP_ID               PIC'9999',
                05 EMP_LAST_NAME        CHAR (30),
                05 EMP_FIRST_NAME       CHAR (20),
                05 EMP_SERVICE_YEARS    PIC  '99',
                05 EMP_PROMOTION_DATE   CHAR (10),
                05 FILLER               CHAR (14);
/********************************************************************
/*              O N   C O N D I T I O N S                           *
********************************************************************/

   ON ENDFILE (EMPVSFIL) SW_END_OF_FILE = '1'B;

   ON KEY(EMPVSFIL) BEGIN;
      SELECT(ONCODE);
         WHEN (51)
            DO;
               PUT SKIP LIST ('KEY NOT FOUND ' || EMP_ID);
               SW_IO_ERROR = '1'B;
            END;
         WHEN (52)
            DO;
               PUT SKIP LIST ('DUPLICATE KEY ' || EMP_ID);
               SW_IO_ERROR = '1'B;
            END;
         OTHERWISE;

      END; /* SELECT */

   END; /* ON KEY */

/********************************************************************
/*              P R O G R A M   M A I N L I N E                     *
********************************************************************/

  CALL P100_INITIALIZATION;
  CALL P200_MAINLINE;
  CALL P300_TERMINATION;

  P100_INITIALIZATION: PROC;

     PUT SKIP LIST ('PLIVS2: VSAM FILE ADD');
     OPEN FILE (EMPVSFIL);
     EMPLOYEE = '';
     SW_ERROR = '0'B;

  END P100_INITIALIZATION;

  P200_MAINLINE: PROC;

     /*   WRITE THE RECORD TO OUTPUT */

     EMP_ID = '1111';
     EMP_LAST_NAME   = 'SMITH';
```

```
       EMP_FIRST_NAME     = 'SANDRA';
       EMP_SERVICE_YEARS  = '09';
       EMP_PROMOTION_DATE = '2017-01-01';

       WRITE FILE (EMPVSFIL) FROM (EMPLOYEE) KEYFROM(EMP_ID);

       IF SW_IO_ERROR THEN
          PUT SKIP LIST ('ADD FAILED FOR EMPLOYEE ' || EMP_ID);
       ELSE
          PUT SKIP LIST ('SUCCESSFUL ADD FOR EMPLOYEE ' || EMP_ID);

  END P200_MAINLINE;

  P300_TERMINATION: PROC;

       CLOSE FILE(EMPVSFIL);

       PUT SKIP LIST ('PLIVS2 - SUCCESSFULLY ENDED');

  END P300_TERMINATION;

  END PLIVS2;
```

And here is the result:

```
       PLIVS2: VSAM FILE INPUT
       SUCCESSFUL ADD FOR RECORD 1111
       PLIVS2 - SUCCESSFULLY ENDED
```

We can test the duplicate record logic by running the program a second time. This time, our output is as follows:

```
       PLIVS2: VSAM FILE ADD
       DUPLICATE KEY 1111
       ADD FAILED FOR EMPLOYEE 1111
       PLIVS2 - SUCCESSFULLY ENDED
```

Great, it correctly reported the error. Always test your error logic to make sure it works!

COBOL Program to Update Records (COBVS3)

For COBVS3 we will update a record. To do that we must first read the record into the record structure, make modifications and then REWRITE the record. Let's say we need to change the years of service for Sandra Smith from 9 to 10. Here is a program that would do this. Note that we opened the file for I-O.

```
       IDENTIFICATION DIVISION.
       PROGRAM-ID. COBVS3.
```

```
      ************************************************
      *     PROGRAM TO RETRIEVE AND UPDATE A RECORD   *
      *        ON THE EMPLOYEE VSAM FILE.             *
      ************************************************

       ENVIRONMENT DIVISION.
       INPUT-OUTPUT SECTION.

           FILE-CONTROL.
              SELECT EMPLOYEE-VS-FILE    ASSIGN TO EMPVSFIL
                 ORGANIZATION IS INDEXED
                 ACCESS MODE  IS RANDOM
                 RECORD KEY   IS EMP-ID
                 FILE STATUS  IS EMP-FILE-STATUS.

       DATA DIVISION.

       FILE SECTION.
       FD EMPLOYEE-VS-FILE.
           01   EMPLOYEE.
                05  EMP-ID               PIC 9(04).
                05  EMP-LAST-NAME        PIC X(30).
                05  EMP-FIRST-NAME       PIC X(20).
                05  EMP-SERVICE-YEARS    PIC 9(02).
                05  EMP-PROMOTION-DATE   PIC X(10).
                05  FILLER               PIC X(14).

       WORKING-STORAGE SECTION.

           01 WS-FLAGS.
                05   SW-END-OF-FILE-SWITCH   PIC X(1) VALUE 'N'.
                   88   SW-END-OF-FILE                VALUE 'Y'.
                   88   SW-NOT-END-OF-FILE            VALUE 'N'.

           01  EMP-FILE-STATUS.
                    05   EMPFILE-STAT1      PIC X.
                    05   EMPFILE-STAT2      PIC X.

       PROCEDURE DIVISION.

           PERFORM P100-INITIALIZATION.
           PERFORM P200-MAINLINE.
           PERFORM P300-TERMINATION.
           GOBACK.

       P100-INITIALIZATION.

           DISPLAY 'COBVS2 - SAMPLE COBOL PROGRAM: VSAM UPDATE'.
           OPEN I-O EMPLOYEE-VS-FILE.

           IF  EMP-FILE-STATUS = '00' OR '97' THEN
              NEXT SENTENCE
           ELSE
```

```
              DISPLAY 'ERROR ON OPEN - FILE STATUS ' EMP-FILE-STATUS.

          INITIALIZE EMPLOYEE.

      P200-MAINLINE.

 *    FIRST READ THE SPECIFIED RECORD.  THEN
 *    MAKE CHANGES TO THE RECORD. FINALLY
 *    REWRITE THE RECORD TO THE VSAM FILE.

      MOVE '1111' TO EMP-ID
      READ EMPLOYEE-VS-FILE

      IF  EMP-FILE-STATUS = '00' THEN
         NEXT SENTENCE
      ELSE
         DISPLAY 'ERROR ON READ - FILE STATUS ' EMP-FILE-STATUS.

      MOVE '10'          TO    EMP-SERVICE-YEARS

      REWRITE EMPLOYEE

      IF  EMP-FILE-STATUS = '00' THEN
         DISPLAY 'UPDATE SUCCESSFUL - DATA IS ' EMPLOYEE
      ELSE
         DISPLAY 'ERROR ON REWRITE - FILE STATUS ' EMP-FILE-STATUS.

      P300-TERMINATION.

          CLOSE EMPLOYEE-VS-FILE.

          DISPLAY 'COBVS3 - SUCCESSFULLY ENDED'.

 *        END OF SOURCE CODE
```

Now let's compile, link and run. Here's the output.

```
COBVS3 - SAMPLE COBOL PROGRAM: VSAM UPDATE
UPDATE SUCCESSFUL - DATA IS 1111SMITH                    SANDRA           102017-01-01
COBVS3 - SUCCESSFULLY ENDED
```

And we can verify that the change took place by checking in File Manager.

```
View               USER01.EMPLOYEE                              Rec 1 of 7
 Command ===>                                                   Scroll PAGE
 Key 1111                   Type KSDS      RBA 0                Format SNGL
                                                      Top Line is 1    of 6
 Current 01: EMPLOYEE                                           Length 80
 Field                 Data
 EMP-ID                1111
 EMP-LAST-NAME         SMITH
 EMP-FIRST-NAME        SANDRA
 EMP-SERVICE-YEARS     10
```

```
EMP-PROMOTION-DATE   2017-01-01
FILLER               ..............
***  End of record  ***
```

PLI Program to Update Records (PLIVS3)

Here is the PLI version of the program. Notice we define the VSAM file for update.

```
PLIVS3: PROC OPTIONS(MAIN) REORDER;
/*******************************************************************
* PROGRAM NAME :   PLIVS3 PROGRAM TO UPDATE A RECORD ON A VSAM FILE.*
********************************************************************/

/*******************************************************************
/*                  F I L E S   U S E D                             *
********************************************************************/

   DCL EMPVSFIL FILE RECORD DIRECT UPDATE KEYED ENV(VSAM);

/*******************************************************************
/*                  W O R K I N G   S T O R A G E                   *
********************************************************************/

   DCL ONCODE                 BUILTIN;
   DCL SW_IO_ERROR            STATIC BIT(01) INIT('0'B);

   DCL 01  EMPLOYEE,
           05 EMP_ID             PIC'9999',
           05 EMP_LAST_NAME      CHAR (30),
           05 EMP_FIRST_NAME     CHAR (20),
           05 EMP_SERVICE_YEARS  PIC  '99',
           05 EMP_PROMOTION_DATE CHAR (10),
           05 FILLER             CHAR (14);

/*******************************************************************
/*                  O N   C O N D I T I O N S                       *
********************************************************************/

   ON KEY(EMPVSFIL) BEGIN;
      SELECT(ONCODE);
         WHEN (51)
            DO;
               PUT SKIP LIST ('KEY NOT FOUND ' || EMP_ID);
               SW_IO_ERROR = '1'B;
            END;
         WHEN (52)
            DO;
               PUT SKIP LIST ('DUPLICATE KEY ' || EMP_ID);
               SW_IO_ERROR = '1'B;
            END;
         OTHERWISE;

      END; /* SELECT */
```

```
      END; /* ON KEY */

/*******************************************************************
/*                  P R O G R A M   M A I N L I N E                *
*******************************************************************/

   CALL P100_INITIALIZATION;
   CALL P200_MAINLINE;
   CALL P300_TERMINATION;

   P100_INITIALIZATION: PROC;

      PUT SKIP LIST ('PLIVS3: VSAM FILE UPDATE');
      OPEN FILE (EMPVSFIL);
      EMPLOYEE = '';

   END P100_INITIALIZATION;

   P200_MAINLINE: PROC;

      /*   WRITE THE RECORD TO OUTPUT */

      EMP_ID = '1111';
      READ FILE (EMPVSFIL) INTO (EMPLOYEE) KEY(EMP_ID);

      IF SW_IO_ERROR THEN
         DO;
            PUT SKIP LIST ('ERROR - RECORD NOT UPDATED');
            RETURN;
         END;

      EMP_SERVICE_YEARS = '10';

      REWRITE FILE (EMPVSFIL) FROM(EMPLOYEE) KEY(EMP_ID);

      IF SW_IO_ERROR THEN
         PUT SKIP LIST ('ERROR - RECORD NOT UPDATED');
      ELSE
         PUT SKIP LIST ('SUCCESSFUL REWRITE FOR EMPLOYEE '
            || EMP_ID);

   END P200_MAINLINE;

   P300_TERMINATION: PROC;

      CLOSE FILE(EMPVSFIL);

      PUT SKIP LIST ('PLIVS3 - SUCCESSFULLY ENDED');

   END P300_TERMINATION;

   END PLIVS3;
```

And the output from running PLIVS3:

```
PLIVS3: VSAM FILE UPDATE
SUCCESSFUL UPDATE FOR RECORD 1111
EMPLOYEE.EMP_ID=1111       EMPLOYEE.EMP_LAST_NAME='SMITH                         '
EMPLOYEE.EMP_FIRST_NAME='SANDRA              '  EMPLOYEE.EMP_SERVICE_YEARS=10
EMPLOYEE.EMP_PROMOTION_DATE='2017-01-01'        EMPLOYEE.FILLER='              '
PLIVS3 - SUCCESSFULLY ENDED
```

COBOL Program to Delete Records (COBVS4)

Now let's write program COBVS4 to delete the Sandra Smith record we just worked with. Actually it will be similar to the update program, except we don't have to first retrieve the record before deleting. And of course we will use the verb DELETE instead of REWRITE.

```
         IDENTIFICATION DIVISION.
         PROGRAM-ID. COBVS4.

        *************************************************
        *      PROGRAM TO DELETE A RECORD FROM THE      *
        *      EMPLOYEE VSAM FILE.                      *
        *************************************************

         ENVIRONMENT DIVISION.
         INPUT-OUTPUT SECTION.

            FILE-CONTROL.
               SELECT EMPLOYEE-VS-FILE    ASSIGN TO EMPVSFIL
               ORGANIZATION IS INDEXED
               ACCESS MODE  IS RANDOM
               RECORD KEY   IS EMP-ID
               FILE STATUS  IS EMP-FILE-STATUS.

         DATA DIVISION.

         FILE SECTION.
         FD EMPLOYEE-VS-FILE.
            01  EMPLOYEE.
                05 EMP-ID                PIC 9(04).
                05 EMP-LAST-NAME         PIC X(30).
                05 EMP-FIRST-NAME        PIC X(20).
                05 EMP-SERVICE-YEARS     PIC 9(02).
                05 EMP-PROMOTION-DATE    PIC X(10).
                05 FILLER                PIC X(14).

         WORKING-STORAGE SECTION.

            01 WS-FLAGS.
                05  SW-END-OF-FILE-SWITCH   PIC X(1) VALUE 'N'.
```

```
                    88  SW-END-OF-FILE                VALUE 'Y'.
                    88  SW-NOT-END-OF-FILE            VALUE 'N'.

            01  EMP-FILE-STATUS.
                    05  EMPFILE-STAT1        PIC X.
                    05  EMPFILE-STAT2        PIC X.

        PROCEDURE DIVISION.

            PERFORM P100-INITIALIZATION.
            PERFORM P200-MAINLINE.
            PERFORM P300-TERMINATION.
            GOBACK.

        P100-INITIALIZATION.

            DISPLAY 'COBVS4 - SAMPLE COBOL PROGRAM: VSAM DELETE'.
            OPEN I-O EMPLOYEE-VS-FILE.

            IF  EMP-FILE-STATUS = '00' OR '97' THEN
                NEXT SENTENCE
            ELSE
                DISPLAY 'ERROR ON OPEN - FILE STATUS ' EMP-FILE-STATUS.

            INITIALIZE EMPLOYEE.

        P200-MAINLINE.

    *       DELETE THE RECORD FROM THE VSAM FILE.

            MOVE '1111' TO EMP-ID
            DELETE EMPLOYEE-VS-FILE

            IF  EMP-FILE-STATUS = '00' THEN
                DISPLAY 'SUCCESS DELETE OF EMPLOYEE ' EMP-ID
            ELSE
                DISPLAY 'ERROR ON DELETE - FILE STATUS ' EMP-FILE-STATUS.

        P300-TERMINATION.

            CLOSE EMPLOYEE-VS-FILE.

            DISPLAY 'COBVS4 - SUCCESSFULLY ENDED'.

    *       END OF SOURCE CODE
```

Here is our execution output:

```
COBVS4 - SAMPLE COBOL PROGRAM: VSAM DELETE
SUCCESS DELETE OF EMPLOYEE 1111
COBVS4 - SUCCESSFULLY ENDED
```

And we can verify that the record was deleted by checking in File Manager. As we can see, there is no longer an employee 1111.

```
View              USER01.EMPLOYEE                             Rec 1 of 6
Command ===>                                                  Scroll PAGE
      Key 1122              Type KSDS    RBA 0                Format TABL
         EMP-ID  EMP-LAST-NAME              EMP-FIRST-NAME    EMP-SERVICE-
         #2  #3                             #4                           #5
         ZD 1:4 AN 5:30                     AN 35:20          ZD 55:2
         <--->  <---+----1----+----2----+---> <---+----1----+---->   <->
000001   1122 JENKINS                       DEBORAH                    5
000002   3217 JOHNSON                       EDWARD                     4
000003   4720 SCHULTZ                       TIM                        9
000004   6288 WILLARD                       JOE                        8
000005   7459 STEWART                       BETTY                      7
000006   9134 FRANKLIN                      BRIANNA                    3
****** ****   End of data    ****
```

Let's go ahead and run the program again to check the error logic. And in fact the program does report the error.

```
COBVS4 - SAMPLE COBOL PROGRAM: VSAM DELETE
ERROR ON DELETE - FILE STATUS 23
COBVS4 - SUCCESSFULLY ENDED
```

If course, you could do more by stating that file status 23 means a requested record was not found. You could even define the various file status codes in working storage with a description (see table at the end of this chapter), and display the text as an error message.

PLI Program to Delete Records (PLIVS4)

Here is the PLI version of the program.

```
PLIVS4: PROC OPTIONS(MAIN) REORDER;
 /*****************************************************************
 * PROGRAM NAME :   PROGRAM TO DELETE A RECORD ON A VSAM FILE.    *
 *****************************************************************/

 /*****************************************************************
 /*                  F I L E S    U S E D                          *
 *****************************************************************/

    DCL EMPVSFIL FILE RECORD DIRECT UPDATE KEYED ENV(VSAM);

 /*****************************************************************
 /*                  W O R K I N G    S T O R A G E               *
 *****************************************************************/

    DCL ONCODE                     BUILTIN;
```

```
   DCL SW_IO_ERROR              STATIC BIT(01) INIT('0'B);


   DCL SW_END_OF_FILE           STATIC BIT(01) INIT('0'B);

   DCL 01  EMPLOYEE,
           05 EMP_ID                PIC'9999',
           05 EMP_LAST_NAME         CHAR (30),
           05 EMP_FIRST_NAME        CHAR (20),
           05 EMP_SERVICE_YEARS     PIC  '99',
           05 EMP_PROMOTION_DATE    CHAR (10),
           05 FILLER                CHAR (14);
/******************************************************************
/*             O N    C O N D I T I O N S                        *
******************************************************************/

   ON KEY(EMPVSFIL) BEGIN;
      SELECT(ONCODE);
         WHEN (51)
            DO;
            PUT SKIP LIST ('KEY NOT FOUND ' || EMP_ID);
            SW_IO_ERROR = '1'B;
            END;
         WHEN (52)
            DO;
               PUT SKIP LIST ('DUPLICATE KEY ' || EMP_ID);
               SW_IO_ERROR = '1'B;
            END;

         OTHERWISE;

      END; /* SELECT */

   END; /* ON KEY */

/******************************************************************
/*             P R O G R A M    M A I N L I N E                  *
******************************************************************/

CALL P100_INITIALIZATION;
CALL P200_MAINLINE;
CALL P300_TERMINATION;

P100_INITIALIZATION: PROC;

   PUT SKIP LIST ('PLIVS4: VSAM FILE DELETE');
   OPEN FILE (EMPVSFIL);
   EMPLOYEE = '';

END P100_INITIALIZATION;

P200_MAINLINE: PROC;
```

```
    /* SET THE RECORD KEY AND THEN DELETE THE RECORD */

    EMP_ID = '1111';
    DELETE FILE(EMPVSFIL) KEY(EMP_ID);

    IF SW_IO_ERROR THEN
       PUT SKIP LIST ('ERROR - RECORD NOT DELETED');
    ELSE
       PUT SKIP LIST ('SUCCESSFUL DELETE OF EMPLOYEE '
          || EMP_ID);

END P200_MAINLINE;

P300_TERMINATION: PROC;

    CLOSE FILE(EMPVSFIL);

    PUT SKIP LIST ('PLIVS4 - SUCCESSFULLY ENDED');

END P300_TERMINATION;

END PLIVS4;
```

And here is the output.

```
    PLIVS4: VSAM FILE DELETE
    SUCCESSFUL DELETE OF EMPLOYEE 1111
    PLIVS4 - SUCCESSFULLY ENDED
```

Let's test the error logic by running the delete a second time. This branches to the ONCODE logic that sets an error switch and announces that the delete was not successful.

```
    PLIVS4: VSAM FILE DELETE
    KEY NOT FOUND 1111
    ERROR - RECORD NOT DELETED
    PLIVS4 - SUCCESSFULLY ENDED
```

The delete error logic works. Let's also go back and check the update error logic in PLIVS3 that updates the same record. As with the delete action, the update should now fail because the record is not there.

```
    PLIVS3: VSAM FILE UPDATE
    KEY NOT FOUND 1111
    ERROR - RECORD NOT UPDATED
    PLIVS3 - SUCCESSFULLY ENDED
```

All is working, great. Let's move on!

COBOL Program to Retrieve Records Sequentially (COBVS5)

Now let's read all of the records sequentially with program COBVS5. We will need to define the file for sequential access, and we'll use a loop which will stop when we reach end of file. Note that end of file is VSAM file status code 10.

```
        IDENTIFICATION DIVISION.
        PROGRAM-ID. COBVS5.

       *********************************************************
       *      PROGRAM TO RETRIEVE RECORDS SEQUENTIALLY          *
       *      FROM THE EMPLOYEE VSAM FILE.                      *
       *********************************************************

        ENVIRONMENT DIVISION.
        INPUT-OUTPUT SECTION.

           FILE-CONTROL.
              SELECT EMPLOYEE-VS-FILE    ASSIGN TO EMPVSFIL
              ORGANIZATION IS INDEXED
              ACCESS MODE  IS SEQUENTIAL
              RECORD KEY   IS EMP-ID
              FILE STATUS  IS EMP-FILE-STATUS.

        DATA DIVISION.

        FILE SECTION.
        FD EMPLOYEE-VS-FILE.
           01  EMPLOYEE.
               05 EMP-ID               PIC 9(04).
               05 EMP-LAST-NAME        PIC X(30).
               05 EMP-FIRST-NAME       PIC X(20).
               05 EMP-SERVICE-YEARS    PIC 9(02).
               05 EMP-PROMOTION-DATE   PIC X(10).
               05 FILLER               PIC X(14).

        WORKING-STORAGE SECTION.

           01 WS-FLAGS.
               05  SW-END-OF-FILE-SWITCH   PIC X(1) VALUE 'N'.
                   88  SW-END-OF-FILE               VALUE 'Y'.
                   88  SW-NOT-END-OF-FILE           VALUE 'N'.

           01 EMP-FILE-STATUS.
                   05  EMPFILE-STAT1      PIC X.
                   05  EMPFILE-STAT2      PIC X.

        PROCEDURE DIVISION.

           PERFORM P100-INITIALIZATION.
           PERFORM P200-MAINLINE.
           PERFORM P300-TERMINATION.
           GOBACK.
```

```
    P100-INITIALIZATION.

        DISPLAY 'COBVS5 - SAMPLE COBOL PROGRAM: READ LOOP'.
        OPEN INPUT   EMPLOYEE-VS-FILE.

        INITIALIZE EMPLOYEE.

    P200-MAINLINE.

        READ EMPLOYEE-VS-FILE
        IF  EMP-FILE-STATUS = '10' THEN
            DISPLAY 'END OF FILE ENCOUNTERED'
            SET SW-END-OF-FILE TO TRUE
        END-IF.

        IF NOT SW-END-OF-FILE THEN
           PERFORM UNTIL SW-END-OF-FILE
*              DISPLAY THE DATA VALUES
               DISPLAY 'EMP-ID               ' EMP-ID
               DISPLAY 'EMP LAST NAME        ' EMP-LAST-NAME
               DISPLAY 'EMP FIRST NAME       ' EMP-FIRST-NAME
               DISPLAY 'EMP YEARS OF SERVICE ' EMP-SERVICE-YEARS
               DISPLAY 'EMP PROMOTION DATE   ' EMP-PROMOTION-DATE

               READ EMPLOYEE-VS-FILE
               IF  EMP-FILE-STATUS = '10' THEN
                  SET SW-END-OF-FILE TO TRUE
                  DISPLAY 'END OF FILE ENCOUNTERED'
               END-IF

           END-PERFORM
        ELSE
           DISPLAY 'NO RECORDS IN FILE'

        END-IF.

    P300-TERMINATION.

        CLOSE EMPLOYEE-VS-FILE.

        DISPLAY 'COBVS5 - SUCCESSFULLY ENDED'.
*       END OF SOURCE CODE
```

Compile, link and run the program.

```
COBVS5 - SAMPLE COBOL PROGRAM: READ LOOP
EMP-ID                 1122
EMP LAST NAME          JENKINS
EMP FIRST NAME         DEBORAH
```

```
EMP YEARS OF SERVICE   05
EMP PROMOTION DATE     2016-09-01
EMP-ID                 3217
EMP LAST NAME          JOHNSON
EMP FIRST NAME         EDWARD
EMP YEARS OF SERVICE   04
EMP PROMOTION DATE     2017-01-01
EMP-ID                 4720
EMP LAST NAME          SCHULTZ
EMP FIRST NAME         TIM
EMP YEARS OF SERVICE   09
EMP PROMOTION DATE     2017-01-01
EMP-ID                 6288
EMP LAST NAME          WILLARD
EMP FIRST NAME         JOE
EMP YEARS OF SERVICE   08
EMP PROMOTION DATE     2016-01-01
EMP-ID                 7459
EMP LAST NAME          STEWART
EMP FIRST NAME         BETTY
EMP YEARS OF SERVICE   07
EMP PROMOTION DATE     2016-07-31
EMP-ID                 9134
EMP LAST NAME          FRANKLIN
EMP FIRST NAME         BRIANNA
EMP YEARS OF SERVICE   03
EMP PROMOTION DATE     2016-10-01
END OF FILE ENCOUNTERED
COBVS5 - SUCCESSFULLY ENDED
```

PLI Program to Retrieve Records Sequentially (PLIVS5)

Now, here's the PLI program source. Note that we define the file for sequential access.

```
PLIVS5: PROC OPTIONS(MAIN) REORDER;
/******************************************************************
* PROGRAM NAME :   PROGRAM TO READ SEQUENTIALLY FROM A VSAM FILE.  *
******************************************************************/

/******************************************************************
/*              F I L E S   U S E D                                *
******************************************************************/

   DCL EMPVSFIL FILE RECORD SEQUENTIAL INPUT KEYED ENV(VSAM);

/******************************************************************
/*              W O R K I N G   S T O R A G E                     *
******************************************************************/

   DCL ONCODE                   BUILTIN;

   DCL SW_END_OF_FILE           STATIC BIT(01) INIT('0'B);
```

```pli
     DCL 01  EMPLOYEE,
             05 EMP_ID                PIC'9999',
             05 EMP_LAST_NAME         CHAR (30),
             05 EMP_FIRST_NAME        CHAR (20),
             05 EMP_SERVICE_YEARS     PIC '99',
             05 EMP_PROMOTION_DATE    CHAR (10),
             05 FILLER                CHAR (14);

/*******************************************************************
/*                  O N   C O N D I T I O N S                      *
*******************************************************************/

   ON ENDFILE (EMPVSFIL) SW_END_OF_FILE =  '1'B;


/*******************************************************************
/*                  P R O G R A M   M A I N L I N E                *
*******************************************************************/

CALL P100_INITIALIZATION;
CALL P200_MAINLINE;
CALL P300_TERMINATION;

P100_INITIALIZATION: PROC;

    PUT SKIP LIST ('PLIVS5: VSAM READ LOOP');
    OPEN FILE (EMPVSFIL);
    EMPLOYEE = '';

END P100_INITIALIZATION;

P200_MAINLINE: PROC;

    /*  DO PRIMING READ THE INPUT FILE */

    READ FILE (EMPVSFIL) INTO (EMPLOYEE);

    IF SW_END_OF_FILE THEN
       PUT SKIP LIST ('NO RECORDS IN FILE');
    ELSE
       DO WHILE (¬SW_END_OF_FILE);

          /*  DISPLAY THE DATA VALUES */

          PUT SKIP DATA (EMPLOYEE);

          READ FILE (EMPVSFIL) INTO (EMPLOYEE);

          IF SW_END_OF_FILE THEN
             PUT SKIP LIST ('END OF FILE ENCOUNTERED');

       END; /* DO UNTIL */
```

```
    END P200_MAINLINE;

P300_TERMINATION: PROC;

    CLOSE FILE(EMPVSFIL);

    PUT SKIP LIST ('PLIVS5 - SUCCESSFULLY ENDED');

END P300_TERMINATION;

END PLIVS5;
```

Compile, link, run, and here is the output:

```
PLIVS5: VSAM READ LOOP
EMPLOYEE.EMP_ID=1122        EMPLOYEE.EMP_LAST_NAME='JENKINS                    '
EMPLOYEE.EMP_FIRST_NAME='DEBORAH              '   EMPLOYEE.EMP_SERVICE_YEARS=05
EMPLOYEE.EMP_PROMOTION_DATE='2016-09-01'          EMPLOYEE.FILLER='034658724   '
EMPLOYEE.EMP_ID=3217        EMPLOYEE.EMP_LAST_NAME='JOHNSON                    '
EMPLOYEE.EMP_FIRST_NAME='EDWARD               '   EMPLOYEE.EMP_SERVICE_YEARS=04
EMPLOYEE.EMP_PROMOTION_DATE='2017-01-01'          EMPLOYEE.FILLER='493082938   '
EMPLOYEE.EMP_ID=4720        EMPLOYEE.EMP_LAST_NAME='SCHULTZ                    '
EMPLOYEE.EMP_FIRST_NAME='TIM                  '   EMPLOYEE.EMP_SERVICE_YEARS=09
EMPLOYEE.EMP_PROMOTION_DATE='2017-01-01'          EMPLOYEE.FILLER='209482059   '
EMPLOYEE.EMP_ID=6288        EMPLOYEE.EMP_LAST_NAME='WILLARD                    '
EMPLOYEE.EMP_FIRST_NAME='JOE                  '   EMPLOYEE.EMP_SERVICE_YEARS=08
EMPLOYEE.EMP_PROMOTION_DATE='2016-01-01'          EMPLOYEE.FILLER='030467384   '
EMPLOYEE.EMP_ID=7459        EMPLOYEE.EMP_LAST_NAME='STEWART                    '
EMPLOYEE.EMP_FIRST_NAME='BETTY                '   EMPLOYEE.EMP_SERVICE_YEARS=07
EMPLOYEE.EMP_PROMOTION_DATE='2016-07-31'          EMPLOYEE.FILLER='991837283   '
EMPLOYEE.EMP_ID=9134        EMPLOYEE.EMP_LAST_NAME='FRANKLIN                   '
EMPLOYEE.EMP_FIRST_NAME='BRIANNA              '   EMPLOYEE.EMP_SERVICE_YEARS=03
EMPLOYEE.EMP_PROMOTION_DATE='2016-10-01'          EMPLOYEE.FILLER='333073948   '
END OF FILE ENCOUNTERED
PLIVS5 - SUCCESSFULLY ENDED
```

So this is a model you can use whenever you need to cycle through a VSAM file sequentially. It should prove useful.

Creating and Accessing Alternate Indexes

So far we've dealt with a VSAM file that has a single index which is associated with the key. Suppose however that you need another index on a file? That is, you need to randomly access your data using another field from the file? You can do this with VSAM, and you can access the data via the alternate index in application programs.

Suppose we want to add a social security number field to our EMPLOYEE file, and that we want an alternate index on it. To do this we will do the following:

1. Modify our file layout to include a social security number field named `EMP-SSN`.
2. Reload the `EMPLOYEE` VSAM file to include the social security numbers.
3. Create the alternate index which will be named `EMPSSN`.
4. Build and test the alternate index.

First, let's update our file layout in the `EMPLOYEE` copybook. Here it is with the `EMP_SSN` added.

```
******************************************************************
* COBOL DECLARATION FOR VSAM FILE EMPLOYEE                        *
******************************************************************
 01  EMPLOYEE.
     05 EMP-ID                PIC 9(04).
     05 EMP-LAST-NAME         PIC X(30).
     05 EMP-FIRST-NAME        PIC X(20).
     05 EMP-SERVICE-YEARS     PIC 9(02).
     05 EMP-PROMOTION-DATE    PIC X(10).
     05 EMP-SSN               PIC X(09).
     05 FILLER                PIC X(05).
```

Then we could add the social security numbers through File Manager. Another alternative is to unload the data first into a flat file, add the social security number values to the flat file, and then scratch and recreate the VSAM file (using the revised unload file. If you want to do the unload, here is some sample JCL.

```
//USER01D JOB 'WINGATE',MSGLEVEL=(1,1),NOTIFY=&SYSUID
//*
//****************************************************************
//* UNLOAD DATA FROM VSAM KSDS TO PS DATA SET
//****************************************************************
//JS010      EXEC PGM=IDCAMS
//SYSPRINT DD SYSOUT=*
//SYSOUT   DD SYSOUT=*
//DD1      DD DSN=USER01.EMPLOYEE,DISP=SHR
//DD2      DD DSN=USER01.EMPLOYEE.UNLOAD,
//            DISP=(NEW,CATLG,DELETE),
//            SPACE=(TRK,(1,1),RLSE),
//            UNIT=SYSDA,VOL=SER=DEVHD1,
//            DCB=(DSORG=PS,RECFM=FB,LRECL=80,BLKSIZE=27920)
//SYSIN    DD *
  REPRO -
  INFILE(DD1) -
  OUTFILE(DD2)
/*
```

I'm going to use File Manager instead. Here's the first record. I am of course adding random nine digit numbers here, not real social security numbers.

```
 Edit             USER01.EMPLOYEE                           Rec 1 of 6
 Command ===>                                               Scroll PAGE
 Key 1122                 Type KSDS       RBA 0             Format SNGL
                                                   Top Line is 1    of 7
 Current 01: EMPLOYEE                                       Length 80
 Field                Data
 EMP-ID               1122
 EMP-LAST-NAME        JENKINS
 EMP-FIRST-NAME       DEBORAH
 EMP-SERVICE-YEARS    5
 EMP-PROMOTION-DATE   2016-09-01
 EMP_SSN              034658724
 FILLER
 ***  End of record   ***
```

Once I've finished adding SSNs, I will verify that all six records have them.

```
 Edit             USER01.EMPLOYEE                           Rec 1 of 6
 Command ===>                                               Scroll PAGE
       Key 1122           Type KSDS       RBA 0             Format TABL
       EMP-SERVICE-YEARS EMP-PROMOTION-DATE EMP_SSN   FILLER
                     #5 #6                 #7        #8
                  ZD 55:2 AN 57:10         AN 67:9   AN 76:5
                     <-> <---+---->        <---+---> <--->
 000001              5   2016-09-01        034658724
 000002              4   2017-01-01        493082938
 000003              9   2017-01-01        209482059
 000004              8   2016-01-01        030467384
 000005              7   2016-07-31        991837283
 000006              3   2016-10-01        333073948
 ****** ****  End of data    ****
```

Now, it's time to build the alternate index. First, we give it a file name and establish the other attributes. We'll give the index file name `USER01.EMPLOYEE.ALX`. And we will define the key as 9 bytes beginning at displacement 66. That's where the social security number is. We also indicate that it is related to the `USER01.EMPLOYEE` cluster.

`DEFINE PATH` is used to relate the alternate index to the base cluster. While defining path we specify the name of the path and the alternate index to which this path is related. This is the actual link between the VSAM cluster and the alternate index.

Finally, the `BLDINDEX` command is used to build the alternate index. `BLDINDEX` reads all the records in the VSAM indexed data set (base cluster) and extracts the data needed to build the alternate index.

```
//USER01D JOB 'WINGATE',MSGLEVEL=(1,1),NOTIFY=&SYSUID
//*
//*****************************************************************
//* DEFINE ALTERNAME INDEX
//*****************************************************************
//JS010    EXEC PGM=IDCAMS
//SYSPRINT DD SYSOUT=*
//SYSOUT   DD SYSOUT=*
//SYSIN    DD *
  DEFINE AIX -
  (NAME(USER01.EMPLOYEE.ALX) -
  RELATE(USER01.EMPLOYEE) -
  CISZ(4096) -
  KEYS(9,66) -
  UNIQUEKEY -
  UPGRADE -
  RECORDSIZE(80,80) -
  TRK(2,1) -
  FREESPACE(10,20) -
  VOLUMES(DEVHD1) -
  )
/*
//*
//*****************************************************************
//* DEFINE PATH
//*****************************************************************
//JS020    EXEC PGM=IDCAMS
//SYSPRINT DD SYSOUT=*
//SYSOUT   DD SYSOUT=*
//SYSIN    DD *
  DEFINE PATH (NAME(USER01.EMPLOYEE.PATH) -
               PATHENTRY(USER01.EMPLOYEE.ALX) UPDATE
/*
//*
//*****************************************************************
//* BUILD INDEX
//*****************************************************************
//JS030    EXEC PGM=IDCAMS
//SYSPRINT DD SYSOUT=*
//SYSOUT   DD SYSOUT=*
//SYSIN    DD *
  BLDINDEX -
       INDATASET(USER01.EMPLOYEE) -
       OUTDATASET(USER01.EMPLOYEE.ALX)
/*
//*
```

COBOL Program to Read Alternate Index (COBVS6)

Now we can use this alternate index to randomly access the data using the EMP-SSN field. We'll write program COBVS6 to demonstrate this. Suppose for example we want to retrieve the record with SSN value 209482059 which is Tim Shultz. We can clone the first program COBVS1 into COBVS6. We do need to change a few things.

First our JCL must include a DD name for the PATH associated with the alternate index. When you use an alternate index, the DD name for the PATH must be the same as the DD name for the cluster except that the PATH DD name must have a 1 at the end of it. Since a DD identifier can be a maximum of 8 bytes, we must shorten the DD name of our EMPLOYEE VSAM file (in the program and JCL) to 7 bytes to so we can include a corresponding DD name for the PATH. We will shorten our cluster DD name to EMPVSFL. We can then define the PATH DD name as EMPVSFL1. Here's our JCL.

```
//USER01D JOB MSGLEVEL=(1,1),NOTIFY=&SYSUID
//*
//*   RUN A COBOL PROGRAM
//*
//STEP01   EXEC PGM=COBVS6
//STEPLIB  DD   DSN=USER01.LOADLIB,DISP=SHR
//SYSOUT   DD   SYSOUT=*
//EMPVSFL  DD DSN=USER01.EMPLOYEE,DISP=SHR
//EMPVSFL1 DD DSN=USER01.EMPLOYEE.PATH,DISP=SHR
//SYSPRINT DD   SYSOUT=*
//SYSUDUMP DD   SYSOUT=*
//SYSOUT   DD   SYSOUT=*
```

Second we need to identify the alternate key in the File Control section, and also change the **ASSIGN TO** clause to match the DD name change we made to the JCL (note that you do **not** need to do an assign statement for the PATH DD). Here is the code change. Notice the reference to the ALTERNATE KEY.

```
FILE-CONTROL.
    SELECT EMPLOYEE-VS-FILE    ASSIGN TO EMPVSFL
        ORGANIZATION    IS INDEXED
        ACCESS MODE     IS RANDOM
        RECORD KEY      IS EMP-ID
        ALTERNATE KEY   IS EMP-SSN
        FILE STATUS     IS EMP-FILE-STATUS.
```

Finally, we need to establish that the alternate key is to be used in the READ. We do this with the KEY IS clause.

```
    READ EMPLOYEE-VS-FILE KEY IS EMP-SSN
```

Here is the final program listing with these features:

```
    IDENTIFICATION DIVISION.
    PROGRAM-ID. COBVS6.

   *******************************************************
   *       PROGRAM TO RETRIEVE A RECORD FROM              *
```

```
*       EMPLOYEE VSAM FILE USING ALTERNATE INDEX.      *
********************************************************

ENVIRONMENT DIVISION.
INPUT-OUTPUT SECTION.

   FILE-CONTROL.
      SELECT EMPLOYEE-VS-FILE    ASSIGN TO EMPVSFL
         ORGANIZATION      IS INDEXED
         ACCESS MODE       IS RANDOM
         RECORD KEY        IS EMP-ID
         **ALTERNATE KEY   IS EMP-SSN**
         FILE STATUS       IS EMP-FILE-STATUS.

DATA DIVISION.

FILE SECTION.
FD EMPLOYEE-VS-FILE.
   01  EMPLOYEE.
       05  EMP-ID              PIC 9(04).
       05  EMP-LAST-NAME       PIC X(30).
       05  EMP-FIRST-NAME      PIC X(20).
       05  EMP-SERVICE-YEARS   PIC 9(02).
       05  EMP-PROMOTION-DATE  PIC X(10).
       05  EMP-SSN             PIC X(09).
       05  FILLER              PIC X(05).

WORKING-STORAGE SECTION.

   01 WS-FLAGS.
      05  SW-END-OF-FILE-SWITCH   PIC X(1) VALUE 'N'.
          88  SW-END-OF-FILE               VALUE 'Y'.
          88  SW-NOT-END-OF-FILE           VALUE 'N'.

   01  EMP-FILE-STATUS.
          05   EMPFILE-STAT1     PIC X.
          05   EMPFILE-STAT2     PIC X.

PROCEDURE DIVISION.

    PERFORM P100-INITIALIZATION.
    PERFORM P200-MAINLINE.
    PERFORM P300-TERMINATION.
    GOBACK.

P100-INITIALIZATION.

    DISPLAY 'COBVS6 - SAMPLE COBOL PROGRAM: VSAM ALT INDEX'.
    OPEN INPUT EMPLOYEE-VS-FILE.

    IF  EMP-FILE-STATUS = '00' OR '97' THEN
        NEXT SENTENCE
    ELSE
```

```
            DISPLAY 'ERROR ON OPEN - FILE STATUS ' EMP-FILE-STATUS.

       INITIALIZE EMPLOYEE.

   P200-MAINLINE.

*      READ THE INPUT FILE TO GET THE REQUESTED RECORD
*      AND DISPLAY THE DATA VALUES

       MOVE '209482059' TO EMP-SSN
       READ EMPLOYEE-VS-FILE KEY IS EMP-SSN

       IF  EMP-FILE-STATUS = '00' THEN
*          DISPLAY THE DATA
           DISPLAY 'EMP-ID                ' EMP-ID
           DISPLAY 'EMP LAST NAME         ' EMP-LAST-NAME
           DISPLAY 'EMP FIRST NAME        ' EMP-FIRST-NAME
           DISPLAY 'EMP YEARS OF SERVICE  ' EMP-SERVICE-YEARS
           DISPLAY 'EMP PROMOTION DATE    ' EMP-PROMOTION-DATE
           DISPLAY 'EMP SOCIAL SECURITY   ' EMP-SSN
       ELSE
           DISPLAY 'RECORD WAS NOT FOUND - RC = ' EMP-FILE-STATUS.

   P300-TERMINATION.

       CLOSE EMPLOYEE-VS-FILE.

       IF  EMP-FILE-STATUS = '00' THEN
          NEXT SENTENCE
       ELSE
           DISPLAY 'ERROR ON CLOSE - FILE STATUS ' EMP-FILE-STATUS.

       DISPLAY 'COBVS6 - SUCCESSFULLY ENDED'.

*      END OF SOURCE CODE
```

Now we can compile, link and execute our program. Here is the result.

```
   COBVS6 - SAMPLE COBOL PROGRAM: VSAM ALT INDEX
   EMP-ID                4720
   EMP LAST NAME         SCHULTZ
   EMP FIRST NAME        TIM
   EMP YEARS OF SERVICE  09
   EMP PROMOTION DATE    2017-01-01
   EMP SOCIAL SECURITY   209482059
   COBVS6 - SUCCESSFULLY ENDED
```

As you can see, we successfully retrieved the record using the alternate index and specifying the KEY IS field.

PLI Program to Read Alternate Index (PLIVS6)

Here's the PLI version of the program. Notice we do not explicitly define an alternate index in our code, but we specify **KEY(EMP_SSN)** to use the alternate key.

```
PLIVS6: PROC OPTIONS(MAIN) REORDER;
/*******************************************************************
* PROGRAM PURPOSE: PROGRAM TO RETRIEVE RECORD ON A VSAM FILE       *
*                  USING AN ALTERNATE INDEX.                       *
*******************************************************************/

/*******************************************************************
/*                F I L E S    U S E D                             *
*******************************************************************/

   DCL EMPVSFL1 FILE RECORD DIRECT INPUT KEYED ENV(VSAM);

/*******************************************************************
/*              W O R K I N G   S T O R A G E                      *
*******************************************************************/

   DCL ONCODE                  BUILTIN;
   DCL SW_IO_ERROR             STATIC BIT(01) INIT('0'B);

   DCL 01   EMPLOYEE,
            05 EMP_ID            PIC'9999',
            05 EMP_LAST_NAME     CHAR (30),
            05 EMP_FIRST_NAME    CHAR (20),
            05 EMP_SERVICE_YEARS PIC  '99',
            05 EMP_PROMOTION_DATE CHAR (10),
            05 EMP_SSN           CHAR (09),
            05 FILLER            CHAR (05);

/*******************************************************************
/*              O N   C O N D I T I O N S                          *
*******************************************************************/

   ON KEY(EMPVSFL1) BEGIN;
      SELECT(ONCODE);
         WHEN (51)
            DO;
               PUT SKIP LIST ('KEY NOT FOUND ' || EMP_SSN);
               SW_IO_ERROR = '1'B;
            END;
         WHEN (52)
            DO;
               PUT SKIP LIST ('DUPLICATE KEY ' || EMP_SSN);
               SW_IO_ERROR = '1'B;
            END;
         OTHERWISE;

      END; /* SELECT */
```

```
        END; /* ON KEY */

   /****************************************************************
   /*              P R O G R A M   M A I N L I N E               *
   ****************************************************************/

   CALL P100_INITIALIZATION;
   CALL P200_MAINLINE;
   CALL P300_TERMINATION;

   P100_INITIALIZATION: PROC;

       PUT SKIP LIST ('PLIVS6: VSAM FILE READ USING ALTERNATE KEY');
       OPEN FILE (EMPVSFL1);
       EMPLOYEE = '';

   END P100_INITIALIZATION;

   P200_MAINLINE: PROC;

       /*   WRITE THE RECORD TO OUTPUT */

       EMP_SSN = '209482059';
       READ FILE (EMPVSFL1) INTO (EMPLOYEE) KEY (EMP_SSN);

       IF SW_IO_ERROR THEN
          PUT SKIP LIST ('ERROR - RECORD NOT READ');
       ELSE
          DO;
             PUT SKIP LIST ('SUCCESSFUL READ OF EMPLOYEE SSN ' || EMP_SSN);
             PUT SKIP DATA (EMPLOYEE);
          END;

   END P200_MAINLINE;

   P300_TERMINATION: PROC;

       CLOSE FILE(EMPVSFL1);

       PUT SKIP LIST ('PLIVS6 - SUCCESSFULLY ENDED');

   END P300_TERMINATION;

   END PLIVS6;
```

Now compile, link, and execute the program. Here's our output.

```
PLIVS6: VSAM FILE READ USING ALTERNATE KEY
SUCCESSFUL READ OF EMPLOYEE SSN 209482059
EMPLOYEE.EMP_ID=4720       EMPLOYEE.EMP_LAST_NAME='SCHULTZ                   '
EMPLOYEE.EMP_FIRST_NAME='TIM            '  EMPLOYEE.EMP_SERVICE_YEARS=09
EMPLOYEE.EMP_PROMOTION_DATE='2017-01-01'   EMPLOYEE.EMP_SSN='209482059'
PLIVS6 - SUCCESSFULLY ENDED
```

Alternate keys give you tremendous flexibility when using VSAM. You can have more than one or more alternate keys on a file and you can specify more than one key in your application programs.

Other VSAM JCL

We haven't gone into much detail about the other file organizations because KSDS is the most common. However, here is some sample JCL for creating the ESDS and RRDS formats.

JCL to CREATE ESDS

```
//**************************************************************
//* DEFINE VSAM ESDS CLUSTER
//**************************************************************
//STEP30   EXEC PGM=IDCAMS
//SYSPRINT DD SYSOUT=*
//SYSOUT   DD SYSOUT=*
//SYSIN    DD *
  DEFINE CLUSTER(NAME(USER01.TEST.ESDS.CLUSTER)  -
  RECORDSIZE(45,45)         -
  CYLINDERS(2,1)            -
  CISZ(4096)                -
  VOLUMES(DEVHD1)           -
  NONINDEXED)               -
  DATA(NAME(USER01.TEST.ESDS.DATA))
/*
//*
```

JCL to CREATE RRDS

```
//*
//**************************************************************
//* DEFINE VSAM RRDS CLUSTER
//**************************************************************
//STEP40   EXEC PGM=IDCAMS
//SYSPRINT DD SYSOUT=*
//SYSOUT   DD SYSOUT=*
//SYSIN    DD *
  DEFINE CLUSTER(NAME(USER01.TEST.RRDS.CLUSTER)  -
  RECORDSIZE(45,45)         -
  CYLINDERS(2,1)            -
  NUMBERED)                 -
  DATA(NAME(USER01.TEST.RRDS.DATA))
/*
```

JCL to LIST DATASET INFORMATION

```
//USER01L JOB 'WINGATE',MSGLEVEL=(1,1),NOTIFY=&SYSUID
//*
//****************************************************************
//* LISTCAT COMMAND
//****************************************************************
//STEP110   EXEC PGM=IDCAMS
//SYSPRINT DD SYSOUT=*
//SYSOUT   DD SYSOUT=*
//SYSIN    DD *
     LISTCAT ENTRIES(USER01.EMPLOYEE) ALL
/*
//*
```

```
IDCAMS  SYSTEM SERVICES                                          TIME: 08:05:59
     LISTCAT ENTRIES(USER01.EMPLOYEE) ALL
CLUSTER ------- USER01.EMPLOYEE
     IN-CAT --- CATALOG.Z113.MASTER
     HISTORY
        DATASET-OWNER-----(NULL)     CREATION--------2018.064
        RELEASE----------------2     EXPIRATION------0000.000
        CA-RECLAIM---------(YES)
        EATTR-------------(NULL)
        BWO STATUS--------(NULL)     BWO TIMESTAMP-----(NULL)
        BWO---------------(NULL)
        PROTECTION-PSWD-----(NULL)   RACF---------------(NO)
     ASSOCIATIONS
        DATA-----USER01.EMPLOYEE.DATA
        INDEX----USER01.EMPLOYEE.INDEX
        AIX------USER01.EMPLOYEE.ALX
  DATA ------- USER01.EMPLOYEE.DATA
     IN-CAT --- CATALOG.Z113.MASTER
     HISTORY
        DATASET-OWNER-----(NULL)     CREATION--------2018.064
        RELEASE----------------2     EXPIRATION------0000.000
        ACCOUNT-INFO----------------------------------(NULL)
        PROTECTION-PSWD-----(NULL)   RACF---------------(NO)
     ASSOCIATIONS
        CLUSTER--USER01.EMPLOYEE
     ATTRIBUTES
        KEYLEN-----------------4     AVGLRECL--------------80    BUFSPACE-------
        RKP--------------------0     MAXLRECL--------------80    EXCPEXIT-------
        SHROPTNS(1,3)  RECOVERY      UNIQUE         NOERASE      INDEXED       N
        NONSPANNED
     STATISTICS   (* - VALUE MAY BE INCORRECT)
        REC-TOTAL--------------7*    SPLITS-CI--------------0*   EXCPS---------
        REC-DELETED------------9*    SPLITS-CA--------------0*   EXTENTS-------
        REC-INSERTED-----------3*    FREESPACE-%CI----------5    SYSTEM-TIMESTAM
        REC-UPDATED-----------11*    FREESPACE-%CA---------10       X'D3FD7137
        REC-RETRIEVED-------191*     FREESPC-----------45056*
     ALLOCATION
```

```
              SPACE-TYPE--------TRACK       HI-A-RBA----------49152
              SPACE-PRI--------------1      HI-U-RBA----------49152
              SPACE-SEC--------------1
           VOLUME
              VOLSER------------DEVHD1      PHYREC-SIZE--------4096    HI-A-RBA-------
              DEVTYPE------X'3010200F'      PHYRECS/TRK----------12    HI-U-RBA-------
              VOLFLAG------------PRIME      TRACKS/CA-------------1
              EXTENTS:
              LOW-CCHH-----X'00AF000E'      LOW-RBA---------------0    TRACKS---------
              HIGH-CCHH----X'00AF000E'      HIGH-RBA----------49151
        INDEX ------ USER01.EMPLOYEE.INDEX
           IN-CAT --- CATALOG.Z113.MASTER
           HISTORY
              DATASET-OWNER-----(NULL)      CREATION--------2018.064
              RELEASE----------------2      EXPIRATION------0000.000
           PROTECTION-PSWD-----(NULL)       RACF---------------(NO)
           ASSOCIATIONS
              CLUSTER--USER01.EMPLOYEE
           ATTRIBUTES
              KEYLEN----------------4       AVGLRECL--------------0    BUFSPACE-------
              RKP-------------------0       MAXLRECL-----------4089    EXCPEXIT-------
              SHROPTNS(1,3)    RECOVERY     UNIQUE           NOERASE   NOWRITECHK
           STATISTICS   (* - VALUE MAY BE INCORRECT)
              REC-TOTAL-------------1*      SPLITS-CI-------------0*   EXCPS----------
              REC-DELETED-----------0*      SPLITS-CA-------------0*   EXTENTS-------
              REC-INSERTED----------0*      FREESPACE-%CI---------0    SYSTEM-TIMESTAM
              REC-UPDATED-----------0*      FREESPACE-%CA---------0        X'D3FD7137
              REC-RETRIEVED---------4*      FREESPC-----------45056*
           ALLOCATION
              SPACE-TYPE--------TRACK       HI-A-RBA----------49152
              SPACE-PRI--------------1      HI-U-RBA-----------4096
              SPACE-SEC--------------1
           VOLUME
              VOLSER------------DEVHD1      PHYREC-SIZE--------4096    HI-A-RBA-------
              DEVTYPE------X'3010200F'      PHYRECS/TRK----------12    HI-U-RBA-------
              VOLFLAG------------PRIME      TRACKS/CA-------------1
              EXTENTS:
              LOW-CCHH-----X'00B60007'      LOW-RBA---------------0    TRACKS---------
              HIGH-CCHH----X'00B60007'      HIGH-RBA----------49151
IDCAMS   SYSTEM SERVICES                                            TIME: 08:05:59
         THE NUMBER OF ENTRIES PROCESSED WAS:
                     AIX ------------------0
                     ALIAS ----------------0
                     CLUSTER --------------1
                     DATA -----------------1
                     GDG ------------------0
                     INDEX ----------------1
                     NONVSAM --------------0
                     PAGESPACE ------------0
                     PATH -----------------0
                     SPACE ----------------0
                     USERCATALOG ----------0
                     TAPELIBRARY ----------0
                     TAPEVOLUME -----------0
                     TOTAL ----------------3
           THE NUMBER OF PROTECTED ENTRIES SUPPRESSED WAS 0
IDC0001I FUNCTION COMPLETED, HIGHEST CONDITION CODE WAS 0

IDC0002I IDCAMS PROCESSING COMPLETE. MAXIMUM CONDITION CODE WAS 0
```

VSAM File Status Codes
Here is a list of the VSAM status codes you might encounter.

Code	Description
00	Operation completed successfully
02	Non-Unique Alternate Index duplicate key found
04	Invalid fixed length record
05	While performing OPEN File and file is not present
10	End of File encountered
14	Attempted to READ a relative record outside file boundary
20	Invalid Key for VSAM KSDS or RRDS
21	Sequence error while performing WRITE or changing key on REWRITE
22	Primary duplicate Key found
23	Record not found or File not found
24	Key outside boundary of file
30	Permanent I/O Error
34	Record outside file boundary
35	While performing OPEN File and file is not present
37	OPEN file with wrong mode
38	Tried to OPEN a Locked file
39	OPEN failed because of conflicting file attributes

```
41  Tried to OPEN a file that is already open

42  Tried to CLOSE a file that is not OPEN

43  Tried to REWRITE without READing a record first

44  Tried to REWRITE a record of a different length

46  Tried to READ beyond End-of-file

47  Tried to READ from a file that was not opened I-O or INPUT

48  Tried to WRITE to a file that was not opened I-O or OUTPUT

49  Tried to DELETE or REWRITE to a file that was not opened I-O

91  Password or authorization failed

92  Logic Error

93  Resources are not available

94  Sequential record unavailable or concurrent OPEN error

95  File Information invalid or incomplete

96  No DD statement for the file

97  OPEN successful and file integrity verified

98  File is Locked - OPEN failed

99  Record Locked - record access failed
```

Chapter One Questions

1. What are the three types of VSAM datasets?

2. How are records stored in an ESDS (entry sequenced) dataset?

3. What VSAM feature enables you to access the records in a KSDS dataset based on a key that is different than the file's primary key?

4. What is the general purpose utility program that provides services for VSAM files?

5. Which AMS function lists information about datasets?

6. If you are mostly going to use a KSDS file for sequential access, should you define a larger or smaller control interval when creating the file?

7. What is the basic AMS command to create a VSAM file?

8. To use the REWRITE command in COBOL, the VSAM file must be opened in what mode?

9. When you define an alternate index, what is the function of the RELATE parameter?

10. When you define a path using DEFINE PATH, what does the PATHENTRY parameter do?

11. After you've defined an alternate index and path, what AMS command must you issue to actually populate the alternate index?

12. After you've created a VSAM file, if you need to add additional DASD volumes that can be used with that file, what command would you use?

13. If you want to set a VSAM file to read only status, what command would you use?

14. What are some ways you can improve the performance of a KSDS file?

15. Do primary key values in a KSDS have to be unique?

16. In the COBOL SELECT statement what organization should be specified for a KSDS file?

17. In the COBOL SELECT statement for a KSDS what are the three possibilities for ACCESS?

18. Is there a performance penalty for using an alternate index compared to using the primary key?

19. What file status code will you receive if an operation succeeded?

Chapter Two: Information Management System (IMS)

Introduction

IMS is a hierarchical database management system (DBMS) that has been around since the 1960's. Although relational DBMSs are more common now, there is still an installed base of IMS users and IBM provides robust support for it. IMS is highly tuned for transaction management and generally provides excellent performance for that environment.

This text deals with IMS-DB, the IMS database manager. IMS also has a transaction manager called IMS-DC. We will be covering IMS-DB in this volume, and IMS-DC in later volume.

There are two modes of running IMS programs. One is DLI which runs within its own address space. There is also Batch Mode Processing (BMP) which runs under the IMS online control region. The practical difference between the two concerns programs that update the database. In DLI mode, a program requires exclusive use of the database to perform updates. In BMP mode, a program does not require exclusive use of the database because it is run in the shared IMS online environment. The IMS online system "referees" the shared online environment.

Before going further I need to point out that in IMS data records are called "segments". I'll use the terms segment and record more or less interchangeably throughout the chapter. There are usually multiple segment types in an IMS database, although not always.

Designing and Creating IMS Databases

Sample System Specification

We're going to create a hierarchical database for a Human Resource system that will involve employees. In fact the database will be named EMPLOYEE and the root segment (highest level segment type) will also be named EMPLOYEE. This segment will include information such as name, years of service and last promotion date.

The EMPLOYEE segment will have a child segment that stores details about the employee's pay. The segment will be named EMPPAY and include the effective date, annual pay and bonus pay.

The EMPPAY segment will have a child segment named EMPPAYHS that includes historical details about each paycheck an employee received.

Note: there can be multiple EMPPAY segments under each EMPLOYEE segment, and there can be multiple EMPPAYHS segments under each EMPPAY segment. The following diagram depicts our EMPLOYEE database visually as a hierarchy.

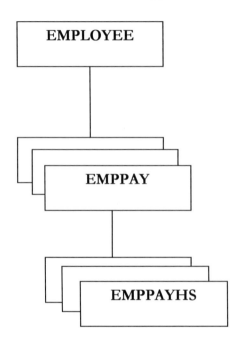

The following shows the segment structure we will be using to organize the three record types. Note that the EMP_ID key is only required on the root segment. You cannot access the child segments except through the root, so this makes sense.

EMPLOYEE Segment (key is EMP_ID).

Field Name	Type
EMP_ID	**INTEGER**
EMP_LAST_NAME	VARCHAR(30)
EMP_FIRST_NAME	VARCHAR(20)
EMP_SERVICE_YEARS	INTEGER
EMP_PROMOTION_DATE	DATE

EMPPAY segment (key is EFF_DATE which means effective date):

Field Name	Type
EFF_DATE	DATE
EMP_REGULAR_PAY	DECIMAL
EMP_BONUS_PAY	DECIMAL
EMP_SEMIMTH_PAY	DECIMAL

EMPPAYHS segment (key is PAY_DATE):

Field Name	Type
PAY_DATE	DATE
ANNUAL_PAY	DECIMAL
PAY_CHECK_AMT	DECIMAL

Having decided the content of our segment types, we can now create a record layout for each of these. We'll do this in COBOL since we will be writing our IMS programs in that language. We'll also create the corresponding PLI record layouts when we write the PLI programs.

Here's the layout for the EMPLOYEE segment:

```
01 IO-EMPLOYEE-RECORD.
   05  EMP-ID          PIC X(04).
   05  FILLER          PIC X(01).
   05  EMPL-LNAME      PIC X(30).
   05  FILLER          PIC X(01).
   05  EMPL-FNAME      PIC X(20).
   05  FILLER          PIC X(01).
   05  EMPL-YRS-SRV    PIC X(02).
   05  FILLER          PIC X(01).
   05  EMPL-PRM-DTE    PIC X(10).
   05  FILLER          PIC X(10).
```

We've provided a bit of filler between fields, and we've left 10 bytes at the end (yes later we will be adding a field so we need some free space). Our total is 80 bytes for this segment type. The record will be keyed on **EMP-ID** which is the first four bytes of the record. We'll need this information to define the database.

Next, the EMPPAY segment layout is as follows:

```
01  IO-EMPPAY-RECORD.
    05  PAY-EFF-DATE   PIC X(8).
    05  PAY-REG-PAY    PIC S9(6)V9(2) USAGE COMP-3.
    05  PAY-BON-PAY    PIC S9(6)V9(2) USAGE COMP-3.
    05  SEMIMTH-PAY    PIC S9(6)V9(2) USAGE COMP-3.
    05  FILLER         PIC X(57).
```

Notice there is no EMP-ID field. As mentioned earlier, child segments do not need to repeat the parent segment key. The hierarchical structure of the database makes this unnecessary. The PAY-EFF-DATE field will be the key for the EMPPAY segment, and it is 8 bytes. The format will be YYYYMMDD.

Also notice that we padded the record with filler to total 80 bytes. We didn't have to do this. The record size is actually 23 bytes without the filler. But often it's a convenience to leave space in the IO layout for future expansion.

Finally, here is the layout for the EMPPAYHS segment. Out key will be PAY-DATE and it will be formatted as YYYYMMDD.

```
01  IO-EMPPAYHS-RECORD.
    05  PAY-DATE       PIC X(8).
    05  PAY-ANN-PAY    PIC S9(6)V9(2) USAGE COMP-3.
    05  PAY-AMT        PIC S9(6)V9(2) USAGE COMP-3.
    05  FILLER         PIC X(57).
```

Now we are ready to build the data base descriptor!

Database Descriptor (DBD)

A database descriptor is required to have an IMS database. The descriptor specifies the name of the database, plus the various segment types. Typically a database administrator will create and maintain DBDs. You should still understand how to read the DBD code to understand the structure of the database.

Here's the DBD code for our EMPLOYEE database.

```
PRINT NOGEN
DBD NAME=EMPLOYEE,ACCESS=HISAM
DATASET DD1=EMPLOYEE,OVFLW=EMPLFLW
SEGM NAME=EMPLOYEE,PARENT=0,BYTES=80
FIELD NAME=(EMPID,SEQ,U),BYTES=04,START=1,TYPE=C
SEGM NAME=EMPPAY,PARENT=EMPLOYEE,BYTES=23
FIELD NAME=(EFFDATE,SEQ,U),START=1,BYTES=8,TYPE=C
```

```
      SEGM  NAME=EMPPAYHS,PARENT=EMPPAY,BYTES=18
      FIELD NAME=(PAYDATE,SEQ,U),START=1,BYTES=8,TYPE=C
DBDGEN
FINISH
END
```

The code above specifies the name of the database which is EMPLOYEE, as well as an access method of HISAM (Hierarchical Indexed Sequential Access Method). HISAM database records are stored in two data sets: a primary data set and an overflow data set. The primary dataset is always a VSAM KSDS and the overflow dataset is a VSAM ESDS. The ESDS dataset is used if the KSDS dataset becomes full. In that case any new records are inserted to the (overflow) ESDS dataset.

There is considerable information available on the IBM web site about how HISAM records are stored, but that information is frankly not very useful for application programmer duties. If you are interested, you can find it here. [i]

Looking at the DBD code, we see that the DATASET DD1 and OVFLW keywords define the DD names of the primary cluster and the overflow dataset, respectively. We defined these values as EMPLOYEE and EMPLFLW. Later when we run batch jobs against the database, the DD name in our JCL must be EMPLOYEE for the KSDS file, and EMPLFLW for the overflow dataset.

Next, we define our segment types using the SEGM NAME= keywords. We also define the parent of each segment unless the segment is the root segment in which case we specify PARENT=0. Next you specify the length of your segment. We've defined the length as the total of the fields we mapped out earlier in the COBOL layouts.

For each segment, if you have any searchable fields (such as keys), they must be defined with the FIELD NAME= keywords. In our case, we will only specify the key fields for each segment. W specify the field name, that the records are to be ordered sequentially (SEQ), and that the field content must be unique(U). Then we specify how many bytes the field is, and it's displacement in the record. We also specify C for character data – the actual data we store can be of any type but we specify C to indicate the default type is character data.

Here's an example of defining the employee id in the DBD from above:

```
      FIELD NAME=(EMPID,SEQ,U),BYTES=04,START=1,TYPE=C
```

Finally, you conclude the DBD with

```
            DBDGEN
            FINISH
            END
```

Now you are ready to run your installation's JCL to generate a DBD. Most likely you will ask a DBA to do this. Here's the JCL I run which executes a proc named DBDGEN. It will be different for your installation.

```
//USER01D JOB MSGLEVEL=(1,1),NOTIFY=&SYSUID
//*
//PLIB     JCLLIB ORDER=SYS1.IMS.PROCLIB
//DGEN     EXEC DBDGEN,
//              MEMBER=EMPLOYEE,                <= DBD SOURCE MEMBER
//              SRCLIB=USER01.IMS.SRCLIB,       <= DBD SOURCE LIBRARY
//              DBDLIB=USER01.IMS.DBDLIB        <= DBD LIBRARY
//*
```

More information about designing, coding and generating DBDs is available on the IBM product web site.

Supporting VSAM Files

Now that we have a DBD generated, we can create the physical files for the database. Actually it can be done in either order, but you do need to know the maximum record size for all segments in order to build the IDCAMS JCL. For IMS datasets we use a VSAM key sequenced data set (KSDS).

Here is the JCL for creating our EMPLOYEE IMS database. Notice that we specify a RECORDSIZE that is 8 bytes longer than the logical record size that we defined in the DBD. And although the key is the first logical byte of each record, we specify the key displacement at byte 6. The IMS system uses the first 5 bytes of each record, so this is required (IMS also uses the last 3 bytes, so we end up with 8 additional bytes for the record size).

Finally, note that we have a second job step to repro a dummy file to our VSAM cluster name to initialize it. This is required. Otherwise we will get an abend the first time we try to access it. Go ahead and run the JCL or ask your DBA to create the physical files.

```
//USER01D JOB MSGLEVEL=(1,1),NOTIFY=&SYSUID
//*
//****************************************************************
//* DEFINE VSAM KSDS CLUSTER FOR EMPLOYEE DATABASE
//****************************************************************
//VDEF     EXEC PGM=IDCAMS
//SYSPRINT DD SYSOUT=*
```

```
//SYSIN    DD  *
  DEFINE CLUSTER(NAME(USER01.IMS.EMPLOYEE.CLUSTER)   -
                 INDEXED                             -
                 KEYS(4,6)                           -
                 RECORDSIZE(88,88)                   -
                 TRACKS(2,1)                         -
                 CISZ(2048)                          -
                 VOLUMES(DEVHD1)                     -
                 )                                   -
         DATA(NAME(USER01.IMS.EMPLOYEE.DATA))
//*
//**************************************************************
//* INITIALIZE THE VSAM FILE TO PLACE EOF MARK
//**************************************************************
//VINIT    EXEC PGM=IDCAMS
//SYSPRINT DD SYSOUT=*
//INF      DD  DUMMY
//OUTF     DD  DSN=USER01.IMS.EMPLOYEE.CLUSTER,DISP=SHR
//SYSIN    DD  *
  REPRO INFILE(INF) OUTFILE(OUTF)
/*
//*
```

Next, here is the JCL for creating the overflow dataset. When your KSDS is full, new records will be placed in the overflow dataset. Again, specify RECORDSIZE 88 (not 80). You must also specify NONINDEXED to get an ESDS file.

```
//USER01D JOB MSGLEVEL=(1,1),NOTIFY=&SYSUID
//*
//**************************************************************
//* DEFINE VSAM ESDS CLUSTER FOR IMS DATA BASE
//**************************************************************
//VDEF     EXEC PGM=IDCAMS
//SYSPRINT DD SYSOUT=*
//SYSOUT   DD SYSOUT=*
//SYSIN    DD  *
  DEFINE CLUSTER(NAME(USER01.IMS.EMPLFLW.CLUSTER)    -
                 NONINDEXED                          -
                 RECORDSIZE(88,88)                   -
                 TRACKS(2,1)                         -
                 CISZ(2048)                          -
                 VOLUMES(DEVHD1)                     -
                 )                                   -
         DATA(NAME(USER01.IMS.EMPLFLW.DATA))
/*
```

Ok, time to move on to our next IMS entity which is a PSB.

Program Specification Block (PSB)

A Program Specification Block (PSB) is an IMS entity that specifies which segments and operations can be performed on one or more databases (using this particular PSB authority). PSBs consist of one or more Program Communication Blocks (PCB) which are logical views of a database. It is typical for each IMS application program to have a separate PSB defined for it, but this is convention, not an IMS requirement. For our programming examples we will mostly use just one PSB, but we will modify it a few times. Here is the code for the PSB that we will be using for most of the examples.

```
PRINT NOGEN
PCB    TYPE=DB,NAME=EMPLOYEE,KEYLEN=20,PROCOPT=AP
SENSEG NAME=EMPLOYEE,PARENT=0
SENSEG NAME=EMPPAY,PARENT=EMPLOYEE
SENSEG NAME=EMPPAYHS,PARENT=EMPPAY
PSBGEN LANG=COBOL,PSBNAME=EMPLOYEE
END
```

Here's the meaning of each keyword for defining the PCB.

PCB – this is where you define a pointer to your database.

TYPE - typically this is DB to indicate a database PCB which provides access to a specific database. There is also a terminal (TP) PCB that is used for teleprocessing calls in IMS DC, but we won't be doing IMS DC in this text.

NAME - identifies the database to be accessed.

PROCOPT - Processing options. This value specifies which operations can be performed such as read, update or delete. The following are the most common options:

G	Get
I	Insert
R	Replace
D	Delete
A	All Options (G, I, R, D)
L	Load Function (Initial Loading)
LS	Load Function (Loading Sequentially)
K	Key Function - Access only key of the segment.
O	Used with G option to indicate that HOLD is not allowed.
P	Path Function (Used during Path Calls)

The PROCOPT can be defined for the entire PCB or it can be more granular by applying it to specific segments. If specified at the segment level, it overrides any PROCOPT at the PCB level. In our case we have specified PROCOPT=AP for the entire PSB. That is powerful. It means All (G, I, R, D) plus authority to do path calls.

KEYLEN – specifies the length of the concatenated key. Concatenated key is the maximum length of all the segment keys added up. This needs to be calculated by adding the longest segment key in each level from top to bottom.

SENSEG means sensitive segment, which means you can access that segment via this PSB. You can specify which segments you want to access. You might not always want all segments to be accessed. In our case we do, so we define a SENSEG for each segment type.

You must then execute a PSBGEN (or ask your DBA to). Here is the JCL I use which executes a proc named PSBGEN, and note that the member name I stored the PSB source under is EMPPSB. Your JCL will be different and specific to the installation:

```
//USER01D JOB MSGLEVEL=(1,1),NOTIFY=&SYSUID
//*
//PLIB    JCLLIB ORDER=SYS1.IMS.PROCLIB
//PGEN    EXEC PSBGEN,
//             MEMBER=EMPPSB,              <= PSB SOURCE MEMBER
//             SRCLIB=USER01.IMS.SRCLIB,   <= PSB SOURCE LIBRARY
//             PSBLIB=USER01.IMS.PSBLIB    <= PSB LIBRARY
//*
```

Now you have the basic building blocks of IMS – a database descriptor (DBD), the physical VSAM files to support the database, and a PSB that provides permissions to access the data within the database via PCBs. We are ready to start programming.

IMS Application Programming Basics

The IMS Program Interface

To request IMS data services in an application program, you must call the IMS interface program for that programming language. The interface program for COBOL is CBLTDLI. This program is called with several parameters which vary depending on the operation being requested. The call also needs to tell CBLTDLI how many parameters are being passed, so we'll declare some constants in our program for that.

```
01 IMS-RET-CODES.
   05 THREE              PIC S9(9) COMP VALUE +3.
   05 FOUR               PIC S9(9) COMP VALUE +4.
   05 FIVE               PIC S9(9) COMP VALUE +5.
   05 SIX                PIC S9(9) COMP VALUE +6.
```

Let's take an example where you want to retrieve an EMPLOYEE segment from the EMPLOYEE database, and you want employee number 3217. Here is the call with appropriate parameters. We'll discuss each of these in turn.

```
CALL 'CBLTDLI' USING FOUR,
               DLI-FUNCGU,
               PCB-MASK,
               SEG-IO-AREA,
               EMP-QUALIFIED-SSA
```

The first parameter specifies the number of parameters being passed. In the case of the above call, the number would be four.

The second parameter is the call type. The following are the common IMS calls used to insert, retrieve, modify and delete data in an IMS database. There are some other calls we'll introduce later such as for checkpointing and rolling back data changes.

DLET	The Delete (DLET) call is used to remove a segment and its dependents from the database.
GN/GHN	The Get Next (GN) call is used to retrieve segments sequentially from the database. The Get Hold Next (GHN) is the hold form for a GN call.
GNP/GHNP	The Get Next in Parent (GNP) call retrieves dependents sequentially. The Get Hold Next in Parent (GHNP) call is the hold form of the GNP call.
GU/GHU	The Get Unique (GU) call is used to directly retrieve segments and to establish a starting position in the database for sequential processing. The Get Hold Unique (GHU) is the hold form for a GU call.
ISRT	The Insert (ISRT) call is used to load a database and to add one or more segments to the database. You can use ISRT to add a record

	to the end of a GSAM database or for an alternate PCB that is set up for IAFP processing.
REPL	The Replace (REPL) call is used to change the values of one or more fields in a segment.

It is a common practice to define a set of constants in your program that specify the value of the specific IMS calls. Here's the COBOL code to put in working storage for this purpose.

```
01 DLI-FUNCTIONS.
   05 DLI-FUNCISRT   PIC X(4) VALUE 'ISRT'.
   05 DLI-FUNCGU     PIC X(4) VALUE 'GU  '.
   05 DLI-FUNCGN     PIC X(4) VALUE 'GN  '.
   05 DLI-FUNCGHU    PIC X(4) VALUE 'GHU '.
   05 DLI-FUNCGHN    PIC X(4) VALUE 'GHN '.
   05 DLI-FUNCGNP    PIC X(4) VALUE 'GNP '.
   05 DLI-FUNCREPL   PIC X(4) VALUE 'REPL'.
   05 DLI-FUNCDLET   PIC X(4) VALUE 'DLET'.
   05 DLI-FUNCXRST   PIC X(4) VALUE 'XRST'.
   05 DLI-FUNCCHKP   PIC X(4) VALUE 'CHKP'.
   05 DLI-FUNCROLL   PIC X(4) VALUE 'ROLL'.
```

As you can see from the call above and the constant definitions, we are doing a Get Unique (GU) call. The DLI-FUNCGU specifies it.

The next parameter is a PCB data area that we defined as PCB-MASK. This returns various information from IMS after the database call. You must define this structure in the Linkage Section of your program since it is passing data back and forth from the CBLTDLI interface program.

```
   LINKAGE SECTION.
01 PCB-MASK.
      03 DBD-NAME       PIC X(8).
      03 SEG-LEVEL      PIC XX.
      03 STATUS-CODE    PIC XX.
      03 PROC-OPT       PIC X(4).
      03 FILLER         PIC X(4).
      03 SEG-NAME       PIC X(8).
      03 KEY-FDBK       PIC S9(5) COMP.
      03 NUM-SENSEG     PIC S9(5) COMP.
      03 KEY-FDBK-AREA.
         05 EMPLOYEE-KEY   PIC X(04).
```

One of the most important data elements in the `PCB-MASK` is the two byte status code returned by the call, the `STATUS-CODE`. A blank status code means that the call was successful. Other status codes indicate the reason why the call failed. Here is a subset of the status codes you may encounter. The complete list of codes is found on the IBM web site. [ii]

IMS Status Codes

PCB Status Code	Description
AC	Hierarchic error in SSAs.
AD	Function parameter incorrect. Only applies to full-function DEQ calls.
AI	Data management OPEN error.
AJ	Incorrect parameter format in I/O area; incorrect SSA format; incorrect command used to insert a logical child segment. I/O area length in AIB is invalid; incorrect class parameter specified in Fast Path Q command code.
AK	Invalid SSA field name.
AM	Call function not compatible with processing option, segment sensitivity, transaction code, definition, or program type.
AU	SSAs too long.
DA	Segment key field or non-replaceable field has been changed.
DJ	No preceding successful `GHU` or `GHN` call or an SSA supplied at a level not retrieved.
FT	Too many SSAs on call.
GB	End of database.
GE	Segment not found.
GG	Segment contains invalid pointer.
GP	No parentage established.
II	Segment already exists.

In your application program control is passed from IMS through an entry point. Your entry point must refer to the PCBs in the order in which they have been defined in the `PSB`. When you code each DL/I call, you must provide the PCB you want to use for that call. Here is the entry point code at the beginning of the procedure division for this program.

```
            ENTRY 'DLITCBL' USING PCB-MASK
```

The next parameter is the segment I/O area. This is where IMS returns the data segment you requested, or where you load data to be inserted/updated on an insert or replace command. For the EMPLOYEE record, we will define the I/O area in COBOL as:

```
01  IO-EMPLOYEE-RECORD.
    05  EMP-ID         PIC X(04).
    05  FILLER         PIC X(01).
    05  EMPL-LNAME     PIC X(30).
    05  FILLER         PIC X(01).
    05  EMPL-FNAME     PIC X(20).
    05  FILLER         PIC X(01).
    05  EMPL-YRS-SRV   PIC X(02).
    05  FILLER         PIC X(01).
    05  EMPL-PRM-DTE   PIC X(10).
    05  FILLER         PIC X(10).
```

The last parameter in our call is a Segment Search Argument (SSA). This is where we specify the type of segment we want and the key value. It is also possible to simply request the next record of a particular segment type without regard to key value. When we specify a key, that means we are using a "qualified" SSA. When we don't specify a key, it means we are using an unqualified SSA.

Here's the COBOL definition of the qualified and unqualified SSAs for the EMPLOYEE segment.

```
01  EMP-QUALIFIED-SSA.
    05  SEGNAME        PIC X(08) VALUE 'EMPLOYEE'.
    05  FILLER         PIC X(01) VALUE '('.
    05  FIELD          PIC X(08) VALUE 'EMPID'.
    05  OPER           PIC X(02) VALUE ' ='.
    05  EMP-ID-VAL     PIC X(04) VALUE '    '.
    05  FILLER         PIC X(01) VALUE ')'.

01  EMP-UNQUALIFIED-SSA.
    05  SEGNAME        PIC X(08) VALUE 'EMPLOYEE'.
    05  FILLER         PIC X(01) VALUE ' '.
```

Both qualified and unqualified SSAs must specify the segment type or name. You specify the key for the qualified SSA in the field we've named EMP-ID-VAL. We'll show many examples of SSAs in the program examples, including the use of Boolean SSA values.

Loading an IMS Database

Ok, finally to our first program. We're going to load the IMS database with a few records from a text file (a.k.a. a flat file). Here is the data file contents:

```
----+----1----+----2----+----3----+----4----+----5----+----6----+----7----+----8
******************************* Top of Data *************************************
1111 VEREEN                     CHARLES                 12 2017-01-01 937253058
1122 JENKINS                    DEBORAH                 05 2017-01-01 435092366
3217 JOHNSON                    EDWARD                  04 2017-01-01 397342007
4175 TURNBULL                   FRED                    01 2016-12-01 542083017
4720 SCHULTZ                    TIM                     09 2017-01-01 650450254
4836 SMITH                      SANDRA                  03 2017-01-01 028374669
6288 WILLARD                    JOE                     06 2016-01-01 209883920
7459 STEWART                    BETTY                   07 2016-07-31 019572830
9134 FRANKLIN                   BRIANNA                 00 2016-10-01 937293598
```

As you can see, we've formatted the records exactly like we want them to be applied to the database. Of course, your input layout could be different than the IMS segment layout, but using the same layout makes it easier because you don't have to do field assignments in the program.

Now let's create a program named COBIMS1 to load the data. We'll define the input file of course. In our program, let's call the file EMPFILE. Let's assume that the DD name for the employee load file is EMPIFILE.

```
        ENVIRONMENT DIVISION.
        INPUT-OUTPUT SECTION.
        FILE-CONTROL.
            SELECT EMPFILE ASSIGN TO EMPIFILE.

        DATA DIVISION.
        FILE SECTION.
        FD  EMPFILE
            RECORDING MODE IS F
            RECORD CONTAINS 80 CHARACTERS.

        01 INSRT-REC.
           05 SEG-IO-AREA PIC X(80).
```

We've specified a SEG-IO-AREA variable to read the input file into and to write the IMS record from. We could have used the fully detailed IO-EMPLOYEE-RECORD instead (and we will later), but I want to demonstrate the value of having your input records structured the same as the IMS segment. When you do this, it really simplifies the coding such that you can both read and write using use a one element structure like SEG-IO-AREA.

Next we'll code the working storage section with a few things including:

- An end of file switch for the loop we'll create to load the records.
- The DLI call constants.
- The Employee segment I/O structure.
- The Employee segment SSA.

```
WORKING-STORAGE SECTION.

 01 WS-FLAGS.
     05  SW-END-OF-FILE-SWITCH    PIC X(1) VALUE 'N'.
         88  SW-END-OF-FILE                VALUE 'Y'.
         88  SW-NOT-END-OF-FILE            VALUE 'N'.

 01 DLI-FUNCTIONS.
     05  DLI-FUNCISRT   PIC X(4) VALUE 'ISRT'.
     05  DLI-FUNCGU     PIC X(4) VALUE 'GU  '.
     05  DLI-FUNCGN     PIC X(4) VALUE 'GN  '.
     05  DLI-FUNCGHU    PIC X(4) VALUE 'GHU '.
     05  DLI-FUNCGNP    PIC X(4) VALUE 'GNP '.
     05  DLI-FUNCREPL   PIC X(4) VALUE 'REPL'.
     05  DLI-FUNCDLET   PIC X(4) VALUE 'DLET'.
     05  DLI-FUNCXRST   PIC X(4) VALUE 'XRST'.
     05  DLI-FUNCCKPT   PIC X(4) VALUE 'CKPT'.

 01 IO-EMPLOYEE-RECORD.
     05   EMPL-ID-IN    PIC X(04).
     05   FILLER        PIC X(01).
     05   EMPL-LNAME    PIC X(30).
     05   FILLER        PIC X(01).
     05   EMPL-FNAME    PIC X(20).
     05   FILLER        PIC X(01).
     05   EMPL-YRS-SRV  PIC X(02).
     05   FILLER        PIC X(01).
     05   EMPL-PRM-DTE  PIC X(10).
     05   FILLER        PIC X(10).

 01 EMP-UNQUALIFIED-SSA.
     05  SEGNAME     PIC X(08) VALUE 'EMPLOYEE'.
     05  FILLER      PIC X(01) VALUE ' '.
```

```
01  EMP-QUALIFIED-SSA.
    05  SEGNAME        PIC X(08) VALUE 'EMPLOYEE'.
    05  FILLER         PIC X(01) VALUE '('.
    05  FIELD          PIC X(08) VALUE 'EMPID'.
    05  OPER           PIC X(02) VALUE ' ='.
    05  EMP-ID-VAL     PIC X(04) VALUE '    '.
    05  FILLER         PIC X(01) VALUE ')'.

01  IMS-RET-CODES.
    05  THREE          PIC S9(9) COMP VALUE +3.
    05  FOUR           PIC S9(9) COMP VALUE +4.
    05  FIVE           PIC S9(9) COMP VALUE +5.
    05  SIX            PIC S9(9) COMP VALUE +6.
```

Finally, we'll code the linkage section which includes the database PCB mask.

```
LINKAGE SECTION.
01  PCB-MASK.
    03  DBD-NAME       PIC X(8).
    03  SEG-LEVEL      PIC XX.
    03  STATUS-CODE    PIC XX.
    03  PROC-OPT       PIC X(4).
    03  FILLER         PIC X(4).
    03  SEG-NAME       PIC X(8).
    03  KEY-FDBK       PIC S9(5) COMP.
    03  NUM-SENSEG     PIC S9(5) COMP.
    03  KEY-FDBK-AREA.
        05 EMPLOYEE-KEY  PIC X(04).
```

We'll work on the procedure division next, which will complete the program. Let's talk about the actual database call. Here's what we'll use:

```
CALL 'CBLTDLI' USING FOUR,
     DLI-FUNCISRT,
     PCB-MASK,
     SEG-IO-AREA,
     EMP-UNQUALIFIED-SSA
```

This is similar to the example we gave earlier with a couple of differences. One difference of course is that we are doing an ISRT call, so we specify the constant DLI-FUNCISRT. The other difference is that we will use an unqualified SSA. On an insert operation, IMS will always establish the record key from the I/O area and therefore it does not use a qualified SSA.

To be clear, any time you are inserting a record, you will use an **unqualified** SSA at the level of the record you are inserting. So if you are inserting a root segment, you will always use an unqualified SSA. If you are inserting a child segment under a root, you will use a qualified SSA on the root segment, and then an unqualified SSA for the child segment. If this seems a bit cryptic now, it should make more sense in later examples where we use child segments and multiple SSAs.

Ok, here's our complete program code. See what you think.

```cobol
            IDENTIFICATION DIVISION.
            PROGRAM-ID. COBIMS1.

           *********************************************************
           *   INSERT A RECORD INTO IMS EMPLOYEE DATABASE           *
           *********************************************************

            ENVIRONMENT DIVISION.
            INPUT-OUTPUT SECTION.
            FILE-CONTROL.
                SELECT EMPFILE ASSIGN TO EMPIFILE.

            DATA DIVISION.
            FILE SECTION.
            FD  EMPFILE
                RECORDING MODE IS F
                RECORD CONTAINS 80 CHARACTERS.

            01 INSRT-REC.
               05 SEG-IO-AREA PIC X(80).

           *********************************************************
           *    W O R K I N G    S T O R A G E    S E C T I O N    *
           *********************************************************

            WORKING-STORAGE SECTION.

              01 WS-FLAGS.
                 05  SW-END-OF-FILE-SWITCH    PIC X(1) VALUE 'N'.
                     88  SW-END-OF-FILE                VALUE 'Y'.
                     88  SW-NOT-END-OF-FILE            VALUE 'N'.

              01 DLI-FUNCTIONS.
                 05 DLI-FUNCISRT  PIC X(4) VALUE 'ISRT'.
                 05 DLI-FUNCGU    PIC X(4) VALUE 'GU  '.
                 05 DLI-FUNCGN    PIC X(4) VALUE 'GN  '.
```

```cobol
       05  DLI-FUNCGHU    PIC X(4) VALUE 'GHU '.
       05  DLI-FUNCGNP    PIC X(4) VALUE 'GNP '.
       05  DLI-FUNCREPL   PIC X(4) VALUE 'REPL'.
       05  DLI-FUNCDLET   PIC X(4) VALUE 'DLET'.
       05  DLI-FUNCXRST   PIC X(4) VALUE 'XRST'.
       05  DLI-FUNCCKPT   PIC X(4) VALUE 'CKPT'.

   01  IN-EMPLOYEE-RECORD.
       05  EMPL-ID-IN     PIC X(04).
       05  FILLER         PIC X(01).
       05  EMPL-LNAME     PIC X(30).
       05  FILLER         PIC X(01).
       05  EMPL-FNAME     PIC X(20).
       05  FILLER         PIC X(01).
       05  EMPL-YRS-SRV   PIC X(02).
       05  FILLER         PIC X(01).
       05  EMPL-PRM-DTE   PIC X(10).
       05  FILLER         PIC X(10).

   01  EMP-UNQUALIFIED-SSA.
       05  SEGNAME        PIC X(08) VALUE 'EMPLOYEE'.
       05  FILLER         PIC X(01) VALUE ' '.

   01  EMP-QUALIFIED-SSA.
       05  SEGNAME        PIC X(08) VALUE 'EMPLOYEE'.
       05  FILLER         PIC X(01) VALUE '('.
       05  FIELD          PIC X(08) VALUE 'EMPID'.
       05  OPER           PIC X(02) VALUE ' ='.
       05  EMP-ID-VAL     PIC X(04) VALUE '    '.
       05  FILLER         PIC X(01) VALUE ')'.

   01  IMS-RET-CODES.
       05  THREE          PIC S9(9) COMP VALUE +3.
       05  FOUR           PIC S9(9) COMP VALUE +4.
       05  FIVE           PIC S9(9) COMP VALUE +5.
       05  SIX            PIC S9(9) COMP VALUE +6.

   LINKAGE SECTION.
    01 PCB-MASK.
       03  DBD-NAME       PIC X(8).
       03  SEG-LEVEL      PIC XX.
       03  STATUS-CODE    PIC XX.
       03  PROC-OPT       PIC X(4).
       03  FILLER         PIC X(4).
       03  SEG-NAME       PIC X(8).
       03  KEY-FDBK       PIC S9(5) COMP.
```

```cobol
       03 NUM-SENSEG       PIC S9(5) COMP.
       03 KEY-FDBK-AREA.
          05 EMPLOYEE-KEY  PIC X(04).
          05 EMPPAYHS-KEY  PIC X(08).


PROCEDURE DIVISION.

    INITIALIZE PCB-MASK
    ENTRY 'DLITCBL' USING PCB-MASK

    PERFORM P100-INITIALIZATION.
    PERFORM P200-MAINLINE.
    PERFORM P300-TERMINATION.
    GOBACK.

P100-INITIALIZATION.

    DISPLAY '** PROGRAM COBIMS1 START **'
    DISPLAY 'PROCESSING IN P100-INITIALIZATION'
    OPEN INPUT EMPFILE.

P200-MAINLINE.

    DISPLAY 'PROCESSING IN P200-MAINLINE'

    READ EMPFILE
        AT END SET SW-END-OF-FILE TO TRUE
    END-READ

    PERFORM UNTIL SW-END-OF-FILE

        CALL 'CBLTDLI' USING FOUR,
            DLI-FUNCISRT,
            PCB-MASK,
            SEG-IO-AREA,
            EMP-UNQUALIFIED-SSA

        IF STATUS-CODE = '  '
           DISPLAY 'SUCCESSFUL INSERT-REC:' SEG-IO-AREA
        ELSE
           PERFORM P400-DISPLAY-ERROR
        END-IF

        READ EMPFILE
            AT END SET SW-END-OF-FILE TO TRUE
```

```
          END-READ

       END-PERFORM.


   P300-TERMINATION.

       DISPLAY 'PROCESSING IN P300-TERMINATION'

       CLOSE EMPFILE
       DISPLAY '** COBIMS1 - SUCCESSFULLY ENDED **'.

   P400-DISPLAY-ERROR.

       DISPLAY 'ERROR ENCOUNTERED - DETAIL FOLLOWS'
       DISPLAY 'SEG-IO-AREA      :' SEG-IO-AREA
       DISPLAY 'DBD-NAME1:'     DBD-NAME
       DISPLAY 'SEG-LEVEL1:'    SEG-LEVEL
       DISPLAY 'STATUS-CODE:'   STATUS-CODE
       DISPLAY 'PROC-OPT1 :'    PROC-OPT
       DISPLAY 'SEG-NAME1 :'    SEG-NAME
       DISPLAY 'KEY-FDBK1 :'    KEY-FDBK
       DISPLAY 'NUM-SENSEG1:'   NUM-SENSEG
       DISPLAY 'KEY-FDBK-AREA1:' KEY-FDBK-AREA.

   *   END OF SOURCE CODE
```

Now we can compile and link the program. You'll need to ask your supervisor or teammate for the compile procedure. I am using JCL as follows to execute a COBOL-IMS compile procedure:

```
//USER01D JOB MSGLEVEL=(1,1),NOTIFY=&SYSUID
//*
//* COMPILE A IMS COBOL PROGRAM
//*
//PLIB     JCLLIB ORDER=SYS1.IMS.PROCLIB
//CL       EXEC IMSCOBCL,
//              MBR=COBIMS1,                   <= COBOL PROGRAM NAME
//              SRCLIB=USER01.COBOL.SRCLIB,    <= COBOL SOURCE LIBRARY
//              COPYLIB=USER01.COPYLIB,        <= COPY BOOK LIBRARY
//              LOADLIB=USER01.IMS.LOADLIB     <= LOAD LIBRARY
```

Finally, one time only you must create and use a special PSB to load the database. The PSB can be identical to the one we already created except it must specify a PROCOPT of **LS** which means Load Sequential. Let's clone EMPPSB into member EMPPSBL:

```
        PRINT NOGEN
        PCB    TYPE=DB,NAME=EMPLOYEE,KEYLEN=20,PROCOPT=LS
        SENSEG NAME=EMPLOYEE,PARENT=0
        SENSEG NAME=EMPPAY,PARENT=EMPLOYEE
        SENSEG NAME=EMPPAYHS,PARENT=EMPPAY
        SENSEG NAME=EMPDEP,PARENT=EMPLOYEE
        PSBGEN LANG=COBOL,PSBNAME=EMPLOYEE
        END
```

Generate this PSB, and then let's execute the program. Execution JCL will look something like this (yours will be whatever you use at your installation). Note that we **MUST** include DD statements for the IMS database and its overflow dataset. Also we include the input file.

```
//USER01D  JOB MSGLEVEL=(1,1),NOTIFY=&SYSUID
//*
//* TO RUN A IMS COBOL PROGRAM
//*
//PLIB     JCLLIB ORDER=SYS1.IMS.PROCLIB
//RUN      EXEC IMSCOBGO,
//              MBR=COBIMS1,                  <= COBOL PROGRAM NAME
//              LOADLIB=USER01.IMS.LOADLIB,   <= LOAD LIBRARY
//              PSB=EMPPSBL,         <= PSB NAME
//              PSBLIB=USER01.IMS.PSBLIB,     <= PSB LIBRARY
//              DBDLIB=USER01.IMS.DBDLIB      <= DBD LIBRARY
//*
//** FLAT FILES IF ANY    **********************
//GO.EMPIFILE DD DSN=USER01.EMPIFILE,DISP=SHR
//*
//** IMS DATABASES (VSAM) ********************
//GO.EMPLOYEE DD DSN=USER01.IMS.EMPLOYEE.CLUSTER,DISP=SHR
//GO.EMPLFLW DD DSN=USER01.IMS.EMPLFLW.CLUSTER,DISP=SHR
//GO.SYSPRINT DD SYSOUT=*
//GO.SYSUDUMP DD SYSOUT=*
//GO.PLIDUMP DD SYSOUT=*
```

And here are the results of the run:

```
** PROGRAM COBIMS1 START **
PROCESSING IN P100-INITIALIZATION
PROCESSING IN P200-MAINLINE
SUCCESSFUL INSERT-REC:1111 VEREEN                     CHARLES
SUCCESSFUL INSERT-REC:1122 JENKINS                    DEBORAH
SUCCESSFUL INSERT-REC:3217 JOHNSON                    EDWARD
```

```
SUCCESSFUL INSERT-REC:4175 TURNBULL              FRED
SUCCESSFUL INSERT-REC:4720 SCHULTZ              TIM
SUCCESSFUL INSERT-REC:4836 SMITH                SANDRA
SUCCESSFUL INSERT-REC:6288 WILLARD              JOE
SUCCESSFUL INSERT-REC:7459 STEWART              BETTY
SUCCESSFUL INSERT-REC:9134 FRANKLIN             BRIANNA
PROCESSING IN P300-TERMINATION
** COBIMS1 - SUCCESSFULLY ENDED **
```

You can browse the IMS data using whatever tool you have such as File Manager IMS. Or you can simply browse the DATA file of the VSAM data set.

```
Browse         USER01.IMS.EMPLOYEE.DATA              Top of 9
Command ===>                                         Scroll PAGE
                    Type DATA     RBA                Format CHAR
                                  Col 1
----+----10---+----2----+----3----+----4----+----5----+----6----+----7----+----
****  Top of data   ****
......1111 VEREEN             CHARLES        12 2017-01-01 93
......1122 JENKINS            DEBORAH        05 2017-01-01 43
......3217 JOHNSON            EDWARD         04 2017-01-01 39
......4175 TURNBULL           FRED           01 2016-12-01 54
......4720 SCHULTZ            TIM            09 2017-01-01 65
......4836 SMITH              SANDRA         03 2017-01-01 02
......6288 WILLARD            JOE            06 2016-01-01 20
......7459 STEWART            BETTY          07 2016-07-31 01
......9134 FRANKLIN           BRIANNA        00 2016-10-01 93
****  End of data   ****
```

For those of you who code in PLI, we must create a different PSB. All you need to do is clone the EMPPSB we are using for COBOL, and on the last line specify that the language is PL/I instead of COBOL.

```
PRINT NOGEN
PCB    TYPE=DB,NAME=EMPLOYEE,KEYLEN=20,PROCOPT=AP
SENSEG NAME=EMPLOYEE,PARENT=0
SENSEG NAME=EMPPAY,PARENT=EMPLOYEE
SENSEG NAME=EMPPAYHS,PARENT=EMPPAY
SENSEG NAME=EMPDEP,PARENT=EMPLOYEE
PSBGEN LANG=PL/I,PSBNAME=EMPLOYEE
END
```

In my case, I created the PLI PSB with member name EMPPSBP so that it won't conflict with the COBOL PSB named EMPPSB. By the way, if you do try to run a PLI program using a COBOL PSB (or vice-versa) you'll get a U0476 abend. Programs must use a PSB that was generated for that particular programming language.

Now, here is the PLI version of the program to load the IMS database.

```pli
PLIIMS1: PROCEDURE (DB_PTR_PCB) OPTIONS(MAIN);
/*********************************************************************
* PROGRAM NAME :    PLIIMS1 - INSERT RECORDS INTO IMS EMPLOYEE DB   *
*********************************************************************/

/*********************************************************************
/*                   F I L E S    U S E D                            *
*********************************************************************/

   DCL EMPIFILE FILE RECORD SEQL INPUT;

/*********************************************************************
/*                W O R K I N G    S T O R A G E                    *
*********************************************************************/

   DCL SW_END_OF_FILE           STATIC BIT(01) INIT('0'B);
   DCL ONCODE                   BUILTIN;
   DCL DB_PTR_PCB               POINTER;

   DCL PLITDLI                  EXTERNAL ENTRY;

   DCL 01 DLI_FUNCTIONS,
          05 DLI_FUNCISRT       CHAR(04) INIT ('ISRT'),
          05 DLI_FUNCGU         CHAR(04) INIT ('GU  '),
          05 DLI_FUNCGN         CHAR(04) INIT ('GN  '),
          05 DLI_FUNCGHU        CHAR(04) INIT ('GHU '),
          05 DLI_FUNCGNP        CHAR(04) INIT ('GNP '),
          05 DLI_FUNCREPL       CHAR(04) INIT ('REPL'),
          05 DLI_FUNCDLET       CHAR(04) INIT ('DLET'),
          05 DLI_FUNCXRST       CHAR(04) INIT ('XRST'),
          05 DLI_FUNCCHKP       CHAR(04) INIT ('CHKP'),
          05 DLI_FUNCROLL       CHAR(04) INIT ('ROLL');

   DCL 01 IN_EMPLOYEE_RECORD,
          05  EMPL_ID_IN        CHAR(04),
          05  FILLER1           CHAR(01),
          05  EMPL_LNAME        CHAR(30),
          05  FILLER2           CHAR(01),
          05  EMPL_FNAME        CHAR(20),
          05  FILLER3           CHAR(01),
          05  EMPL_YRS_SRV      CHAR(02),
          05  FILLER4           CHAR(01),
          05  EMPL_PRM_DTE      CHAR(10),
          05  FILLER5           CHAR(10);

   DCL 01 PCB_MASK              BASED(DB_PTR_PCB),
          05 DBD_NAME            CHAR(08),
          05 SEG_LEVEL           CHAR(02),
          05 STATUS_CODE         CHAR(02),
          05 PROC_OPT            CHAR(04),
          05 FILLER6             FIXED BIN (31),
          05 SEG_NAME             CHAR(08),
```

```
              05  KEY_FDBK              FIXED BIN (31),
              05  NUM_SENSEG            FIXED BIN (31),
              05  KEY_FDBK_AREA,
                  10  EMPLOYEE_ID       CHAR(04);

       DCL 01 EMP_UNQUALIFIED_SSA,
              05  SEGNAME               CHAR(08) INIT ('EMPLOYEE'),
              05  FILLER7               CHAR(01) INIT (' ');

       DCL 01 EMP_QUALIFIED_SSA,
              05  SEGNAME               CHAR(08) INIT('EMPLOYEE'),
              05  FILLER8               CHAR(01) INIT('('),
              05  FIELD                 CHAR(08) INIT('EMPID'),
              05  OPER                  CHAR(02) INIT(' ='),
              05  EMP_ID_VAL            CHAR(04) INIT('    '),
              05  FILLER9               CHAR(01) INIT(')');

       DCL SEG_IO_AREA                  CHAR(80) INIT (' ');

       DCL THREE                        FIXED BIN (31) INIT(3);
       DCL FOUR                         FIXED BIN (31) INIT(4);
       DCL FIVE                         FIXED BIN (31) INIT(5);
       DCL SIX                          FIXED BIN (31) INIT(6);
/**********************************************************************
/*               O N   C O N D I T I O N S                            *
**********************************************************************/

    ON ENDFILE (EMPIFILE) SW_END_OF_FILE = '1'B;

/**********************************************************************
/*             P R O G R A M   M A I N L I N E                        *
**********************************************************************/

CALL P100_INITIALIZATION;
CALL P200_MAINLINE;
CALL P300_TERMINATION;

P100_INITIALIZATION: PROC;

    PUT SKIP LIST ('PLIIMS1: INSERT RECORDS');
    OPEN FILE (EMPIFILE);

    IN_EMPLOYEE_RECORD  = '';
    PCB_MASK = '';

END P100_INITIALIZATION;

P200_MAINLINE: PROC;

       /* MAIN LOOP _ READ THE INPUT FILE, LOAD THE OUTPUT
                      STRUCTURE AND WRITE THE RECORD TO OUTPUT */
```

```
        READ FILE (EMPIFILE) INTO (IN_EMPLOYEE_RECORD);

        DO WHILE (¬SW_END_OF_FILE);

           SEG_IO_AREA = STRING(IN_EMPLOYEE_RECORD);

           CALL PLITDLI (FOUR,
                         DLI_FUNCISRT,
                         PCB_MASK,
                         SEG_IO_AREA,
                         EMP_UNQUALIFIED_SSA);

           IF STATUS_CODE = '  ' THEN
              PUT SKIP LIST ('SUCCESSFUL INSERT-REC:' || SEG_IO_AREA);
           ELSE
              DO;
                 CALL P400_DISPLAY_ERROR;
                 RETURN;
              END;

           READ FILE (EMPIFILE) INTO (IN_EMPLOYEE_RECORD);

        END; /* DO WHILE */

END P200_MAINLINE;

P300_TERMINATION: PROC;

     CLOSE FILE(EMPIFILE);

     PUT SKIP LIST ('PLIIMS1 - SUCCESSFULLY ENDED');

END P300_TERMINATION;

P400_DISPLAY_ERROR: PROC;

     PUT SKIP LIST ('ERROR ENCOUNTERED - DETAIL FOLLOWS');
     PUT SKIP LIST ('SEG_IO_AREA      :' || SEG_IO_AREA);
     PUT SKIP LIST ('DBD_NAME1:' ||   DBD_NAME);
     PUT SKIP LIST ('SEG_LEVEL1:' || SEG_LEVEL);
     PUT SKIP LIST ('STATUS_CODE:' || STATUS_CODE);
     PUT SKIP LIST ('PROC_OPT1 :' || PROC_OPT);
     PUT SKIP LIST ('SEG_NAME1 :' || SEG_NAME);
     PUT SKIP LIST ('KEY_FDBK1 :' || KEY_FDBK);
     PUT SKIP LIST ('NUM_SENSEG1:' || NUM_SENSEG);
     PUT SKIP LIST ('KEY_FDBK_AREA1:' || KEY_FDBK_AREA);

END P400_DISPLAY_ERROR;

END PLIIMS1;
```

Reading a Segment (GU)

Our next program will be named `COBIMS2`, and the purpose is simply to retrieve a record from the `EMPLOYEE` database. In this case, we want the record for employee 3217.

Our basic program structure will be similar to the load program except we will need to perform a Get Unique (`GU`) call, and we'll use a qualified SSA. Remember our qualified SSA structure looks like this:

```
01  EMP-QUALIFIED-SSA.
    05  SEGNAME     PIC X(08) VALUE 'EMPLOYEE'.
    05  FILLER      PIC X(01) VALUE '('.
    05  FIELD       PIC X(08) VALUE 'EMPID'.
    05  OPER        PIC X(02) VALUE ' ='.
    05  EMP-ID-VAL  PIC X(04) VALUE '    '.
    05  FILLER      PIC X(01) VALUE ')'.
```

So we must load the `EMP-ID-VAL` variable with character value '3217'. Our call will look like this.

```
CALL 'CBLTDLI' USING FOUR,
               DLI-FUNCGU,
               PCB-MASK,
               SEG-IO-AREA,
               EMP-QUALIFIED-SSA
```

Now we can code the entire program. We don't need a loop because we are retrieving a single record. So the program is quite simple. Note that we check for a blank status code after the IMS call, and we report an error if it is not blank.

```
       ID DIVISION.
       PROGRAM-ID. COBIMS2.

      ******************************************************
      *    RETRIEVE A RECORD FROM IMS EMPLOYEE DATABASE    *
      ******************************************************

       ENVIRONMENT DIVISION.
       DATA DIVISION.

      ******************************************************
      *  W O R K I N G   S T O R A G E   S E C T I O N    *
      ******************************************************
```

```
       WORKING-STORAGE SECTION.

       01 SEG-IO-AREA     PIC X(80).

       01 DLI-FUNCTIONS.
          05 DLI-FUNCISRT  PIC X(4) VALUE 'ISRT'.
          05 DLI-FUNCGU    PIC X(4) VALUE 'GU  '.
          05 DLI-FUNCGN    PIC X(4) VALUE 'GN  '.
          05 DLI-FUNCGHU   PIC X(4) VALUE 'GHU '.
          05 DLI-FUNCGNP   PIC X(4) VALUE 'GNP '.
          05 DLI-FUNCREPL  PIC X(4) VALUE 'REPL'.
          05 DLI-FUNCDLET  PIC X(4) VALUE 'DLET'.
          05 DLI-FUNCXRST  PIC X(4) VALUE 'XRST'.
          05 DLI-FUNCCKPT  PIC X(4) VALUE 'CKPT'.

       01 EMP-UNQUALIFIED-SSA.
          05  SEGNAME      PIC X(08) VALUE 'EMPLOYEE'.
          05  FILLER       PIC X(01) VALUE ' '.

       01 EMP-QUALIFIED-SSA.
          05  SEGNAME      PIC X(08) VALUE 'EMPLOYEE'.
          05  FILLER       PIC X(01) VALUE '('.
          05  FIELD        PIC X(08) VALUE 'EMPID'.
          05  OPER         PIC X(02) VALUE ' ='.
          05  EMP-ID-VAL   PIC X(04) VALUE '    '.
          05  FILLER       PIC X(01) VALUE ')'.

       01 IMS-RET-CODES.
          05 THREE         PIC S9(9) COMP VALUE +3.
          05 FOUR          PIC S9(9) COMP VALUE +4.
          05 FIVE          PIC S9(9) COMP VALUE +5.
          05 SIX           PIC S9(9) COMP VALUE +6.

       LINKAGE SECTION.
        01 PCB-MASK.
           03 DBD-NAME      PIC X(8).
           03 SEG-LEVEL     PIC XX.
           03 STATUS-CODE   PIC XX.
           03 PROC-OPT      PIC X(4).
           03 FILLER        PIC X(4).
           03 SEG-NAME      PIC X(8).
           03 KEY-FDBK      PIC S9(5) COMP.
           03 NUM-SENSEG    PIC S9(5) COMP.
           03 KEY-FDBK-AREA.
              05 EMPLOYEE-ID  PIC X(04).
              05 EMPPAYHS     PIC X(08).
```

```
       PROCEDURE DIVISION.

           INITIALIZE PCB-MASK
           ENTRY 'DLITCBL' USING PCB-MASK

           PERFORM P100-INITIALIZATION.
           PERFORM P200-MAINLINE.
           PERFORM P300-TERMINATION.
           GOBACK.

       P100-INITIALIZATION.

           DISPLAY '** PROGRAM COBIMS2 START **'
           DISPLAY 'PROCESSING IN P100-INITIALIZATION'.

       P200-MAINLINE.

           DISPLAY 'PROCESSING IN P200-MAINLINE'

           MOVE '3217' TO EMP-ID-VAL

           CALL 'CBLTDLI' USING FOUR,
                        DLI-FUNCGU,
                        PCB-MASK,
                        SEG-IO-AREA,
                        EMP-QUALIFIED-SSA

           IF STATUS-CODE = ' '
              DISPLAY 'SUCCESSFUL GET CALL   '
              DISPLAY 'SEG-IO-ARE : ' SEG-IO-AREA
           ELSE
              DISPLAY 'ERROR IN FETCH :' STATUS-CODE
              PERFORM P400-DISPLAY-ERROR
           END-IF.

       P300-TERMINATION.

           DISPLAY 'PROCESSING IN P300-TERMINATION'
           DISPLAY '** COBIMS2 - SUCCESSFULLY ENDED **'.

       P400-DISPLAY-ERROR.

           DISPLAY 'ERROR ENCOUNTERED - DETAIL FOLLOWS'
           DISPLAY 'SEG-IO-AREA      :' SEG-IO-AREA
           DISPLAY 'DBD-NAME1:'      DBD-NAME
```

```
            DISPLAY 'SEG-LEVEL1:'      SEG-LEVEL
            DISPLAY 'STATUS-CODE:'     STATUS-CODE
            DISPLAY 'PROC-OPT1 :'      PROC-OPT
            DISPLAY 'SEG-NAME1 :'      SEG-NAME
            DISPLAY 'KEY-FDBK1 :'      KEY-FDBK
            DISPLAY 'NUM-SENSEG1:'     NUM-SENSEG
            DISPLAY 'KEY-FDBK-AREA1:'  KEY-FDBK-AREA.

      *     END OF SOURCE CODE
```

Now compile, link and run the program. Here is the output showing that the data was successfully retrieved.

```
** PROGRAM COBIMS2 START **
PROCESSING IN P100-INITIALIZATION
PROCESSING IN P200-MAINLINE
SUCCESSFUL GET CALL
SEG-IO-ARE : 3217 JOHNSON              EDWARD             04 2017-01-01 397342007
PROCESSING IN P300-TERMINATION
** COBIMS2 - SUCCESSFULLY ENDED **
```

Also, we need to test a case where we try to retrieve an employee number which doesn't exist. Let's modify the program to look for `EMP-ID` 3218 which doesn't exist. Now recompile and re-execute the program. Here's the result:

```
** PROGRAM COBIMS2 START **
PROCESSING IN P100-INITIALIZATION
PROCESSING IN P200-MAINLINE
ERROR IN FETCH :GE
ERROR ENCOUNTERED - DETAIL FOLLOWS
SEG-IO-AREA     :
DBD-NAME1:EMPLOYEE
SEG-LEVEL1:00
STATUS-CODE:GE
PROC-OPT1 :AP
SEG-NAME1 :
KEY-FDBK1 :00000
NUM-SENSEG1:00004
KEY-FDBK-AREA1:
PROCESSING IN P300-TERMINATION
** COBIMS2 - SUCCESSFULLY ENDED **
```

Excellent, we captured and reported the error. IMS returned a `GE` return code which means the record was not found.

You'll use GU processing anytime you have a need to access data for a particular record in the database for read-only. Here we read all the root segments. Later we will read segments lower in the database hierarchy.

Here is the PLI source code for the same program.

```
PLIIMS2: PROCEDURE (DB_PTR_PCB) OPTIONS(MAIN);
/******************************************************************
* PROGRAM NAME :    PLIIMS2 - RETRIEVE A RECORD FROM EMPLOYEE DB   *
******************************************************************/

/******************************************************************
/*              W O R K I N G   S T O R A G E                     *
******************************************************************/

     DCL ONCODE                   BUILTIN;
     DCL DB_PTR_PCB               POINTER;
     DCL PLITDLI                  EXTERNAL ENTRY;

     DCL 01 DLI_FUNCTIONS,
            05 DLI_FUNCISRT       CHAR(04) INIT ('ISRT'),
            05 DLI_FUNCGU         CHAR(04) INIT ('GU  '),
            05 DLI_FUNCGN         CHAR(04) INIT ('GN  '),
            05 DLI_FUNCGHU        CHAR(04) INIT ('GHU '),
            05 DLI_FUNCGNP        CHAR(04) INIT ('GNP '),
            05 DLI_FUNCREPL       CHAR(04) INIT ('REPL'),
            05 DLI_FUNCDLET       CHAR(04) INIT ('DLET'),
            05 DLI_FUNCXRST       CHAR(04) INIT ('XRST'),
            05 DLI_FUNCCHKP       CHAR(04) INIT ('CHKP'),
            05 DLI_FUNCROLL       CHAR(04) INIT ('ROLL');

     DCL 01 IO_EMPLOYEE_RECORD,
            05  EMPL_ID_IN        CHAR(04),
            05  FILLER1           CHAR(01),
            05  EMPL_LNAME        CHAR(30),
            05  FILLER2           CHAR(01),
            05  EMPL_FNAME        CHAR(20),
            05  FILLER3           CHAR(01),
            05  EMPL_YRS_SRV      CHAR(02),
            05  FILLER4           CHAR(01),
            05  EMPL_PRM_DTE      CHAR(10),
            05  FILLER5           CHAR(10);

     DCL 01 PCB_MASK              BASED(DB_PTR_PCB),
            05 DBD_NAME           CHAR(08),
            05 SEG_LEVEL          CHAR(02),
            05 STATUS_CODE        CHAR(02),
            05 PROC_OPT           CHAR(04),
            05 FILLER6            FIXED BIN (31),
            05 SEG_NAME           CHAR(08),
            05 KEY_FDBK           FIXED BIN (31),
            05 NUM_SENSEG         FIXED BIN (31),
            05 KEY_FDBK_AREA,
               10 EMPLOYEE_ID     CHAR(04);

     DCL 01 EMP_UNQUALIFIED_SSA,
```

```
              05  SEGNAME              CHAR(08) INIT ('EMPLOYEE'),
              05  FILLER7              CHAR(01) INIT (' ');

      DCL 01 EMP_QUALIFIED_SSA,
              05  SEGNAME              CHAR(08) INIT('EMPLOYEE'),
              05  FILLER8              CHAR(01) INIT('('),
              05  FIELD                CHAR(08) INIT('EMPID'),
              05  OPER                 CHAR(02) INIT(' ='),
              05  EMP_ID_VAL           CHAR(04) INIT('    '),
              05  FILLER9              CHAR(01) INIT(')');

      DCL THREE                        FIXED BIN (31) INIT(3);
      DCL FOUR                         FIXED BIN (31) INIT(4);
      DCL FIVE                         FIXED BIN (31) INIT(5);
      DCL SIX                          FIXED BIN (31) INIT(6);

   /******************************************************************
   /*              P R O G R A M   M A I N L I N E                   *
   ******************************************************************/

   CALL P100_INITIALIZATION;
   CALL P200_MAINLINE;
   CALL P300_TERMINATION;

   P100_INITIALIZATION: PROC;

      PUT SKIP LIST ('PLIIMS2: RETRIEVE RECORD FROM EMPLOYEE DB');
      IO_EMPLOYEE_RECORD  = '';

   END P100_INITIALIZATION;

   P200_MAINLINE: PROC;

      /*  SET THE EMPLOYEE SEGMENT SEARCH ARGUMENT AND CALL PLITDLI */

      EMP_ID_VAL = '3217';

      CALL PLITDLI (FOUR,
                    DLI_FUNCGU,
                    PCB_MASK,
                    IO_EMPLOYEE_RECORD,
                    EMP_QUALIFIED_SSA);

      IF STATUS_CODE = '  ' THEN
         DO;
             PUT SKIP LIST ('SUCCESSFUL RETRIEVAL :');
             PUT SKIP DATA(IO_EMPLOYEE_RECORD);
         END;
      ELSE
         CALL P400_DISPLAY_ERROR;

   END P200_MAINLINE;
```

```
P300_TERMINATION: PROC;

    PUT SKIP LIST ('PLIIMS2 - ENDED SUCCESSFULLY');

END P300_TERMINATION;

P400_DISPLAY_ERROR: PROC;

    PUT SKIP LIST ('ERROR ENCOUNTERED - DETAIL FOLLOWS');
    PUT SKIP LIST ('SEG_IO_AREA      :' || SEG_IO_AREA);
    PUT SKIP LIST ('DBD_NAME1:' ||  DBD_NAME);
    PUT SKIP LIST ('SEG_LEVEL1:' || SEG_LEVEL);
    PUT SKIP LIST ('STATUS_CODE:' || STATUS_CODE);
    PUT SKIP LIST ('PROC_OPT1 :' || PROC_OPT);
    PUT SKIP LIST ('SEG_NAME1 :' || SEG_NAME);
    PUT SKIP LIST ('KEY_FDBK1 :' || KEY_FDBK);
    PUT SKIP LIST ('NUM_SENSEG1:' || NUM_SENSEG);
    PUT SKIP LIST ('KEY_FDBK_AREA1:' || KEY_FDBK_AREA);

END P400_DISPLAY_ERROR;

END PLIIMS2;
```

And here is the output for retrieving employee 3217.

```
PLIIMS2: RETRIEVE RECORD FROM EMPLOYEE DB
SUCCESSFUL RETRIEVAL :
IO_EMPLOYEE_RECORD.EMPL_ID_IN='3217'           IO_EMPLOYEE_RECORD.FILLER1=' '
IO_EMPLOYEE_RECORD.EMPL_LNAME='JOHNSON               '              IO_EMPLO
IO_EMPLOYEE_RECORD.EMPL_FNAME='EDWARD          '              IO_EMPLO
IO_EMPLOYEE_RECORD.EMPL_YRS_SRV='04'           IO_EMPLOYEE_RECORD.FILLER4=' '
IO_EMPLOYEE_RECORD.EMPL_PRM_DTE='2017-01-01'   IO_EMPLOYEE_RECORD.FILLER5=' 397
PLIIMS2 - ENDED SUCCESSFULLY
```

If we change the record number to employee 3218, we get this output:

```
PLIIMS2: RETRIEVE RECORD FROM EMPLOYEE DB
ERROR ENCOUNTERED - DETAIL FOLLOWS
SEG_IO_AREA      :
DBD_NAME1:EMPLOYEE
SEG_LEVEL1:00
STATUS_CODE:GE
PROC_OPT1 :AP
SEG_NAME1 :
KEY_FDBK1 :                  0
NUM_SENSEG1:                 4
KEY_FDBK_AREA1:
PLIIMS2 - ENDED SUCCESSFULLY
```

Reading a Database Sequentially (GN)

Our next program `COBIMS3` will read the entire database sequentially. This scenario isn't unusual (a payroll program might process the database sequentially to generate pay checks) so you'll want to have a model of how to carry it out.

Basically we are going to create a loop that will walk through the database sequentially getting each EMPLOYEE segment using Get Next (GN) calls. We'll need a switch to indicate a stopping point which will be the end of the database (IMS status code GB). We'll also use an unqualified SSA since we don't need to know the key of each record to traverse the database. Here is the code.

```cobol
       IDENTIFICATION DIVISION.
       PROGRAM-ID. COBIMS3.

      **********************************************************
      *   WALK THROUGH THE EMPLOYEE (ROOT) SEGMENTS OF         *
      *   THE ENTIRE EMPLOYEE IMS DATABASE.                    *
      **********************************************************

       ENVIRONMENT DIVISION.
       INPUT-OUTPUT SECTION.
       DATA DIVISION.

      **********************************************************
      *   W O R K I N G    S T O R A G E    S E C T I O N     *
      **********************************************************

       WORKING-STORAGE SECTION.

        01 WS-FLAGS.
           05  SW-END-OF-DB-SWITCH     PIC X(1) VALUE 'N'.
               88  SW-END-OF-DB                 VALUE 'Y'.
               88  SW-NOT-END-OF-DB             VALUE 'N'.


        01 DLI-FUNCTIONS.
           05 DLI-FUNCISRT    PIC X(4) VALUE 'ISRT'.
           05 DLI-FUNCGU      PIC X(4) VALUE 'GU  '.
           05 DLI-FUNCGN      PIC X(4) VALUE 'GN  '.
           05 DLI-FUNCGHU     PIC X(4) VALUE 'GHU '.
           05 DLI-FUNCGNP     PIC X(4) VALUE 'GNP '.
           05 DLI-FUNCREPL    PIC X(4) VALUE 'REPL'.
           05 DLI-FUNCDLET    PIC X(4) VALUE 'DLET'.
           05 DLI-FUNCXRST    PIC X(4) VALUE 'XRST'.
           05 DLI-FUNCCKPT    PIC X(4) VALUE 'CKPT'.

        01 IN-EMPLOYEE-RECORD.
           05   EMPL-ID-IN     PIC X(04).
           05   FILLER         PIC X(01).
           05   EMPL-LNAME     PIC X(30).
           05   FILLER         PIC X(01).
           05   EMPL-FNAME     PIC X(20).
           05   FILLER         PIC X(01).
           05   EMPL-YRS-SRV   PIC X(02).
           05   FILLER         PIC X(01).
           05   EMPL-PRM-DTE   PIC X(10).
```

```
           05  FILLER        PIC X(10).

       01 EMP-UNQUALIFIED-SSA.
           05  SEGNAME       PIC X(08) VALUE 'EMPLOYEE'.
           05  FILLER        PIC X(01) VALUE ' '.

       01 EMP-QUALIFIED-SSA.
           05  SEGNAME       PIC X(08) VALUE 'EMPLOYEE'.
           05  FILLER        PIC X(01) VALUE '('.
           05  FIELD         PIC X(08) VALUE 'EMPID'.
           05  OPER          PIC X(02) VALUE ' ='.
           05  EMP-ID-VAL    PIC X(04) VALUE '    '.
           05  FILLER        PIC X(01) VALUE ')'.

       01 SEG-IO-AREA        PIC X(80).

       01 IMS-RET-CODES.
           05  THREE         PIC S9(9) COMP VALUE +3.
           05  FOUR          PIC S9(9) COMP VALUE +4.
           05  FIVE          PIC S9(9) COMP VALUE +5.
           05  SIX           PIC S9(9) COMP VALUE +6.

       LINKAGE SECTION.
        01 PCB-MASK.
           03  DBD-NAME      PIC X(8).
           03  SEG-LEVEL     PIC XX.
           03  STATUS-CODE   PIC XX.
           03  PROC-OPT      PIC X(4).
           03  FILLER        PIC X(4).
           03  SEG-NAME      PIC X(8).
           03  KEY-FDBK      PIC S9(5) COMP.
           03  NUM-SENSEG    PIC S9(5) COMP.
           03  KEY-FDBK-AREA.
              05  EMPLOYEE-KEY  PIC X(04).
              05  EMPPAYHS-KEY  PIC X(08).

       PROCEDURE DIVISION.

           INITIALIZE PCB-MASK
           ENTRY 'DLITCBL' USING PCB-MASK

           PERFORM P100-INITIALIZATION.
           PERFORM P200-MAINLINE.
           PERFORM P300-TERMINATION.
           GOBACK.

       P100-INITIALIZATION.

           DISPLAY '** PROGRAM COBIMS3 START **'
           DISPLAY 'PROCESSING IN P100-INITIALIZATION'.

      *    DO INITIAL DB READ FOR FIRST EMPLOYEE RECORD
```

```
        CALL 'CBLTDLI' USING FOUR,
              DLI-FUNCGN,
              PCB-MASK,
              SEG-IO-AREA,
              EMP-UNQUALIFIED-SSA

        IF STATUS-CODE = '  ' THEN
           NEXT SENTENCE
        ELSE
           IF STATUS-CODE = 'GB' THEN
              SET SW-END-OF-DB TO TRUE
              DISPLAY 'END OF DATABASE :'
           ELSE
              PERFORM P400-DISPLAY-ERROR
              GOBACK
           END-IF

        END-IF.

   P200-MAINLINE.

        DISPLAY 'PROCESSING IN P200-MAINLINE'

*     CHECK STATUS CODE AND FIRST RECORD

        IF SW-END-OF-DB THEN
           DISPLAY 'NO RECORDS TO PROCESS!!'
        ELSE
           PERFORM UNTIL SW-END-OF-DB
              DISPLAY 'SUCCESSFUL READ :' SEG-IO-AREA

              CALL 'CBLTDLI' USING FOUR,
                    DLI-FUNCGN,
                    PCB-MASK,
                    SEG-IO-AREA,
                    EMP-UNQUALIFIED-SSA

              IF STATUS-CODE = 'GB' THEN
                 SET SW-END-OF-DB TO TRUE
                 DISPLAY 'END OF DATABASE'
              ELSE
                 IF STATUS-CODE NOT EQUAL SPACES THEN
                    PERFORM P400-DISPLAY-ERROR
                    GOBACK
                 END-IF
              END-IF

           END-PERFORM.

        DISPLAY 'FINISHED PROCESSING IN P200-MAINLINE'.

   P300-TERMINATION.
```

```
            DISPLAY 'PROCESSING IN P300-TERMINATION'
            DISPLAY '** COBIMS3 - SUCCESSFULLY ENDED **'.

        P400-DISPLAY-ERROR.

            DISPLAY 'ERROR ENCOUNTERED - DETAIL FOLLOWS'
            DISPLAY 'SEG-IO-AREA       :' SEG-IO-AREA
            DISPLAY 'DBD-NAME1:'         DBD-NAME
            DISPLAY 'SEG-LEVEL1:'        SEG-LEVEL
            DISPLAY 'STATUS-CODE:'       STATUS-CODE
            DISPLAY 'PROC-OPT1 :'        PROC-OPT
            DISPLAY 'SEG-NAME1 :'        SEG-NAME
            DISPLAY 'KEY-FDBK1 :'        KEY-FDBK
            DISPLAY 'NUM-SENSEG1:'       NUM-SENSEG
            DISPLAY 'KEY-FDBK-AREA1:'    KEY-FDBK-AREA.

    *    END OF SOURCE CODE
```

Now let's compile and link, and then execute COBIMS3. Here's the run output.

```
** PROGRAM COBIMS3 START **
PROCESSING IN P100-INITIALIZATION
PROCESSING IN P200-MAINLINE
SUCCESSFUL READ :1111 VEREEN              CHARLES          12 201
SUCCESSFUL READ :1122 JENKINS             DEBORAH          05 201
SUCCESSFUL READ :3217 JOHNSON             EDWARD           04 201
SUCCESSFUL READ :4175 TURNBULL            FRED             01 201
SUCCESSFUL READ :4720 SCHULTZ             TIM              09 201
SUCCESSFUL READ :4836 SMITH               SANDRA           03 201
SUCCESSFUL READ :6288 WILLARD             JOE              06 201
SUCCESSFUL READ :7459 STEWART             BETTY            07 201
SUCCESSFUL READ :9134 FRANKLIN            BRIANNA          00 201
END OF DATABASE
FINISHED PROCESSING IN P200-MAINLINE
PROCESSING IN P300-TERMINATION
** COBIMS3 - SUCCESSFULLY ENDED **
```

You now have a model for any kind of sequential processing you want to do on root segments. Processing child segments is a bit more involved, but not much. We'll show an example of that later.

Here's the PLI source for the program:

```
PLIIMS3: PROCEDURE (DB_PTR_PCB) OPTIONS(MAIN);
 /****************************************************************
  * PROGRAM NAME: PLIIMS3 - WALK THROUGH THE EMPLOYEE (ROOT)     *
  *                         SEGMENTS OF THE EMPLOYEE IMS DATABASE. *
  ****************************************************************/

 /****************************************************************
 /*                    W O R K I N G   S T O R A G E             *
```

```
        *******************************************************************/

        DCL SW_END_OF_DB              STATIC BIT(01) INIT('0'B);
        DCL ONCODE                    BUILTIN;
        DCL DB_PTR_PCB                POINTER;

        DCL PLITDLI                   EXTERNAL ENTRY;

        DCL 01 DLI_FUNCTIONS,
            05 DLI_FUNCISRT           CHAR(04) INIT ('ISRT'),
            05 DLI_FUNCGU             CHAR(04) INIT ('GU  '),
            05 DLI_FUNCGN             CHAR(04) INIT ('GN  '),
            05 DLI_FUNCGHU            CHAR(04) INIT ('GHU '),
            05 DLI_FUNCGNP            CHAR(04) INIT ('GNP '),
            05 DLI_FUNCREPL           CHAR(04) INIT ('REPL'),
            05 DLI_FUNCDLET           CHAR(04) INIT ('DLET'),
            05 DLI_FUNCXRST           CHAR(04) INIT ('XRST'),
            05 DLI_FUNCCHKP           CHAR(04) INIT ('CHKP'),
            05 DLI_FUNCROLL           CHAR(04) INIT ('ROLL');

        DCL 01 IO_EMPLOYEE_RECORD,
            05  EMPL_ID_IN            CHAR(04),
            05  FILLER1               CHAR(01),
            05  EMPL_LNAME            CHAR(30),
            05  FILLER2               CHAR(01),
            05  EMPL_FNAME            CHAR(20),
            05  FILLER3               CHAR(01),
            05  EMPL_YRS_SRV          CHAR(02),
            05  FILLER4               CHAR(01),
            05  EMPL_PRM_DTE          CHAR(10),
            05  FILLER5               CHAR(10);

        DCL 01 PCB_MASK               BASED(DB_PTR_PCB),
            05 DBD_NAME               CHAR(08),
            05 SEG_LEVEL              CHAR(02),
            05 STATUS_CODE            CHAR(02),
            05 PROC_OPT               CHAR(04),
            05 FILLER6                FIXED BIN (31),
            05 SEG_NAME               CHAR(08),
            05 KEY_FDBK               FIXED BIN (31),
            05 NUM_SENSEG             FIXED BIN (31),
            05 KEY_FDBK_AREA,
              10 EMPLOYEE_ID          CHAR(04);

        DCL 01 EMP_UNQUALIFIED_SSA,
            05  SEGNAME               CHAR(08) INIT ('EMPLOYEE'),
            05  FILLER7               CHAR(01) INIT (' ');

        DCL 01 EMP_QUALIFIED_SSA,
            05  SEGNAME               CHAR(08) INIT('EMPLOYEE'),
            05  FILLER8               CHAR(01) INIT('('),
            05  FIELD                 CHAR(08) INIT('EMPID'),
            05  OPER                  CHAR(02) INIT(' ='),
```

```
               05  EMP_ID_VAL          CHAR(04) INIT('    '),
               05  FILLER9             CHAR(01) INIT(')');

    DCL THREE                          FIXED BIN (31) INIT(3);
    DCL FOUR                           FIXED BIN (31) INIT(4);
    DCL FIVE                           FIXED BIN (31) INIT(5);
    DCL SIX                            FIXED BIN (31) INIT(6);

/********************************************************************
/*              P R O G R A M    M A I N L I N E                    *
********************************************************************/

CALL P100_INITIALIZATION;
CALL P200_MAINLINE;
CALL P300_TERMINATION;

P100_INITIALIZATION: PROC;

    PUT SKIP LIST ('PLIIMS3: TRAVERSE EMPLOYEE DATABASE ROOT SEGS');
    PCB_MASK = '';
    IO_EMPLOYEE_RECORD = '';

 /* DO INITIAL DB READ FOR FIRST EMPLOYEE RECORD */

    CALL PLITDLI (FOUR,
                  DLI_FUNCGN,
                  PCB_MASK,
                  IO_EMPLOYEE_RECORD,
                  EMP_UNQUALIFIED_SSA);

    IF STATUS_CODE = '  ' THEN;
    ELSE
       IF STATUS_CODE = 'GB' THEN
          DO;
              SW_END_OF_DB = '1'B;
              PUT SKIP LIST ('** END OF DATABASE');
          END;
       ELSE
          DO;
              CALL P400_DISPLAY_ERROR;
              RETURN;
          END;

END P100_INITIALIZATION;

P200_MAINLINE: PROC;

    /*  MAIN LOOP - CYCLE THROUGH ALL ROOT SEGMENTS IN THE DB,
                    DISPLAYING THE DATA RETRIEVED                 */

         IF SW_END_OF_DB THEN
            PUT SKIP LIST ('NO RECORDS TO PROCESS!!');
```

```
            ELSE
                DO WHILE (¬SW_END_OF_DB);
                    PUT SKIP LIST ('SUCCESSFUL READ :'
                        || IO_EMPLOYEE_RECORD);

                    CALL PLITDLI (FOUR,
                                  DLI_FUNCGN,
                                  PCB_MASK,
                                  IO_EMPLOYEE_RECORD,
                                  EMP_UNQUALIFIED_SSA);

                    IF STATUS_CODE = '  ' THEN;
                    ELSE
                        IF STATUS_CODE = 'GB' THEN
                            DO;
                                SW_END_OF_DB = '1'B;
                                PUT SKIP LIST ('** END OF DATABASE');
                            END;
                        ELSE
                            DO;
                                CALL P400_DISPLAY_ERROR;
                                RETURN;
                            END;

                END; /* DO WHILE */

            PUT SKIP LIST ('FINISHED PROCESSING IN P200_MAINLINE');

END P200_MAINLINE;

P300_TERMINATION: PROC;
    CLOSE FILE(EMPIFILE);

    PUT SKIP LIST ('PLIIMS3 - SUCCESSFULLY ENDED');

END P300_TERMINATION;

P400_DISPLAY_ERROR: PROC;

    PUT SKIP LIST ('ERROR ENCOUNTERED - DETAIL FOLLOWS');
    PUT SKIP LIST ('SEG_IO_AREA     :' || SEG_IO_AREA);
    PUT SKIP LIST ('DBD_NAME1:' ||  DBD_NAME);
    PUT SKIP LIST ('SEG_LEVEL1:' || SEG_LEVEL);
    PUT SKIP LIST ('STATUS_CODE:' || STATUS_CODE);
    PUT SKIP LIST ('PROC_OPT1 :' || PROC_OPT);
    PUT SKIP LIST ('SEG_NAME1 :' || SEG_NAME);
    PUT SKIP LIST ('KEY_FDBK1 :' || KEY_FDBK);
    PUT SKIP LIST ('NUM_SENSEG1:' || NUM_SENSEG);
    PUT SKIP LIST ('KEY_FDBK_AREA1:' || KEY_FDBK_AREA);

END P400_DISPLAY_ERROR;

END PLIIMS3;
```

The output from `PLIIMS3` is here:

```
PLIIMS3: TRAVERSE EMPLOYEE DATABASE ROOT SEGS
SUCCESSFUL READ :1111    SUCCESSFUL READ :       SUCCESSFUL READ :VEREEN
SUCCESSFUL READ :CHARLES                          SUCCESSFUL READ :         SUCCESSF
SUCCESSFUL READ :2017-01-01                       SUCCESSFUL READ : 937253058
SUCCESSFUL READ :1122    SUCCESSFUL READ :       SUCCESSFUL READ :JENKINS
SUCCESSFUL READ :DEBORAH                          SUCCESSFUL READ :         SUCCESSF
SUCCESSFUL READ :2017-01-01                       SUCCESSFUL READ : 435092366
SUCCESSFUL READ :3217    SUCCESSFUL READ :       SUCCESSFUL READ :JOHNSON
SUCCESSFUL READ :EDWARD                           SUCCESSFUL READ :         SUCCESSF
SUCCESSFUL READ :2017-01-01                       SUCCESSFUL READ : 397342007
SUCCESSFUL READ :4175    SUCCESSFUL READ :       SUCCESSFUL READ :TURNBULL
SUCCESSFUL READ :FRED                             SUCCESSFUL READ :         SUCCESSF
SUCCESSFUL READ :2016-12-01                       SUCCESSFUL READ : 542083017
SUCCESSFUL READ :4720    SUCCESSFUL READ :       SUCCESSFUL READ :SCHULTZ
SUCCESSFUL READ :TIM                              SUCCESSFUL READ :         SUCCESSF
SUCCESSFUL READ :2017-01-01                       SUCCESSFUL READ : 650450254
SUCCESSFUL READ :4836    SUCCESSFUL READ :       SUCCESSFUL READ :SMITH
SUCCESSFUL READ :SANDRA                           SUCCESSFUL READ :         SUCCESSF
SUCCESSFUL READ :2017-01-01                       SUCCESSFUL READ : 028374669
SUCCESSFUL READ :6288    SUCCESSFUL READ :       SUCCESSFUL READ :WILLARD
SUCCESSFUL READ :JOE                              SUCCESSFUL READ :         SUCCESSF
SUCCESSFUL READ :2016-01-01                       SUCCESSFUL READ : 209883920
SUCCESSFUL READ :7459    SUCCESSFUL READ :       SUCCESSFUL READ :STEWART
SUCCESSFUL READ :BETTY                            SUCCESSFUL READ :         SUCCESSF
SUCCESSFUL READ :2016-07-31                       SUCCESSFUL READ : 019572830
SUCCESSFUL READ :9134    SUCCESSFUL READ :       SUCCESSFUL READ :FRANKLIN
SUCCESSFUL READ :BRIANNA                          SUCCESSFUL READ :         SUCCESSF
SUCCESSFUL READ :2016-10-01                       SUCCESSFUL READ : 937293598
** END OF DATABASE
FINISHED PROCESSING IN P200_MAINLINE
PLIIMS3 - SUCCESSFULLY ENDED
```

Updating a Segment (`GHU`/`REPL`)

In `COBIMS4` we will update a record. Updating (either changing or deleting a record) always involves two steps in IMS. You must first get and lock the record you are operating on so that no other process can make updates to it. Second you issue either a `REPL` or `DLET` call.

A Get Hold Unique (`GHU`) call prevents any other process from making modifications to the record until you are finished with it. Similar calls are Get Hold Next (`GHN`) and Get Hold Next in Parent (`GHNP`).

For this example, let's change the promotion date on employee 9134 to Sept 1, 2016. To do that we need a `GHU` call with a qualified SSA that we have loaded with the employee id value of 9134.

```
MOVE '9134' TO EMP-ID-VAL
```

Here is the `GHU` call, and notice we are using `IO-EMPLOYEE-RECORD` as our segment I/O area. This is because it has the full record layout with all the fields which makes it easy to change the promotion date by field assignment.

```
CALL 'CBLTDLI' USING FOUR,
               DLI-FUNCGHU,
               PCB-MASK,
               IO-EMPLOYEE-RECORD,
               EMP-QUALIFIED-SSA
```

Once you've done the `GHU` call you can change the value of the promotion date.

```
MOVE '2016-09-01' TO EMPL-PRM-DTE
```

Finally you issue the `REPL` call. A `REPL` does not use any SSA since the record is already held in memory. It simply uses the segment I/O area to perform the update to the database. So you only have three parameters.

```
CALL 'CBLTDLI' USING THREE,
               DLI-FUNCREPL,
               PCB-MASK,
               IO-EMPLOYEE-RECORD
```

Here is the entire program listing for `COBIMS4`.

```
        ID DIVISION.
 PROGRAM-ID. COBIMS4.

 ********************************************************
 *     UPDATE A RECORD FROM IMS EMPLOYEE DATABASE       *
 ********************************************************

 ENVIRONMENT DIVISION.
 DATA DIVISION.

 ********************************************************
 *   W O R K I N G    S T O R A G E    S E C T I O N   *
 ********************************************************

 WORKING-STORAGE SECTION.

 01 SEG-IO-AREA      PIC X(80).

 01 IO-EMPLOYEE-RECORD.
     05   EMPL-ID-IN     PIC X(04).
     05   FILLER         PIC X(01).
     05   EMPL-LNAME     PIC X(30).
     05   FILLER         PIC X(01).
```

```
        05  EMPL-FNAME    PIC X(20).
        05  FILLER        PIC X(01).
        05  EMPL-YRS-SRV  PIC X(02).
        05  FILLER        PIC X(01).
        05  EMPL-PRM-DTE  PIC X(10).
        05  FILLER        PIC X(10).

    01 DLI-FUNCTIONS.
        05  DLI-FUNCISRT  PIC X(4) VALUE 'ISRT'.
        05  DLI-FUNCGU    PIC X(4) VALUE 'GU  '.
        05  DLI-FUNCGN    PIC X(4) VALUE 'GN  '.
        05  DLI-FUNCGHU   PIC X(4) VALUE 'GHU '.
        05  DLI-FUNCGNP   PIC X(4) VALUE 'GNP '.
        05  DLI-FUNCREPL  PIC X(4) VALUE 'REPL'.
        05  DLI-FUNCDLET  PIC X(4) VALUE 'DLET'.
        05  DLI-FUNCXRST  PIC X(4) VALUE 'XRST'.
        05  DLI-FUNCCKPT  PIC X(4) VALUE 'CKPT'.

    01 EMP-UNQUALIFIED-SSA.
        05  SEGNAME       PIC X(08) VALUE 'EMPLOYEE'.
        05  FILLER        PIC X(01) VALUE ' '.

    01 EMP-QUALIFIED-SSA.
        05  SEGNAME       PIC X(08) VALUE 'EMPLOYEE'.
        05  FILLER        PIC X(01) VALUE '('.
        05  FIELD         PIC X(08) VALUE 'EMPID'.
        05  OPER          PIC X(02) VALUE ' ='.
        05  EMP-ID-VAL    PIC X(04) VALUE '    '.
        05  FILLER        PIC X(01) VALUE ')'.

    01 IMS-RET-CODES.
        05 THREE          PIC S9(9) COMP VALUE +3.
        05 FOUR           PIC S9(9) COMP VALUE +4.
        05 FIVE           PIC S9(9) COMP VALUE +5.
        05 SIX            PIC S9(9) COMP VALUE +6.

    LINKAGE SECTION.
     01 PCB-MASK.
        03 DBD-NAME       PIC X(8).
        03 SEG-LEVEL      PIC XX.
        03 STATUS-CODE    PIC XX.
        03 PROC-OPT       PIC X(4).
        03 FILLER         PIC X(4).
        03 SEG-NAME       PIC X(8).
        03 KEY-FDBK       PIC S9(5) COMP.
        03 NUM-SENSEG     PIC S9(5) COMP.
        03 KEY-FDBK-AREA.
            05 EMPLOYEE-ID  PIC X(04).
            05 EMPPAYHS     PIC X(08).

    PROCEDURE DIVISION.

        INITIALIZE PCB-MASK
```

```
        ENTRY 'DLITCBL' USING PCB-MASK

        PERFORM P100-INITIALIZATION.
        PERFORM P200-MAINLINE.
        PERFORM P300-TERMINATION.
        GOBACK.

    P100-INITIALIZATION.

        DISPLAY '** PROGRAM COBIMS4 START **'
        DISPLAY 'PROCESSING IN P100-INITIALIZATION'.

    P200-MAINLINE.

        DISPLAY 'PROCESSING IN P200-MAINLINE'
        MOVE '9134' TO EMP-ID-VAL

*   AQCUIRE THE SEGMENT WITH HOLD

        CALL 'CBLTDLI' USING FOUR,
                    DLI-FUNCGHU,
                    PCB-MASK,
                    IO-EMPLOYEE-RECORD,
                    EMP-QUALIFIED-SSA

        IF STATUS-CODE = '  '
           DISPLAY 'SUCCESSFUL GET HOLD CALL  '
           DISPLAY 'IO-EMPLOYEE-RECORD : ' IO-EMPLOYEE-RECORD

*   NOW MAKE THE CHANGE AND REPLACE THE SEGMENT

            MOVE '2016-09-01' TO EMPL-PRM-DTE

            CALL 'CBLTDLI' USING THREE,
                        DLI-FUNCREPL,
                        PCB-MASK,
                        IO-EMPLOYEE-RECORD

           IF STATUS-CODE = '  '
              DISPLAY 'SUCCESSFUL REPLACEMENT '
              DISPLAY 'IO-EMPLOYEE-RECORD : ' IO-EMPLOYEE-RECORD
           ELSE
              DISPLAY 'ERROR IN REPLACE :' STATUS-CODE
              PERFORM P400-DISPLAY-ERROR
           END-IF

        ELSE
           DISPLAY 'ERROR IN GET HOLD :' STATUS-CODE
           PERFORM P400-DISPLAY-ERROR
        END-IF.

    P300-TERMINATION.
```

```
            DISPLAY 'PROCESSING IN P300-TERMINATION'
            DISPLAY '** COBIMS4 - SUCCESSFULLY ENDED **'.

        P400-DISPLAY-ERROR.

            DISPLAY 'ERROR ENCOUNTERED - DETAIL FOLLOWS'
            DISPLAY 'SEG-IO-AREA     :' SEG-IO-AREA
            DISPLAY 'DBD-NAME1:'       DBD-NAME
            DISPLAY 'SEG-LEVEL1:'      SEG-LEVEL
            DISPLAY 'STATUS-CODE:'     STATUS-CODE
            DISPLAY 'PROC-OPT1 :'      PROC-OPT
            DISPLAY 'SEG-NAME1 :'      SEG-NAME
            DISPLAY 'KEY-FDBK1 :'      KEY-FDBK
            DISPLAY 'NUM-SENSEG1:'     NUM-SENSEG
            DISPLAY 'KEY-FDBK-AREA1:'  KEY-FDBK-AREA.

     *      END OF SOURCE CODE
```

Now let's compile and link, and then run the program.

```
** PROGRAM COBIMS4 START **
PROCESSING IN P100-INITIALIZATION
PROCESSING IN P200-MAINLINE
SUCCESSFUL GET HOLD CALL
IO-EMPLOYEE-RECORD : 9134 FRANKLIN         BRIANNA         00  2016-10-01 937293598
SUCCESSFUL REPLACEMENT
IO-EMPLOYEE-RECORD : 9134 FRANKLIN         BRIANNA         00  2016-09-01 937293598
PROCESSING IN P300-TERMINATION
** COBIMS4 - SUCCESSFULLY ENDED **
```

This is the basic model for doing updates to a database segment. Here is the PLI code for those of you who are following along in PLI.

```
   PLIIMS4: PROCEDURE (DB_PTR_PCB) OPTIONS(MAIN);
   /******************************************************************
   * PROGRAM NAME :   PLIIMS4 - UPDATE A RECORD FROM EMPLOYEE DB     *
   ******************************************************************/

   /******************************************************************
   /*            W O R K I N G   S T O R A G E                       *
   ******************************************************************/

      DCL ONCODE                   BUILTIN;
      DCL DB_PTR_PCB               POINTER;
      DCL PLITDLI                  EXTERNAL ENTRY;

      DCL 01 DLI_FUNCTIONS,
             05 DLI_FUNCISRT       CHAR(04) INIT ('ISRT'),
             05 DLI_FUNCGU         CHAR(04) INIT ('GU  '),
             05 DLI_FUNCGN         CHAR(04) INIT ('GN  '),
             05 DLI_FUNCGHU        CHAR(04) INIT ('GHU '),
             05 DLI_FUNCGNP        CHAR(04) INIT ('GNP '),
```

```
        05  DLI_FUNCREPL          CHAR(04) INIT ('REPL'),
        05  DLI_FUNCDLET          CHAR(04) INIT ('DLET'),
        05  DLI_FUNCXRST          CHAR(04) INIT ('XRST'),
        05  DLI_FUNCCHKP          CHAR(04) INIT ('CHKP'),
        05  DLI_FUNCROLL          CHAR(04) INIT ('ROLL');

    DCL 01 IO_EMPLOYEE_RECORD,
        05   EMPL_ID_IN           CHAR(04),
        05   FILLER1              CHAR(01),
        05   EMPL_LNAME           CHAR(30),
        05   FILLER2              CHAR(01),
        05   EMPL_FNAME           CHAR(20),
        05   FILLER3              CHAR(01),
        05   EMPL_YRS_SRV         CHAR(02),
        05   FILLER4              CHAR(01),
        05   EMPL_PRM_DTE         CHAR(10),
        05   FILLER5              CHAR(10);

    DCL 01 PCB_MASK               BASED(DB_PTR_PCB),
        05  DBD_NAME              CHAR(08),
        05  SEG_LEVEL             CHAR(02),
        05  STATUS_CODE           CHAR(02),
        05  PROC_OPT              CHAR(04),
        05  FILLER6               FIXED BIN (31),
        05  SEG_NAME              CHAR(08),
        05  KEY_FDBK              FIXED BIN (31),
        05  NUM_SENSEG            FIXED BIN (31),
        05  KEY_FDBK_AREA,
           10 EMPLOYEE_ID         CHAR(04);

    DCL 01 EMP_UNQUALIFIED_SSA,
        05   SEGNAME              CHAR(08) INIT ('EMPLOYEE'),
        05   FILLER7              CHAR(01) INIT (' ');

    DCL 01 EMP_QUALIFIED_SSA,
        05   SEGNAME              CHAR(08) INIT('EMPLOYEE'),
        05   FILLER8              CHAR(01) INIT('('),
        05   FIELD                CHAR(08) INIT('EMPID'),
        05   OPER                 CHAR(02) INIT(' ='),
        05   EMP_ID_VAL           CHAR(04) INIT('    '),
        05   FILLER9              CHAR(01) INIT(')');

    DCL THREE                     FIXED BIN (31) INIT(3);
    DCL FOUR                      FIXED BIN (31) INIT(4);
    DCL F1VE                      FIXED BIN (31) INIT(5);

/******************************************************************
/*                P R O G R A M   M A I N L I N E                 *
******************************************************************/

CALL P100_INITIALIZATION;
CALL P200_MAINLINE;
CALL P300_TERMINATION;
```

```
P100_INITIALIZATION: PROC;

    PUT SKIP LIST ('PLIIMS4: UPDATE RECORD FROM EMPLOYEE DB');
    IO_EMPLOYEE_RECORD = '';
    PCB_MASK = '';

END P100_INITIALIZATION;

P200_MAINLINE: PROC;

    /*  SET THE EMPLOYEE SEGMENT SEARCH ARGUMENT AND CALL PLITDLI */

    EMP_ID_VAL = '9134';

    CALL PLITDLI (FOUR,
                  DLI_FUNCGHU,
                  PCB_MASK,
                  IO_EMPLOYEE_RECORD,
                  EMP_QUALIFIED_SSA);

    IF STATUS_CODE = ' ' THEN
       DO;
          PUT SKIP LIST ('SUCCESSFUL GET-HOLD CALL :');
          PUT SKIP DATA(IO_EMPLOYEE_RECORD);

      /*  NOW MAKE THE CHANGE AND REPLACE THE SEGMENT */

          EMPL_PRM_DTE = '2016-09-01';

          CALL PLITDLI (THREE,
                        DLI_FUNCREPL,
                        PCB_MASK,
                        IO_EMPLOYEE_RECORD);

          IF STATUS_CODE = ' ' THEN
             DO;
                PUT SKIP LIST ('SUCCESSFUL REPLACE CALL :');
                PUT SKIP DATA(IO_EMPLOYEE_RECORD);
             END;
          ELSE
             DO;
                PUT SKIP LIST ('ERROR IN REPLACE: ' || STATUS_CODE);
                CALL P400_DISPLAY_ERROR;
             END;

       END;

    ELSE
       DO;
          PUT SKIP LIST ('ERROR IN GET HOLD :' || STATUS_CODE);
          CALL P400_DISPLAY_ERROR;
       END;
```

```
      END P200_MAINLINE;

      P300_TERMINATION: PROC;

          PUT SKIP LIST ('PLIIMS4 - ENDED SUCCESSFULLY');

      END P300_TERMINATION;

      P400_DISPLAY_ERROR: PROC;

          PUT SKIP LIST ('ERROR ENCOUNTERED - DETAIL FOLLOWS');
          PUT SKIP LIST ('SEG_IO_AREA     :' || SEG_IO_AREA);
          PUT SKIP LIST ('DBD_NAME1:' ||  DBD_NAME);
          PUT SKIP LIST ('SEG_LEVEL1:' || SEG_LEVEL);
          PUT SKIP LIST ('STATUS_CODE:' || STATUS_CODE);
          PUT SKIP LIST ('PROC_OPT1 :' || PROC_OPT);
          PUT SKIP LIST ('SEG_NAME1 :' || SEG_NAME);
          PUT SKIP LIST ('KEY_FDBK1 :' || KEY_FDBK);
          PUT SKIP LIST ('NUM_SENSEG1:' || NUM_SENSEG);
          PUT SKIP LIST ('KEY_FDBK_AREA1:' || KEY_FDBK_AREA);

      END P400_DISPLAY_ERROR;

      END PLIIMS4;
```

Deleting a Segment (GHU/DLET)

For COBIMS5 we are going to delete a record. Basically the code is exactly the same as for COBIMS4 except we are deleting instead of updating a record. Let's delete employee 9134, the one we just updated. You can simply copy the COBIMS4 code and make modifications to turn it into a delete program.

Here's the source code.

```
           ID DIVISION.
           PROGRAM-ID. COBIMS5.

          ***********************************************
          *     DELETE A RECORD FROM IMS EMPLOYEE DATABASE     *
          ***********************************************

           ENVIRONMENT DIVISION.
           DATA DIVISION.

          ***********************************************
          *   W O R K I N G    S T O R A G E    S E C T I O N   *
          ***********************************************

           WORKING-STORAGE SECTION.

           01 SEG-IO-AREA       PIC X(80).
```

```cobol
01  IO-EMPLOYEE-RECORD.
    05  EMPL-ID-IN     PIC X(04).
    05  FILLER         PIC X(01).
    05  EMPL-LNAME     PIC X(30).
    05  FILLER         PIC X(01).
    05  EMPL-FNAME     PIC X(20).
    05  FILLER         PIC X(01).
    05  EMPL-YRS-SRV   PIC X(02).
    05  FILLER         PIC X(01).
    05  EMPL-PRM-DTE   PIC X(10).
    05  FILLER         PIC X(10).

01  DLI-FUNCTIONS.
    05  DLI-FUNCISRT   PIC X(4) VALUE 'ISRT'.
    05  DLI-FUNCGU     PIC X(4) VALUE 'GU  '.
    05  DLI-FUNCGN     PIC X(4) VALUE 'GN  '.
    05  DLI-FUNCGHU    PIC X(4) VALUE 'GHU '.
    05  DLI-FUNCGNP    PIC X(4) VALUE 'GNP '.
    05  DLI-FUNCREPL   PIC X(4) VALUE 'REPL'.
    05  DLI-FUNCDLET   PIC X(4) VALUE 'DLET'.
    05  DLI-FUNCXRST   PIC X(4) VALUE 'XRST'.
    05  DLI-FUNCCKPT   PIC X(4) VALUE 'CKPT'.

01  EMP-UNQUALIFIED-SSA.
    05  SEGNAME        PIC X(08) VALUE 'EMPLOYEE'.
    05  FILLER         PIC X(01) VALUE ' '.

01  EMP-QUALIFIED-SSA.
    05  SEGNAME        PIC X(08) VALUE 'EMPLOYEE'.
    05  FILLER         PIC X(01) VALUE '('.
    05  FIELD          PIC X(08) VALUE 'EMPID'.
    05  OPER           PIC X(02) VALUE ' ='.
    05  EMP-ID-VAL     PIC X(04) VALUE '    '.
    05  FILLER         PIC X(01) VALUE ')'.

01  IMS-RET-CODES.
    05  THREE          PIC S9(9) COMP VALUE +3.
    05  FOUR           PIC S9(9) COMP VALUE +4.
    05  FIVE           PIC S9(9) COMP VALUE +5.
    05  SIX            PIC S9(9) COMP VALUE +6.


LINKAGE SECTION.
 01  PCB-MASK.
     03  DBD-NAME      PIC X(8).
     03  SEG-LEVEL     PIC XX.
     03  STATUS-CODE   PIC XX.
     03  PROC-OPT      PIC X(4).
     03  FILLER        PIC X(4).
     03  SEG-NAME      PIC X(8).
     03  KEY-FDBK      PIC S9(5) COMP.
     03  NUM-SENSEG    PIC S9(5) COMP.
```

```
       03 KEY-FDBK-AREA.
          05 EMPLOYEE-ID   PIC X(04).
          05 EMPPAYHS      PIC X(08).

   PROCEDURE DIVISION.

       INITIALIZE PCB-MASK
       ENTRY 'DLITCBL' USING PCB-MASK

       PERFORM P100-INITIALIZATION.
       PERFORM P200-MAINLINE.
       PERFORM P300-TERMINATION.
       GOBACK.

   P100-INITIALIZATION.

       DISPLAY '** PROGRAM COBIMS5 START **'
       DISPLAY 'PROCESSING IN P100-INITIALIZATION'.

   P200-MAINLINE.

       DISPLAY 'PROCESSING IN P200-MAINLINE'
       MOVE '9134' TO EMP-ID-VAL

*      AQCUIRE THE SEGMENT WITH HOLD

           CALL 'CBLTDLI' USING FOUR,
                   DLI-FUNCGHU,
                   PCB-MASK,
                   IO-EMPLOYEE-RECORD,
                   EMP-QUALIFIED-SSA

       IF STATUS-CODE = '  '
          DISPLAY 'SUCCESSFUL GET HOLD CALL  '
          DISPLAY 'IO-EMPLOYEE-RECORD : ' IO-EMPLOYEE-RECORD

*      NOW DELETE THE SEGMENT

           CALL 'CBLTDLI' USING THREE,
                   DLI-FUNCDLET,
                   PCB-MASK,
                   IO-EMPLOYEE-RECORD

          IF STATUS-CODE = '  '
             DISPLAY 'SUCCESSFUL DELETION OF ' EMP-ID-VAL
          ELSE
             DISPLAY 'ERROR IN DELETE :' STATUS-CODE
             PERFORM P400-DISPLAY-ERROR
          END-IF

       ELSE
          DISPLAY 'ERROR IN GET HOLD :' STATUS-CODE
          PERFORM P400-DISPLAY-ERROR
```

```
            END-IF.

        P300-TERMINATION.

            DISPLAY 'PROCESSING IN P300-TERMINATION'
            DISPLAY '** COBIMS5 - SUCCESSFULLY ENDED **'.

        P400-DISPLAY-ERROR.

            DISPLAY 'ERROR ENCOUNTERED - DETAIL FOLLOWS'
            DISPLAY 'SEG-IO-AREA      :' SEG-IO-AREA
            DISPLAY 'DBD-NAME1:'       DBD-NAME
            DISPLAY 'SEG-LEVEL1:'      SEG-LEVEL
            DISPLAY 'STATUS-CODE:'     STATUS-CODE
            DISPLAY 'PROC-OPT1 :'      PROC-OPT
            DISPLAY 'SEG-NAME1 :'      SEG-NAME
            DISPLAY 'KEY-FDBK1 :'      KEY-FDBK
            DISPLAY 'NUM-SENSEG1:'     NUM-SENSEG
            DISPLAY 'KEY-FDBK-AREA1:' KEY-FDBK-AREA.

    *   END OF SOURCE CODE
```

Now compile, link and run:

```
** PROGRAM COBIMS5 START **
PROCESSING IN P100-INITIALIZATION
PROCESSING IN P200-MAINLINE
SUCCESSFUL GET HOLD CALL
IO-EMPLOYEE-RECORD : 9134 FRANKLIN            BRIANNA                00 2016-09-01
937293598
SUCCESSFUL DELETION OF 9134
PROCESSING IN P300-TERMINATION
** COBIMS5 - SUCCESSFULLY ENDED **
```

As you can see, the record was deleted. Here is the PLI code to perform the delete.

```
PLIIMS5: PROCEDURE (DB_PTR_PCB) OPTIONS(MAIN);
/***************************************************************
* PROGRAM NAME :   PLIIMS5 - DELETE A RECORD FROM EMPLOYEE DB  *
***************************************************************/

/***************************************************************
/*              W O R K I N G   S T O R A G E                  *
***************************************************************/

    DCL ONCODE                  BUILTIN;
    DCL DB_PTR_PCB              POINTER;
    DCL PLITDLI                 EXTERNAL ENTRY;

    DCL 01 DLI_FUNCTIONS,
         05 DLI_FUNCISRT        CHAR(04) INIT ('ISRT'),
```

```
         05  DLI_FUNCGU           CHAR(04) INIT ('GU  '),
         05  DLI_FUNCGN           CHAR(04) INIT ('GN  '),
         05  DLI_FUNCGHU          CHAR(04) INIT ('GHU '),
         05  DLI_FUNCGNP          CHAR(04) INIT ('GNP '),
         05  DLI_FUNCREPL         CHAR(04) INIT ('REPL'),
         05  DLI_FUNCDLET         CHAR(04) INIT ('DLET'),
         05  DLI_FUNCXRST         CHAR(04) INIT ('XRST'),
         05  DLI_FUNCCHKP         CHAR(04) INIT ('CHKP'),
         05  DLI_FUNCROLL         CHAR(04) INIT ('ROLL');

     DCL 01 IO_EMPLOYEE_RECORD,
         05  EMPL_ID              CHAR(04),
         05  FILLER1              CHAR(01),
         05  EMPL_LNAME           CHAR(30),
         05  FILLER2              CHAR(01),
         05  EMPL_FNAME           CHAR(20),
         05  FILLER3              CHAR(01),
         05  EMPL_YRS_SRV         CHAR(02),
         05  FILLER4              CHAR(01),
         05  EMPL_PRM_DTE         CHAR(10),
         05  FILLER5              CHAR(10);

     DCL 01 PCB_MASK              BASED(DB_PTR_PCB),
         05  DBD_NAME             CHAR(08),
         05  SEG_LEVEL            CHAR(02),
         05  STATUS_CODE          CHAR(02),
         05  PROC_OPT             CHAR(04),
         05  FILLER6              FIXED BIN (31),
         05  SEG_NAME             CHAR(08),
         05  KEY_FDBK             FIXED BIN (31),
         05  NUM_SENSEG           FIXED BIN (31),
         05  KEY_FDBK_AREA,
             10 EMPLOYEE_ID       CHAR(04);

     DCL 01 EMP_UNQUALIFIED_SSA,
         05  SEGNAME              CHAR(08) INIT ('EMPLOYEE'),
         05  FILLER7              CHAR(01) INIT (' ');

     DCL 01 EMP_QUALIFIED_SSA,
         05  SEGNAME              CHAR(08) INIT('EMPLOYEE'),
         05  FILLER8              CHAR(01) INIT('('),
         05  FIELD                CHAR(08) INIT('EMPID'),
         05  OPER                 CHAR(02) INIT(' ='),
         05  EMP_ID_VAL           CHAR(04) INIT('    '),
         05  FILLER9              CHAR(01) INIT(')');

     DCL THREE                    FIXED BIN (31) INIT(3);
     DCL FOUR                     FIXED BIN (31) INIT(4);
     DCL FIVE                     FIXED BIN (31) INIT(5);
     DCL SIX                      FIXED BIN (31) INIT(6);

/******************************************************************
/*                P R O G R A M   M A I N L I N E                 *
```

```
    ****************************************************************/

     CALL P100_INITIALIZATION;
     CALL P200_MAINLINE;
     CALL P300_TERMINATION;

  P100_INITIALIZATION: PROC;

     PUT SKIP LIST ('PLIIMS5: DELETE RECORD FROM EMPLOYEE DB');
     IO_EMPLOYEE_RECORD = '';
     PCB_MASK = '';

  END P100_INITIALIZATION;

  P200_MAINLINE: PROC;

     /*   SET THE EMPLOYEE SEGMENT SEARCH ARGUMENT AND CALL PLITDLI   */

     EMP_ID_VAL = '9134';

     CALL PLITDLI (FOUR,
                   DLI_FUNCGHU,
                   PCB_MASK,
                   IO_EMPLOYEE_RECORD,
                   EMP_QUALIFIED_SSA);

     IF STATUS_CODE = '  ' THEN
        DO;
           PUT SKIP LIST ('SUCCESSFUL GET-HOLD CALL :');
           PUT SKIP DATA(IO_EMPLOYEE_RECORD);

     /*   NOW DELETE THE SEGMENT  */

           CALL PLITDLI (THREE,
                         DLI_FUNCDLET,
                         PCB_MASK,
                         IO_EMPLOYEE_RECORD);

           IF STATUS_CODE = '  ' THEN
              DO;
                 PUT SKIP LIST ('SUCCESSFUL DELETE CALL :');
                 PUT SKIP LIST ('EMPLOYEE ' || EMPL_ID);
              END;
           ELSE
              DO;
                 PUT SKIP LIST ('ERROR IN DELETE: ' || STATUS_CODE);
                 CALL P400_DISPLAY_ERROR;
              END;

        END;

     ELSE
        DO;
```

```
            PUT SKIP LIST ('ERROR IN GET HOLD :' || STATUS_CODE);
            CALL P400_DISPLAY_ERROR;
         END;

   END P200_MAINLINE;

   P300_TERMINATION: PROC;

      PUT SKIP LIST ('PLIIMS5 - ENDED SUCCESSFULLY');

   END P300_TERMINATION;

   P400_DISPLAY_ERROR: PROC;

      PUT SKIP LIST ('ERROR ENCOUNTERED - DETAIL FOLLOWS');
      PUT SKIP LIST ('SEG_IO_AREA     :' || SEG_IO_AREA);
      PUT SKIP LIST ('DBD_NAME1:' || DBD_NAME);
      PUT SKIP LIST ('SEG_LEVEL1:' || SEG_LEVEL);
      PUT SKIP LIST ('STATUS_CODE:' || STATUS_CODE);
      PUT SKIP LIST ('PROC_OPT1 :' || PROC_OPT);
      PUT SKIP LIST ('SEG_NAME1 :' || SEG_NAME);
      PUT SKIP LIST ('KEY_FDBK1 :' || KEY_FDBK);
      PUT SKIP LIST ('NUM_SENSEG1:' || NUM_SENSEG);
      PUT SKIP LIST ('KEY_FDBK_AREA1:' || KEY_FDBK_AREA);

   END P400_DISPLAY_ERROR;

   END PLIIMS5;
```

Inserting Child Segments

So far we've only dealt with root segments. That was pretty straightforward. Now let's introduce child segments. In COBIMS6 we are going to create an EMPPAY segment under each EMPLOYEE root segment. This will be similar to how we inserted root segments except we need to specify which root segment to insert the child segment under.

First, let's look at our input file:

```
       ----+----1----+----2----+----3----+----4----+----5
       ****************************** Top of Data ****
       1111      8700000   670000   362500   20170101
       1122      8200000   600000   341666   20170101
       3217      6500000   550000   270833   20170101
       4175      5500000   150000   229166   20170101
       4720      8000000   250000   333333   20170101
       4836      6200000   220000   258333   20170101
       6288      7000000   200000   291666   20170101
       7459      8500000   450000   354166   20170101
       9134      7500000   250000   312500   20170101
```

To decrypt here a little, the file above contains employee id numbers with annual salary, annual bonus pay, twice-per-month paycheck dollar amount, and the effective date for all this information. Let's create a record structure in COBOL for this file.

```
01  IN-EMPPAY-RECORD.
    05  EMP-ID-IN      PIC X(04).
    05  FILLER         PIC X(05).
    05  REG-PAY-IN     PIC 99999V99.
    05  FILLER         PIC X(02).
    05  BON-PAY-IN     PIC 9999V99.
    05  FILLER         PIC X(02).
    05  SEMIMTH-IN     PIC 9999V99.
    05  FILLER         PIC X(02).
    05  EFF-DATE-IN    PIC X(08).
    05  FILLER         PIC X(38).
```

We'll also need an IMS I/O area for the EMPPAY segment. How about this one? We'll map data from the input record into this I/O area before we do the ISRT action. Note that we are using packed data fields for the IMS segment. This will save some space.

```
01  IO-EMPPAY-RECORD.
    05  PAY-EFF-DATE   PIC X(8).
    05  PAY-REG-PAY    PIC S9(6)V9(2) USAGE COMP-3.
    05  PAY-BON-PAY    PIC S9(6)V9(2) USAGE COMP-3.
    05  SEMIMTH-PAY    PIC S9(6)V9(2) USAGE COMP-3.
    05  FILLER         PIC X(57).
```

Finally, we need our SSA structures. We'll be using the unqualified EMPPAY SSA, but we'll go ahead and add both the qualified and unqualified SSAs to the program.

```
01  EMPPAY-UNQUALIFIED-SSA.
    05  SEGNAME        PIC X(08) VALUE 'EMPPAY  '.
    05  FILLER         PIC X(01) VALUE ' '.

01  EMPPAY-QUALIFIED-SSA.
    05  SEGNAME        PIC X(08) VALUE 'EMPPAY  '.
    05  FILLER         PIC X(01) VALUE '('.
    05  FIELD          PIC X(08) VALUE 'EFFDATE '.
    05  OPER           PIC X(02) VALUE ' ='.
    05  EFFDATE-VAL    PIC X(08) VALUE '        '.
    05  FILLER         PIC X(01) VALUE ')'.
```

So given this information, our ISRT call should look like this. Notice that we use a qualified SSA for the EMPLOYEE root segment, and an unqualified SSA for the EMPPAY segment.

```
        CALL 'CBLTDLI' USING FIVE,
              DLI-FUNCISRT,
```

```
            PCB-MASK,
            IO-EMPPAY-RECORD,
            EMP-QUALIFIED-SSA
            EMPPAY-UNQUALIFIED-SSA
```

Of course we will need a loop for reading the input pay file, and we'll need code to map the input fields to the EMPPAY fields. And we must move the employee id on the input file to the EMPLOYEE qualified SSA. Finally, recall that we deleted employee 9134, but there is a record in the input file for 9134. Have we coded to handle this missing root? We'll soon see.

Here is our completed code for COBIMS6.

```
              IDENTIFICATION DIVISION.
       PROGRAM-ID. COBIMS6.

      ********************************************************
      *    INSERT EMPLOYEE PAY RECORDS INTO THE EMPLOYEE     *
      *    IMS DATABASE. ROOT KEY MUST BE SPECIFIED.         *
      ********************************************************

       ENVIRONMENT DIVISION.
       INPUT-OUTPUT SECTION.

           FILE-CONTROL.
               SELECT EMPPAY-IN-FILE   ASSIGN TO EMPPAYFL.

       DATA DIVISION.

       FILE SECTION.
       FD EMPPAY-IN-FILE
           RECORDING MODE IS F
           RECORD CONTAINS 80 CHARACTERS
           DATA RECORD IS IN-EMPPAY-RECORD.

           01 IN-EMPPAY-RECORD.
               05   EMP-ID-IN     PIC X(04).
               05   FILLER        PIC X(05).
               05   REG-PAY-IN    PIC 99999V99.
               05   FILLER        PIC X(02).
               05   BON-PAY-IN    PIC 9999V99.
               05   FILLER        PIC X(02).
               05   SEMIMTH-IN    PIC 9999V99.
               05   FILLER        PIC X(02).
               05   EFF-DATE-IN   PIC X(08).
               05   FILLER        PIC X(38).

      ********************************************************
      *   W O R K I N G    S T O R A G E    S E C T I O N   *
      ********************************************************
```

```cobol
       WORKING-STORAGE SECTION.

       01  WS-FLAGS.
           05  SW-END-OF-FILE-SWITCH   PIC X(1) VALUE 'N'.
               88  SW-END-OF-FILE               VALUE 'Y'.
               88  SW-NOT-END-OF-FILE           VALUE 'N'.

       01  IO-EMPLOYEE-RECORD.
           05  EMPL-ID-IN     PIC X(04).
           05  FILLER         PIC X(01).
           05  EMPL-LNAME     PIC X(30).
           05  FILLER         PIC X(01).
           05  EMPL-FNAME     PIC X(20).
           05  FILLER         PIC X(01).
           05  EMPL-YRS-SRV   PIC X(02).
           05  FILLER         PIC X(01).
           05  EMPL-PRM-DTE   PIC X(10).
           05  FILLER         PIC X(10).

       01  IO-EMPPAY-RECORD.
           05  PAY-EFF-DATE   PIC X(8).
           05  PAY-REG-PAY    PIC S9(6)V9(2) USAGE COMP-3.
           05  PAY-BON-PAY    PIC S9(6)V9(2) USAGE COMP-3.
           05  SEMIMTH-PAY    PIC S9(6)V9(2) USAGE COMP-3.
           05  FILLER         PIC X(57).

       01  SEG-IO-AREA     PIC X(80).

       01  DLI-FUNCTIONS.
           05  DLI-FUNCISRT   PIC X(4) VALUE 'ISRT'.
           05  DLI-FUNCGU     PIC X(4) VALUE 'GU  '.
           05  DLI-FUNCGN     PIC X(4) VALUE 'GN  '.
           05  DLI-FUNCGHU    PIC X(4) VALUE 'GHU '.
           05  DLI-FUNCGNP    PIC X(4) VALUE 'GNP '.
           05  DLI-FUNCREPL   PIC X(4) VALUE 'REPL'.
           05  DLI-FUNCDLET   PIC X(4) VALUE 'DLET'.
           05  DLI-FUNCXRST   PIC X(4) VALUE 'XRST'.
           05  DLI-FUNCCKPT   PIC X(4) VALUE 'CKPT'.

         01  EMP-UNQUALIFIED-SSA.
             05  SEGNAME    PIC X(08) VALUE 'EMPLOYEE'.
             05  FILLER     PIC X(01) VALUE ' '.

         01  EMP-QUALIFIED-SSA.
             05  SEGNAME    PIC X(08) VALUE 'EMPLOYEE'.
             05  FILLER     PIC X(01) VALUE '('.
             05  FIELD      PIC X(08) VALUE 'EMPID'.
             05  OPER       PIC X(02) VALUE ' ='.
             05  EMP-ID-VAL PIC X(04) VALUE '    '.
             05  FILLER     PIC X(01) VALUE ')'.

         01  EMPPAY-UNQUALIFIED-SSA.
```

```
           05  SEGNAME       PIC X(08) VALUE 'EMPPAY  '.
           05  FILLER        PIC X(01) VALUE ' '.

       01  EMPPAY-QUALIFIED-SSA.
           05  SEGNAME       PIC X(08) VALUE 'EMPPAY  '.
           05  FILLER        PIC X(01) VALUE '('.
           05  FIELD         PIC X(08) VALUE 'EFFDATE '.
           05  OPER          PIC X(02) VALUE ' ='.
           05  EFFDATE-VAL   PIC X(08) VALUE '        '.
           05  FILLER        PIC X(01) VALUE ')'.

       01  IMS-RET-CODES.
           05  THREE         PIC S9(9) COMP VALUE +3.
           05  FOUR          PIC S9(9) COMP VALUE +4.
           05  FIVE          PIC S9(9) COMP VALUE +5.
           05  SIX           PIC S9(9) COMP VALUE +6.


       LINKAGE SECTION.
        01  PCB-MASK.
            03  DBD-NAME      PIC X(8).
            03  SEG-LEVEL     PIC XX.
            03  STATUS-CODE   PIC XX.
            03  PROC-OPT      PIC X(4).
            03  FILLER        PIC X(4).
            03  SEG-NAME      PIC X(8).
            03  KEY-FDBK      PIC S9(5) COMP.
            03  NUM-SENSEG    PIC S9(5) COMP.
            03  KEY-FDBK-AREA.
                05  EMPLOYEE-ID  PIC X(04).
                05  EMPPAYHS     PIC X(08).

       PROCEDURE DIVISION.

           INITIALIZE PCB-MASK
           ENTRY 'DLITCBL' USING PCB-MASK

           PERFORM P100-INITIALIZATION.
           PERFORM P200-MAINLINE.
           PERFORM P300-TERMINATION.
           GOBACK.

       P100-INITIALIZATION.

           DISPLAY '** PROGRAM COBIMS6 START **'
           DISPLAY 'PROCESSING IN P100-INITIALIZATION'
           OPEN INPUT EMPPAY-IN-FILE.

       P200-MAINLINE.

           DISPLAY 'PROCESSING IN P200-MAINLINE'
```

```
    READ EMPPAY-IN-FILE
       AT END SET SW-END-OF-FILE TO TRUE
    END-READ

    PERFORM UNTIL SW-END-OF-FILE

       DISPLAY 'MAPPING FIELDS FOR EMPLOYEE ' EMP-ID-IN
       DISPLAY 'EFF-DATE-IN ' EFF-DATE-IN
       DISPLAY 'REG-PAY-IN  ' REG-PAY-IN
       DISPLAY 'BON-PAY-IN  ' BON-PAY-IN
       DISPLAY 'SEMIMTH-IN  ' SEMIMTH-IN
       MOVE EMP-ID-IN    TO EMP-ID-VAL
       MOVE EFF-DATE-IN  TO PAY-EFF-DATE
       MOVE REG-PAY-IN   TO PAY-REG-PAY
       MOVE BON-PAY-IN   TO PAY-BON-PAY
       MOVE SEMIMTH-IN   TO SEMIMTH-PAY

       CALL 'CBLTDLI' USING FIVE,
            DLI-FUNCISRT,
            PCB-MASK,
            IO-EMPPAY-RECORD,
            EMP-QUALIFIED-SSA
            EMPPAY-UNQUALIFIED-SSA

       IF STATUS-CODE = '  '
          DISPLAY 'SUCCESSFUL INSERT-REC FOR EMP: ' EMP-ID-VAL
          DISPLAY 'SUCCESSFUL INSERT-REC VALUES : '
          IO-EMPPAY-RECORD
       ELSE
          PERFORM P400-DISPLAY-ERROR
       END-IF

       READ EMPPAY-IN-FILE
          AT END SET SW-END-OF-FILE TO TRUE
       END-READ

    END-PERFORM.

P300-TERMINATION.

    DISPLAY 'PROCESSING IN P300-TERMINATION'
    CLOSE EMPPAY-IN-FILE.
    DISPLAY '** COBIMS6 - SUCCESSFULLY ENDED **'.

P400-DISPLAY-ERROR.

    DISPLAY 'ERROR ENCOUNTERED - DETAIL FOLLOWS'
    DISPLAY 'DBD-NAME1:'     DBD-NAME
    DISPLAY 'SEG-LEVEL1:'    SEG-LEVEL
    DISPLAY 'STATUS-CODE:'   STATUS-CODE
    DISPLAY 'PROC-OPT1 :'    PROC-OPT
    DISPLAY 'SEG-NAME1 :'    SEG-NAME
    DISPLAY 'KEY-FDBK1 :'    KEY-FDBK
```

```
            DISPLAY 'NUM-SENSEG1:'   NUM-SENSEG
            DISPLAY 'KEY-FDBK-AREA1:' KEY-FDBK-AREA.

     *      END OF SOURCE CODE
```

Compile and link, and then run the program. Here is the output.

```
** PROGRAM COBIMS6 START **
PROCESSING IN P100-INITIALIZATION
PROCESSING IN P200-MAINLINE
MAPPING FIELDS FOR EMPLOYEE 1111
EFF-DATE-IN 20170101
REG-PAY-IN  8700000
BON-PAY-IN  670000
SEMIMTH-IN  362500
SUCCESSFUL INSERT-REC FOR EMP: 1111
SUCCESSFUL INSERT-REC VALUES : 20170101 g            &
MAPPING FIELDS FOR EMPLOYEE 1122
EFF-DATE-IN 20170101
REG-PAY-IN  8200000
BON-PAY-IN  600000
SEMIMTH-IN  341666
SUCCESSFUL INSERT-REC FOR EMP: 1122
SUCCESSFUL INSERT-REC VALUES : 20170101 b            %
MAPPING FIELDS FOR EMPLOYEE 3217
EFF-DATE-IN 20170101
REG-PAY-IN  6500000
BON-PAY-IN  550000
SEMIMTH-IN  270833
SUCCESSFUL INSERT-REC FOR EMP: 3217
SUCCESSFUL INSERT-REC VALUES : 20170101        &     c
MAPPING FIELDS FOR EMPLOYEE 4175
EFF-DATE-IN 20170101
REG-PAY-IN  5500000
BON-PAY-IN  150000
SEMIMTH-IN  229166
SUCCESSFUL INSERT-REC FOR EMP: 4175
SUCCESSFUL INSERT-REC VALUES : 20170101        &     %
MAPPING FIELDS FOR EMPLOYEE 4720
EFF-DATE-IN 20170101
REG-PAY-IN  8000000
BON-PAY-IN  250000
SEMIMTH-IN  333333
SUCCESSFUL INSERT-REC FOR EMP: 4720
SUCCESSFUL INSERT-REC VALUES : 20170101        &
MAPPING FIELDS FOR EMPLOYEE 4836
EFF-DATE-IN 20170101
REG-PAY-IN  6200000
BON-PAY-IN  220000
SEMIMTH-IN  258333
SUCCESSFUL INSERT-REC FOR EMP: 4836
SUCCESSFUL INSERT-REC VALUES : 20170101
MAPPING FIELDS FOR EMPLOYEE 6288
```

```
EFF-DATE-IN 20170101
REG-PAY-IN  7000000
BON-PAY-IN  200000
SEMIMTH-IN  291666
SUCCESSFUL INSERT-REC FOR EMP: 6288
SUCCESSFUL INSERT-REC VALUES : 20170101              j %
MAPPING FIELDS FOR EMPLOYEE 7459
EFF-DATE-IN 20170101
REG-PAY-IN  8500000
BON-PAY-IN  450000
SEMIMTH-IN  354166
SUCCESSFUL INSERT-REC FOR EMP: 7459
SUCCESSFUL INSERT-REC VALUES : 20170101 e     &      %
MAPPING FIELDS FOR EMPLOYEE 9134
EFF-DATE-IN 20170101
REG-PAY-IN  7500000
BON-PAY-IN  250000
SEMIMTH-IN  312500
```
ERROR ENCOUNTERED - DETAIL FOLLOWS
DBD-NAME1:EMPLOYEE
SEG-LEVEL1:00
STATUS-CODE:GE
PROC-OPT1 :AP
SEG-NAME1 :
KEY-FDBK1 :00000
NUM-SENSEG1:00004
KEY-FDBK-AREA1:   20170101
```
PROCESSING IN P300-TERMINATION
** COBIMS6 - SUCCESSFULLY ENDED **
```

The bolded text above shows that our error code caught the missing root segment and reported it. In this case we took a "soft landing" by not terminating the program. In the real world we might have forced an abend.[2] Or we might possibly have written the record to an exception report for someone to review and correct.

So now you have a model for inserting new data to child segments in an IMS database. Here is the PLI code that corresponds to COBIMS6.

```
PLIIMS6: PROCEDURE (DB_PTR_PCB) OPTIONS(MAIN);
/****************************************************************
* PROGRAM NAME :    PLIIMS6 - INSERT EMPLOYEE PAY RECORDS INTO THE *
*                   EMPLOYEE IMS DB. ROOT KEY MUST BE SPECIFIED.   *
****************************************************************/

/****************************************************************
```

---

[2] You can force an abend with a memory dump by calling LE program CEE3DMP. Details for how to do that are at the link below. We will only take soft abends in this text, so we won't abend with CEE3DMP. https://www.ibm.com/support/knowledgecenter/en/SSLTBW_2.3.0/com.ibm.zos.v2r3.ccca100/ccca1mst78.htm

```
/*                  F I L E S   U S E D                                *
***********************************************************************/

    DCL EMPPAYFL FILE RECORD SEQL INPUT;

/**********************************************************************
/*                W O R K I N G   S T O R A G E                        *
***********************************************************************/

    DCL SW_END_OF_FILE           STATIC BIT(01) INIT('0'B);
    DCL ONCODE                   BUILTIN;
    DCL DB_PTR_PCB               POINTER;

    DCL PLITDLI                  EXTERNAL ENTRY;

    DCL 01 DLI_FUNCTIONS,
        05 DLI_FUNCISRT          CHAR(04) INIT ('ISRT'),
        05 DLI_FUNCGU            CHAR(04) INIT ('GU  '),
        05 DLI_FUNCGN            CHAR(04) INIT ('GN  '),
        05 DLI_FUNCGHU           CHAR(04) INIT ('GHU '),
        05 DLI_FUNCGNP           CHAR(04) INIT ('GNP '),
        05 DLI_FUNCREPL          CHAR(04) INIT ('REPL'),
        05 DLI_FUNCDLET          CHAR(04) INIT ('DLET'),
        05 DLI_FUNCXRST          CHAR(04) INIT ('XRST'),
        05 DLI_FUNCCHKP          CHAR(04) INIT ('CHKP'),
        05 DLI_FUNCROLL          CHAR(04) INIT ('ROLL');

    DCL 01 IN_EMPPAY_RECORD,
        05  EMP_ID_IN            CHAR(04),
        05  FILLER1              CHAR(05),
        05  REG_PAY_IN           PIC '99999V99',
        05  FILLER2              CHAR(02),
        05  BON_PAY_IN           PIC '9999V99',
        05  FILLER3              CHAR(02),
        05  SEMIMTH_IN           PIC '9999V99',
        05  FILLER4              CHAR(02),
        05  EFF_DATE_IN          CHAR(08),
        05  FILLER5              CHAR(38);

    DCL 01 IO_EMPPAY_RECORD,
        05  PAY_EFF_DATE         CHAR(8),
        05  PAY_REG_PAY          FIXED DEC (8,2),
        05  PAY_BON_PAY          FIXED DEC (8,2),
        05  SEMIMTH_PAY          FIXED DEC (8,2),
        05  FILLER55             CHAR(57);

    DCL 01 PCB_MASK              BASED(DB_PTR_PCB),
        05  DBD_NAME             CHAR(08),
        05  SEG_LEVEL            CHAR(02),
        05  STATUS_CODE          CHAR(02),
        05  PROC_OPT             CHAR(04),
        05  FILLER6              FIXED BIN (31),
        05  SEG_NAME             CHAR(08),
```

```
          05  KEY_FDBK            FIXED BIN (31),
          05  NUM_SENSEG          FIXED BIN (31),
          05  KEY_FDBK_AREA,
               10 EMPLOYEE_ID     CHAR(04),
               10 EMP_PAY_DATE    CHAR(08);

   DCL 01 EMP_UNQUALIFIED_SSA,
          05  SEGNAME             CHAR(08) INIT ('EMPLOYEE'),
          05  FILLER7             CHAR(01) INIT (' ');

   DCL 01 EMP_QUALIFIED_SSA,
          05  SEGNAME             CHAR(08) INIT('EMPLOYEE'),
          05  FILLER8             CHAR(01) INIT('('),
          05  FIELD               CHAR(08) INIT('EMPID'),
          05  OPER                CHAR(02) INIT(' ='),
          05  EMP_ID_VAL          CHAR(04) INIT('    '),
          05  FILLER9             CHAR(01) INIT(')');

   DCL 01 EMPPAY_UNQUALIFIED_SSA,
          05  SEGNAME             CHAR(08) INIT('EMPPAY   '),
          05  FILLER10            CHAR(01) INIT(' ');

   DCL 01 EMPPAY_QUALIFIED_SSA,
          05  SEGNAME             CHAR(08) INIT('EMPPAY   '),
          05  FILLER11            CHAR(01) INIT('('),
          05  FIELD               CHAR(08) INIT('EFFDATE '),
          05  OPER                CHAR(02) INIT(' ='),
          05  EFFDATE_VAL         CHAR(08) INIT('        '),
          05  FILLER12            CHAR(01) INIT(')');

   DCL SEG_IO_AREA                CHAR(80) INIT (' ');

   DCL THREE                      FIXED BIN (31) INIT(3);
   DCL FOUR                       FIXED BIN (31) INIT(4);
   DCL FIVE                       FIXED BIN (31) INIT(5);
   DCL SIX                        FIXED BIN (31) INIT(6);
/******************************************************************
/*             ON  CONDITIONS                                     *
******************************************************************/

   ON ENDFILE (EMPIFILE) SW_END_OF_FILE = '1'B;

/******************************************************************
/*             PROGRAM  MAINLINE                                  *
******************************************************************/

CALL P100_INITIALIZATION;
CALL P200_MAINLINE;
CALL P300_TERMINATION;

P100_INITIALIZATION: PROC;
```

```
        PUT SKIP LIST ('PLIIMS6: INSERT RECORDS');
        OPEN FILE (EMPPAYFL);

        IN_EMPPAY_RECORD  = '';
        PCB_MASK = '';

END P100_INITIALIZATION;

P200_MAINLINE: PROC;

    /*  MAIN LOOP - READ THE INPUT FILE, LOAD THE OUTPUT
                    STRUCTURE AND WRITE PAY RECORD TO OUTPUT */

    READ FILE (EMPPAYFL) INTO (IN_EMPPAY_RECORD);

    DO WHILE (¬SW_END_OF_FILE);

       /* ASSIGN KEY FOR EMPLOYEE LEVEL SSA */

       EMP_ID_VAL    = EMP_ID_IN;

       /* ASSIGN PAY FIELDS */

       PAY_EFF_DATE = EFF_DATE_IN;
       PAY_REG_PAY  = REG_PAY_IN;
       PAY_BON_PAY  = BON_PAY_IN;
       SEMIMTH_PAY  = SEMIMTH_IN;

       CALL PLITDLI (FIVE,
                     DLI_FUNCISRT,
                     PCB_MASK,
                     IO_EMPPAY_RECORD,
                     EMP_QUALIFIED_SSA,
                     EMPPAY_UNQUALIFIED_SSA);

       IF STATUS_CODE = '  ' THEN
          DO;
             PUT SKIP LIST ('SUCCESSFUL INSERT PAY REC:');
             PUT SKIP DATA (IO_EMPPAY_RECORD);
          END;
       ELSE
          DO;
             CALL P400_DISPLAY_ERROR;
             RETURN;
          END;

       READ FILE (EMPPAYFL) INTO (IN_EMPPAY_RECORD);

    END; /* DO WHILE */

END P200_MAINLINE;

P300_TERMINATION: PROC;
```

```
           CLOSE FILE(EMPPAYFL);

        PUT SKIP LIST ('PLIIMS6 - SUCCESSFULLY ENDED');

END P300_TERMINATION;

P400_DISPLAY_ERROR: PROC;

        PUT SKIP LIST ('ERROR ENCOUNTERED - DETAIL FOLLOWS');
        PUT SKIP DATA (IO_EMPPAY_RECORD);
        PUT SKIP LIST ('DBD_NAME1:'    ||   DBD_NAME);
        PUT SKIP LIST ('SEG_LEVEL1:'   ||   SEG_LEVEL);
        PUT SKIP LIST ('STATUS_CODE:'  ||   STATUS_CODE);
        PUT SKIP LIST ('PROC_OPT1 :'   ||   PROC_OPT);
        PUT SKIP LIST ('SEG_NAME1 :'   ||   SEG_NAME);
        PUT SKIP LIST ('KEY_FDBK1 :'   ||   KEY_FDBK);
        PUT SKIP LIST ('NUM_SENSEG1:'  ||   NUM_SENSEG);
        PUT SKIP LIST ('KEY_FDBK_AREA1:'  ||  KEY_FDBK_AREA);

END P400_DISPLAY_ERROR;

END PLIIMS6;
```

Reading Child Segments Sequentially (GNP)

Now let's use COBIMS7 to read back the records we just added to the database. We can traverse the database using GN for the root segments and GNP (Get Next Within Parent) calls for the children. So we'll borrow the code from COBIMS3 for walking through the root segments. And then we'll add code for retrieving GNP.

Keep in mind that we've only added a single EMPPAY child under each root segment. If there were more than one child, our code would need to allow for that. But for now, our spec will ask us to simply get a root and then get the first child under that root. Then we will display the pay information for the employee.

We already know how to traverse the root segment. So once we get a root segment, we need to take the EMP-ID returned in the IO-EMPLOYEE-RECORD and use it to set the qualified SSA for EMPLOYEE. We could use the unqualified SSA for the EMPPAY segment, but since we already know the exact key we can as easily use the qualified SSA. And we'll load the segment data into the IO-EMPPAY-RECORD I/O area. This is what our call will look like.

```
           MOVE EMPL-ID-IN TO EMP-ID-VAL
           MOVE '20170101' TO EFFDATE-VAL

           CALL 'CBLTDLI' USING FIVE,
                DLI-FUNCGNP,
```

```
              PCB-MASK,
              IO-EMPPAY-RECORD,
              EMP-QUALIFIED-SSA,
              EMPPAY-UNQUALIFIED-SSA
```

Other than that, our program doesn't need to use any new techniques. Here is the completed program listing.

```
               IDENTIFICATION DIVISION.
        PROGRAM-ID. COBIMS7.

       *********************************************************
       *  WALK THROUGH THE EMPLOYEE AND EMPPAY SEGS OF          *
       *  THE ENTIRE EMPLOYEE IMS DATABASE.                     *
       *********************************************************

        ENVIRONMENT DIVISION.
        INPUT-OUTPUT SECTION.
        DATA DIVISION.

       *********************************************************
       *  W O R K I N G   S T O R A G E   S E C T I O N        *
       *********************************************************

        WORKING-STORAGE SECTION.

         01 WS-FLAGS.
             05  SW-END-OF-DB-SWITCH    PIC X(1) VALUE 'N'.
                 88  SW-END-OF-DB                VALUE 'Y'.
                 88  SW-NOT-END-OF-DB            VALUE 'N'.

         01 IO-EMPLOYEE-RECORD.
             05  EMPL-ID-IN     PIC X(04).
             05  FILLER         PIC X(01).
             05  EMPL-LNAME     PIC X(30).
             05  FILLER         PIC X(01).
             05  EMPL-FNAME     PIC X(20).
             05  FILLER         PIC X(01).
             05  EMPL-YRS-SRV   PIC X(02).
             05  FILLER         PIC X(01).
             05  EMPL-PRM-DTE   PIC X(10).
             05  FILLER         PIC X(10).

         01 IO-EMPPAY-RECORD.
             05  PAY-EFF-DATE   PIC X(8).
             05  PAY-REG-PAY    PIC S9(6)V9(2) USAGE COMP-3.
             05  PAY-BON-PAY    PIC S9(6)V9(2) USAGE COMP-3.
             05  SEMIMTH-PAY    PIC S9(6)V9(2) USAGE COMP-3.
             05  FILLER         PIC X(57).

         01 DISPLAY-EMPLOYEE-PIC.
             05  DIS-REG-PAY    PIC ZZ999.99-.
```

```
          05  DIS-BON-PAY    PIC ZZ999.99-.
          05  DIS-SMT-PAY    PIC ZZ999.99-.

      01  EMP-UNQUALIFIED-SSA.
          05  SEGNAME        PIC X(08) VALUE 'EMPLOYEE'.
          05  FILLER         PIC X(01) VALUE ' '.

      01  EMP-QUALIFIED-SSA.
          05  SEGNAME        PIC X(08) VALUE 'EMPLOYEE'.
          05  FILLER         PIC X(01) VALUE '('.
          05  FIELD          PIC X(08) VALUE 'EMPID'.
          05  OPER           PIC X(02) VALUE ' ='.
          05  EMP-ID-VAL     PIC X(04) VALUE '    '.
          05  FILLER         PIC X(01) VALUE ')'.

      01  EMPPAY-UNQUALIFIED-SSA.
          05  SEGNAME        PIC X(08) VALUE 'EMPPAY  '.
          05  FILLER         PIC X(01) VALUE ' '.

      01  EMPPAY-QUALIFIED-SSA.
          05  SEGNAME        PIC X(08) VALUE 'EMPPAY  '.
          05  FILLER         PIC X(01) VALUE '('.
          05  FIELD          PIC X(08) VALUE 'EFFDATE '.
          05  OPER           PIC X(02) VALUE ' ='.
          05  EFFDATE-VAL    PIC X(08) VALUE '        '.
          05  FILLER         PIC X(01) VALUE ')'.

      01  DLI-FUNCTIONS.
          05  DLI-FUNCISRT   PIC X(4) VALUE 'ISRT'.
          05  DLI-FUNCGU     PIC X(4) VALUE 'GU  '.
          05  DLI-FUNCGN     PIC X(4) VALUE 'GN  '.
          05  DLI-FUNCGHU    PIC X(4) VALUE 'GHU '.
          05  DLI-FUNCGNP    PIC X(4) VALUE 'GNP '.
          05  DLI-FUNCREPL   PIC X(4) VALUE 'REPL'.
          05  DLI-FUNCDLET   PIC X(4) VALUE 'DLET'.
          05  DLI-FUNCXRST   PIC X(4) VALUE 'XRST'.
          05  DLI-FUNCCKPT   PIC X(4) VALUE 'CKPT'.

      01  IMS-RET-CODES.
          05  THREE          PIC S9(9) COMP VALUE +3.
          05  FOUR           PIC S9(9) COMP VALUE +4.
          05  FIVE           PIC S9(9) COMP VALUE +5.
          05  SIX            PIC S9(9) COMP VALUE +6.


       LINKAGE SECTION.
       01  PCB-MASK.
           03  DBD-NAME      PIC X(8).
           03  SEG-LEVEL     PIC XX.
           03  STATUS-CODE   PIC XX.
           03  PROC-OPT      PIC X(4).
           03  FILLER        PIC X(4).
           03  SEG-NAME      PIC X(8).
```

```cobol
           03 KEY-FDBK        PIC S9(5) COMP.
           03 NUM-SENSEG      PIC S9(5) COMP.
           03 KEY-FDBK-AREA.
              05 EMPLOYEE-KEY  PIC X(04).
              05 EMPPAYHS-KEY  PIC X(08).

       PROCEDURE DIVISION.

           INITIALIZE PCB-MASK
           ENTRY 'DLITCBL' USING PCB-MASK

           PERFORM P100-INITIALIZATION.
           PERFORM P200-MAINLINE.
           PERFORM P300-TERMINATION.
           GOBACK.

       P100-INITIALIZATION.

           DISPLAY '** PROGRAM COBIMS7 START **'
           DISPLAY 'PROCESSING IN P100-INITIALIZATION'.

      *    DO INITIAL DB READ FOR FIRST EMPLOYEE RECORD

           CALL 'CBLTDLI' USING FOUR,
                 DLI-FUNCGN,
                 PCB-MASK,
                 IO-EMPLOYEE-RECORD,
                 EMP-UNQUALIFIED-SSA

           IF STATUS-CODE = '  ' THEN
              NEXT SENTENCE
           ELSE
              IF STATUS-CODE = 'GB' THEN
                 SET SW-END-OF-DB TO TRUE
                 DISPLAY 'END OF DATABASE :'
              ELSE
                 PERFORM P400-DISPLAY-ERROR
                 GOBACK
              END-IF

           END-IF.

       P200-MAINLINE.

           DISPLAY 'PROCESSING IN P200-MAINLINE'

      *    CHECK STATUS CODE AND FIRST RECORD

           IF SW-END-OF-DB THEN
              DISPLAY 'NO RECORDS TO PROCESS!!'
           ELSE
              DISPLAY 'SUCCESSFUL READ :' IO-EMPLOYEE-RECORD
              PERFORM UNTIL SW-END-OF-DB
```

```cobol
        PERFORM P500-GET-PAY-SEG

        CALL 'CBLTDLI' USING FOUR,
             DLI-FUNCGN,
             PCB-MASK,
             IO-EMPLOYEE-RECORD,
             EMP-UNQUALIFIED-SSA

        IF STATUS-CODE = 'GB' THEN
           SET SW-END-OF-DB TO TRUE
           DISPLAY 'END OF DATABASE'
        ELSE
           IF STATUS-CODE NOT EQUAL SPACES THEN
              PERFORM P400-DISPLAY-ERROR
           ELSE
              DISPLAY 'SUCCESSFUL READ :' IO-EMPLOYEE-RECORD
           END-IF
        END-IF

    END-PERFORM.

    DISPLAY 'FINISHED PROCESSING IN P200-MAINLINE'.

P300-TERMINATION.

    DISPLAY 'PROCESSING IN P300-TERMINATION'
    DISPLAY '** COBIMS7 - SUCCESSFULLY ENDED **'.

P400-DISPLAY-ERROR.

    DISPLAY 'PROCESSING IN P400-DISPLAY-ERROR'
    DISPLAY 'ERROR ENCOUNTERED - DETAIL FOLLOWS'
    DISPLAY 'DBD-NAME1:'     DBD-NAME
    DISPLAY 'SEG-LEVEL1:'    SEG-LEVEL
    DISPLAY 'STATUS-CODE:'   STATUS-CODE
    DISPLAY 'PROC-OPT1 :'    PROC-OPT
    DISPLAY 'SEG-NAME1 :'    SEG-NAME
    DISPLAY 'KEY-FDBK1 :'    KEY-FDBK
    DISPLAY 'NUM-SENSEG1:'   NUM-SENSEG
    DISPLAY 'KEY-FDBK-AREA1:' KEY-FDBK-AREA.

P500-GET-PAY-SEG.

    DISPLAY 'PROCESSING IN P500-GET-PAY-SEG'

    MOVE EMPL-ID-IN TO EMP-ID-VAL
    MOVE '20170101' TO EFFDATE-VAL

    CALL 'CBLTDLI' USING FIVE,
         DLI-FUNCGNP,
         PCB-MASK,
         IO-EMPPAY-RECORD,
         EMP-QUALIFIED-SSA,
```

```
                EMPPAY-QUALIFIED-SSA

           IF STATUS-CODE NOT EQUAL SPACES THEN
               PERFORM P400-DISPLAY-ERROR
           ELSE
    *      MAP FIELDS
               MOVE PAY-REG-PAY TO DIS-REG-PAY
               MOVE PAY-BON-PAY TO DIS-BON-PAY
               MOVE SEMIMTH-PAY TO DIS-SMT-PAY
               DISPLAY 'SUCCESSFUL PAY READ :'
               DISPLAY '   EFFECTIVE DATE = ' PAY-EFF-DATE
               DISPLAY '   PAY-REG-PAY = ' DIS-REG-PAY
               DISPLAY '   PAY-BON-PAY = ' DIS-BON-PAY
               DISPLAY '   SEMIMTH-PAY = ' DIS-SMT-PAY
           END-IF.

    *      END OF SOURCE CODE
```

Once again, let's compile and link, and then run the program. Here is the output showing both root and child segments.

```
** PROGRAM COBIMS7 START **
PROCESSING IN P100-INITIALIZATION
PROCESSING IN P200-MAINLINE
SUCCESSFUL READ :1111 VEREEN                CHARLES            12 201
PROCESSING IN P500-GET-PAY-SEG
SUCCESSFUL PAY READ :
   EFFECTIVE DATE = 20170101
   PAY-REG-PAY = 87000.00
   PAY-BON-PAY =  6700.00
   SEMIMTH-PAY =  3625.00
SUCCESSFUL READ :1122 JENKINS               DEBORAH            05 201
PROCESSING IN P500-GET-PAY-SEG
SUCCESSFUL PAY READ :
   EFFECTIVE DATE = 20170101
   PAY-REG-PAY = 82000.00
   PAY-BON-PAY =  6000.00
   SEMIMTH-PAY =  3416.66
SUCCESSFUL READ :3217 JOHNSON               EDWARD             04 201
PROCESSING IN P500-GET-PAY-SEG
SUCCESSFUL PAY READ :
   EFFECTIVE DATE = 20170101
   PAY-REG-PAY = 65000.00
   PAY-BON-PAY =  5500.00
   SEMIMTH-PAY =  2708.33
SUCCESSFUL READ :4175 TURNBULL              FRED               01 201
PROCESSING IN P500-GET-PAY-SEG
SUCCESSFUL PAY READ :
   EFFECTIVE DATE = 20170101
   PAY-REG-PAY = 55000.00
   PAY-BON-PAY =  1500.00
   SEMIMTH-PAY =  2291.66
SUCCESSFUL READ :4720 SCHULTZ               TIM                09 201
PROCESSING IN P500-GET-PAY-SEG
SUCCESSFUL PAY READ :
   EFFECTIVE DATE = 20170101
```

```
     PAY-REG-PAY =  80000.00
     PAY-BON-PAY =   2500.00
     SEMIMTH-PAY =   3333.33
SUCCESSFUL READ :4836 SMITH                SANDRA              03 201
PROCESSING IN P500-GET-PAY-SEG
SUCCESSFUL PAY READ :
     EFFECTIVE DATE = 20170101
     PAY-REG-PAY =  62000.00
     PAY-BON-PAY =   2200.00
     SEMIMTH-PAY =   2583.33
SUCCESSFUL READ :6288 WILLARD              JOE                 06 201
PROCESSING IN P500-GET-PAY-SEG
SUCCESSFUL PAY READ :
     EFFECTIVE DATE = 20170101
     PAY-REG-PAY =  70000.00
     PAY-BON-PAY =   2000.00
     SEMIMTH-PAY =   2916.66
SUCCESSFUL READ :7459 STEWART              BETTY               07 201
PROCESSING IN P500-GET-PAY-SEG
SUCCESSFUL PAY READ :
     EFFECTIVE DATE = 20170101
     PAY-REG-PAY =  85000.00
     PAY-BON-PAY =   4500.00
     SEMIMTH-PAY =   3541.66
END OF DATABASE
FINISHED PROCESSING IN P200-MAINLINE
PROCESSING IN P300-TERMINATION
** COBIMS7 - SUCCESSFULLY ENDED **
```

Here is the PLI source code for this program:

```
   PLIIMS7: PROCEDURE (DB_PTR_PCB) OPTIONS(MAIN);
   /*****************************************************************
    * PROGRAM NAME: PLIIMS7 - WALK THROUGH THE EMPLOYEE AND EMPPAY  *
    *                SEGMENTS OF THE EMPLOYEE IMS DATABASE.         *
    *****************************************************************/

   /*****************************************************************
   /*                  W O R K I N G   S T O R A G E               *
    *****************************************************************/

       DCL SW_END_OF_DB           STATIC BIT(01) INIT('0'B);
       DCL SW_NO_MORE_SEGS        STATIC BIT(01) INIT('0'B);
       DCL ONCODE                 BUILTIN;
       DCL DB_PTR_PCB             POINTER;

       DCL PLITDLI                EXTERNAL ENTRY;

       DCL 01 DLI_FUNCTIONS,
           05 DLI_FUNCISRT        CHAR(04) INIT ('ISRT'),
           05 DLI_FUNCGU          CHAR(04) INIT ('GU  '),
           05 DLI_FUNCGN          CHAR(04) INIT ('GN  '),
           05 DLI_FUNCGHU         CHAR(04) INIT ('GHU '),
           05 DLI_FUNCGNP         CHAR(04) INIT ('GNP '),
           05 DLI_FUNCREPL        CHAR(04) INIT ('REPL'),
```

```
        05 DLI_FUNCDLET          CHAR(04) INIT ('DLET'),
        05 DLI_FUNCXRST          CHAR(04) INIT ('XRST'),
        05 DLI_FUNCCHKP          CHAR(04) INIT ('CHKP'),
        05 DLI_FUNCROLL          CHAR(04) INIT ('ROLL');

DCL 01 IO_EMPLOYEE_RECORD,
        05  EMPL_ID_IN           CHAR(04),
        05  FILLER1              CHAR(01),
        05  EMPL_LNAME           CHAR(30),
        05  FILLER2              CHAR(01),
        05  EMPL_FNAME           CHAR(20),
        05  FILLER3              CHAR(01),
        05  EMPL_YRS_SRV         CHAR(02),
        05  FILLER4              CHAR(01),
        05  EMPL_PRM_DTE         CHAR(10),
        05  FILLER5              CHAR(10);

DCL 01 IO_EMPPAY_RECORD,
        05  PAY_EFF_DATE         CHAR(8),
        05  PAY_REG_PAY          FIXED DEC (8,2),
        05  PAY_BON_PAY          FIXED DEC (8,2),
        05  SEMIMTH_PAY          FIXED DEC (8,2),
        05  FILLER6              CHAR(57);

DCL 01 IO_EMPPAYHS_RECORD.
        05  PAY-DATE             CHAR(8),
        05  PAY-ANN-PAY          FIXED DEC (8,2),
        05  PAY-AMT              FIXED DEC (8,2),
        05  FILLER65             CHAR(62);

DCL 01 PCB_MASK                  BASED(DB_PTR_PCB),
        05 DBD_NAME              CHAR(08),
        05 SEG_LEVEL             CHAR(02),
        05 STATUS_CODE           CHAR(02),
        05 PROC_OPT              CHAR(04),
        05 FILLER99              FIXED BIN (31),
        05 SEG_NAME              CHAR(08),
        05 KEY_FDBK              FIXED BIN (31),
        05 NUM_SENSEG            FIXED BIN (31),
        05 KEY_FDBK_AREA,
           10 EMPLOYEE_ID        CHAR(04);

DCL 01 EMP_UNQUALIFIED_SSA,
        05  SEGNAME              CHAR(08) INIT ('EMPLOYEE'),
        05  FILLER7              CHAR(01) INIT (' ');

DCL 01 EMP_QUALIFIED_SSA,
        05  SEGNAME              CHAR(08) INIT('EMPLOYEE'),
        05  FILLER8              CHAR(01) INIT('('),
        05  FIELD                CHAR(08) INIT('EMPID'),
        05  OPER                 CHAR(02) INIT(' ='),
        05  EMP_ID_VAL           CHAR(04) INIT('    '),
        05  FILLER9              CHAR(01) INIT(')');
```

```
     DCL 01 EMPPAY_UNQUALIFIED_SSA,
            05   SEGNAME              CHAR(08) INIT('EMPPAY  '),
            05   FILLER10             CHAR(01) INIT(' ');

     DCL 01 EMPPAY_QUALIFIED_SSA,
            05   SEGNAME              CHAR(08) INIT('EMPPAY  '),
            05   FILLER11             CHAR(01) INIT('('),
            05   FIELD                CHAR(08) INIT('EFFDATE '),
            05   OPER                 CHAR(02) INIT(' ='),
            05   EFFDATE_VAL          CHAR(08) INIT('        '),
            05   FILLER12             CHAR(01) INIT(')');

     DCL THREE                        FIXED BIN (31) INIT(3);
     DCL FOUR                         FIXED BIN (31) INIT(4);
     DCL FIVE                         FIXED BIN (31) INIT(5);
     DCL SIX                          FIXED BIN (31) INIT(6);

 /********************************************************************
 /*              P R O G R A M    M A I N L I N E                    *
 ********************************************************************/

 CALL P100_INITIALIZATION;
 CALL P200_MAINLINE;
 CALL P300_TERMINATION;

 P100_INITIALIZATION: PROC;

     PUT SKIP LIST ('PLIIMS7: TRAVERSE EMPLOYEE DATABASE PAY SEGS');
     PUT SKIP LIST ('PROCESSING IN P100-INITIALIZATION');

     PCB_MASK = '';
     IO_EMPLOYEE_RECORD  = '';
     IO_EMPPAY_RECORD    = '';

  /* DO INITIAL DB READ FOR FIRST EMPLOYEE RECORD */

     CALL PLITDLI (FOUR,
                   DLI_FUNCGN,
                   PCB_MASK,
                   IO_EMPLOYEE_RECORD,
                   EMP_UNQUALIFIED_SSA);

     IF STATUS_CODE = '  ' THEN;
     ELSE
        IF STATUS_CODE = 'GB' THEN
           DO;
               SW_END_OF_DB = '1'B;
               PUT SKIP LIST ('** END OF DATABASE');
           END;
        ELSE
           DO;
               CALL P400_DISPLAY_ERROR;
```

```
                RETURN;
            END;

END P100_INITIALIZATION;

P200_MAINLINE: PROC;

    /*  MAIN LOOP - CYCLE THROUGH ALL ROOT SEGMENTS IN THE DB,
                 DISPLAYING THE DATA RETRIEVED              */

        IF SW_END_OF_DB THEN
            PUT SKIP LIST ('NO RECORDS TO PROCESS!!');
        ELSE
            DO WHILE (¬SW_END_OF_DB);
                PUT SKIP LIST ('SUCCESSFUL EMPLOYEE READ : ' ||
                EMPL_ID);

                SW_NO_MORE_SEGS = '0'B;

                DO WHILE (¬SW_END_OF_DB & ¬SW_NO_MORE_SEGS);
                    CALL P500_GET_PAY_SEG;
                END; /* DO WHILE */

                /* GET NEXT ROOT */

                CALL PLITDLI (FOUR,
                              DLI_FUNCGN,
                              PCB_MASK,
                              IO_EMPLOYEE_RECORD,
                              EMP_UNQUALIFIED_SSA);

                IF STATUS_CODE = ' ' THEN;
                ELSE
                    IF STATUS_CODE = 'GB' THEN
                        DO;
                            SW_END_OF_DB = '1'B;
                            PUT SKIP LIST ('** END OF DATABASE');
                        END;
                    ELSE
                        DO;
                            CALL P400_DISPLAY_ERROR;
                            RETURN;
                        END;

            END; /* DO WHILE */

        PUT SKIP LIST ('FINISHED PROCESSING IN P200_MAINLINE');

END P200_MAINLINE;

P300_TERMINATION: PROC;

    CLOSE FILE(EMPIFILE);
```

```
         PUT SKIP LIST ('PLIIMS7 - SUCCESSFULLY ENDED');

END P300_TERMINATION;

P400_DISPLAY_ERROR: PROC;

     PUT SKIP LIST ('ERROR ENCOUNTERED - DETAIL FOLLOWS');
     PUT SKIP LIST ('SEG_IO_AREA      :' || SEG_IO_AREA);
     PUT SKIP LIST ('DBD_NAME1:' ||  DBD_NAME);
     PUT SKIP LIST ('SEG_LEVEL1:' || SEG_LEVEL);
     PUT SKIP LIST ('STATUS_CODE:' || STATUS_CODE);
     PUT SKIP LIST ('PROC_OPT1 :' || PROC_OPT);
     PUT SKIP LIST ('SEG_NAME1 :' || SEG_NAME);
     PUT SKIP LIST ('KEY_FDBK1 :' || KEY_FDBK);
     PUT SKIP LIST ('NUM_SENSEG1:' || NUM_SENSEG);
     PUT SKIP LIST ('KEY_FDBK_AREA1:' || KEY_FDBK_AREA);

END P400_DISPLAY_ERROR;

P500_GET_PAY_SEG: PROC;

     PUT SKIP LIST ('PROCESSING IN P500_GET_PAY_SEG');
     EMP_ID_VAL  = EMPL_ID;
     EFFDATE_VAL = '20170101';

     CALL PLITDLI (FIVE,
                   DLI_FUNCGNP,
                   PCB_MASK,
                   IO_EMPPAY_RECORD,
                   EMP_QUALIFIED_SSA,
                   EMPPAY_QUALIFIED_SSA);

     SELECT (STATUS_CODE);

        WHEN (' ')
           DO;
              PUT SKIP LIST ('SUCCESSFUL EMPPAY RETRIEVAL');
              PUT SKIP LIST ('PAY_EFF_DATE ' || PAY_EFF_DATE);
              PUT SKIP LIST ('PAY_REG_PAY  ' || PAY_REG_PAY);
              PUT SKIP LIST ('PAY_BON_PAY  ' || PAY_BON_PAY);
              PUT SKIP LIST ('SEMIMTH_PAY  ' || SEMIMTH_PAY);
           END;

        WHEN ('GE')
           DO;
              SW_NO_MORE_SEGS = '1'B;
              PUT SKIP LIST ('** NO MORE PAY SEGMENTS');
           END;

        WHEN ('GB')
           DO;
              SW_END_OF_DB = '1'B;
```

```
            PUT SKIP LIST ('** END OF DATABASE');
         END;
      OTHERWISE
         CALL P400_DISPLAY_ERROR;

   END; /* SELECT */

END P500_GET_PAY_SEG;

END PLIIMS7;
```

Inserting Child Segments Down the Hierarchy (3 levels)

Ok, I think we have a pretty good handle on the adding and retrieving of child segments. But just to be sure, let's work with the `EMPPAYHS` segment, adding and retrieving records. That's slightly different that what we've done already, but not much.

For `COBIMS8`, let's add a pay history segment `EMPPAYHS` for all employees using pay date January 15, 2017, and using the twice-monthly pay information from the `EMPPAY` segment. So we need to position ourselves at the `EMPPAY` child segment under each `EMPLOYEE` root segment, and then `ISRT` an `EMPPAYHS` segment.

I think we've covered all the techniques required to write this program. Why don't you give it a try first, and then we'll get back together and compare our code? Take a good break and then code up your version.

. . . .

Ok, I'm back with a good cup of coffee. Here's my version of the code. I added the segment I/O and SSAs for the `EMPPAYHS` segment. The `INSERT` call for the `EMPPAYHS` segment is as follows:

```
         CALL 'CBLTDLI' USING SIX,
              DLI-FUNCISRT,
              PCB-MASK,
              IO-EMPPAYHS-RECORD,
              EMP-QUALIFIED-SSA,
              EMPPAY-QUALIFIED-SSA,
              EMPPAYHS-UNQUALIFIED-SSA.
```

Should be no surprises there. Just a bit more navigation and slightly different database calls. Note that we must use qualified SSAs for `EMPLOYEE` and `EMPPAY`. Here's the full program.

```
         ID DIVISION.
         PROGRAM-ID. COBIMS8.

     ******************************************************
```

```
*     INSERT EMPLOYEE PAY HISTORY RECS INTO THE       *
*     EMPLOYEE IMS DATABASE. THIS EXAMPLE WALKS       *
*     THROUGH THE ROOT AND EMPPAY SEGS AND THEN       *
*     INSERTS THE PAY HISTORY SEGMENT UNDER THE       *
*     EMPPAY SEGMENT.                                 *
*******************************************************

ENVIRONMENT DIVISION.
DATA DIVISION.


*******************************************************
*    W O R K I N G    S T O R A G E    S E C T I O N  *
*******************************************************

WORKING-STORAGE SECTION.

01 WS-FLAGS.
    05  SW-END-OF-FILE-SWITCH     PIC X(1) VALUE 'N'.
        88  SW-END-OF-FILE                 VALUE 'Y'.
        88  SW-NOT-END-OF-FILE             VALUE 'N'.
    05  SW-END-OF-DB-SWITCH       PIC X(1) VALUE 'N'.
        88  SW-END-OF-DB                   VALUE 'Y'.
        88  SW-NOT-END-OF-DB               VALUE 'N'.

01 IO-EMPLOYEE-RECORD.
    05   EMPL-ID        PIC X(04).
    05   FILLER         PIC X(01).
    05   EMPL-LNAME     PIC X(30).
    05   FILLER         PIC X(01).
    05   EMPL-FNAME     PIC X(20).
    05   FILLER         PIC X(01).
    05   EMPL-YRS-SRV   PIC X(02).
    05   FILLER         PIC X(01).
    05   EMPL-PRM-DTE   PIC X(10).
    05   FILLER         PIC X(10).

01 IO-EMPPAY-RECORD.
    05   PAY-EFF-DATE   PIC X(8).
    05   PAY-REG-PAY    PIC S9(6)V9(2) USAGE COMP-3.
    05   PAY-BON-PAY    PIC S9(6)V9(2) USAGE COMP-3.
    05   SEMIMTH-PAY    PIC S9(6)V9(2) USAGE COMP-3.
    05   FILLER         PIC X(57).

01 IO-EMPPAYHS-RECORD.
    05   PAY-DATE       PIC X(8).
    05   PAY-ANN-PAY    PIC S9(6)V9(2) USAGE COMP-3.
    05   PAY-AMT        PIC S9(6)V9(2) USAGE COMP-3.
    05   FILLER         PIC X(62).

01 SEG-IO-AREA      PIC X(80).

01 DLI-FUNCTIONS.
    05 DLI-FUNCISRT    PIC X(4) VALUE 'ISRT'.
```

```cobol
           05 DLI-FUNCGU      PIC X(4) VALUE 'GU  '.
           05 DLI-FUNCGN      PIC X(4) VALUE 'GN  '.
           05 DLI-FUNCGHU     PIC X(4) VALUE 'GHU '.
           05 DLI-FUNCGNP     PIC X(4) VALUE 'GNP '.
           05 DLI-FUNCREPL    PIC X(4) VALUE 'REPL'.
           05 DLI-FUNCDLET    PIC X(4) VALUE 'DLET'.
           05 DLI-FUNCXRST    PIC X(4) VALUE 'XRST'.
           05 DLI-FUNCCKPT    PIC X(4) VALUE 'CKPT'.

       01 EMP-UNQUALIFIED-SSA.
           05  SEGNAME       PIC X(08) VALUE 'EMPLOYEE'.
           05  FILLER        PIC X(01) VALUE ' '.

       01 EMP-QUALIFIED-SSA.
           05  SEGNAME       PIC X(08) VALUE 'EMPLOYEE'.
           05  FILLER        PIC X(01) VALUE '('.
           05  FIELD         PIC X(08) VALUE 'EMPID'.
           05  OPER          PIC X(02) VALUE ' ='.
           05  EMP-ID-VAL    PIC X(04) VALUE '    '.
           05  FILLER        PIC X(01) VALUE ')'.

       01 EMPPAY-UNQUALIFIED-SSA.
           05  SEGNAME       PIC X(08) VALUE 'EMPPAY  '.
           05  FILLER        PIC X(01) VALUE ' '.

       01 EMPPAY-QUALIFIED-SSA.
           05  SEGNAME       PIC X(08) VALUE 'EMPPAY  '.
           05  FILLER        PIC X(01) VALUE '('.
           05  FIELD         PIC X(08) VALUE 'EFFDATE '.
           05  OPER          PIC X(02) VALUE ' ='.
           05  EFFDATE-VAL   PIC X(08) VALUE '        '.
           05  FILLER        PIC X(01) VALUE ')'.

       01 EMPPAYHS-UNQUALIFIED-SSA.
           05  SEGNAME       PIC X(08) VALUE 'EMPPAYHS'.
           05  FILLER        PIC X(01) VALUE ' '.

       01 IMS-RET-CODES.
           05 THREE           PIC S9(9) COMP VALUE +3.
           05 FOUR            PIC S9(9) COMP VALUE +4.
           05 FIVE            PIC S9(9) COMP VALUE +5.
           05 SIX             PIC S9(9) COMP VALUE +6.

       77 WS-PAY-DATE     PIC X(08) VALUE '20170115'.

       LINKAGE SECTION.
       01 PCB-MASK.
           03 DBD-NAME        PIC X(8).
           03 SEG-LEVEL       PIC XX.
           03 STATUS-CODE     PIC XX.
           03 PROC-OPT        PIC X(4).
           03 FILLER          PIC X(4).
           03 SEG-NAME        PIC X(8).
```

```cobol
           03 KEY-FDBK        PIC S9(5) COMP.
           03 NUM-SENSEG      PIC S9(5) COMP.
           03 KEY-FDBK-AREA.
              05 EMPLOYEE-ID  PIC X(04).
              05 EMPPAYHS     PIC X(08).

       PROCEDURE DIVISION.

           INITIALIZE PCB-MASK
           ENTRY 'DLITCBL' USING PCB-MASK

           PERFORM P100-INITIALIZATION.
           PERFORM P200-MAINLINE.
           PERFORM P300-TERMINATION.
           GOBACK.

       P100-INITIALIZATION.

           DISPLAY '** PROGRAM COBIMS8 START **'
           DISPLAY 'PROCESSING IN P100-INITIALIZATION'.

      *    DO INITIAL DB READ FOR FIRST EMPLOYEE ROOT SEGMENT

           CALL 'CBLTDLI' USING ,
               DLI-FUNCGN,
               PCB-MASK,
               IO-EMPLOYEE-RECORD,
               EMP-UNQUALIFIED-SSA

           IF STATUS-CODE = '  ' THEN
              NEXT SENTENCE
           ELSE
              IF STATUS-CODE = 'GB' THEN
                 SET SW-END-OF-DB TO TRUE
                 DISPLAY 'END OF DATABASE :'
              ELSE
                 PERFORM P9000-DISPLAY-ERROR
                 GOBACK
              END-IF

           END-IF.

        P200-MAINLINE.
           DISPLAY 'PROCESSING IN P200-MAINLINE'

      *    CHECK STATUS CODE AND FIRST RECORD

           IF SW-END-OF-DB THEN
              DISPLAY 'NO RECORDS TO PROCESS!!'
           ELSE
              PERFORM UNTIL SW-END-OF-DB
                 DISPLAY 'SUCCESSFUL READ :' IO-EMPLOYEE-RECORD
                 MOVE EMPL-ID TO EMP-ID-VAL
```

```
        PERFORM P2000-GET-EMPPAY
        IF STATUS-CODE NOT EQUAL SPACES THEN
           PERFORM P9000-DISPLAY-ERROR
           GOBACK
        ELSE
           DISPLAY 'SUCCESSFUL PAY READ :' IO-EMPPAY-RECORD
           MOVE PAY-EFF-DATE TO EFFDATE-VAL
           MOVE WS-PAY-DATE TO PAY-DATE
           MOVE PAY-REG-PAY TO PAY-ANN-PAY
           MOVE SEMIMTH-PAY TO PAY-AMT
           PERFORM P3000-INSERT-EMPPAYHS
           IF STATUS-CODE NOT EQUAL SPACES THEN
              PERFORM P9000-DISPLAY-ERROR
              GOBACK
           ELSE
              DISPLAY 'SUCCESSFUL INSERT EMPPAYHS : '
                 EMP-ID-VAL
              DISPLAY 'SUCCESSFUL INSERT VALUES   : '
                 IO-EMPPAYHS-RECORD
        END-IF

           PERFORM P1000-GET-NEXT-ROOT
           IF STATUS-CODE = 'GB' THEN
              SET SW-END-OF-DB TO TRUE
              DISPLAY 'END OF DATABASE'
           END-IF

        END-IF

     END-PERFORM.

   DISPLAY 'FINISHED PROCESSING IN P200-MAINLINE'.

P300-TERMINATION.

   DISPLAY 'PROCESSING IN P300-TERMINATION'
   DISPLAY '** COBIMS8 - SUCCESSFULLY ENDED **'.

P1000-GET-NEXT-ROOT.

   DISPLAY 'PROCESSING IN P1000-GET-NEXT-ROOT'.

   CALL 'CBLTDLI' USING FOUR,
        DLI-FUNCGN,
        PCB-MASK,
        IO-EMPLOYEE-RECORD,
        EMP-UNQUALIFIED-SSA.

P2000-GET-EMPPAY.

   DISPLAY 'PROCESSING IN P2000-GET-EMPPAY'.

   CALL 'CBLTDLI' USING FIVE,
```

```
                    DLI-FUNCGNP,
                    PCB-MASK,
                    IO-EMPPAY-RECORD,
                    EMP-QUALIFIED-SSA,
                    EMPPAY-UNQUALIFIED-SSA.

       P3000-INSERT-EMPPAYHS.

            DISPLAY 'PROCESSING IN P3000-INSERT-EMPPAYHS'.

            CALL 'CBLTDLI' USING SIX,
                    DLI-FUNCISRT,
                    PCB-MASK,
                    IO-EMPPAYHS-RECORD,
                    EMP-QUALIFIED-SSA,
                    EMPPAY-QUALIFIED-SSA,
                    EMPPAYHS-UNQUALIFIED-SSA.

       P9000-DISPLAY-ERROR.

            DISPLAY 'ERROR ENCOUNTERED - DETAIL FOLLOWS'
            DISPLAY 'DBD-NAME1:'       DBD-NAME
            DISPLAY 'SEG-LEVEL1:'      SEG-LEVEL
            DISPLAY 'STATUS-CODE:'     STATUS-CODE
            DISPLAY 'PROC-OPT1 :'      PROC-OPT
            DISPLAY 'SEG-NAME1 :'      SEG-NAME
            DISPLAY 'KEY-FDBK1 :'      KEY-FDBK
            DISPLAY 'NUM-SENSEG1:'     NUM-SENSEG
            DISPLAY 'KEY-FDBK-AREA1:'  KEY-FDBK-AREA.

       *    END OF SOURCE CODE
```

Now let's compile, link and run the program. Here is the output.

```
** PROGRAM COBIMS8 START **
PROCESSING IN P100-INITIALIZATION
PROCESSING IN P200-MAINLINE
SUCCESSFUL READ :1111 VEREEN                     CHARLES            12 201
PROCESSING IN P2000-GET-EMPPAY
SUCCESSFUL PAY READ :20170101 g            &
PROCESSING IN P3000-INSERT-EMPPAYHS
SUCCESSFUL INSERT EMPPAYHS : 1111
SUCCESSFUL INSERT VALUES   : 20170115 g        &
PROCESSING IN P1000-GET-NEXT-ROOT
SUCCESSFUL READ :1122 JENKINS                    DEBORAH            05 201
PROCESSING IN P2000-GET-EMPPAY
SUCCESSFUL PAY READ :20170101 b            %
PROCESSING IN P3000-INSERT-EMPPAYHS
SUCCESSFUL INSERT EMPPAYHS : 1122
SUCCESSFUL INSERT VALUES   : 20170115 b        %
PROCESSING IN P1000-GET-NEXT-ROOT
SUCCESSFUL READ :3217 JOHNSON                    EDWARD             04 201
PROCESSING IN P2000-GET-EMPPAY
SUCCESSFUL PAY READ :20170101         &    c
PROCESSING IN P3000-INSERT-EMPPAYHS
```

```
SUCCESSFUL INSERT EMPPAYHS : 3217
SUCCESSFUL INSERT VALUES   : 20170115       c
PROCESSING IN P1000-GET-NEXT-ROOT
SUCCESSFUL READ :4175 TURNBULL              FRED            01 201
PROCESSING IN P2000-GET-EMPPAY
SUCCESSFUL PAY READ :20170101        &    %
PROCESSING IN P3000-INSERT-EMPPAYHS
SUCCESSFUL INSERT EMPPAYHS : 4175
SUCCESSFUL INSERT VALUES   : 20170115       %
PROCESSING IN P1000-GET-NEXT-ROOT
SUCCESSFUL READ :4720 SCHULTZ               TIM             09 201
PROCESSING IN P2000-GET-EMPPAY
SUCCESSFUL PAY READ :20170101        &
PROCESSING IN P3000-INSERT-EMPPAYHS
SUCCESSFUL INSERT EMPPAYHS : 4720
SUCCESSFUL INSERT VALUES   : 20170115
PROCESSING IN P1000-GET-NEXT-ROOT
SUCCESSFUL READ :4836 SMITH                 SANDRA          03 201
PROCESSING IN P2000-GET-EMPPAY
SUCCESSFUL PAY READ :20170101
PROCESSING IN P3000-INSERT-EMPPAYHS
SUCCESSFUL INSERT EMPPAYHS : 4836
SUCCESSFUL INSERT VALUES   : 20170115
PROCESSING IN P1000-GET-NEXT-ROOT
SUCCESSFUL READ :6288 WILLARD               JOE             06 201
PROCESSING IN P2000-GET-EMPPAY
SUCCESSFUL PAY READ :20170101       j  %
PROCESSING IN P3000-INSERT-EMPPAYHS
SUCCESSFUL INSERT EMPPAYHS : 6288
SUCCESSFUL INSERT VALUES   : 20170115      j %
PROCESSING IN P1000-GET-NEXT-ROOT
SUCCESSFUL READ :7459 STEWART               BETTY           07 201
PROCESSING IN P2000-GET-EMPPAY
SUCCESSFUL PAY READ :20170101 e      &    %
PROCESSING IN P3000-INSERT-EMPPAYHS
SUCCESSFUL INSERT EMPPAYHS : 7459
SUCCESSFUL INSERT VALUES   : 20170115 e     %
PROCESSING IN P1000-GET-NEXT-ROOT
END OF DATABASE
FINISHED PROCESSING IN P200-MAINLINE
PROCESSING IN P300-TERMINATION
** COBIMS8 - SUCCESSFULLY ENDED **
```

So that's how to insert a child segment under a higher level child. To make this more interesting, change the value of the pay date to January 31, 2017. Then compile and link and run again. Do this twice more using pay dates February 15, 2017 and February 28, 2017. Now we have four paychecks for each employee. We'll read all this data back in the next training program.

Here is the PLI code that corresponds to COBIMS8.

```
PLIIMS8: PROCEDURE (DB_PTR_PCB) OPTIONS(MAIN);
 /******************************************************************
  * PROGRAM NAME :    PLIIMS8 - INSERT EMPLOYEE HISTORY PAY RECORDS  *
```

```
*                 UNDER THEIR EMPPAY PARENTS. QUALIFIED SSA'S      *
*                 MUST BE PROVIDED FOR BOTH THE EMPLOYEE AND       *
*                 EMPPAY SEGMENTS.                                 *
********************************************************************/

/*******************************************************************
/*                  W O R K I N G   S T O R A G E                   *
********************************************************************/

    DCL SW_END_OF_DB            STATIC BIT(01) INIT('0'B);
    DCL ONCODE                  BUILTIN;
    DCL DB_PTR_PCB              POINTER;

    DCL PLITDLI                 EXTERNAL ENTRY;

    DCL 01 DLI_FUNCTIONS,
         05  DLI_FUNCISRT       CHAR(04) INIT ('ISRT'),
         05  DLI_FUNCGU         CHAR(04) INIT ('GU  '),
         05  DLI_FUNCGN         CHAR(04) INIT ('GN  '),
         05  DLI_FUNCGHU        CHAR(04) INIT ('GHU '),
         05  DLI_FUNCGNP        CHAR(04) INIT ('GNP '),
         05  DLI_FUNCREPL       CHAR(04) INIT ('REPL'),
         05  DLI_FUNCDLET       CHAR(04) INIT ('DLET'),
         05  DLI_FUNCXRST       CHAR(04) INIT ('XRST'),
         05  DLI_FUNCCHKP       CHAR(04) INIT ('CHKP'),
         05  DLI_FUNCROLL       CHAR(04) INIT ('ROLL');

    DCL 01 IO_EMPLOYEE_RECORD,
         05  EMPL_ID            CHAR(04),
         05  FILLER1            CHAR(01),
         05  EMPL_LNAME         CHAR(30),
         05  FILLER2            CHAR(01),
         05  EMPL_FNAME         CHAR(20),
         05  FILLER3            CHAR(01),
         05  EMPL_YRS_SRV       CHAR(02),
         05  FILLER4            CHAR(01),
         05  EMPL_PRM_DTE       CHAR(10),
         05  FILLER5            CHAR(10);

    DCL 01 IO_EMPPAY_RECORD,
         05  PAY_EFF_DATE       CHAR(8),
         05  PAY_REG_PAY        FIXED DEC (8,2),
         05  PAY_BON_PAY        FIXED DEC (8,2),
         05  SEMIMTH_PAY        FIXED DEC (8,2),
         05  FILLER55           CHAR(57);

    DCL 01 IO_EMPPAYHS_RECORD,
         05  PAY_DATE           CHAR(8),
         05  PAY_ANN_PAY        FIXED DEC (8,2),
         05  PAY_AMT            FIXED DEC (8,2),
         05  FILLER65           CHAR(62);

    DCL 01 PCB_MASK             BASED(DB_PTR_PCB),
```

```
            05  DBD_NAME            CHAR(08),
            05  SEG_LEVEL           CHAR(02),
            05  STATUS_CODE         CHAR(02),
            05  PROC_OPT            CHAR(04),
            05  FILLER6             FIXED BIN (31),
            05  SEG_NAME            CHAR(08),
            05  KEY_FDBK            FIXED BIN (31),
            05  NUM_SENSEG          FIXED BIN (31),
            05  KEY_FDBK_AREA,
                10  EMPLOYEE_ID     CHAR(04),
                10  EMP_PAY_DATE    CHAR(08);

    DCL 01 EMP_UNQUALIFIED_SSA,
            05  SEGNAME             CHAR(08) INIT ('EMPLOYEE'),
            05  FILLER7             CHAR(01) INIT (' ');

    DCL 01 EMP_QUALIFIED_SSA,
            05  SEGNAME             CHAR(08) INIT('EMPLOYEE'),
            05  FILLER8             CHAR(01) INIT('('),
            05  FIELD               CHAR(08) INIT('EMPID'),
            05  OPER                CHAR(02) INIT(' ='),
            05  EMP_ID_VAL          CHAR(04) INIT('    '),
            05  FILLER9             CHAR(01) INIT(')');

    DCL 01 EMPPAY_UNQUALIFIED_SSA,
            05  SEGNAME             CHAR(08) INIT('EMPPAY  '),
            05  FILLER10            CHAR(01) INIT(' ');

    DCL 01 EMPPAY_QUALIFIED_SSA,
            05  SEGNAME             CHAR(08) INIT('EMPPAY  '),
            05  FILLER11            CHAR(01) INIT('('),
            05  FIELD               CHAR(08) INIT('EFFDATE '),
            05  OPER                CHAR(02) INIT(' ='),
            05  EFFDATE_VAL         CHAR(08) INIT('        '),
            05  FILLER12            CHAR(01) INIT(')');

    DCL 01 EMPPAYHS_UNQUALIFIED_SSA,
            05  SEGNAME             CHAR(08) INIT('EMPPAYHS'),
            05  FILLER13            CHAR(01) INIT(' ');

    DCL WS_PAY_DATE                 CHAR(08) INIT ('20170228');

    DCL SEG_IO_AREA                 CHAR(80) INIT (' ');

    DCL THREE                       FIXED BIN (31) INIT(3);
    DCL FOUR                        FIXED BIN (31) INIT(4);
    DCL FIVE                        FIXED BIN (31) INIT(5);
    DCL SIX                         FIXED BIN (31) INIT(6);
/********************************************************************
/*              P R O G R A M   M A I N L I N E                     *
********************************************************************/
```

```
     CALL P100_INITIALIZATION;
     CALL P200_MAINLINE;
     CALL P300_TERMINATION;

P100_INITIALIZATION: PROC;

    PUT SKIP LIST ('PLIIMS8: INSERT RECORDS');
    PUT SKIP LIST ('PROCESSING IN P100_INITIALIZATION');

    IO_EMPLOYEE_RECORD  = '';
    IO_EMPPAY_RECORD    = '';
    IO_EMPPAYHS_RECORD  = '';
    PCB_MASK = '';

    /* DO INITIAL DB READ FOR FIRST EMPLOYEE RECORD */

    CALL PLITDLI (FOUR,
                  DLI_FUNCGN,
                  PCB_MASK,
                  IO_EMPLOYEE_RECORD,
                  EMP_UNQUALIFIED_SSA);

    IF STATUS_CODE = '  ' THEN;
    ELSE
       IF STATUS_CODE = 'GB' THEN
          DO;
              SW_END_OF_DB = '1'B;
              PUT SKIP LIST ('** END OF DATABASE');
          END;
       ELSE
          DO;
              CALL P9000_DISPLAY_ERROR;
              RETURN;
          END;

END P100_INITIALIZATION;

P200_MAINLINE: PROC;

    /*  MAIN LOOP - WALK THROUGH THE DATABASE GETTING EMPLOYEE
                PAY HISTORY SEGMENTS.                         */

    IF SW_END_OF_DB THEN
       PUT SKIP LIST ('NO RECORDS TO PROCESS!!');
    ELSE
       DO WHILE (¬SW_END_OF_DB);

           PUT SKIP LIST ('SUCCESSFUL READ OF EMPLOYEE ' || EMPL_ID);

           /* ASSIGN KEY FOR EMPLOYEE LEVEL SSA AND GET EMPPAY SEG */

           EMP_ID_VAL = EMPL_ID;
           CALL P2000_GET_EMPPAY;
```

```
            IF STATUS_CODE ¬= ' ' THEN
                DO;
                    PUT SKIP LIST ('ERROR READING EMPPAY');
                    CALL P9000_DISPLAY_ERROR;
                    RETURN;
                END;
            ELSE
                DO;
                    PUT SKIP LIST ('SUCCESSFUL PAY READ : '
                        || IO_EMPPAY_RECORD);

                    /* ASSIGN KEY FOR EMPPAY LEVEL SSA FOR SEG */

                    EFFDATE_VAL = PAY_EFF_DATE;

                    PAY_DATE    = WS_PAY_DATE;
                    PAY_ANN_PAY = PAY_REG_PAY;
                    PAY_AMT     = SEMIMTH_PAY;

                    CALL P3000_INSERT_EMPPAYHS;
                    IF STATUS_CODE ¬= ' ' THEN
                        DO;
                            CALL P9000_DISPLAY_ERROR;
                            RETURN;
                        END;
                    ELSE
                        DO;
                            PUT SKIP LIST ('SUCCESSFUL INSERT EMPPAYHS : '
                                || EMP_ID_VAL);
                            PUT SKIP LIST ('SUCCESSFUL INSERT VALUES   : ' );
                            PUT SKIP DATA (IO_EMPPAYHS_RECORD);
                        END;

                    CALL P1000_GET_NEXT_ROOT;
                    IF STATUS_CODE = 'GB' THEN
                        DO;
                            SW_END_OF_DB = '1'B;
                            PUT SKIP LIST ('** END OF DATABASE');
                        END;
                    ELSE
                        IF STATUS_CODE = ' ' THEN;
                        ELSE
                            DO;
                                CALL P9000_DISPLAY_ERROR;
                                RETURN;
                            END;

                END; /* SUCCESSFULLY RETRIEVED PAY SEG */

        END; /* DO WHILE */

    PUT SKIP LIST ('FINISHED PROCESSING IN P200_MAINLINE');
```

```
      END P200_MAINLINE;

   P300_TERMINATION: PROC;

        PUT SKIP LIST ('PLIIMS8 - SUCCESSFULLY ENDED');

   END P300_TERMINATION;

   P1000_GET_NEXT_ROOT: PROC;

      PUT SKIP LIST ('PROCESSING IN P1000_GET_NEXT_ROOT');

      CALL PLITDLI (FOUR,
                    DLI_FUNCGN,
                    PCB_MASK,
                    IO_EMPLOYEE_RECORD,
                    EMP_UNQUALIFIED_SSA);

   END P1000_GET_NEXT_ROOT;

   P2000_GET_EMPPAY: PROC;

       PUT SKIP LIST ('PROCESSING IN P2000_GET_EMPPAY');

       CALL PLITDLI (FIVE,
                     DLI_FUNCGNP,
                     PCB_MASK,
                     IO_EMPPAY_RECORD,
                     EMP_QUALIFIED_SSA,
                     EMPPAY_UNQUALIFIED_SSA);

   END P2000_GET_EMPPAY;

   P3000_INSERT_EMPPAYHS: PROC;

        PUT SKIP LIST ('PROCESSING IN P3000-INSERT-EMPPAYHS');

        CALL PLITDLI (SIX,
                      DLI_FUNCISRT,
                      PCB_MASK,
                      IO_EMPPAYHS_RECORD,
                      EMP_QUALIFIED_SSA,
                      EMPPAY_QUALIFIED_SSA,
                      EMPPAYHS_UNQUALIFIED_SSA);

   END P3000_INSERT_EMPPAYHS;

   P9000_DISPLAY_ERROR: PROC;

        PUT SKIP LIST ('ERROR ENCOUNTERED - DETAIL FOLLOWS');
        PUT SKIP DATA (IO_EMPPAY_RECORD);
        PUT SKIP LIST ('DBD_NAME1:' ||  DBD_NAME);
        PUT SKIP LIST ('SEG_LEVEL1:' || SEG_LEVEL);
```

```
            PUT SKIP LIST ('STATUS_CODE:' || STATUS_CODE);
            PUT SKIP LIST ('PROC_OPT1 :' || PROC_OPT);
            PUT SKIP LIST ('SEG_NAME1 :' || SEG_NAME);
            PUT SKIP LIST ('KEY_FDBK1 :' || KEY_FDBK);
            PUT SKIP LIST ('NUM_SENSEG1:' || NUM_SENSEG);
            PUT SKIP LIST ('KEY_FDBK_AREA1:' || KEY_FDBK_AREA);

        END P9000_DISPLAY_ERROR;

        END PLIIMS8;
```

Read Child Segments Down the Hierarchy (3 levels)

For COBIMS9 you'll need to retrieve and display all the pay history segments for each employee. This should be fairly straightforward by now. Yes you'll need one more loop, and more navigation. But we need the practice to really drill the techniques in. Give this one a try, then take a long break and we'll compare code.

. . . .

Ok, I hope you are enjoying coding IMS in COBOL! I'll bet you got your version of the program to work without any serious problems. Let me give you my code and see what you think. Note that I have switches both for end of database and for end of EMPPAYHS segments. The latter is needed for looping through the multiple EMPPAYHS segments.

```
          ID DIVISION.
          PROGRAM-ID. COBIMS9.

         **********************************************************
         *    READ AND DISPLAY EMP HISTORY RECS FROM THE          *
         *    EMPLOYEE IMS DATABASE.  THIS EXAMPLE WALKS          *
         *    THROUGH THE ROOT AND EMPPAY SEGS AND THEN           *
         *    READS THE PAY HISTORY SEGMENTS UNDER THE            *
         *    EMPPAY SEGMENT.                                     *
         **********************************************************

          ENVIRONMENT DIVISION.
          DATA DIVISION.

         **********************************************************
         *   W O R K I N G    S T O R A G E    S E C T I O N     *
         **********************************************************

          WORKING-STORAGE SECTION.

          01 WS-FLAGS.
             05  SW-END-OF-FILE-SWITCH    PIC X(1) VALUE 'N'.
                 88  SW-END-OF-FILE                VALUE 'Y'.
                 88  SW-NOT-END-OF-FILE            VALUE 'N'.
```

```cobol
        05  SW-END-OF-DB-SWITCH      PIC X(1) VALUE 'N'.
            88  SW-END-OF-DB                  VALUE 'Y'.
            88  SW-NOT-END-OF-DB              VALUE 'N'.
        05  SW-END-OF-EMPPAYHS-SW    PIC X(1) VALUE 'N'.
            88  SW-END-OF-EMPPAYHS            VALUE 'Y'.
            88  SW-NOT-END-OF-EMPPAYHS        VALUE 'N'.

    01  IO-EMPLOYEE-RECORD.
        05  EMPL-ID       PIC X(04).
        05  FILLER        PIC X(01).
        05  EMPL-LNAME    PIC X(30).
        05  FILLER        PIC X(01).
        05  EMPL-FNAME    PIC X(20).
        05  FILLER        PIC X(01).
        05  EMPL-YRS-SRV  PIC X(02).
        05  FILLER        PIC X(01).
        05  EMPL-PRM-DTE  PIC X(10).
        05  FILLER        PIC X(10).

    01  IO-EMPPAY-RECORD.
        05  PAY-EFF-DATE  PIC X(8).
        05  PAY-REG-PAY   PIC S9(6)V9(2) USAGE COMP-3.
        05  PAY-BON-PAY   PIC S9(6)V9(2) USAGE COMP-3.
        05  SEMIMTH-PAY   PIC S9(6)V9(2) USAGE COMP-3.
        05  FILLER        PIC X(57).

    01  IO-EMPPAYHS-RECORD.
        05  PAY-DATE      PIC X(8).
        05  PAY-ANN-PAY   PIC S9(6)V9(2) USAGE COMP-3.
        05  PAY-AMT       PIC S9(6)V9(2) USAGE COMP-3.
        05  FILLER        PIC X(62).

    01  SEG-IO-AREA       PIC X(80).

    01  DLI-FUNCTIONS.
        05  DLI-FUNCISRT  PIC X(4) VALUE 'ISRT'.
        05  DLI-FUNCGU    PIC X(4) VALUE 'GU  '.
        05  DLI-FUNCGN    PIC X(4) VALUE 'GN  '.
        05  DLI-FUNCGHU   PIC X(4) VALUE 'GHU '.
        05  DLI-FUNCGNP   PIC X(4) VALUE 'GNP '.
        05  DLI-FUNCREPL  PIC X(4) VALUE 'REPL'.
        05  DLI-FUNCDLET  PIC X(4) VALUE 'DLET'.
        05  DLI-FUNCXRST  PIC X(4) VALUE 'XRST'.
        05  DLI-FUNCCKPT  PIC X(4) VALUE 'CKPT'.

    01  DISPLAY-EMPPAYHS-PIC.
        05  DIS-REG-PAY   PIC ZZ999.99-.
        05  DIS-SMT-PAY   PIC ZZ999.99-.

    01  EMP-UNQUALIFIED-SSA.
        05  SEGNAME       PIC X(08) VALUE 'EMPLOYEE'.
        05  FILLER        PIC X(01) VALUE ' '.
```

```
       01  EMP-QUALIFIED-SSA.
           05  SEGNAME      PIC X(08) VALUE 'EMPLOYEE'.
           05  FILLER       PIC X(01) VALUE '('.
           05  FIELD        PIC X(08) VALUE 'EMPID'.
           05  OPER         PIC X(02) VALUE ' ='.
           05  EMP-ID-VAL   PIC X(04) VALUE '    '.
           05  FILLER       PIC X(01) VALUE ')'.

       01  EMPPAY-UNQUALIFIED-SSA.
           05  SEGNAME      PIC X(08) VALUE 'EMPPAY  '.
           05  FILLER       PIC X(01) VALUE ' '.

       01  EMPPAY-QUALIFIED-SSA.
           05  SEGNAME      PIC X(08) VALUE 'EMPPAY  '.
           05  FILLER       PIC X(01) VALUE '('.
           05  FIELD        PIC X(08) VALUE 'EFFDATE '.
           05  OPER         PIC X(02) VALUE ' ='.
           05  EFFDATE-VAL  PIC X(08) VALUE '        '.
           05  FILLER       PIC X(01) VALUE ')'.

       01  EMPPAYHS-UNQUALIFIED-SSA.
           05  SEGNAME      PIC X(08) VALUE 'EMPPAYHS'.
           05  FILLER       PIC X(01) VALUE ' '.

       01  IMS-RET-CODES.
           05  THREE        PIC S9(9) COMP VALUE +3.
           05  FOUR         PIC S9(9) COMP VALUE +4.
           05  FIVE         PIC S9(9) COMP VALUE +5.
           05  SIX          PIC S9(9) COMP VALUE +6.

       77  WS-PAY-DATE      PIC X(08) VALUE '20170228'.

       LINKAGE SECTION.
       01  PCB-MASK.
           03  DBD-NAME        PIC X(8).
           03  SEG-LEVEL       PIC XX.
           03  STATUS-CODE     PIC XX.
           03  PROC-OPT        PIC X(4).
           03  FILLER          PIC X(4).
           03  SEG-NAME        PIC X(8).
           03  KEY-FDBK        PIC S9(5) COMP.
           03  NUM-SENSEG      PIC S9(5) COMP.
           03  KEY-FDBK-AREA.
               05  EMPLOYEE-ID PIC X(04).
               05  EMPPAYHS    PIC X(08).

       PROCEDURE DIVISION.

           INITIALIZE PCB-MASK
           ENTRY 'DLITCBL' USING PCB-MASK

           PERFORM P100-INITIALIZATION.
           PERFORM P200-MAINLINE.
```

```
        PERFORM P300-TERMINATION.
        GOBACK.

 P100-INITIALIZATION.

        DISPLAY '** PROGRAM COBIMS9 START **'
        DISPLAY 'PROCESSING IN P100-INITIALIZATION'.

*       DO INITIAL DB READ FOR FIRST EMPLOYEE ROOT SEGMENT

        CALL 'CBLTDLI' USING FOUR,
             DLI-FUNCGN,
             PCB-MASK,
             IO-EMPLOYEE-RECORD,
             EMP-UNQUALIFIED-SSA

        IF STATUS-CODE = '  ' THEN
           DISPLAY '********************************'
        ELSE
           IF STATUS-CODE = 'GB' THEN
              SET SW-END-OF-DB TO TRUE
              DISPLAY 'END OF DATABASE :'
           ELSE
              PERFORM P9000-DISPLAY-ERROR
              GOBACK
           END-IF

        END-IF.

 P200-MAINLINE.

        DISPLAY 'PROCESSING IN P200-MAINLINE'

*       CHECK STATUS CODE AND FIRST RECORD

        IF SW-END-OF-DB THEN
           DISPLAY 'NO RECORDS TO PROCESS!!'
        ELSE
           PERFORM UNTIL SW-END-OF-DB
              DISPLAY 'SUCCESSFUL READ :' IO-EMPLOYEE-RECORD
              MOVE EMPL-ID TO EMP-ID-VAL
              PERFORM P2000-GET-EMPPAY
              IF STATUS-CODE NOT EQUAL SPACES THEN
                 PERFORM P9000-DISPLAY-ERROR
                 GOBACK
              ELSE
                 MOVE PAY-EFF-DATE TO EFFDATE-VAL
                 SET SW-NOT-END-OF-EMPPAYHS TO TRUE
                 PERFORM P3000-GET-NEXT-EMPPAYHS
                    UNTIL SW-END-OF-EMPPAYHS
              END-IF

              PERFORM P1000-GET-NEXT-ROOT
```

```cobol
               IF STATUS-CODE = 'GB' THEN
                  SET SW-END-OF-DB TO TRUE
                  DISPLAY 'END OF DATABASE'
               END-IF

           **END-PERFORM**

        END-IF.

        DISPLAY 'FINISHED PROCESSING IN P200-MAINLINE'.

    P300-TERMINATION.

        DISPLAY 'PROCESSING IN P300-TERMINATION'
        DISPLAY '** COBIMS9 - SUCCESSFULLY ENDED **'.

    P1000-GET-NEXT-ROOT.

        DISPLAY '*********************************'
        DISPLAY 'PROCESSING IN P1000-GET-NEXT-ROOT'.

        CALL 'CBLTDLI' USING FOUR,
             DLI-FUNCGN,
             PCB-MASK,
             **IO-EMPLOYEE-RECORD**,
             **EMP-UNQUALIFIED-SSA**.

    P2000-GET-EMPPAY.

        DISPLAY 'PROCESSING IN P2000-GET-EMPPAY'.

        CALL 'CBLTDLI' USING FIVE,
             DLI-FUNCGNP,
             PCB-MASK,
             **IO-EMPPAY-RECORD**,
             **EMP-QUALIFIED-SSA**,
             **EMPPAY-UNQUALIFIED-SSA**.

    P3000-GET-NEXT-EMPPAYHS.

        DISPLAY 'PROCESSING IN P3000-GET-NEXT-EMPPAYHS'.

        CALL 'CBLTDLI' USING SIX,
             DLI-FUNCGNP,
             PCB-MASK,
             IO-EMPPAYHS-RECORD,
             **EMP-QUALIFIED-SSA**,
             **EMPPAY-QUALIFIED-SSA**,
             **EMPPAYHS-UNQUALIFIED-SSA**.

               EVALUATE STATUS-CODE
                  WHEN '  '
                     DISPLAY 'GOOD READ OF EMPPAYHS : '
```

```
                EMP-ID-VAL
              MOVE PAY-ANN-PAY TO DIS-REG-PAY
              MOVE PAY-AMT      TO DIS-SMT-PAY
              DISPLAY 'PAY-DATE   : ' PAY-DATE
              DISPLAY 'PAY-ANN-PAY: ' DIS-REG-PAY
              DISPLAY 'PAY-AMT    : ' DIS-SMT-PAY
           WHEN 'GE'
           WHEN 'GB'
              SET SW-END-OF-EMPPAYHS TO TRUE
              DISPLAY 'NO MORE PAY HISTORY SEGMENTS'
           WHEN OTHER
              PERFORM P9000-DISPLAY-ERROR
              SET SW-END-OF-EMPPAYHS TO TRUE
              GOBACK
           END-EVALUATE.

       P9000-DISPLAY-ERROR.

           DISPLAY 'ERROR ENCOUNTERED - DETAIL FOLLOWS'
           DISPLAY 'DBD-NAME1:'     DBD-NAME
           DISPLAY 'SEG-LEVEL1:'    SEG-LEVEL
           DISPLAY 'STATUS-CODE:'   STATUS-CODE
           DISPLAY 'PROC-OPT1 :'    PROC-OPT
           DISPLAY 'SEG-NAME1 :'    SEG-NAME
           DISPLAY 'KEY-FDBK1 :'    KEY-FDBK
           DISPLAY 'NUM-SENSEG1:'   NUM-SENSEG
           DISPLAY 'KEY-FDBK-AREA1:' KEY-FDBK-AREA.

      *    END OF SOURCE CODE
```

Compile, link, run. Here is the output.

```
** PROGRAM COBIMS9 START **
PROCESSING IN P100-INITIALIZATION
*********************************
PROCESSING IN P200-MAINLINE
SUCCESSFUL READ :1111 VEREEN                       CHARLES            12 201
PROCESSING IN P2000-GET-EMPPAY
PROCESSING IN P3000-GET-NEXT-EMPPAYHS
GOOD READ OF EMPPAYHS : 1111
PAY-DATE   : 20170115
PAY-ANN-PAY: 87000.00
PAY-AMT    : 3625.00
PROCESSING IN P3000-GET-NEXT-EMPPAYHS
GOOD READ OF EMPPAYHS : 1111
PAY-DATE   : 20170130
PAY-ANN-PAY: 87000.00
PAY-AMT    : 3625.00
PROCESSING IN P3000-GET-NEXT-EMPPAYHS
GOOD READ OF EMPPAYHS : 1111
PAY-DATE   : 20170215
PAY-ANN-PAY: 87000.00
PAY-AMT    : 3625.00
PROCESSING IN P3000-GET-NEXT-EMPPAYHS
GOOD READ OF EMPPAYHS : 1111
```

```
PAY-DATE   : 20170228
PAY-ANN-PAY: 87000.00
PAY-AMT    :  3625.00
PROCESSING IN P3000-GET-NEXT-EMPPAYHS
NO MORE PAY HISTORY SEGMENTS
********************************
PROCESSING IN P1000-GET-NEXT-ROOT
SUCCESSFUL READ :1122 JENKINS                    DEBORAH            05 201
PROCESSING IN P2000-GET-EMPPAY
PROCESSING IN P3000-GET-NEXT-EMPPAYHS
GOOD READ OF EMPPAYHS : 1122
PAY-DATE   : 20170115
PAY-ANN-PAY: 82000.00
PAY-AMT    :  3416.66
PROCESSING IN P3000-GET-NEXT-EMPPAYHS
GOOD READ OF EMPPAYHS : 1122
PAY-DATE   : 20170130
PAY-ANN-PAY: 82000.00
PAY-AMT    :  3416.66
PROCESSING IN P3000-GET-NEXT-EMPPAYHS
GOOD READ OF EMPPAYHS : 1122
PAY-DATE   : 20170215
PAY-ANN-PAY: 82000.00
PAY-AMT    :  3416.66
PROCESSING IN P3000-GET-NEXT-EMPPAYHS
GOOD READ OF EMPPAYHS : 1122
PAY-DATE   : 20170228
PAY-ANN-PAY: 82000.00
PAY-AMT    :  3416.66
PROCESSING IN P3000-GET-NEXT-EMPPAYHS
NO MORE PAY HISTORY SEGMENTS
********************************
PROCESSING IN P1000-GET-NEXT-ROOT
SUCCESSFUL READ :3217 JOHNSON                    EDWARD             04 201
PROCESSING IN P2000-GET-EMPPAY
PROCESSING IN P3000-GET-NEXT-EMPPAYHS
GOOD READ OF EMPPAYHS : 3217
PAY-DATE   : 20170115
PAY-ANN-PAY: 65000.00
PAY-AMT    :  2708.33
PROCESSING IN P3000-GET-NEXT-EMPPAYHS
GOOD READ OF EMPPAYHS : 3217
PAY-DATE   : 20170130
PAY-ANN-PAY: 65000.00
PAY-AMT    :  2708.33
PROCESSING IN P3000-GET-NEXT-EMPPAYHS
GOOD READ OF EMPPAYHS : 3217
PAY-DATE   : 20170215
PAY-ANN-PAY: 65000.00
PAY-AMT    :  2708.33
PROCESSING IN P3000-GET-NEXT-EMPPAYHS
GOOD READ OF EMPPAYHS : 3217
PAY-DATE   : 20170228
PAY-ANN-PAY: 65000.00
PAY-AMT    :  2708.33
PROCESSING IN P3000-GET-NEXT-EMPPAYHS
NO MORE PAY HISTORY SEGMENTS
********************************
PROCESSING IN P1000-GET-NEXT-ROOT
SUCCESSFUL READ :4175 TURNBULL                   FRED               01 201
```

```
PROCESSING IN P2000-GET-EMPPAY
PROCESSING IN P3000-GET-NEXT-EMPPAYHS
GOOD READ OF EMPPAYHS : 4175
PAY-DATE   : 20170115
PAY-ANN-PAY: 55000.00
PAY-AMT    :  2291.66
PROCESSING IN P3000-GET-NEXT-EMPPAYHS
GOOD READ OF EMPPAYHS : 4175
PAY-DATE   : 20170130
PAY-ANN-PAY: 55000.00
PAY-AMT    :  2291.66
PROCESSING IN P3000-GET-NEXT-EMPPAYHS
GOOD READ OF EMPPAYHS : 4175
PAY-DATE   : 20170215
PAY-ANN-PAY: 55000.00
PAY-AMT    :  2291.66
PROCESSING IN P3000-GET-NEXT-EMPPAYHS
GOOD READ OF EMPPAYHS : 4175
PAY-DATE   : 20170228
PAY-ANN-PAY: 55000.00
PAY-AMT    :  2291.66
PROCESSING IN P3000-GET-NEXT-EMPPAYHS
NO MORE PAY HISTORY SEGMENTS
*********************************
PROCESSING IN P1000-GET-NEXT-ROOT
SUCCESSFUL READ :4720 SCHULTZ                TIM             09 201
PROCESSING IN P2000-GET-EMPPAY
PROCESSING IN P3000-GET-NEXT-EMPPAYHS
GOOD READ OF EMPPAYHS : 4720
PAY-DATE   : 20170115
PAY-ANN-PAY: 80000.00
PAY-AMT    :  3333.33
PROCESSING IN P3000-GET-NEXT-EMPPAYHS
GOOD READ OF EMPPAYHS : 4720
PAY-DATE   : 20170130
PAY-ANN-PAY: 80000.00
PAY-AMT    :  3333.33
PROCESSING IN P3000-GET-NEXT-EMPPAYHS
GOOD READ OF EMPPAYHS : 4720
PAY-DATE   : 20170215
PAY-ANN-PAY: 80000.00
PAY-AMT    :  3333.33
PROCESSING IN P3000-GET-NEXT-EMPPAYHS
GOOD READ OF EMPPAYHS : 4720
PAY-DATE   : 20170228
PAY-ANN-PAY: 80000.00
PAY-AMT    :  3333.33
PROCESSING IN P3000-GET-NEXT-EMPPAYHS
NO MORE PAY HISTORY SEGMENTS
*********************************
PROCESSING IN P1000-GET-NEXT-ROOT
SUCCESSFUL READ :4836 SMITH                  SANDRA          03 201
PROCESSING IN P2000-GET-EMPPAY
PROCESSING IN P3000-GET-NEXT-EMPPAYHS
GOOD READ OF EMPPAYHS : 4836
PAY-DATE   : 20170115
PAY-ANN-PAY: 62000.00
PAY-AMT    :  2583.33
PROCESSING IN P3000-GET-NEXT-EMPPAYHS
GOOD READ OF EMPPAYHS : 4836
```

```
PAY-DATE    : 20170130
PAY-ANN-PAY: 62000.00
PAY-AMT     :  2583.33
PROCESSING IN P3000-GET-NEXT-EMPPAYHS
GOOD READ OF EMPPAYHS : 4836
PAY-DATE    : 20170215
PAY-ANN-PAY: 62000.00
PAY-AMT     :  2583.33
PROCESSING IN P3000-GET-NEXT-EMPPAYHS
GOOD READ OF EMPPAYHS : 4836
PAY-DATE    : 20170228
PAY-ANN-PAY: 62000.00
PAY-AMT     :  2583.33
PROCESSING IN P3000-GET-NEXT-EMPPAYHS
NO MORE PAY HISTORY SEGMENTS
********************************
PROCESSING IN P1000-GET-NEXT-ROOT
SUCCESSFUL READ :6288 WILLARD              JOE              06 201
PROCESSING IN P2000-GET-EMPPAY
PROCESSING IN P3000-GET-NEXT-EMPPAYHS
GOOD READ OF EMPPAYHS : 6288
PAY-DATE    : 20170115
PAY-ANN-PAY: 70000.00
PAY-AMT     :  2916.66
PROCESSING IN P3000-GET-NEXT-EMPPAYHS
GOOD READ OF EMPPAYHS : 6288
PAY-DATE    : 20170130
PAY-ANN-PAY: 70000.00
PAY-AMT     :  2916.66
PROCESSING IN P3000-GET-NEXT-EMPPAYHS
GOOD READ OF EMPPAYHS : 6288
PAY-DATE    : 20170215
PAY-ANN-PAY: 70000.00
PAY-AMT     :  2916.66
PROCESSING IN P3000-GET-NEXT-EMPPAYHS
GOOD READ OF EMPPAYHS : 6288
PAY-DATE    : 20170228
PAY-ANN-PAY: 70000.00
PAY-AMT     :  2916.66
PROCESSING IN P3000-GET-NEXT-EMPPAYHS
NO MORE PAY HISTORY SEGMENTS
********************************
PROCESSING IN P1000-GET-NEXT-ROOT
SUCCESSFUL READ :7459 STEWART              BETTY            07 201
PROCESSING IN P2000-GET-EMPPAY
PROCESSING IN P3000-GET-NEXT-EMPPAYHS
GOOD READ OF EMPPAYHS : 7459
PAY-DATE    : 20170115
PAY-ANN-PAY: 85000.00
PAY-AMT     :  3541.66
PROCESSING IN P3000-GET-NEXT-EMPPAYHS
GOOD READ OF EMPPAYHS : 7459
PAY-DATE    : 20170130
PAY-ANN-PAY: 85000.00
PAY-AMT     :  3541.66
PROCESSING IN P3000-GET-NEXT-EMPPAYHS
GOOD READ OF EMPPAYHS : 7459
PAY-DATE    : 20170215
PAY-ANN-PAY: 85000.00
PAY-AMT     :  3541.66
```

```
PROCESSING IN P3000-GET-NEXT-EMPPAYHS
GOOD READ OF EMPPAYHS : 7459
PAY-DATE   : 20170228
PAY-ANN-PAY: 85000.00
PAY-AMT    :  3541.66
PROCESSING IN P3000-GET-NEXT-EMPPAYHS
NO MORE PAY HISTORY SEGMENTS
********************************
PROCESSING IN P1000-GET-NEXT-ROOT
END OF DATABASE
FINISHED PROCESSING IN P200-MAINLINE
PROCESSING IN P300-TERMINATION
** COBIMS9 - SUCCESSFULLY ENDED **
```

Ok I think we've covered the root-child relationships enough. You have some models to use for most anything you'd want to do in the hierarchy. Time to move on to other topics. First, here's the PLI code that corresponds to the COBIMS9 program.

```
       PLIIMS9: PROCEDURE (DB_PTR_PCB) OPTIONS(MAIN);
      /******************************************************************
       * PROGRAM NAME :    PLIIMS9 - READ EMPLOYEE HISTORY PAY RECORDS   *
       *                   UNDER THEIR EMPPAY PARENTS. QUALIFIED SSA'S   *
       *                   MUST BE PROVIDED FOR BOTH THE EMPLOYEE AND    *
       *                   EMPPAY SEGMENTS.                              *
       ******************************************************************/

      /******************************************************************
      /*                W O R K I N G   S T O R A G E                   *
       ******************************************************************/

           DCL SW_END_OF_DB            STATIC BIT(01) INIT('0'B);
           DCL SW_END_OF_EMPPAYHS      STATIC BIT(01) INIT('0'B);
           DCL ONCODE                  BUILTIN;
           DCL DB_PTR_PCB              POINTER;

           DCL PLITDLI                 EXTERNAL ENTRY;

           DCL 01 DLI_FUNCTIONS,
                05  DLI_FUNCISRT       CHAR(04) INIT ('ISRT'),
                05  DLI_FUNCGU         CHAR(04) INIT ('GU  '),
                05  DLI_FUNCGN         CHAR(04) INIT ('GN  '),
                05  DLI_FUNCGHU        CHAR(04) INIT ('GHU '),
                05  DLI_FUNCGNP        CHAR(04) INIT ('GNP '),
                05  DLI_FUNCREPL       CHAR(04) INIT ('REPL'),
                05  DLI_FUNCDLET       CHAR(04) INIT ('DLET'),
                05  DLI_FUNCXRST       CHAR(04) INIT ('XRST'),
                05  DLI_FUNCCHKP       CHAR(04) INIT ('CHKP'),
                05  DLI_FUNCROLL       CHAR(04) INIT ('ROLL');

           DCL 01 IO_EMPLOYEE_RECORD,
                05   EMPL_ID           CHAR(04),
                05   FILLER1           CHAR(01),
```

```
          05  EMPL_LNAME           CHAR(30),
          05  FILLER2              CHAR(01),
          05  EMPL_FNAME           CHAR(20),
          05  FILLER3              CHAR(01),
          05  EMPL_YRS_SRV         CHAR(02),
          05  FILLER4              CHAR(01),
          05  EMPL_PRM_DTE         CHAR(10),
          05  FILLER5              CHAR(10);

     DCL 01 IO_EMPPAY_RECORD,
          05  PAY_EFF_DATE         CHAR(8),
          05  PAY_REG_PAY          FIXED DEC (8,2),
          05  PAY_BON_PAY          FIXED DEC (8,2),
          05  SEMIMTH_PAY          FIXED DEC (8,2),
          05  FILLER55             CHAR(57);

     DCL 01 IO_EMPPAYHS_RECORD,
          05  PAY_DATE             CHAR(8),
          05  PAY_ANN_PAY          FIXED DEC (8,2),
          05  PAY_AMT              FIXED DEC (8,2),
          05  FILLER65             CHAR(62);

     DCL 01 PCB_MASK               BASED(DB_PTR_PCB),
          05  DBD_NAME             CHAR(08),
          05  SEG_LEVEL            CHAR(02),
          05  STATUS_CODE          CHAR(02),
          05  PROC_OPT             CHAR(04),
          05  FILLER6              FIXED BIN (31),
          05  SEG_NAME             CHAR(08),
          05  KEY_FDBK             FIXED BIN (31),
          05  NUM_SENSEG           FIXED BIN (31),
          05  KEY_FDBK_AREA,
             10  EMPLOYEE_ID       CHAR(04),
             10  EMP_PAY_DATE      CHAR(08);

     DCL 01 EMP_UNQUALIFIED_SSA,
          05  SEGNAME              CHAR(08) INIT ('EMPLOYEE'),
          05  FILLER7              CHAR(01) INIT (' ');

     DCL 01 EMP_QUALIFIED_SSA,
          05  SEGNAME              CHAR(08) INIT('EMPLOYEE'),
          05  FILLER8              CHAR(01) INIT('('),
          05  FIELD                CHAR(08) INIT('EMPID'),
          05  OPER                 CHAR(02) INIT(' ='),
          05  EMP_ID_VAL           CHAR(04) INIT('    '),
          05  FILLER9              CHAR(01) INIT(')');

     DCL 01 EMPPAY_UNQUALIFIED_SSA,
          05  SEGNAME              CHAR(08) INIT('EMPPAY   '),
          05  FILLER10             CHAR(01) INIT(' ');

     DCL 01 EMPPAY_QUALIFIED_SSA,
          05  SEGNAME              CHAR(08) INIT('EMPPAY   '),
```

```
            05  FILLER11           CHAR(01) INIT('('),
            05  FIELD              CHAR(08) INIT('EFFDATE '),
            05  OPER               CHAR(02) INIT(' ='),
            05  EFFDATE_VAL        CHAR(08) INIT('        '),
            05  FILLER12           CHAR(01) INIT(')');

    DCL 01 EMPPAYHS_UNQUALIFIED_SSA,
            05  SEGNAME            CHAR(08) INIT('EMPPAYHS'),
            05  FILLER13           CHAR(01) INIT(' ');

    DCL WS_PAY_DATE                CHAR(08) INIT ('20170215');

    DCL SEG_IO_AREA                CHAR(80) INIT (' ');

    DCL THREE                      FIXED BIN (31) INIT(3);
    DCL FOUR                       FIXED BIN (31) INIT(4);
    DCL FIVE                       FIXED BIN (31) INIT(5);
    DCL SIX                        FIXED BIN (31) INIT(6);

 /*********************************************************************
 /*              P R O G R A M    M A I N L I N E                     *
 *********************************************************************/

 CALL P100_INITIALIZATION;
 CALL P200_MAINLINE;
 CALL P300_TERMINATION;

 P100_INITIALIZATION: PROC;

     PUT SKIP LIST ('PLIIMS9: READ EMPPAYHS RECORDS');
     PUT SKIP LIST ('PROCESSING IN P100_INITIALIZATION');

     IO_EMPLOYEE_RECORD = '';
     IO_EMPPAY_RECORD   = '';
     IO_EMPPAYHS_RECORD = '';
     PCB_MASK = '';

     /* DO INITIAL DB READ FOR FIRST EMPLOYEE RECORD */

     CALL PLITDLI (FOUR,
                   DLI_FUNCGN,
                   PCB_MASK,
                   IO_EMPLOYEE_RECORD,
                   EMP_UNQUALIFIED_SSA);

     IF STATUS_CODE = '  ' THEN;
     ELSE
        IF STATUS_CODE = 'GB' THEN
           DO;
              SW_END_OF_DB = '1'B;
              PUT SKIP LIST ('** END OF DATABASE');
           END;
        ELSE
```

```
            DO;
                CALL P9000_DISPLAY_ERROR;
                RETURN;
            END;

END P100_INITIALIZATION;

P200_MAINLINE: PROC;

    /*  MAIN LOOP - WALK THROUGH THE DATABASE GETTING EMPLOYEE
                    PAY HISTORY SEGMENTS.                       */

    IF SW_END_OF_DB THEN
        PUT SKIP LIST ('NO RECORDS TO PROCESS!!');
    ELSE
        DO WHILE (¬SW_END_OF_DB);

            PUT SKIP LIST ('SUCCESSFUL READ OF EMPLOYEE ' || EMPL_ID);

            /* ASSIGN KEY FOR EMPLOYEE LEVEL SSA AND GET EMPPAY SEG */

            EMP_ID_VAL = EMPL_ID;
            CALL P2000_GET_EMPPAY;
            IF STATUS_CODE ¬= ' ' THEN
                DO;
                    PUT SKIP LIST ('ERROR READING EMPPAY');
                    CALL P9000_DISPLAY_ERROR;
                    RETURN;
                END;
            ELSE
                DO;
                    PUT SKIP LIST ('SUCCESSFUL PAY READ : '
                        || IO_EMPPAY_RECORD);

                    /* ASSIGN KEY FOR EMPPAY LEVEL SSA FOR SEG */

                    EFFDATE_VAL = PAY_EFF_DATE;

                    SW_END_OF_EMPPAYHS = '0'B;
                    DO WHILE (¬SW_END_OF_EMPPAYHS);
                       CALL P3000_GET_NEXT_EMPPAYHS;
                    END; /* DO WHILE */

                    CALL P1000_GET_NEXT_ROOT;
                    IF STATUS_CODE = 'GB' THEN
                       DO;
                           SW_END_OF_DB = '1'B;
                           PUT SKIP LIST ('** END OF DATABASE');
                       END;
                    ELSE
                       IF STATUS_CODE = ' ' THEN;
                       ELSE
                          DO;
```

```
                    CALL P9000_DISPLAY_ERROR;
                    RETURN;
                END;

            END; /* SUCCESSFULLY RETRIEVED PAY SEG */

        END; /* DO WHILE */

        PUT SKIP LIST ('FINISHED PROCESSING IN P200_MAINLINE');

END P200_MAINLINE;

P300_TERMINATION: PROC;

    PUT SKIP LIST ('PLIIMS9 - SUCCESSFULLY ENDED');

END P300_TERMINATION;

P1000_GET_NEXT_ROOT: PROC;

    PUT SKIP LIST ('PROCESSING IN P1000_GET_NEXT_ROOT');

    CALL PLITDLI (FOUR,
                  DLI_FUNCGN,
                  PCB_MASK,
                  IO_EMPLOYEE_RECORD,
                  EMP_UNQUALIFIED_SSA);

END P1000_GET_NEXT_ROOT;

P2000_GET_EMPPAY: PROC;

    PUT SKIP LIST ('PROCESSING IN P2000_GET_EMPPAY');

    CALL PLITDLI (FIVE,
                  DLI_FUNCGNP,
                  PCB_MASK,
                  IO_EMPPAY_RECORD,
                  EMP_QUALIFIED_SSA,
                  EMPPAY_UNQUALIFIED_SSA);

END P2000_GET_EMPPAY;

P3000_GET_NEXT_EMPPAYHS: PROC;

    PUT SKIP LIST ('PROCESSING IN P3000_GET_NEXT_EMPPAYHS');

    CALL PLITDLI (SIX,
                  DLI_FUNCGNP,
                  PCB_MASK,
                  IO_EMPPAYHS_RECORD,
                  EMP_QUALIFIED_SSA,
                  EMPPAY_QUALIFIED_SSA,
```

```
                EMPPAYHS_UNQUALIFIED_SSA);

     SELECT (STATUS_CODE);
        WHEN (' ')
           DO;
              PUT SKIP LIST ('GOOD READ OF EMPPAYHS : '
                 || EMP_ID_VAL);
              PUT SKIP LIST ('PAY_DATE   : ' || PAY_DATE);
              PUT SKIP LIST ('PAY_ANN_PAY: ' || PAY_ANN_PAY);
              PUT SKIP LIST ('PAY_AMT    : ' || PAY_AMT);
           END;
        WHEN ('GE','GB')
           DO;
              SW_END_OF_EMPPAYHS = '1'B;
              PUT SKIP LIST ('NO MORE PAY HISTORY SEGMENTS');
           END;
        OTHERWISE
           DO;
              CALL P9000_DISPLAY_ERROR;
              SW_END_OF_EMPPAYHS = '1'B;
           END;

     END; /* SELECT */

END P3000_GET_NEXT_EMPPAYHS;

P9000_DISPLAY_ERROR: PROC;

     PUT SKIP LIST ('ERROR ENCOUNTERED - DETAIL FOLLOWS');
     PUT SKIP DATA (IO_EMPPAY_RECORD);
     PUT SKIP LIST ('DBD_NAME1:' || DBD_NAME);
     PUT SKIP LIST ('SEG_LEVEL1:' || SEG_LEVEL);
     PUT SKIP LIST ('STATUS_CODE:' || STATUS_CODE);
     PUT SKIP LIST ('PROC_OPT1 :' || PROC_OPT);
     PUT SKIP LIST ('SEG_NAME1 :' || SEG_NAME);
     PUT SKIP LIST ('KEY_FDBK1 :' || KEY_FDBK);
     PUT SKIP LIST ('NUM_SENSEG1:' || NUM_SENSEG);
     PUT SKIP LIST ('KEY_FDBK_AREA1:' || KEY_FDBK_AREA);

END P9000_DISPLAY_ERROR;

END PLIIMS9;
```

Additional IMS Programming Features
Retrieve Segments Using Searchable Fields

So far all the qualified SSA retrievals we've done have been based on a segment **key**. It is also possible to retrieve IMS segments by a searchable field that is not the key. For this example with program COBIMSA we will create a new field for our EMPLOYEE record layout, and then define this field in our DBD. Then we will write a program to search based on the new EMPSSN field which is the employee social security number.

Ok, where shall we put the field? We have a 9 byte social security number field, and we have 10 bytes of filler at the end of the record. Let's use the last 9 bytes of the record. Here is our new layout.

```
01  IO-EMPLOYEE-RECORD.
    05  FILLER         PIC X(06).
    05  EMP-ID         PIC X(04).
    05  FILLER         PIC X(01).
    05  EMPL-LNAME     PIC X(30).
    05  FILLER         PIC X(01).
    05  EMPL-FNAME     PIC X(20).
    05  FILLER         PIC X(01).
    05  EMPL-YRS-SRV   PIC X(02).
    05  FILLER         PIC X(01).
    05  EMPL-PRM-DTE   PIC X(10).
    05  FILLER         PIC X(01).
    05  EMPL-SSN       PIC X(09).
```

Now let's assign `EMPL-SSN` values to the original flat file we used to load the database. Here it is:

```
BROWSE     USER01.EMPIFILE                      Line 00000000 Col 001 080
----+----1----+----2----+----3----+----4----+----5----+----6----+----7----+----8
Command ===>                                           Scroll ===> CSR
******************************* Top of Data *********************************
1111 VEREEN                    CHARLES          12 2017-01-01 937253058
1122 JENKINS                   DEBORAH          05 2017-01-01 435092366
3217 JOHNSON                   EDWARD           04 2017-01-01 397342007
4175 TURNBULL                  FRED             01 2016-12-01 542083017
4720 SCHULTZ                   TIM              09 2017-01-01 650450254
4836 SMITH                     SANDRA           03 2017-01-01 028374669
6288 WILLARD                   JOE              06 2016-01-01 209883920
7459 STEWART                   BETTY            07 2016-07-31 019572830
9134 FRANKLIN                  BRIANNA          00 2016-10-01 937293598
****************************** Bottom of Data *******************************
```

Now let's delete all existing records in the database (you can use File Manager for this as explained earlier in the chapter). Then let's run `COBIMS1` to reload the database from our flat file which now includes the `EMPL-SSN` values. Now we can browse the database and verify that the `EMPL-SSN` field is populated (you will need to scroll to the right to see the `EMPSSN` field).

```
Browse           USER01.IMS.EMPLOYEE.CLUSTER             Top of 9
Command ===>                                             Scroll PAGE
                      Type KSDS     RBA                  Format CHAR
Key                                       Col 10
>----+----20---+----3----+----4----+----5----+----6----+----7----+----8----+---
****    Top of data    ****
1 VEREEN                    CHARLES          12 2017-01-01 937253058..
2 JENKINS                   DEBORAH          05 2017-01-01 435092366..
7 JOHNSON                   EDWARD           04 2017-01-01 397342007..
5 TURNBULL                  FRED             01 2016-12-01 542083017..
```

```
0 SCHULTZ              TIM                09 2017-01-01 650450254..
6 SMITH                SANDRA             03 2017-01-01 028374669..
8 WILLARD              JOE                06 2016-01-01 209883920..
9 STEWART              BETTY              07 2016-07-31 019572830..
4 FRANKLIN             BRIANNA            00 2016-10-01 937293598..
```

Ok, next step. To be able to search on a field in an IMS segment, the field must be defined in the DBD. Recall our original code for the DBD is as follows:

```
PRINT NOGEN
DBD NAME=EMPLOYEE,ACCESS=HISAM
DATASET DD1=EMPLOYEE,OVFLW=EMPLFLW
SEGM NAME=EMPLOYEE,PARENT=0,BYTES=80
FIELD NAME=(EMPID,SEQ,U),BYTES=04,START=1,TYPE=C
SEGM NAME=EMPPAY,PARENT=EMPLOYEE,BYTES=23
FIELD NAME=(EFFDATE,SEQ,U),START=1,BYTES=8,TYPE=C
SEGM  NAME=EMPPAYHS,PARENT=EMPPAY,BYTES=18
FIELD NAME=(PAYDATE,SEQ,U),START=1,BYTES=8,TYPE=C
DBDGEN
FINISH
END
```

The only searchable field right now on the EMPLOYEE segment is the primary key EMPID. To make the EMPSSN field searchable we must add it to the DBD. The appropriate code is bolded below. Note that EMPSSN starts in position 72 of the record and is 9 bytes in length.

```
PRINT NOGEN
DBD NAME=EMPLOYEE,ACCESS=HISAM
DATASET DD1=EMPLOYEE,OVFLW=EMPLFLW
SEGM NAME=EMPLOYEE,PARENT=0,BYTES=80
FIELD NAME=(EMPID,SEQ,U),BYTES=04,START=1,TYPE=C
FIELD NAME=EMPSSN,START=72,BYTES=9,TYPE=C
SEGM NAME=EMPPAY,PARENT=EMPLOYEE,BYTES=23
FIELD NAME=(EFFDATE,SEQ,U),START=1,BYTES=8,TYPE=C
SEGM  NAME=EMPPAYHS,PARENT=EMPPAY,BYTES=18
FIELD NAME=(PAYDATE,SEQ,U),START=1,BYTES=8,TYPE=C
DBDGEN
FINISH
END
```

Go ahead and run the DBD gen process.

Next we can write a program to search on the EMPSSN field. We can clone the COBIMS2 program to make COBIMSA. One change we must make is to use a different qualified SSA than the one we started with. We need only change the field name in the SSA and create a value field with an appropriate specification (in this case a 9 position character field for the SSN key).

Here is our new structure:

```
01 EMP-QUALIFIED-SSA-EMPSSN.
   05  SEGNAME      PIC X(08) VALUE 'EMPLOYEE'.
   05  FILLER       PIC X(01) VALUE '('.
   05  FIELD        PIC X(08) VALUE 'EMPSSN'.
   05  OPER         PIC X(02) VALUE ' ='.
   05  EMPSSN-VAL   PIC X(09) VALUE '         '.
   05  FILLER       PIC X(01) VALUE ')'.
```

Naturally you must load the EMPSSN-VAL variable with the value you are looking for. Let's use the social security number 937253058 for Charles Vereen who is employee number 1111. Here is our COBOL program source.

```
ID DIVISION.
PROGRAM-ID. COBIMSA.

************************************************************
*   RETRIEVE A RECORD FROM IMS EMPLOYEE DATABASE            *
*   USING SEARCHABLE FIELD EMPSSN                           *
************************************************************

ENVIRONMENT DIVISION.
DATA DIVISION.

************************************************************
*    W O R K I N G    S T O R A G E    S E C T I O N       *
************************************************************

WORKING-STORAGE SECTION.

01 SEG-IO-AREA      PIC X(80).


01 DLI-FUNCTIONS.
   05  DLI-FUNCISRT  PIC X(4) VALUE 'ISRT'.
   05  DLI-FUNCGU    PIC X(4) VALUE 'GU  '.
   05  DLI-FUNCGN    PIC X(4) VALUE 'GN  '.
   05  DLI-FUNCGHU   PIC X(4) VALUE 'GHU '.
   05  DLI-FUNCGNP   PIC X(4) VALUE 'GNP '.
   05  DLI-FUNCREPL  PIC X(4) VALUE 'REPL'.
   05  DLI-FUNCDLET  PIC X(4) VALUE 'DLET'.
   05  DLI-FUNCXRST  PIC X(4) VALUE 'XRST'.
   05  DLI-FUNCCKPT  PIC X(4) VALUE 'CKPT'.

 01 EMP-UNQUALIFIED-SSA.
    05  SEGNAME      PIC X(08) VALUE 'EMPLOYEE'.
    05  FILLER       PIC X(01) VALUE ' '.

 01 EMP-QUALIFIED-SSA.
    05  SEGNAME      PIC X(08) VALUE 'EMPLOYEE'.
    05  FILLER       PIC X(01) VALUE '('.
```

```cobol
           05  FIELD        PIC X(08) VALUE 'EMPID'.
           05  OPER         PIC X(02) VALUE ' ='.
           05  EMP-ID-VAL   PIC X(04) VALUE '    '.
           05  FILLER       PIC X(01) VALUE ')'.

       01  EMP-QUALIFIED-SSA-EMPSSN.
           05  SEGNAME      PIC X(08) VALUE 'EMPLOYEE'.
           05  FILLER       PIC X(01) VALUE '('.
           05  FIELD        PIC X(08) VALUE 'EMPSSN'.
           05  OPER         PIC X(02) VALUE ' ='.
           05  EMPSSN-VAL   PIC X(09) VALUE '         '.
           05  FILLER       PIC X(01) VALUE ')'.

       01  IMS-RET-CODES.
           05 THREE         PIC S9(9) COMP VALUE +3.
           05 FOUR          PIC S9(9) COMP VALUE +4.
           05 FIVE          PIC S9(9) COMP VALUE +5.
           05 SIX           PIC S9(9) COMP VALUE +6.


       LINKAGE SECTION.
        01 PCB-MASK.
           03 DBD-NAME      PIC X(8).
           03 SEG-LEVEL     PIC XX.
           03 STATUS-CODE   PIC XX.
           03 PROC-OPT      PIC X(4).
           03 FILLER        PIC X(4).
           03 SEG-NAME      PIC X(8).
           03 KEY-FDBK      PIC S9(5) COMP.
           03 NUM-SENSEG    PIC S9(5) COMP.
           03 KEY-FDBK-AREA.
              05 EMPLOYEE-ID  PIC X(04).
              05 EMPPAYHS     PIC X(08).

       PROCEDURE DIVISION.

           INITIALIZE PCB-MASK
           ENTRY 'DLITCBL' USING PCB-MASK

           PERFORM P100-INITIALIZATION.
           PERFORM P200-MAINLINE.
           PERFORM P300-TERMINATION.
           GOBACK.

       P100-INITIALIZATION.

           DISPLAY '** PROGRAM COBIMSA START **'
           DISPLAY 'PROCESSING IN P100-INITIALIZATION'.

       P200-MAINLINE.

           DISPLAY 'PROCESSING IN P200-MAINLINE'
```

```
          MOVE '937253058' TO EMPSSN-VAL

      DISPLAY 'EMP-QUALIFIED-SSA-EMPSSN '
         EMP-QUALIFIED-SSA-EMPSSN

      CALL 'CBLTDLI' USING FOUR,
                     DLI-FUNCGU,
                     PCB-MASK,
                     SEG-IO-AREA,
                     EMP-QUALIFIED-SSA-EMPSSN

      IF STATUS-CODE = '  '
         DISPLAY 'SUCCESSFUL GET CALL  '
         DISPLAY 'SEG-IO-ARE : ' SEG-IO-AREA
      ELSE
         DISPLAY 'ERROR IN FETCH :' STATUS-CODE
         PERFORM P400-DISPLAY-ERROR
      END-IF.

  P300-TERMINATION.

      DISPLAY 'PROCESSING IN P300-TERMINATION'
      DISPLAY '** COBIMSA - SUCCESSFULLY ENDED **'.

  P400-DISPLAY-ERROR.

      DISPLAY 'ERROR ENCOUNTERED - DETAIL FOLLOWS'
      DISPLAY 'SEG-IO-AREA     :' SEG-IO-AREA
      DISPLAY 'DBD-NAME1:'     DBD-NAME
      DISPLAY 'SEG-LEVEL1:'    SEG-LEVEL
      DISPLAY 'STATUS-CODE:'   STATUS-CODE
      DISPLAY 'PROC-OPT1 :'    PROC-OPT
      DISPLAY 'SEG-NAME1 :'    SEG-NAME
      DISPLAY 'KEY-FDBK1 :'    KEY-FDBK
      DISPLAY 'NUM-SENSEG1:'   NUM-SENSEG
      DISPLAY 'KEY-FDBK-AREA1:' KEY-FDBK-AREA.

  *   END OF SOURCE CODE
```

Again we compile, link and execute. Here's the output:

```
** PROGRAM COBIMSA START **
PROCESSING IN P100-INITIALIZATION
PROCESSING IN P200-MAINLINE
EMP-QUALIFIED-SSA-EMPSSN EMPLOYEE(EMPSSN   =937253058)
SUCCESSFUL GET CALL
SEG-IO-ARE : 1111 VEREEN              CHARLES              12 2017-01-01 937253058
PROCESSING IN P300-TERMINATION
** COBIMSA - SUCCESSFULLY ENDED **
```

As you can see, we retrieved the desired record using the EMPSSN search field. So keep in mind that you can search on fields other than the key field as long as they are defined in the DBD. If you are going to be searching on a non-indexed field often, you'll want to check with your DBA about possibly defining a secondary index.

Here's the PLI code for this example.

```
PLIIMSA: PROCEDURE (DB_PTR_PCB) OPTIONS(MAIN);
/******************************************************************
 * PROGRAM NAME :    PLIIMSA - RETRIEVE A RECORD FROM EMPLOYEE DB  *
 *                         USING SEARCH FIELD EMPSSN.              *
 ******************************************************************/

/******************************************************************
/*                  W O R K I N G   S T O R A G E                  *
 ******************************************************************/
    DCL ONCODE                  BUILTIN;
    DCL DB_PTR_PCB              POINTER;
    DCL PLITDLI                 EXTERNAL ENTRY;

    DCL 01 DLI_FUNCTIONS,
         05 DLI_FUNCISRT        CHAR(04) INIT ('ISRT'),
         05 DLI_FUNCGU          CHAR(04) INIT ('GU  '),
         05 DLI_FUNCGN          CHAR(04) INIT ('GN  '),
         05 DLI_FUNCGHU         CHAR(04) INIT ('GHU '),
         05 DLI_FUNCGNP         CHAR(04) INIT ('GNP '),
         05 DLI_FUNCREPL        CHAR(04) INIT ('REPL'),
         05 DLI_FUNCDLET        CHAR(04) INIT ('DLET'),
         05 DLI_FUNCXRST        CHAR(04) INIT ('XRST'),
         05 DLI_FUNCCHKP        CHAR(04) INIT ('CHKP'),
         05 DLI_FUNCROLL        CHAR(04) INIT ('ROLL');

    DCL 01 IO_EMPLOYEE_RECORD,
         05  EMPL_ID_IN         CHAR(04),
         05  FILLER1            CHAR(01),
         05  EMPL_LNAME         CHAR(30),
         05  FILLER2            CHAR(01),
         05  EMPL_FNAME         CHAR(20),
         05  FILLER3            CHAR(01),
         05  EMPL_YRS_SRV       CHAR(02),
         05  FILLER4            CHAR(01),
         05  EMPL_PRM_DTE       CHAR(10),
         05  FILLER5            CHAR(01),
         05  EMPL_SSN           CHAR(09);

    DCL 01 PCB_MASK             BASED(DB_PTR_PCB),
         05 DBD_NAME             CHAR(08),
         05 SEG_LEVEL            CHAR(02),
         05 STATUS_CODE          CHAR(02),
         05 PROC_OPT             CHAR(04),
```

```
            05  FILLER6              FIXED BIN (31),
            05  SEG_NAME             CHAR(08),
            05  KEY_FDBK             FIXED BIN (31),
            05  NUM_SENSEG           FIXED BIN (31),
            05  KEY_FDBK_AREA,
                10  EMPLOYEE_ID      CHAR(04);

    DCL 01 EMP_UNQUALIFIED_SSA,
            05  SEGNAME              CHAR(08) INIT ('EMPLOYEE'),
            05  FILLER7              CHAR(01) INIT (' ');

    DCL 01 EMP_QUALIFIED_SSA,
            05  SEGNAME              CHAR(08) INIT('EMPLOYEE'),
            05  FILLER8              CHAR(01) INIT('('),
            05  FIELD                CHAR(08) INIT('EMPID'),
            05  OPER                 CHAR(02) INIT(' ='),
            05  EMP_ID_VAL           CHAR(04) INIT('    '),
            05  FILLER9              CHAR(01) INIT(')');

    DCL 01 EMP_QUALIFIED_SSA_EMPSSN,
            05  SEGNAME              CHAR(08) INIT('EMPLOYEE'),
            05  FILLER10             CHAR(01) INIT('('),
            05  FIELD                CHAR(08) INIT('EMPSSN'),
            05  OPER                 CHAR(02) INIT(' ='),
            05  EMPSSN_VAL           CHAR(09) INIT('         '),
            05  FILLER11             CHAR(01) INIT(')');

    DCL THREE                        FIXED BIN (31) INIT(3);
    DCL FOUR                         FIXED BIN (31) INIT(4);
    DCL FIVE                         FIXED BIN (31) INIT(5);
    DCL SIX                          FIXED BIN (31) INIT(6);

/*********************************************************************
/*              P R O G R A M   M A I N L I N E                      *
*********************************************************************/

CALL P100_INITIALIZATION;
CALL P200_MAINLINE;
CALL P300_TERMINATION;

P100_INITIALIZATION: PROC;

    PUT SKIP LIST ('PLIIMSA: GET RECORD FROM EMPLOYEE DB USING EMPSS');
    IO_EMPLOYEE_RECORD  = '';

END P100_INITIALIZATION;

P200_MAINLINE: PROC;

   /*  SET THE EMPLOYEE SEGMENT SEARCH ARGUMENT AND CALL PLITDLI  */

   EMPSSN_VAL = '937253058';
```

```
       CALL PLITDLI (FOUR,
                     DLI_FUNCGU,
                     PCB_MASK,
                     IO_EMPLOYEE_RECORD,
                     EMP_QUALIFIED_SSA_EMPSSN);

    IF STATUS_CODE = '   ' THEN
       DO;
           PUT SKIP LIST ('SUCCESSFUL RETRIEVAL - SSN: ' || EMPL_SSN);
           PUT SKIP DATA(IO_EMPLOYEE_RECORD);
       END;
    ELSE
       CALL P400_DISPLAY_ERROR;

END P200_MAINLINE;

P300_TERMINATION: PROC;

    PUT SKIP LIST ('PLIIMSA - ENDED SUCCESSFULLY');

END P300_TERMINATION;

P400_DISPLAY_ERROR: PROC;

    PUT SKIP LIST ('ERROR ENCOUNTERED - DETAIL FOLLOWS');
    PUT SKIP LIST ('SEG_IO_AREA      :' || SEG_IO_AREA);
    PUT SKIP LIST ('DBD_NAME1:' ||   DBD_NAME);
    PUT SKIP LIST ('SEG_LEVEL1:' || SEG_LEVEL);
    PUT SKIP LIST ('STATUS_CODE:' || STATUS_CODE);
    PUT SKIP LIST ('PROC_OPT1 :' || PROC_OPT);
    PUT SKIP LIST ('SEG_NAME1 :' || SEG_NAME);
    PUT SKIP LIST ('KEY_FDBK1 :' || KEY_FDBK);
    PUT SKIP LIST ('NUM_SENSEG1:' || NUM_SENSEG);
    PUT SKIP LIST ('KEY_FDBK_AREA1:' || KEY_FDBK_AREA);

END P400_DISPLAY_ERROR;

END PLIIMSA;
```

Retrieve Segments Using Boolean SSAs

The qualified SSA retrievals we've done so far have searched using a field value that is equal to a single searchable field. It is also possible to retrieve IMS segments using other Boolean operators such as greater than or less than. Additionally, you can specify more than one operator, such as > VALUE1 and < VALUE2.

For this example with program COBIMSB we will retrieve root segments for all employees whose EMPID is greater than 3000 and less than 7000. For that we simply need to create and use a new SSA. Here it is:

```
       01 EMP-QUALIFIED-SSA-BOOL.
```

```
          05   SEGNAME      PIC X(08) VALUE 'EMPLOYEE'.
          05   FILLER       PIC X(01) VALUE '('.
          05   FIELD        PIC X(08) VALUE 'EMPID'.
          05   OPER         PIC X(02) VALUE '>='.
          05   EMP-ID-VAL1  PIC X(04) VALUE '    '.
          05   OPER         PIC X(01) VALUE '&'.
          05   FIELD2       PIC X(08) VALUE 'EMPID'.
          05   OPER2        PIC X(02) VALUE '<='.
          05   EMP-ID-VAL2  PIC X(04) VALUE '    '.
          05   FILLER       PIC X(01) VALUE ')'.
```

For the above we must load (or initialize) the minimum value 3000 into EMP-ID-VAL1, and the ceiling value 7000 into EMP-ID-VAL2. Then we'll call the database using the EMP-QUALIFIED-SSA-BOOL SSA. We'll do a loop through the database and our retrieval loop should only return those employee records that satisfy the Boolean SSA.

Note that to end our read loop, we check both for IMS status codes GB and GE. This is because the last record that satisfies the database call may not be the physical end of the database. Consequently reading beyond the end of the "result set" of your database call will result in a GE status code unless it happens to also be the end of the database. So you have to check for both GB and GE.

Here is our program source code.

```
        IDENTIFICATION DIVISION.
        PROGRAM-ID. COBIMSB.

       **********************************************************
       *   WALK THROUGH THE EMPLOYEE SEGMENTS OF THE ENTIRE     *
       *   EMPLOYEE IMS DATABASE USING BOOLEAN SSA.             *
       **********************************************************

        ENVIRONMENT DIVISION.
        INPUT-OUTPUT SECTION.
        DATA DIVISION.

       **********************************************************
       *   W O R K I N G    S T O R A G E    S E C T I O N     *
       **********************************************************

        WORKING-STORAGE SECTION.

          01 WS-FLAGS.
             05   SW-END-OF-DB-SWITCH     PIC X(1) VALUE 'N'.
                  88   SW-END-OF-DB                VALUE 'Y'.
                  88   SW-NOT-END-OF-DB            VALUE 'N'.

          01 DLI-FUNCTIONS.
             05 DLI-FUNCISRT   PIC X(4) VALUE 'ISRT'.
             05 DLI-FUNCGU     PIC X(4) VALUE 'GU  '.
```

```
       05  DLI-FUNCGN     PIC X(4) VALUE 'GN  '.
       05  DLI-FUNCGHU    PIC X(4) VALUE 'GHU '.
       05  DLI-FUNCGNP    PIC X(4) VALUE 'GNP '.
       05  DLI-FUNCREPL   PIC X(4) VALUE 'REPL'.
       05  DLI-FUNCDLET   PIC X(4) VALUE 'DLET'.
       05  DLI-FUNCXRST   PIC X(4) VALUE 'XRST'.
       05  DLI-FUNCCKPT   PIC X(4) VALUE 'CKPT'.

   01  IO-EMPLOYEE-RECORD.
       05  EMPL-ID-IN     PIC X(04).
       05  FILLER         PIC X(01).
       05  EMPL-LNAME     PIC X(30).
       05  FILLER         PIC X(01).
       05  EMPL-FNAME     PIC X(20).
       05  FILLER         PIC X(01).
       05  EMPL-YRS-SRV   PIC X(02).
       05  FILLER         PIC X(01).
       05  EMPL-PRM-DTE   PIC X(10).
       05  FILLER         PIC X(10).

   01  EMP-UNQUALIFIED-SSA.
       05  SEGNAME        PIC X(08) VALUE 'EMPLOYEE'.
       05  FILLER         PIC X(01) VALUE ' '.

   01  EMP-QUALIFIED-SSA.
       05  SEGNAME        PIC X(08) VALUE 'EMPLOYEE'.
       05  FILLER         PIC X(01) VALUE '('.
       05  FIELD          PIC X(08) VALUE 'EMPID'.
       05  OPER           PIC X(02) VALUE ' ='.
       05  EMP-ID-VAL     PIC X(04) VALUE '    '.
       05  FILLER         PIC X(01) VALUE ')'.

   01  **EMP-QUALIFIED-SSA-BOOL.**
       05  **SEGNAME        PIC X(08) VALUE 'EMPLOYEE'.**
       05  **FILLER         PIC X(01) VALUE '('.**
       05  **FIELD          PIC X(08) VALUE 'EMPID'.**
       05  **OPER           PIC X(02) VALUE '>='.**
       05  **EMP-ID-VAL1    PIC X(04) VALUE '    '.**
       05  **OPER           PIC X(01) VALUE '&'.**
       05  **FIELD2         PIC X(08) VALUE 'EMPID'.**
       05  **OPER2          PIC X(02) VALUE '<='.**
       05  **EMP-ID-VAL2    PIC X(04) VALUE '    '.**
       05  **FILLER         PIC X(01) VALUE ')'.**

   01  SEG-TO-AREA        PIC X(80).

   01  IMS-RET-CODES.
       05  THREE          PIC S9(9) COMP VALUE +3.
       05  FOUR           PIC S9(9) COMP VALUE +4.
       05  FIVE           PIC S9(9) COMP VALUE +5.
       05  SIX            PIC S9(9) COMP VALUE +6.
```

```cobol
       LINKAGE SECTION.
        01 PCB-MASK.
           03 DBD-NAME        PIC X(8).
           03 SEG-LEVEL       PIC XX.
           03 STATUS-CODE     PIC XX.
           03 PROC-OPT        PIC X(4).
           03 FILLER          PIC X(4).
           03 SEG-NAME        PIC X(8).
           03 KEY-FDBK        PIC S9(5) COMP.
           03 NUM-SENSEG      PIC S9(5) COMP.
           03 KEY-FDBK-AREA.
              05 EMPLOYEE-KEY  PIC X(04).
              05 EMPPAYHS-KEY  PIC X(08).

       PROCEDURE DIVISION.

           INITIALIZE PCB-MASK
           ENTRY 'DLITCBL' USING PCB-MASK

           PERFORM P100-INITIALIZATION.
           PERFORM P200-MAINLINE.
           PERFORM P300-TERMINATION.
           GOBACK.

       P100-INITIALIZATION.

           DISPLAY '** PROGRAM COBIMSB START **'
           DISPLAY 'PROCESSING IN P100-INITIALIZATION'.
           MOVE '3000' TO EMP-ID-VAL1
           MOVE '7000' TO EMP-ID-VAL2

      *    DO INITIAL DB READ FOR FIRST EMPLOYEE RECORD

           CALL 'CBLTDLI' USING FOUR,
               DLI-FUNCGN,
               PCB-MASK,
               SEG-IO-AREA,
               EMP-QUALIFIED-SSA-BOOL

           IF STATUS-CODE = '  ' THEN
              NEXT SENTENCE
           ELSE
              IF STATUS-CODE = 'GE' OR
                 STATUS-CODE = 'GB' THEN
                 SET SW-END-OF-DB TO TRUE
                  DISPLAY 'END OF DATABASE :'
              ELSE
                 PERFORM P400-DISPLAY-ERROR
                  GOBACK
              END-IF

           END-IF.
```

```
    P200-MAINLINE.

        DISPLAY 'PROCESSING IN P200-MAINLINE'

*       CHECK STATUS CODE AND FIRST RECORD

        IF SW-END-OF-DB THEN
           DISPLAY 'NO RECORDS TO PROCESS!!'
        ELSE
           PERFORM UNTIL SW-END-OF-DB
              DISPLAY 'SUCCESSFUL READ :' SEG-IO-AREA
              CALL 'CBLTDLI' USING FOUR,
                  DLI-FUNCGN,
                  PCB-MASK,
                  SEG-IO-AREA,
                  EMP-QUALIFIED-SSA-BOOL

              IF STATUS-CODE = 'GB' OR 'GE' THEN
              SET SW-END-OF-DB TO TRUE
                 DISPLAY 'END OF DATABASE'
              ELSE
                 IF STATUS-CODE NOT EQUAL SPACES THEN
                    PERFORM P400-DISPLAY-ERROR
                    GOBACK
                 END-IF
              END-IF

           END-PERFORM.

        DISPLAY 'FINISHED PROCESSING IN P200-MAINLINE'.

    P300-TERMINATION.

        DISPLAY 'PROCESSING IN P300-TERMINATION'
        DISPLAY '** COBIMSB - SUCCESSFULLY ENDED **'.

    P400-DISPLAY-ERROR.

        DISPLAY 'ERROR ENCOUNTERED - DETAIL FOLLOWS'
        DISPLAY 'SEG-IO-AREA     :' SEG-IO-AREA
        DISPLAY 'DBD-NAME1:'       DBD-NAME
        DISPLAY 'SEG-LEVEL1:'      SEG-LEVEL
        DISPLAY 'STATUS-CODE:'     STATUS-CODE
        DISPLAY 'PROC-OPT1 :'      PROC-OPT
        DISPLAY 'SEG-NAME1 :'      SEG-NAME
        DISPLAY 'KEY-FDBK1 :'      KEY-FDBK
        DISPLAY 'NUM-SENSEG1:'     NUM-SENSEG
        DISPLAY 'KEY-FDBK-AREA1:'  KEY-FDBK-AREA.

*       END OF SOURCE CODE
```

After we compile, link and execute, here is the output. As you can see, the only employees retrieved are those whose ids fall between 3,000 and 7,000 inclusive.

```
** PROGRAM COBIMSB START **
PROCESSING IN P100-INITIALIZATION
EMP-QUALIFIED-SSA-BOOL EMPLOYEE(EMPID    >=3000&EMPID    <=7000)
PROCESSING IN P200-MAINLINE
SUCCESSFUL READ :3217 JOHNSON                EDWARD             04 201
SUCCESSFUL READ :4175 TURNBULL               FRED               01 201
SUCCESSFUL READ :4720 SCHULTZ                TIM                09 201
SUCCESSFUL READ :4836 SMITH                  SANDRA             03 201
SUCCESSFUL READ :6288 WILLARD                JOE                06 201
END OF DATABASE
FINISHED PROCESSING IN P200-MAINLINE
PROCESSING IN P300-TERMINATION
** COBIMSB - SUCCESSFULLY ENDED **
```

Extended Boolean SSAs can be very handy when you need to ready a range of values, or for any retrieval that must satisfy multiple conditions.

Here's the PLI source code for this example.

```
PLIIMSB: PROCEDURE (DB_PTR_PCB) OPTIONS(MAIN);
/*******************************************************************
* PROGRAM NAME :    PLIIMSB - WALK THROUGH THE ROOT SEGMENTS OF    *
*                   EMPLOYEE DB USING BOOLEAN SSA.                 *
*******************************************************************/

/*******************************************************************
/*              W O R K I N G    S T O R A G E                     *
*******************************************************************/
     DCL ONCODE                   BUILTIN;
     DCL DB_PTR_PCB               POINTER;
     DCL PLITDLI                  EXTERNAL ENTRY;
     DCL SW_END_OF_DB             STATIC BIT(01) INIT('0'B);

     DCL 01 DLI_FUNCTIONS,
            05 DLI_FUNCISRT       CHAR(04) INIT ('ISRT'),
            05 DLI_FUNCGU         CHAR(04) INIT ('GU  '),
            05 DLI_FUNCGN         CHAR(04) INIT ('GN  '),
            05 DLI_FUNCGHU        CHAR(04) INIT ('GHU '),
            05 DLI_FUNCGNP        CHAR(04) INIT ('GNP '),
            05 DLI_FUNCREPL       CHAR(04) INIT ('REPL'),
            05 DLI_FUNCDLET       CHAR(04) INIT ('DLET'),
            05 DLI_FUNCXRST       CHAR(04) INIT ('XRST'),
            05 DLI_FUNCCHKP       CHAR(04) INIT ('CHKP'),
            05 DLI_FUNCROLL       CHAR(04) INIT ('ROLL');

     DCL 01 IO_EMPLOYEE_RECORD,
            05  EMPL_ID_IN        CHAR(04),
```

```
        05  FILLER1             CHAR(01),
        05  EMPL_LNAME          CHAR(30),
        05  FILLER2             CHAR(01),
        05  EMPL_FNAME          CHAR(20),
        05  FILLER3             CHAR(01),
        05  EMPL_YRS_SRV        CHAR(02),
        05  FILLER4             CHAR(01),
        05  EMPL_PRM_DTE        CHAR(10),
        05  FILLER5             CHAR(01),
        05  EMPL_SSN            CHAR(09);

DCL 01 PCB_MASK                 BASED(DB_PTR_PCB),
        05  DBD_NAME            CHAR(08),
        05  SEG_LEVEL           CHAR(02),
        05  STATUS_CODE         CHAR(02),
        05  PROC_OPT            CHAR(04),
        05  FILLER6             FIXED BIN (31),
        05  SEG_NAME            CHAR(08),
        05  KEY_FDBK            FIXED BIN (31),
        05  NUM_SENSEG          FIXED BIN (31),
        05  KEY_FDBK_AREA,
           10 EMPLOYEE_ID       CHAR(04);

DCL 01 EMP_UNQUALIFIED_SSA,
        05  SEGNAME             CHAR(08) INIT ('EMPLOYEE'),
        05  FILLER7             CHAR(01) INIT (' ');

DCL 01 EMP_QUALIFIED_SSA,
        05  SEGNAME             CHAR(08) INIT('EMPLOYEE'),
        05  FILLER8             CHAR(01) INIT('('),
        05  FIELD               CHAR(08) INIT('EMPID'),
        05  OPER                CHAR(02) INIT(' ='),
        05  EMP_ID_VAL          CHAR(04) INIT('    '),
        05  FILLER9             CHAR(01) INIT(')');

**DCL 01 EMP_QUALIFIED_SSA_BOOL,**
        **05  SEGNAME             CHAR(08) INIT('EMPLOYEE'),**
        **05  FILLER10            CHAR(01) INIT('('),**
        **05  FIELD               CHAR(08) INIT('EMPID'),**
        **05  OPER                CHAR(02) INIT('>='),**
        **05  EMP_ID_VAL1         CHAR(04) INIT('    '),**
        **05  OPER2               CHAR(01) INIT('&'),**
        **05  FIELD2              CHAR(08) INIT('EMPID'),**
        **05  OPER3               CHAR(02) INIT('<='),**
        **05  EMP_ID_VAL2         CHAR(04) INIT('    '),**
        **05  FILLER11            CHAR(01) INIT(')');**

DCL THREE                       FIXED BIN (31) INIT(3);
DCL FOUR                        FIXED BIN (31) INIT(4);
DCL FIVE                        FIXED BIN (31) INIT(5);
DCL SIX                         FIXED BIN (31) INIT(6);

/*****************************************************************
```

```
/*                  P R O G R A M   M A I N L I N E                    *
**********************************************************************/

   CALL P100_INITIALIZATION;
   CALL P200_MAINLINE;
   CALL P300_TERMINATION;

   P100_INITIALIZATION: PROC;

      PUT SKIP LIST ('PLIIMSB: TRAVERSE EMPLOYEE DB ROOT SEGS USING BOOL
         SSAs');
      PCB_MASK = '';
      IO_EMPLOYEE_RECORD  = '';

    /*  SET THE EMPLOYEE SEGMENT SEARCH ARGUMENT */

      EMP_ID_VAL1 = '3000';
      EMP_ID_VAL2 = '7000';

    /* DO INITIAL DB READ FOR FIRST EMPLOYEE RECORD */

      CALL PLITDLI (FOUR,
                    DLI_FUNCGN,
                    PCB_MASK,
                    IO_EMPLOYEE_RECORD,
                    EMP_QUALIFIED_SSA_BOOL);

      IF STATUS_CODE = '  ' THEN;
      ELSE
         IF STATUS_CODE = 'GB' |
            STATUS_CODE = 'GE' THEN
            DO;
               SW_END_OF_DB = '1'B;
               PUT SKIP LIST ('** END OF DATABASE');
            END;
         ELSE
            DO;
               CALL P400_DISPLAY_ERROR;
               RETURN;
            END;

   END P100_INITIALIZATION;

   P200_MAINLINE: PROC;

      /*  MAIN LOOP - CYCLE THROUGH ALL ROOT SEGMENTS IN THE DB,
                      DISPLAYING THE DATA RETRIEVED                   */

      IF SW_END_OF_DB THEN
         PUT SKIP LIST ('NO RECORDS TO PROCESS!!');
      ELSE
         DO WHILE (¬SW_END_OF_DB);
            PUT SKIP LIST ('SUCCESSFUL READ USING BOOLEAN SSA : ');
```

```
              PUT SKIP DATA (IO_EMPLOYEE_RECORD);

              CALL PLITDLI (FOUR,
                            DLI_FUNCGN,
                            PCB_MASK,
                            IO_EMPLOYEE_RECORD,
                            EMP_QUALIFIED_SSA_BOOL);

              IF STATUS_CODE = ' ' THEN;
              ELSE
                 IF STATUS_CODE = 'GB' |
                    STATUS_CODE = 'GE' THEN
                    DO;
                       SW_END_OF_DB = '1'B;
                       PUT SKIP LIST ('** END OF DATABASE');
                    END;
                 ELSE
                    DO;
                       CALL P400_DISPLAY_ERROR;
                       RETURN;
                    END;

         END; /* DO WHILE */

      PUT SKIP LIST ('FINISHED PROCESSING IN P200_MAINLINE');

   END P200_MAINLINE;

   P300_TERMINATION: PROC;

      PUT SKIP LIST ('PLIIMSB - ENDED SUCCESSFULLY');

   END P300_TERMINATION;

   P400_DISPLAY_ERROR: PROC;

      PUT SKIP LIST ('ERROR ENCOUNTERED - DETAIL FOLLOWS');
      PUT SKIP LIST ('IO_EMPLOYEE_RECORD :'
         || IO_EMPLOYEE_RECORD);
      PUT SKIP LIST ('DBD_NAME1:' || DBD_NAME);
      PUT SKIP LIST ('SEG_LEVEL1:' || SEG_LEVEL);
      PUT SKIP LIST ('STATUS_CODE:' || STATUS_CODE);
      PUT SKIP LIST ('PROC_OPT1 :' || PROC_OPT);
      PUT SKIP LIST ('SEG_NAME1 :' || SEG_NAME);
      PUT SKIP LIST ('KEY_FDBK1 :' || KEY_FDBK);
      PUT SKIP LIST ('NUM_SENSEG1:' || NUM_SENSEG);
      PUT SKIP LIST ('KEY_FDBK_AREA1:' || KEY_FDBK_AREA);

   END P400_DISPLAY_ERROR;

END PLIIMSB;
```

Command Codes

IMS command codes change and/or extend the way an IMS call works. There are about 18 command codes that serve various purposes. See the table at the end of this topic for all the command codes and what they do.

We'll do an example of the C command code. The C command code allows you to issue a qualified SSA using the concatenated key for a child segment rather than using separate SSAs for the various parent/child segments. For example suppose we want to retrieve the paycheck record of employee 3217 for pay effective January 1, 2017, and for payday February 15, 2017. The concatenated key for that is as follows:

```
32172017010120170215
```

This is the key for the root segment (3217) plus the key for the EMPPAY segment (20170101), plus the key for the EMPPAYHS segment (20170215).

To use the C command code, we must create a new SSA structure that uses both the C command code, and accommodates the concatenated key. It will look like this:

```
01  EMPPAYHS-CCODE-SSA.
    05  SEGNAME     PIC X(08) VALUE 'EMPPAYHS'.
    05  FILLER      PIC X(02) VALUE '*C'.
    05  FILLER      PIC X(01) VALUE '('.
    05  CONCATKEY   PIC X(20) VALUE SPACES.
    05  FILLER      PIC X(01) VALUE ')'.
```

Like all SSAs, our new one includes the segment name. Position 9 of the SSA will contain an asterisk (*) or blank if a command code is not being used. We put a C in position 10 to indicate we are using a concatenated key command code. We've named our concatenated key variable CONCATKEY (the name is arbitrary – you could use any name for this variable).

The CONCATKEY length is 20 bytes (4 for the employee id, and 8 each for the salary effective date and the pay date. We have initialized the concatenated key variable to the value we are looking for. You could also load it using a MOVE statement.

Ok here is the complete code for COBIMSC. It should look very familiar except for the SSA. For comparison, we will first use the regular multiple SSA method to call the 2/15 pay record. Then we will use a second call with the C command code method and a concatenated key. The results should be identical.

```cobol
       IDENTIFICATION DIVISION.
       PROGRAM-ID. COBIMSC.

      **********************************************************
      *    READ AND DISPLAY EMP HISTORY RECORD FROM            *
      *    EMPLOYEE IMS DATABASE. THIS EXAMPLE USES A          *
      *    C COMMAND CODE TO PROVIDE THE CONCATENATED          *
      *    KEY SSA RATHER THAN A QUALIFICATION STATEMENT       *
      *    SSA (second example).                               *
      **********************************************************

       ENVIRONMENT DIVISION.
       DATA DIVISION.

      **********************************************************
      *   W O R K I N G   S T O R A G E   S E C T I O N        *
      **********************************************************

       WORKING-STORAGE SECTION.

       01 WS-FLAGS.
           05  SW-END-OF-DB-SWITCH    PIC X(1) VALUE 'N'.
               88  SW-END-OF-DB                VALUE 'Y'.
               88  SW-NOT-END-OF-DB            VALUE 'N'.
           05  SW-END-OF-EMPPAYHS-SW  PIC X(1) VALUE 'N'.
               88  SW-END-OF-EMPPAYHS          VALUE 'Y'.
               88  SW-NOT-END-OF-EMPPAYHS      VALUE 'N'.

       01 IO-EMPLOYEE-RECORD.
           05  EMPL-ID       PIC X(04).
           05  FILLER        PIC X(01).
           05  EMPL-LNAME    PIC X(30).
           05  FILLER        PIC X(01).
           05  EMPL-FNAME    PIC X(20).
           05  FILLER        PIC X(01).
           05  EMPL-YRS-SRV  PIC X(02).
           05  FILLER        PIC X(01).
           05  EMPL-PRM-DTE  PIC X(10).
           05  FILLER        PIC X(10).

       01 IO-EMPPAY-RECORD.
           05  PAY-EFF-DATE  PIC X(8).
           05  PAY-REG-PAY   PIC S9(6)V9(2) USAGE COMP-3.
           05  PAY-BON-PAY   PIC S9(6)V9(2) USAGE COMP-3.
           05  SEMIMTH-PAY   PIC S9(6)V9(2) USAGE COMP-3.
           05  FILLER        PIC X(57).
```

```cobol
01 IO-EMPPAYHS-RECORD.
   05  PAY-DATE      PIC X(8).
   05  PAY-ANN-PAY   PIC S9(6)V9(2) USAGE COMP-3.
   05  PAY-AMT       PIC S9(6)V9(2) USAGE COMP-3.
   05  FILLER        PIC X(62).

01 SEG-IO-AREA      PIC X(80).

01 IMS-RET-CODES.
   05 THREE         PIC S9(9) COMP VALUE +3.
   05 FOUR          PIC S9(9) COMP VALUE +4.
   05 FIVE          PIC S9(9) COMP VALUE +5.
   05 SIX           PIC S9(9) COMP VALUE +6.

01 DLI-FUNCTIONS.
   05 DLI-FUNCISRT  PIC X(4) VALUE 'ISRT'.
   05 DLI-FUNCGU    PIC X(4) VALUE 'GU  '.
   05 DLI-FUNCGN    PIC X(4) VALUE 'GN  '.
   05 DLI-FUNCGHU   PIC X(4) VALUE 'GHU '.
   05 DLI-FUNCGNP   PIC X(4) VALUE 'GNP '.
   05 DLI-FUNCREPL  PIC X(4) VALUE 'REPL'.
   05 DLI-FUNCDLET  PIC X(4) VALUE 'DLET'.
   05 DLI-FUNCXRST  PIC X(4) VALUE 'XRST'.
   05 DLI-FUNCCKPT  PIC X(4) VALUE 'CKPT'.

01 DISPLAY-EMPPAYHS-PIC.
   05  DIS-REG-PAY  PIC ZZ999.99-.
   05  DIS-SMT-PAY  PIC ZZ999.99-.

 01 EMP-UNQUALIFIED-SSA.
    05  SEGNAME     PIC X(08) VALUE 'EMPLOYEE'.
    05  FILLER      PIC X(01) VALUE ' '.

 01 EMP-QUALIFIED-SSA.
    05  SEGNAME     PIC X(08) VALUE 'EMPLOYEE'.
    05  FILLER      PIC X(01) VALUE '('.
    05  FIELD       PIC X(08) VALUE 'EMPID'.
    05  OPER        PIC X(02) VALUE ' ='.
    05  EMP-ID-VAL  PIC X(04) VALUE '    '.
    05  FILLER      PIC X(01) VALUE ')'.

 01 EMPPAY-UNQUALIFIED-SSA.
    05  SEGNAME     PIC X(08) VALUE 'EMPPAY  '.
    05  FILLER      PIC X(01) VALUE ' '.

 01 EMPPAY-QUALIFIED-SSA.
```

```
           05  SEGNAME       PIC X(08) VALUE 'EMPPAY  '.
           05  FILLER        PIC X(01) VALUE '('.
           05  FIELD         PIC X(08) VALUE 'EFFDATE '.
           05  OPER          PIC X(02) VALUE ' ='.
           05  EFFDATE-VAL   PIC X(08) VALUE '        '.
           05  FILLER        PIC X(01) VALUE ')'.

       01 EMPPAYHS-UNQUALIFIED-SSA.
           05  SEGNAME       PIC X(08) VALUE 'EMPPAYHS'.
           05  FILLER        PIC X(01) VALUE ' '.

       01 EMPPAYHS-QUALIFIED-SSA.
           05  SEGNAME       PIC X(08) VALUE 'EMPPAYHS'.
           05  FILLER        PIC X(01) VALUE '('.
           05  FIELD         PIC X(08) VALUE 'PAYDATE '.
           05  OPER          PIC X(02) VALUE ' ='.
           05  PAYDATE-VAL   PIC X(08) VALUE '        '.
           05  FILLER        PIC X(01) VALUE ')'.

       01 **EMPPAYHS-CCODE-SSA**.
           05  **SEGNAME**       **PIC X(08) VALUE 'EMPPAYHS'**.
           05  **FILLER**        **PIC X(02) VALUE '*C'**.
           05  **FILLER**        **PIC X(01) VALUE '('**.
           05  **CONCATKEY**     **PIC X(20) VALUE '32172017010120170215'**.
           05  **FILLER**        **PIC X(01) VALUE ')'**.


       LINKAGE SECTION.
        01 PCB-MASK.
           03 DBD-NAME       PIC X(8).
           03 SEG-LEVEL      PIC XX.
           03 STATUS-CODE    PIC XX.
           03 PROC-OPT       PIC X(4).
           03 FILLER         PIC X(4).
           03 SEG-NAME       PIC X(8).
           03 KEY-FDBK       PIC S9(5) COMP.
           03 NUM-SENSEG     PIC S9(5) COMP.
           03 KEY-FDBK-AREA.
              05 EMPLOYEE-ID  PIC X(04).
              05 EMPPAYHS     PIC X(08).

       PROCEDURE DIVISION.

           INITIALIZE PCB-MASK
           ENTRY 'DLITCBL' USING PCB-MASK
```

```
           PERFORM P100-INITIALIZATION.
           PERFORM P200-MAINLINE.
           PERFORM P300-TERMINATION.
           GOBACK.

       P100-INITIALIZATION.

           DISPLAY '** PROGRAM COBIMSC START **'
           DISPLAY 'PROCESSING IN P100-INITIALIZATION'.


       P200-MAINLINE.

           DISPLAY 'PROCESSING IN P200-MAINLINE'

           MOVE '3217'      TO EMP-ID-VAL
           MOVE '20170101' TO EFFDATE-VAL
           MOVE '201700215' TO PAYDATE-VAL

           CALL 'CBLTDLI' USING SIX,
                DLI-FUNCGU,
                PCB-MASK,
                IO-EMPPAYHS-RECORD,
                EMP-QUALIFIED-SSA,
                EMPPAY-QUALIFIED-SSA,
                EMPPAYHS-QUALIFIED-SSA.

           EVALUATE STATUS-CODE
              WHEN '  '
                 DISPLAY 'GOOD READ OF EMPPAYHS : '
                    EMP-ID-VAL
                 MOVE PAY-ANN-PAY TO DIS-REG-PAY
                 MOVE PAY-AMT     TO DIS-SMT-PAY
                 DISPLAY 'PAY-DATE    : ' PAY-DATE
                 DISPLAY 'PAY-ANN-PAY: ' DIS-REG-PAY
                 DISPLAY 'PAY-AMT     : ' DIS-SMT-PAY
              WHEN 'GE'
              WHEN 'GB'
                 DISPLAY 'PAY HISTORY SEGMENT NOT FOUND'
              WHEN OTHER
                 PERFORM P9000-DISPLAY-ERROR
                 GOBACK
           END-EVALUATE.

           DISPLAY 'NOW CALLING THE 2/15/2017 REC USING C COMMAND CODE'
```

```cobol
        CALL 'CBLTDLI' USING FOUR,
             DLI-FUNCGU,
             PCB-MASK,
             IO-EMPPAYHS-RECORD,
             EMPPAYHS-CCODE-SSA.

        EVALUATE STATUS-CODE
           WHEN ' '
              DISPLAY 'GOOD READ OF EMPPAYHS : '
                  EMP-ID-VAL
              MOVE PAY-ANN-PAY TO DIS-REG-PAY
              MOVE PAY-AMT     TO DIS-SMT-PAY
              DISPLAY 'PAY-DATE   : ' PAY-DATE
              DISPLAY 'PAY-ANN-PAY: ' DIS-REG-PAY
              DISPLAY 'PAY-AMT    : ' DIS-SMT-PAY
           WHEN 'GE'
           WHEN 'GB'
              DISPLAY 'PAY HISTORY SEGMENT NOT FOUND'
           WHEN OTHER
              PERFORM P9000-DISPLAY-ERROR
              GOBACK
        END-EVALUATE.

        DISPLAY 'FINISHED PROCESSING IN P200-MAINLINE'.

    P300-TERMINATION.

        DISPLAY 'PROCESSING IN P300-TERMINATION'
        DISPLAY '** COBIMSC - SUCCESSFULLY ENDED **'.

    P9000-DISPLAY-ERROR.

        DISPLAY 'ERROR ENCOUNTERED - DETAIL FOLLOWS'
        DISPLAY 'DBD-NAME1:'      DBD-NAME
        DISPLAY 'SEG-LEVEL1:'     SEG-LEVEL
        DISPLAY 'STATUS-CODE:'    STATUS-CODE
        DISPLAY 'PROC-OPT1 :'     PROC-OPT
        DISPLAY 'SEG-NAME1 :'     SEG-NAME
        DISPLAY 'KEY-FDBK1 :'     KEY-FDBK
        DISPLAY 'NUM-SENSEG1:'    NUM-SENSEG
        DISPLAY 'KEY-FDBK-AREA1:' KEY-FDBK-AREA.

    *   END OF SOURCE CODE
```

Ok, once again we compile, link and execute. Here is our output.

```
** PROGRAM COBIMSC START **
PROCESSING IN P100-INITIALIZATION
PROCESSING IN P200-MAINLINE
FIRST CALL THE 2/15/2017 PAY REC WITH 3 SSA METHOD
GOOD READ OF EMPPAYHS : 3217
PAY-DATE   : 20170215
PAY-ANN-PAY: 65000.00
PAY-AMT    :  2708.33
```
NOW CALLING THE 2/15/2017 REC USING C COMMAND CODE
GOOD READ OF EMPPAYHS : 3217
PAY-DATE   : 20170215
PAY-ANN-PAY: 65000.00
PAY-AMT   : 2708.33
```
FINISHED PROCESSING IN P200-MAINLINE
PROCESSING IN P300-TERMINATION
** COBIMSC - SUCCESSFULLY ENDED **
```

PLI source code for this example is here:

```
PLIIMSC: PROCEDURE (DB_PTR_PCB) OPTIONS(MAIN);
/******************************************************************
* PROGRAM NAME :    PLIIMSC - RETRIEVE A RECORD FROM EMPLOYEE DB  *
*                   USING C COMMAND CODE TO PROVIDE A             *
*                   CONCATENATED KEY SSA.                         *
******************************************************************/

/******************************************************************
/*              W O R K I N G   S T O R A G E                     *
******************************************************************/

    DCL ONCODE                  BUILTIN;
    DCL DB_PTR_PCB              POINTER;
    DCL PLITDLI                 EXTERNAL ENTRY;

    DCL 01 DLI_FUNCTIONS,
          05 DLI_FUNCISRT       CHAR(04) INIT ('ISRT'),
          05 DLI_FUNCGU         CHAR(04) INIT ('GU  '),
          05 DLI_FUNCGN         CHAR(04) INIT ('GN  '),
          05 DLI_FUNCGHU        CHAR(04) INIT ('GHU '),
          05 DLI_FUNCGNP        CHAR(04) INIT ('GNP '),
          05 DLI_FUNCREPL       CHAR(04) INIT ('REPL'),
          05 DLI_FUNCDLET       CHAR(04) INIT ('DLET'),
          05 DLI_FUNCXRST       CHAR(04) INIT ('XRST'),
          05 DLI_FUNCCHKP       CHAR(04) INIT ('CHKP'),
          05 DLI_FUNCROLL       CHAR(04) INIT ('ROLL');

    DCL 01 IO_EMPLOYEE_RECORD,
          05  EMPL_ID_IN        CHAR(04),
          05  FILLER1           CHAR(01),
          05  EMPL_LNAME        CHAR(30),
          05  FILLER2           CHAR(01),
          05  EMPL_FNAME        CHAR(20),
          05  FILLER3           CHAR(01),
```

```
        05  EMPL_YRS_SRV      CHAR(02),
        05  FILLER4           CHAR(01),
        05  EMPL_PRM_DTE      CHAR(10),
        05  FILLER5           CHAR(01),
        05  EMPL_SSN          CHAR(09);

DCL 01 IO_EMPPAY_RECORD,
        05  PAY_EFF_DATE      CHAR(8),
        05  PAY_REG_PAY       FIXED DEC (8,2),
        05  PAY_BON_PAY       FIXED DEC (8,2),
        05  SEMIMTH_PAY       FIXED DEC (8,2),
        05  FILLER6           CHAR(57);

DCL 01 IO_EMPPAYHS_RECORD,
        05  PAY_DATE          CHAR(8),
        05  PAY_ANN_PAY       FIXED DEC (8,2),
        05  PAY_AMT           FIXED DEC (8,2),
        05  FILLER65          CHAR(62);

DCL 01 PCB_MASK               BASED(DB_PTR_PCB),
        05  DBD_NAME          CHAR(08),
        05  SEG_LEVEL         CHAR(02),
        05  STATUS_CODE       CHAR(02),
        05  PROC_OPT          CHAR(04),
        05  FILLER99          FIXED BIN (31),
        05  SEG_NAME          CHAR(08),
        05  KEY_FDBK          FIXED BIN (31),
        05  NUM_SENSEG        FIXED BIN (31),
        05  KEY_FDBK_AREA,
            10 EMPLOYEE_ID    CHAR(04);

DCL 01 EMP_UNQUALIFIED_SSA,
        05  SEGNAME           CHAR(08) INIT ('EMPLOYEE'),
        05  FILLER7           CHAR(01) INIT (' ');

DCL 01 EMP_QUALIFIED_SSA,
        05  SEGNAME           CHAR(08) INIT('EMPLOYEE'),
        05  FILLER8           CHAR(01) INIT('('),
        05  FIELD             CHAR(08) INIT('EMPID'),
        05  OPER              CHAR(02) INIT(' ='),
        05  EMP_ID_VAL        CHAR(04) INIT('    '),
        05  FILLER9           CHAR(01) INIT(')');

DCL 01 EMPPAY_UNQUALIFIED_SSA,
        05  SEGNAME           CHAR(08) INIT('EMPPAY  '),
        05  FILLER10          CHAR(01) INIT(' ');

DCL 01 EMPPAY_QUALIFIED_SSA,
        05  SEGNAME           CHAR(08) INIT('EMPPAY  '),
        05  FILLER11          CHAR(01) INIT('('),
        05  FIELD             CHAR(08) INIT('EFFDATE '),
        05  OPER              CHAR(02) INIT(' ='),
        05  EFFDATE_VAL       CHAR(08) INIT('        '),
```

```
            05  FILLER12            CHAR(01) INIT(')');

    DCL 01 EMP_QUALIFIED_SSA_EMPSSN,
            05  SEGNAME             CHAR(08) INIT('EMPLOYEE'),
            05  FILLER10            CHAR(01) INIT('('),
            05  FIELD               CHAR(08) INIT('EMPSSN'),
            05  OPER                CHAR(02) INIT(' ='),
            05  EMPSSN_VAL          CHAR(09) INIT('         '),
            05  FILLER11            CHAR(01) INIT(')');

    DCL 01 EMPPAYHS_UNQUALIFIED_SSA,
            05  SEGNAME             CHAR(08) INIT('EMPPAYHS'),
            05  FILLER12            CHAR(01) INIT(' ');

    DCL 01 EMPPAYHS_QUALIFIED_SSA,
            05  SEGNAME             CHAR(08) INIT('EMPPAYHS'),
            05  FILLER13            CHAR(01) INIT('('),
            05  FIELD               CHAR(08) INIT('PAYDATE '),
            05  OPER                CHAR(02) INIT(' ='),
            05  PAYDATE_VAL         CHAR(08) INIT('        '),
            05  FILLER14            CHAR(01) INIT(')');

    DCL 01 EMPPAYHS_CCODE_SSA,
            05  SEGNAME             CHAR(08) INIT('EMPPAYHS'),
            05  FILLER15            CHAR(02) INIT('*C'),
            05  FILLER16            CHAR(01) INIT('('),
            05  CONCATKEY           CHAR(20) INIT('                    '),
            05  FILLER17            CHAR(01) INIT(')');

    DCL THREE                       FIXED BIN (31) INIT(3);
    DCL FOUR                        FIXED BIN (31) INIT(4);
    DCL FIVE                        FIXED BIN (31) INIT(5);
    DCL SIX                         FIXED BIN (31) INIT(6);

/*******************************************************************
/*              P R O G R A M   M A I N L I N E                    *
*******************************************************************/

CALL P100_INITIALIZATION;
CALL P200_MAINLINE;
CALL P300_TERMINATION;

P100_INITIALIZATION: PROC;

    PUT SKIP LIST ('PLIIMSC: GET EMPPAYHS REC FROM DB USING CMD CODE');
    PUT SKIP LIST ('PROCESSING IN P100_INITIALIZATION');
    IO_EMPLOYEE_RECORD    = '';
    IO_EMPPAY_RECORD      = '';
    IO_EMPPAYHS_RECORD    = '';

END P100_INITIALIZATION;

P200_MAINLINE: PROC;
```

```
             /*  SET THE EMPLOYEE SEGMENT SEARCH ARGUMENT AND CALL PLITDLI  */

          EMP_ID_VAL    = '3217';
          EFFDATE_VAL   = '20170101';
          PAYDATE_VAL   = '20170215';

          PUT SKIP LIST ('1ST CALL THE 2/15/2017 PAY REC WITH 3 SSA METHOD');

          CALL PLITDLI (SIX,
                        DLI_FUNCGU,
                        PCB_MASK,
                        IO_EMPPAYHS_RECORD,
                        EMP_QUALIFIED_SSA,
                        EMPPAY_QUALIFIED_SSA,
                        EMPPAYHS_QUALIFIED_SSA);

          SELECT (STATUS_CODE);
             WHEN (' ')
                DO;
                   PUT SKIP LIST ('GOOD READ OF EMPPAYHS : ' || EMP_ID_VAL);
                   PUT SKIP DATA (IO_EMPPAYHS_RECORD);
                END;
             WHEN ('GE','GB')
                PUT SKIP LIST ('PAY HIST SEG NOT FOUND FOR ' || EMP_ID_VAL);
             OTHERWISE
                DO;
                   CALL P400_DISPLAY_ERROR;
                   RETURN;
                END;

           END; /* SELECT */

          PUT SKIP LIST ('2ND CALL THE 2/15/2017 PAY REC WITH CMD CODE C');

          CONCATKEY = '321720170101201702l5';

          CALL PLITDLI (FOUR,
                        DLI_FUNCGU,
                        PCB_MASK,
                        IO_EMPPAYHS_RECORD,
                        EMPPAYHS_CCODE_SSA);

          SELECT (STATUS_CODE);
             WHEN (' ')
                DO;
                   PUT SKIP LIST ('GOOD READ OF EMPPAYHS : ' || EMP_ID_VAL);
                   PUT SKIP DATA (IO_EMPPAYHS_RECORD);
                END;
             WHEN ('GE','GB')
                PUT SKIP LIST ('PAY HIST SEG NOT FOUND FOR ' || EMP_ID_VAL);
             OTHERWISE
                DO;
```

```
            CALL P400_DISPLAY_ERROR;
            RETURN;
        END;

    END; /* SELECT */

END P200_MAINLINE;

P300_TERMINATION: PROC;

    PUT SKIP LIST ('PLIIMSC - ENDED SUCCESSFULLY');

END P300_TERMINATION;

P400_DISPLAY_ERROR: PROC;

    PUT SKIP LIST ('ERROR ENCOUNTERED - DETAIL FOLLOWS');
    PUT SKIP LIST ('IO_EMPPAYHS_RECORD: ' || IO_EMPLOYEE_RECORD);
    PUT SKIP LIST ('DBD_NAME1:'   ||  DBD_NAME);
    PUT SKIP LIST ('SEG_LEVEL1:'  || SEG_LEVEL);
    PUT SKIP LIST ('STATUS_CODE:' || STATUS_CODE);
    PUT SKIP LIST ('PROC_OPT1 :'  || PROC_OPT);
    PUT SKIP LIST ('SEG_NAME1 :'  || SEG_NAME);
    PUT SKIP LIST ('KEY_FDBK1 :'  || KEY_FDBK);
    PUT SKIP LIST ('NUM_SENSEG1:' || NUM_SENSEG);
    PUT SKIP LIST ('KEY_FDBK_AREA1:' || KEY_FDBK_AREA);

END P400_DISPLAY_ERROR;

END PLIIMSC;
```

Command codes can be very useful when you need the features they offer. Check out the following table of the command codes and how they are used. This information is from the IBM product web site. [iii] You'll find more detail about each command code there as well.

Summary of Command Codes

Command Code	Description
A	Clear positioning and start the call at the beginning of the database.
C	Use the concatenated key of a segment to identify the segment.
D	Retrieve or insert a sequence of segments in a hierarchic path using only one call, instead of using a separate (path) call for each segment.
F	Back up to the first occurrence of a segment under its parent when searching for a particular segment occurrence. Disregarded for

Command Code	Description
	a root segment.
G	Prevent randomization or the calling of the HALDB Partition Selection exit routine and search the database sequentially.
L	Retrieve the last occurrence of a segment under its parent.
M	Move a subset pointer to the next segment occurrence after your current position. (Used with DEDBs only.)
N	Designate segments that you do not want replaced when replacing segments after a Get Hold call. Typically used when replacing a path of segments.
O	Either field names or both segment position and lengths can be contained in the SSA qualification for combine field position.
P	Set parentage at a higher level than what it usually is (the lowest-level SSA of the call).
Q	Reserve a segment so that other programs cannot update it until you have finished processing and updating it.
R	Retrieve the first segment occurrence in a subset. (Used with DEDBs only.)
S	Unconditionally set a subset pointer to the current position. (Used with DEDBs only.)
U	Limit the search for a segment to the dependents of the segment occurrence on which position is established.
V	Use the hierarchic level at the current position and higher as qualification for the segment.
W	Set a subset pointer to your current position, if the subset pointer is not already set. (Used with DEDBs only.)
Z	Set a subset pointer to 0, so it can be reused. (Used with DEDBs only.)
-	NULL. Use an SSA in command code format without specifying the command code. Can be replaced during execution with the command codes that you want.

Committing and Rolling Back Changes

Let's look at how we commit updated data to the database. This is not difficult to do using checkpoint calls. Using checkpoint **restart** is somewhat more involved, especially for running in DLI mode where you must use a log file. We'll provide examples of both checkpointing and checkpoint restarting. It will be better if we take it in two chunks with two programs, so that's what we'll do.

For COBIMSD our objective is to delete all the records in the database. We use the same walkthrough-the-database code we used in COBIMS3 except we will use GHN to do the walking, and we will add a DLET call after each GHN to delete the root segment. Note: all child segments are automatically deleted when a root segment is deleted. In fact the principle is even broader - all children under a parent segment are deleted if the parent segment is deleted.

We will also set up checkpointing to show it's usage. We will need to do four things before checkpointing can work.

1. Change the PSB to include an IO-PCB
2. Add an XRST call before any data related IMS calls are done
3. Add CHKP calls at specified intervals
4. Add code to reset database position after a checkpoint

Modifying the PSB to Add An IO-PCB

We have to back up a bit to make a fundamental change to our PSB. In order to issue IMS service commands like CHKP (as opposed to database retrieval or update commands) you must use a special PCB called the IO-PCB. Programs that run in BMP mode are always defined to use an IO-PCB, but those that run in DLI mode by default do not have to use an IO-PCB (unless they are doing IMS service calls).

Since we have only been running in DLI mode and not issuing IMS service calls, we didn't define our PSB to include an IOPCB. Since we must now use an IO-PCB to use CHKP calls, let's modify our PSB accordingly. The change is very simple and involves adding a **CMPAT=Y** clause after the PSBNAME= clause. Let's create a separate PSB named EMPPSBZ. It will be a clone of the EMPPSB except for the CMPAT=Y. Here is the code:

```
PRINT NOGEN
PCB    TYPE=DB,NAME=EMPLOYEE,KEYLEN=20,PROCOPT=AP
SENSEG NAME=EMPLOYEE,PARENT=0
SENSEG NAME=EMPPAY,PARENT=EMPLOYEE
SENSEG NAME=EMPPAYHS,PARENT=EMPPAY
SENSEG NAME=EMPDEP,PARENT=EMPLOYEE
PSBGEN LANG=COBOL,PSBNAME=EMPLOYEE,CMPAT=YES
END
```

Let's save this as member `EMPPSBZ` in our library and run the `PSBGEN` process.

So what practical effect does this have if we use the `EMPPSBZ` `PSB` to run a program? Basically this `PSB` **implicitly** includes an `IO-PCB`, meaning you don't see an `IO-PCB` defined in the `PSB`, but it must be the first `PCB` pointer in the linkage between your program and IMS. Since we defined the `PSB` this way, you **must** handle the `IO-PCB` in your program by:

- Including a structure for the `IO-PCB`.

- Including the `IO-PCB` structure name in the `ENTRY` statement in the procedure division.

Here is our new `IO-PCB` structure:

```
01 IO-PCB.
   05 FILLER           PICTURE X(10).
   05 IO-STATUS-CODE   PICTURE XX.
   05 FILLER           PICTURE X(20).
```

And here is the change to the `ENTRY` coded in the procedure division. Notice it now includes both the `IO-PCB` and the `PCB-MASK` structures.

```
ENTRY 'DLITCBL' USING IO-PCB, PCB-MASK
```

You MUST put the `IO-PCB` first in the parameter list before any database PCBs. The database PCBs that follow should be in the same order that they are defined in the `PSB`. Now we can move on to doing the restart call.

Adding an XRST Call to Initialization Routine

Now we need to include an `XRST` (Extended Restart Facility) call to check for restart. Don't worry that we won't actually be restarting with this program yet (the reason is because we aren't logging our changes yet – be patient, we'll get there in the next program). The `XRST` call is part of the procedure that we need to do symbolic checkpoints and eventually perform IMS restarts, so we include it here. [3]

First, add these structures and variables to your working storage section.

---

[3] In this text we will only deal with symbolic checkpoints. IMS also offers basic checkpoints, but these do not work with the extended restart facility (the `XRST` call and automated repositions, etc), so with basic checkpoints your program must do 100% of the code to perform a restart. Consequently basic checkpoints are of limited value and I don't deal with them in this text.

```cobol
01 XRST-IOAREA.
   05 XRST-ID        PIC X(08) VALUE SPACES.
   05 FILLER         PIC X(04) VALUE SPACES.

77 IO-AREALEN       PIC S9(9) USAGE IS BINARY VALUE 12.

77 CHKP-ID          PIC X(08) VALUE 'IMSD    '.

77 CHKP-NBR         PIC 999   VALUE ZERO.
77 CHKP-COUNT       PIC S9(9) USAGE IS BINARY VALUE ZERO.

01 CHKP-MESSAGE.
   05 FILLER              PIC X(24) VALUE
      'COBIMSD   CHECK POINT NO:'.
   05 CHKP-MESS-NBR       PIC 999      VALUE ZERO.
   05 FILLER              PIC X(15)    VALUE ',AT INPUT REC#:'.
   05 CHKP-MESS-REC       PIC ZZZZZ9   VALUE SPACES.
   05 FILLER              PIC X(10)    VALUE ',AT EMP#:'.
   05 CHKP-MESS-EMP       PIC X(08)    VALUE SPACES.

01 IMS-CHKP-AREA-LTH.
   05 LEN              PIC S9(9) USAGE IS BINARY VALUE +7.

01 IMS-CHKP-AREA.
   05 CHKP-EMP-ID    PIC X(04) VALUE SPACES.
   05 CHKP-NBR-LAST  PIC 999   VALUE 0.
```

Second, add this code at the beginning of your Initialization paragraph.

```cobol
* CHECK FOR RESTART

   CALL 'CBLTDLI' USING SIX,
        DLI-FUNCXRST,
        PCB-MASK,
        IO-AREALEN,
        XRST-IOAREA,
        IMS-CHKP-AREA-LTH,
        IMS-CHKP-AREA

   IF STATUS-CODE NOT EQUAL SPACES THEN
      PERFORM P9000-DISPLAY-ERROR
      GOBACK
   END-IF

   IF XRST-ID NOT EQUAL SPACES THEN
      MOVE CHKP-NBR-LAST TO CHKP-NBR
      DISPLAY '*** COBIMSD IMS RESTART ***'
      DISPLAY '*   LAST CHECK POINT :' XRST-ID
      DISPLAY '*   EMPLOYEE NUMBER  :' CHKP-EMP-ID
   ELSE
      DISPLAY '****** COBIMSD IMS NORMAL START ***'
      PERFORM P8000-TAKE-CHECKPOINT
```

```
        END-IF.
```

This code checks to see if our execution is being run as a restart. If it is, then we announce that it is a restart. If it is not, we announce a normal start. That's all we need to do with XRST right now. Later we will add code to perform the various restart actions, and we'll explain the parameters at that time.

Adding the CHKP Call

Now let's add code for taking a checkpoint. We'll code a separate procedure for this. The required parameters for the call are the CHKP function, the IO-PCB structure, the length of an IO area that contains the checkpoint id, the IO area that contains the checkpoint id, the length of the checkpoint area, and the checkpoint area structure. The latter is where you save anything you want to save for restart, such as the last processed EMP-ID, record counters and anything else you want to save for a restart. Here is the code for doing the checkpoint call.

```
    P8000-TAKE-CHECKPOINT.

        DISPLAY 'PROCESSING IN P8000-TAKE-CHECKPOINT'
        ADD +1             TO CHKP-NBR
        MOVE CHKP-NBR      TO CHKP-NBR-LAST
        MOVE CHKP-NBR-LAST TO CHKP-ID(6:3)
        MOVE EMP-ID        TO CHKP-EMP-ID

        CALL 'CBLTDLI' USING SIX,
             DLI-FUNCCHKP,
             IO-PCB,              Replaces PCB-MASK?
             IO-AREALEN,
             CHKP-ID,
             IMS-CHKP-AREA-LTH,
             IMS-CHKP-AREA

        IF IO-STATUS-CODE NOT EQUAL SPACES THEN
           DISPLAY 'TOOK AN ERROR DOING THE CHECKPOINT'
           DISPLAY 'IO-STATUS-CODE ' IO-STATUS-CODE
           PERFORM P9000-DISPLAY-ERROR
           PERFORM P9000-DISPLAY-ERROR
           GOBACK
        ELSE
           MOVE 0 TO CHKP-COUNT
           MOVE CHKP-NBR       TO CHKP-MESS-NBR
           MOVE CHKP-EMP-ID    TO CHKP-MESS-EMP
           DISPLAY CHKP-MESSAGE
        END-IF.
```

One final note: the third parameter in the CHKP call (the IO area length) is not actually used by IMS, but it must still be included for backward compatibility. You need only define a variable for it in the program.

Adding Code to Reposition in the Database After Checkpoint
Finally, we must create code to reposition the database after taking a checkpoint. The reason is that the checkpoint call causes the database position to be lost. If you continue GHN calls at this point without reestablishing your database position, you'll get an error.

So what we'll do is to ensure we have the next record to process and we'll include that in the checkpoint IO area that we are going to save. So our code will:

DLET a record

Read the next record and capture the employee id

If it is time to take a checkpoint then

Take a check point using the captured employee id that was just read

Reposition in the database using the captured employee id

The reposition code is as follows. Notice it is using a qualified SSA to get the exact record that is needed to reposition. Of course we must use a qualified SSA, and the EMP-ID that was retrieved in the GHN call before we took the checkpoint.

```
P1000-RESET-POSITION.

    DISPLAY 'PROCESSING IN P1000-RESET-POSITION'

    CALL 'CBLTDLI' USING FOUR,
        DLI-FUNCGHU,
        PCB-MASK,
        IO-EMPLOYEE-RECORD,
        EMP-QUALIFIED-SSA

    IF STATUS-CODE NOT EQUAL SPACES THEN
       PERFORM P9000-DISPLAY-ERROR
       GOBACK
    ELSE
       DISPLAY 'SUCCESSFUL REPOSITION AT EMP ID ' EMP-ID.
```

Ok, now we've performed all four items that will enable us to commit data updates by taking checkpoints at some interval. Let's make our record interval 5. So we have eight records in the database, and we'll take a checkpoints as follows:

- At the beginning of the program.

- After each 5 records have been processed.

- At the end of the program.

Here is our complete program code for COBIMSD. As mentioned earlier, we haven't completed the code yet for a restart. But we now have the functionality to commit our data changes with the checkpoint call.

```
        IDENTIFICATION DIVISION.
        PROGRAM-ID. COBIMSD.

       **********************************************************
       *   WALK THROUGH THE EMPLOYEE (ROOT) SEGMENTS OF          *
       *   THE ENTIRE EMPLOYEE DATABASE. DELETE ALL RECORDS.*
       **********************************************************

        ENVIRONMENT DIVISION.
        INPUT-OUTPUT SECTION.
        DATA DIVISION.

       **********************************************************
       *    W O R K I N G    S T O R A G E    S E C T I O N     *
       **********************************************************

        WORKING-STORAGE SECTION.

         01 WS-FLAGS.
            05   SW-END-OF-DB-SWITCH     PIC X(1) VALUE 'N'.
                 88   SW-END-OF-DB                VALUE 'Y'.
                 88   SW-NOT-END-OF-DB            VALUE 'N'.

         01 DLI-FUNCTIONS.
            05 DLI-FUNCISRT   PIC X(4) VALUE 'ISRT'.
            05 DLI-FUNCGU     PIC X(4) VALUE 'GU  '.
            05 DLI-FUNCGN     PIC X(4) VALUE 'GN  '.
            05 DLI-FUNCGHU    PIC X(4) VALUE 'GHU '.
            05 DLI-FUNCGHN    PIC X(4) VALUE 'GHN '.
            05 DLI-FUNCGNP    PIC X(4) VALUE 'GNP '.
            05 DLI-FUNCREPL   PIC X(4) VALUE 'REPL'.
            05 DLI-FUNCDLET   PIC X(4) VALUE 'DLET'.
            05 DLI-FUNCXRST   PIC X(4) VALUE 'XRST'.
            05 DLI-FUNCCHKP   PIC X(4) VALUE 'CHKP'.

         01 IO-EMPLOYEE-RECORD.
            05   EMP-ID       PIC X(04).
            05   FILLER       PIC X(01).
            05   EMPL-LNAME   PIC X(30).
```

```
           05  FILLER         PIC X(01).
           05  EMPL-FNAME     PIC X(20).
           05  FILLER         PIC X(01).
           05  EMPL-YRS-SRV   PIC X(02).
           05  FILLER         PIC X(01).
           05  EMPL-PRM-DTE   PIC X(10).
           05  FILLER         PIC X(10).

       01 EMP-UNQUALIFIED-SSA.
           05  SEGNAME        PIC X(08) VALUE 'EMPLOYEE'.
           05  FILLER         PIC X(01) VALUE ' '.

       01 EMP-QUALIFIED-SSA.
           05  SEGNAME        PIC X(08) VALUE 'EMPLOYEE'.
           05  FILLER         PIC X(01) VALUE '('.
           05  FIELD          PIC X(08) VALUE 'EMPID'.
           05  OPER           PIC X(02) VALUE ' ='.
           05  EMP-ID-VAL     PIC X(04) VALUE '    '.
           05  FILLER         PIC X(01) VALUE ')'.

       01 SEG-IO-AREA         PIC X(80).

       01 IMS-RET-CODES.
           05  ONE            PIC S9(9) COMP VALUE +1.
           05  TWO            PIC S9(9) COMP VALUE +2.
           05  THREE          PIC S9(9) COMP VALUE +3.
           05  FOUR           PIC S9(9) COMP VALUE +4.
           05  FIVE           PIC S9(9) COMP VALUE +5.
           05  SIX            PIC S9(9) COMP VALUE +6.


       01 XRST-IOAREA.
           05 XRST-ID         PIC X(08) VALUE SPACES.
           05 FILLER          PIC X(04) VALUE SPACES.

       77 IO-AREALEN          PIC S9(9) USAGE IS BINARY VALUE 12.

       77 CHKP-ID             PIC X(08) VALUE 'IMSD    '.

       77 CHKP-NBR            PIC 999    VALUE ZERO.
       77 CHKP-COUNT          PIC S9(9) USAGE IS BINARY VALUE ZERO.

       01 CHKP-MESSAGE.
           05 FILLER              PIC X(24) VALUE
              'COBIMSD   CHECK POINT NO:'.
           05 CHKP-MESS-NBR       PIC 999      VALUE ZERO.
           05 FILLER              PIC X(15)    VALUE ',AT INPUT REC#:'.
           05 CHKP-MESS-REC       PIC ZZZZZ9   VALUE SPACES.
           05 FILLER              PIC X(10)    VALUE ',AT EMP#:'.
           05 CHKP-MESS-EMP       PIC X(08)    VALUE SPACES.

       01 IMS-CHKP-AREA-LTH.
           05 LEN              PIC S9(9) USAGE IS BINARY VALUE +7.
```

```
    01 IMS-CHKP-AREA.
        05 CHKP-EMP-ID       PIC X(04) VALUE SPACES.
        05 CHKP-NBR-LAST     PIC 999   VALUE 0.

LINKAGE SECTION.

    01 IO-PCB.
        05 FILLER            PICTURE X(10).
        05 IO-STATUS-CODE    PICTURE XX.
        05 FILLER            PICTURE X(20).

    01 PCB-MASK.
        03 DBD-NAME          PIC X(8).
        03 SEG-LEVEL         PIC XX.
        03 STATUS-CODE       PIC XX.
        03 PROC-OPT          PIC X(4).
        03 FILLER            PIC X(4).
        03 SEG-NAME          PIC X(8).
        03 KEY-FDBK          PIC S9(5) COMP.
        03 NUM-SENSEG        PIC S9(5) COMP.
        03 KEY-FDBK-AREA.
            05 EMPLOYEE-KEY  PIC X(04).
            05 EMPPAYHS-KEY  PIC X(08).


PROCEDURE DIVISION.

    INITIALIZE IO-PCB PCB-MASK
    ENTRY 'DLITCBL' USING IO-PCB, PCB-MASK

    PERFORM P100-INITIALIZATION.
    PERFORM P200-MAINLINE.
    PERFORM P300-TERMINATION.
    GOBACK.

P100-INITIALIZATION.

    DISPLAY '** PROGRAM COBIMSD START **'
    DISPLAY 'PROCESSING IN P100-INITIALIZATION'.

* CHECK FOR RESTART

    CALL 'CBLTDLI' USING SIX,
         DLI-FUNCXRST,
         PCB-MASK,
         IO-AREALEN,
         XRST-IOAREA,
         IMS-CHKP-AREA-LTH,
         IMS-CHKP-AREA

    IF STATUS-CODE NOT EQUAL SPACES THEN
         PERFORM P9000-DISPLAY-ERROR
```

```
            GOBACK
        END-IF

        IF XRST-ID NOT EQUAL SPACES THEN
            MOVE CHKP-NBR-LAST TO CHKP-NBR
            DISPLAY '*** COBIMSD IMS RESTART ***'
            DISPLAY '*   LAST CHECK POINT :' XRST-ID
            DISPLAY '*   EMPLOYEE NUMBER  :' CHKP-EMP-ID
        ELSE
            DISPLAY '****** COBIMSD IMS NORMAL START ***'
            PERFORM P8000-TAKE-CHECKPOINT
        END-IF.

*       DO INITIAL DB READ FOR FIRST EMPLOYEE RECORD

        CALL 'CBLTDLI' USING FOUR,
             DLI-FUNCGHN,
             PCB-MASK,
             IO-EMPLOYEE-RECORD,
             EMP-UNQUALIFIED-SSA

        IF STATUS-CODE = '  ' THEN
           NEXT SENTENCE
        ELSE
           IF STATUS-CODE = 'GB' THEN
              SET SW-END-OF-DB TO TRUE
              DISPLAY 'END OF DATABASE :'
           ELSE
              PERFORM P9000-DISPLAY-ERROR
              GOBACK
           END-IF

        END-IF.

   P200-MAINLINE.

        DISPLAY 'PROCESSING IN P200-MAINLINE'

*       CHECK STATUS CODE AND FIRST RECORD

        IF SW-END-OF-DB THEN
           DISPLAY 'NO RECORDS TO PROCESS!!'
        ELSE

           PERFORM UNTIL SW-END-OF-DB

              CALL 'CBLTDLI' USING THREE,
                   DLI-FUNCDLET,
                   PCB-MASK,
                   IO-EMPLOYEE-RECORD

              IF STATUS-CODE NOT EQUAL SPACES THEN
                 PERFORM P9000-DISPLAY-ERROR
```

```
                    GOBACK
                ELSE
                    DISPLAY 'SUCCESSFUL DELETE OF EMPLOYEE ' EMP-ID
                END-IF

*       GET THE NEXT RECORD

            CALL 'CBLTDLI' USING FOUR,
                DLI-FUNCGHN,
                PCB-MASK,
                IO-EMPLOYEE-RECORD,
                EMP-UNQUALIFIED-SSA

            IF STATUS-CODE = 'GB' THEN
                SET SW-END-OF-DB TO TRUE
                DISPLAY 'END OF DATABASE'
            ELSE
                IF STATUS-CODE NOT EQUAL SPACES THEN
                    PERFORM P9000-DISPLAY-ERROR
                    SET SW-END-OF-DB TO TRUE
                    GOBACK
                ELSE
                    DISPLAY 'SUCCESSFUL GET HOLD :'
                        IO-EMPLOYEE-RECORD
                    MOVE EMP-ID TO EMP-ID-VAL
                    ADD +1 TO CHKP-COUNT
                    IF CHKP-COUNT GREATER THAN OR EQUAL TO 5
                        PERFORM P8000-TAKE-CHECKPOINT
                        PERFORM P1000-RESET-POSITION
                    END-IF
                END-IF
            END-IF

        END-PERFORM.
        DISPLAY 'FINISHED PROCESSING IN P200-MAINLINE'.

    P300-TERMINATION.

        DISPLAY 'PROCESSING IN P300-TERMINATION'
        ADD +1 TO CHKP-COUNT
        PERFORM P8000-TAKE-CHECKPOINT
        DISPLAY '** COBIMSD - SUCCESSFULLY ENDED **'.

    P1000-RESET-POSITION.

        DISPLAY 'PROCESSING IN P1000-RESET-POSITION'

        CALL 'CBLTDLI' USING FOUR,
            DLI-FUNCGHU,
            PCB-MASK,
            IO-EMPLOYEE-RECORD,
            EMP-QUALIFIED-SSA
```

```
            IF STATUS-CODE NOT EQUAL SPACES THEN
                PERFORM P9000-DISPLAY-ERROR
                GOBACK
            ELSE
                DISPLAY 'SUCCESSFUL REPOSITION AT EMP ID ' EMP-ID.

        P8000-TAKE-CHECKPOINT.

            DISPLAY 'PROCESSING IN P8000-TAKE-CHECKPOINT'

            ADD +1              TO CHKP-NBR
            MOVE CHKP-NBR       TO CHKP-NBR-LAST
            MOVE CHKP-NBR-LAST  TO CHKP-ID(6:3)
            MOVE EMP-ID         TO CHKP-EMP-ID

            CALL 'CBLTDLI' USING SIX,
                 DLI-FUNCCHKP,
                 IO-PCB,
                 IO-AREALEN,
                 CHKP-ID,
                 IMS-CHKP-AREA-LTH,
                 IMS-CHKP-AREA

            IF IO-STATUS-CODE NOT EQUAL SPACES THEN
                DISPLAY 'TOOK AN ERROR DOING THE CHECKPOINT'
                DISPLAY 'IO-STATUS-CODE ' IO-STATUS-CODE
                PERFORM P9000-DISPLAY-ERROR
                GOBACK
            ELSE
                MOVE 0 TO CHKP-COUNT
                MOVE CHKP-NBR       TO CHKP-MESS-NBR
                MOVE CHKP-EMP-ID    TO CHKP-MESS-EMP
                DISPLAY CHKP-MESSAGE
            END-IF.

        P9000-DISPLAY-ERROR.

            DISPLAY 'ERROR ENCOUNTERED - DETAIL FOLLOWS'
            DISPLAY 'SEG-IO-AREA     :' SEG-IO-AREA
            DISPLAY 'DBD-NAME1:'     DBD-NAME
            DISPLAY 'SEG-LEVEL1:'    SEG-LEVEL
            DISPLAY 'STATUS-CODE:'   STATUS-CODE
            DISPLAY 'PROC-OPT1 :'    PROC-OPT
            DISPLAY 'SEG-NAME1 :'    SEG-NAME
            DISPLAY 'KEY-FDBK1 :'    KEY-FDBK
            DISPLAY 'NUM-SENSEG1:'   NUM-SENSEG
            DISPLAY 'KEY-FDBK-AREA1:' KEY-FDBK-AREA.

        *   END OF SOURCE CODE
```

At this point, we can compile and link, and then run the program. Make sure your JCL specifies the EMPPSBZ PSB or you'll get an error.

```
** PROGRAM COBIMSD START **
PROCESSING IN P100-INITIALIZATION
****** COBIMSD IMS NORMAL START ***
PROCESSING IN P8000-TAKE-CHECKPOINT
COBIMSD   CHECK POINT NO:001,AT INPUT REC#:         ,AT EMP#:
PROCESSING IN P200-MAINLINE
SUCCESSFUL DELETE OF EMPLOYEE 1111
SUCCESSFUL GET HOLD :1122 JENKINS                DEBORAH           05
SUCCESSFUL DELETE OF EMPLOYEE 1122
SUCCESSFUL GET HOLD :3217 JOHNSON                EDWARD            04
SUCCESSFUL DELETE OF EMPLOYEE 3217
SUCCESSFUL GET HOLD :4175 TURNBULL               FRED              01
SUCCESSFUL DELETE OF EMPLOYEE 4175
SUCCESSFUL GET HOLD :4720 SCHULTZ                TIM               09
SUCCESSFUL DELETE OF EMPLOYEE 4720
SUCCESSFUL GET HOLD :4836 SMITH                  SANDRA            03
PROCESSING IN P8000-TAKE-CHECKPOINT
COBIMSD   CHECK POINT NO:002,AT INPUT REC#:         ,AT EMP#: 4836
PROCESSING IN P1000-RESET-POSITION
SUCCESSFUL REPOSITION AT EMP ID 4836
SUCCESSFUL DELETE OF EMPLOYEE 4836
SUCCESSFUL GET HOLD :6288 WILLARD                JOE               06
SUCCESSFUL DELETE OF EMPLOYEE 6288
SUCCESSFUL GET HOLD :7459 STEWART                BETTY             07
SUCCESSFUL DELETE OF EMPLOYEE 7459
END OF DATABASE
FINISHED PROCESSING IN P200-MAINLINE
PROCESSING IN P300-TERMINATION
PROCESSING IN P8000-TAKE-CHECKPOINT
COBIMSD   CHECK POINT NO:003,AT INPUT REC#:         ,AT EMP#: 7459
** COBIMSD - SUCCESSFULLY ENDED **
```

We now have an empty database. You can verify this by looking in your File Manager IMS if you have it, or you can try browsing the DATA file of the KSDS. Since it is empty, you'll get an error.

```
VSAM POINT RC X"08", Error Code X"20"
VSAM GET RC X"08", Error Code X"58"
Function terminated
***
```

We have shown we can commit updates to the database at some interval. In a real production environment we would not checkpoint every 5 records. More likely we would checkpoint at 500 records or 1,000 records or 2,000 records. You don't want to lock your data for too long, so find a record interval that commits at about once a minute, or whatever your DBA recommends.

Here is the corresponding PLI code for COBIMSD.

```
PLIIMSD: PROCEDURE (IO_PTR_PCB,DB_PTR_PCB) OPTIONS(MAIN);
```

```
/****************************************************************
* PROGRAM NAME: PLIIMSD - WALK THROUGH THE EMPLOYEE (ROOT)      *
*                        SEGMENTS OF THE EMPLOYEE IMS DATABASE, *
*                        AND DELETE EACH ONE.                   *
****************************************************************/

/****************************************************************
/*              W O R K I N G   S T O R A G E                   *
****************************************************************/

     DCL SW_END_OF_DB            STATIC BIT(01) INIT('0'B);
     DCL ONCODE                  BUILTIN;
     DCL DB_PTR_PCB              POINTER;
     DCL IO_PTR_PCB              POINTER;

     DCL PLITDLI                 EXTERNAL ENTRY;

     DCL 01 DLI_FUNCTIONS,
            05 DLI_FUNCISRT      CHAR(04) INIT ('ISRT'),
            05 DLI_FUNCGU        CHAR(04) INIT ('GU  '),
            05 DLI_FUNCGN        CHAR(04) INIT ('GN  '),
            05 DLI_FUNCGHU       CHAR(04) INIT ('GHU '),
            05 DLI_FUNCGNP       CHAR(04) INIT ('GNP '),
            05 DLI_FUNCREPL      CHAR(04) INIT ('REPL'),
            05 DLI_FUNCDLET      CHAR(04) INIT ('DLET'),
            05 DLI_FUNCXRST      CHAR(04) INIT ('XRST'),
            05 DLI_FUNCCHKP      CHAR(04) INIT ('CHKP'),
            05 DLI_FUNCROLL      CHAR(04) INIT ('ROLL');

     DCL 01 IO_EMPLOYEE_RECORD,
            05  EMPL_ID          CHAR(04),
            05  FILLER1          CHAR(01),
            05  EMPL_LNAME       CHAR(30),
            05  FILLER2          CHAR(01),
            05  EMPL_FNAME       CHAR(20),
            05  FILLER3          CHAR(01),
            05  EMPL_YRS_SRV     CHAR(02),
            05  FILLER4          CHAR(01),
            05  EMPL_PRM_DTE     CHAR(10),
            05  FILLER5          CHAR(10);

     DCL 01 EMP_UNQUALIFIED_SSA,
            05  SEGNAME          CHAR(08) INIT ('EMPLOYEE'),
            05  FILLER7          CHAR(01) INIT (' ');

     DCL 01 EMP_QUALIFIED_SSA,
            05  SEGNAME          CHAR(08) INIT('EMPLOYEE'),
            05  FILLER8          CHAR(01) INIT('('),
            05  FIELD            CHAR(08) INIT('EMPID'),
            05  OPER             CHAR(02) INIT(' ='),
            05  EMP_ID_VAL       CHAR(04) INIT('    '),
            05  FILLER9          CHAR(01) INIT(')');
```

```
        DCL THREE                   FIXED BIN (31) INIT(3);
        DCL FOUR                    FIXED BIN (31) INIT(4);
        DCL FIVE                    FIXED BIN (31) INIT(5);
        DCL SIX                     FIXED BIN (31) INIT(6);

        DCL 01 XRST_IOAREA,
             05 XRST_ID      CHAR(08) INIT('        '),
             05 FILLER10     CHAR(04) INIT('    ');

        DCL XRST_IO_AREALEN    FIXED BIN(31) INIT (12);
        DCL IO_AREALEN         FIXED BIN(31) INIT (08);
        DCL CHKP_ID            CHAR(08) INIT( 'IMSD-   ');
        DCL CHKP_NBR           FIXED DEC (3)  INIT(0);
        DCL CHKP_COUNT         FIXED BIN (31) INIT(0);

        DCL 01 CHKP_MESSAGE,
             05 FILLER11         CHAR(24)    INIT(
                'COBIMSD   CHECK POINT NO:'),
             05 CHKP_MESS_NBR    PIC '999',
             05 FILLER12         CHAR(15)    INIT( ',AT INPUT REC#:'),
             05 CHKP_MESS_REC    PIC 'ZZZZZ9',
             05 FILLER13         CHAR(10)    INIT(',AT EMP#:'),
             05 CHKP_MESS_EMP    CHAR(08)    INIT(' ');

        DCL IMS_CHKP_AREA_LTH    FIXED BIN (31) INIT(07);

        DCL 01 IMS_CHKP_AREA,
             05 CHKP_EMP_ID      CHAR(04)    INIT('0000'),
             05 CHKP_NBR_LAST    CHAR(03)    INIT('000');

        DCL 01 IO_PCB               BASED(IO_PTR_PCB),
             05 FILLER97            CHAR(10)   INIT(' '),
             05 IO_STATUS_CODE      CHAR(02)   INIT (' ');

        DCL 01 PCB_MASK             BASED(DB_PTR_PCB),
             05 DBD_NAME            CHAR(08),
             05 SEG_LEVEL           CHAR(02),
             05 STATUS_CODE         CHAR(02),
             05 PROC_OPT            CHAR(04),
             05 FILLER99            FIXED BIN (31),
             05 SEG_NAME            CHAR(08),
             05 KEY_FDBK            FIXED BIN (31),
             05 NUM_SENSEG          FIXED BIN (31),
             05 KEY_FDBK_AREA,
                10 KFB_EMPLOYEE_ID CHAR(04);
/*******************************************************************
/*                P R O G R A M    M A I N L I N E                 *
*******************************************************************/

CALL P100_INITIALIZATION;
CALL P200_MAINLINE;
CALL P300_TERMINATION;
```

```pli
P100_INITIALIZATION: PROC;

    PUT SKIP LIST ('PLIIMSD: TRAVERSE EMPLOYEE DATABASE ROOT SEGS');
    PUT SKIP LIST ('PROCESSING IN P100_INITIALIZATION');
    IO_PCB   = '';
    PCB_MASK = '';
    IO_EMPLOYEE_RECORD  = '';

    /* CHECK FOR RESTART */

    CALL PLITDLI (SIX,
                  DLI_FUNCXRST,
                  IO_PCB,
                  XRST_IO_AREALEN,
                  XRST_IOAREA,
                  IMS_CHKP_AREA_LTH,
                  IMS_CHKP_AREA);

    IF IO_STATUS_CODE ¬= '  ' THEN
       DO;
          CALL P9000_DISPLAY_ERROR;
          RETURN;
       END;

    IF XRST_ID ¬= '  ' THEN
       DO;
          CHKP_NBR = CHKP_NBR_LAST;
          PUT SKIP LIST ('*** COBIMSD IMS RESTART ***');
          PUT SKIP LIST ('*  LAST CHECK POINT :' || XRST_ID);
          PUT SKIP LIST ('*  EMPLOYEE NUMBER  :' || CHKP_EMP_ID);
       END;
    ELSE
       DO;
          PUT SKIP LIST ('****** COBIMSD IMS NORMAL START ***');
          CALL P8000_TAKE_CHECKPOINT;
       END;

 /* DO INITIAL DB READ FOR FIRST EMPLOYEE RECORD */

    CALL PLITDLI (FOUR,
                  DLI_FUNCGHN,
                  PCB_MASK,
                  IO_EMPLOYEE_RECORD,
                  EMP_UNQUALIFIED_SSA);

    IF STATUS_CODE = '  ' THEN;
    ELSE
       IF STATUS_CODE = 'GB' THEN
          DO;
             SW_END_OF_DB = '1'B;
             PUT SKIP LIST ('** END OF DATABASE');
          END;
```

```
            ELSE
               DO;
                  CALL P9000_DISPLAY_ERROR;
                  RETURN;
               END;

END P100_INITIALIZATION;

P200_MAINLINE: PROC;

      /*  MAIN LOOP - CYCLE THROUGH ALL ROOT SEGMENTS IN THE DB,
                      DISPLAYING THE DATA RETRIEVED                */

      IF SW_END_OF_DB THEN
         PUT SKIP LIST ('NO RECORDS TO PROCESS!!');
      ELSE
         DO WHILE (¬SW_END_OF_DB);
            PUT SKIP LIST ('SUCCESSFUL GET-HOLD :'
               || EMPL_ID);

            /* DELETE THE SWGMENT */

            CALL PLITDLI (THREE,
                          DLI_FUNCDLET,
                          PCB_MASK,
                          IO_EMPLOYEE_RECORD);

            IF STATUS_CODE ¬= ' ' THEN
               DO;
                  CALL P9000_DISPLAY_ERROR;
                  RETURN;
               END;
            ELSE
               PUT SKIP LIST ('SUCCESSFUL DELETE OF EMP ' || EMPL_ID);

            /* NOW GET THE NEXT ROOT TO DELETE */

            CALL PLITDLI (FOUR,
                          DLI_FUNCGN,
                          PCB_MASK,
                          IO_EMPLOYEE_RECORD,
                          EMP_UNQUALIFIED_SSA);

            IF STATUS_CODE = ' ' THEN
               DO;
                  PUT SKIP LIST ('SUCCESSFUL GET HOLD: ' || EMPL_ID);
                  EMP_ID_VAL = EMPL_ID;
                  CHKP_COUNT = CHKP_COUNT + 1;
                  IF CHKP_COUNT >= 5 THEN
                     DO;
                        CALL P8000_TAKE_CHECKPOINT;
                        CALL P1000_RESET_POSITION;
                     END;
```

```
                    END;
                ELSE
                    IF STATUS_CODE = 'GB' THEN
                        DO;
                            SW_END_OF_DB = '1'B;
                            PUT SKIP LIST ('** END OF DATABASE');
                        END;
                    ELSE
                        DO;
                            CALL P9000_DISPLAY_ERROR;
                            RETURN;
                        END;

        END; /* DO WHILE */

    PUT SKIP LIST ('FINISHED PROCESSING IN P200_MAINLINE');

END P200_MAINLINE;

P300_TERMINATION: PROC;

    PUT SKIP LIST ('PROCESSING IN P300_TERMINATION');

    CHKP_COUNT = CHKP_COUNT + 1;
    CALL P8000_TAKE_CHECKPOINT;

    PUT SKIP LIST ('PLIIMSD - SUCCESSFULLY ENDED');

END P300_TERMINATION;

P1000_RESET_POSITION: PROC;

    PUT SKIP LIST ('PROCESSING IN P1000_RESET_POSITION');

    CALL PLITDLI (FOUR,
                  DLI_FUNCGHU,
                  PCB_MASK,
                  IO_EMPLOYEE_RECORD,
                  EMP_QUALIFIED_SSA);

    IF STATUS_CODE ¬= '  ' THEN
        DO;
            CALL P9000_DISPLAY_ERROR;
            RETURN;
        END;
    ELSE
        PUT SKIP LIST ('SUCCESSFUL REPOSITION AT EMP ID ' || EMPL_ID);

END P1000_RESET_POSITION;

P8000_TAKE_CHECKPOINT: PROC;

    PUT SKIP LIST ('PROCESSING IN P8000_TAKE_CHECKPOINT');
```

```
        CHKP_NBR                = CHKP_NBR + 1;
        CHKP_NBR_LAST           = CHKP_NBR;
        SUBSTR(CHKP_ID,6,3)     = CHKP_NBR_LAST;
        CHKP_EMP_ID             = EMPL_ID;

        PUT SKIP LIST ('IO_AREALEN ' || IO_AREALEN);
        PUT SKIP LIST ('IMS_CHKP_AREA_LTH ' || IMS_CHKP_AREA_LTH);

        PUT SKIP LIST ('CHKP_ID = ' || CHKP_ID);
        PUT SKIP LIST (' ');

        CALL PLITDLI (SIX,
                      DLI_FUNCCHKP,
                      IO_PCB,
                      IO_AREALEN,
                      CHKP_ID,
                      IMS_CHKP_AREA_LTH,
                      IMS_CHKP_AREA);

     IF IO_STATUS_CODE ¬= ' ' THEN
        DO;
            PUT SKIP LIST ('TOOK AN ERROR DOING THE CHECKPOINT');
            PUT SKIP LIST ('IO_STATUS_CODE ' || IO_STATUS_CODE);
            CALL P9000_DISPLAY_ERROR;
            RETURN;
        END;
     ELSE
        DO;
            CHKP_COUNT = 0;
            CHKP_MESS_NBR = CHKP_NBR;
            CHKP_MESS_EMP = CHKP_EMP_ID;
            PUT SKIP LIST (CHKP_MESSAGE);
        END;

END P8000_TAKE_CHECKPOINT;

P9000_DISPLAY_ERROR: PROC;

    PUT SKIP LIST ('ERROR ENCOUNTERED - DETAIL FOLLOWS');
    PUT SKIP LIST ('SEG_IO_AREA     :' || SEG_IO_AREA);
    PUT SKIP LIST ('DBD_NAME1:' || DBD_NAME);
    PUT SKIP LIST ('SEG_LEVEL1:' || SEG_LEVEL);
    PUT SKIP LIST ('STATUS_CODE:' || STATUS_CODE);
    PUT SKIP LIST ('PROC_OPT1 :' || PROC_OPT);
    PUT SKIP LIST ('SEG_NAME1 :' || SEG_NAME);
    PUT SKIP LIST ('KEY_FDBK1 :' || KEY_FDBK);
    PUT SKIP LIST ('NUM_SENSEG1:' || NUM_SENSEG);
    PUT SKIP LIST ('KEY_FDBK_AREA1:' || KEY_FDBK_AREA);

END P9000_DISPLAY_ERROR;

END PLIIMSD;
```

Performing Checkpoint Restart

At this point, we've successfully committed data using checkpoints. However, we have not yet demonstrated how to perform a restart using the extended restart facility (XRST). To do that, we need to introduce IMS logging.

Using the IMS Log

To allow for IMS restartability, you must log all the transactions and checkpoints you take. When you stop the program (or when IMS stops it for an abend), your data modifications (ISRT, REPL, DLET) are automatically backed out to the last checkpoint. So typically, you will want to fix whatever the problem was, and then restart your program from the last checkpoint.

In your execution JCL for running IMS programs, there should be two DD statements that are probably dummied out.[4] The IEFRDER DD should definitely be there, and the IMSLOGR may be there (it is only referenced on restart so it might not be).

```
//IMSLOGR   DD DUMMY
//IEFRDER   DD DUMMY
```

Here's what these are used for when they are not dummied out (when actual file names are specified):

- IMSLOGR – the previous (existing) generation of IMS log file created for your DLI execution.

- IEFRDER – the new generation of the IMS log file created for your DLI execution to log any updates to the database performed by your program.

You'll want to create a generation data group for your IMS log file, and then define these DDs to use the 0 and +1 generation of this data set. I created USER01.IMSLOG with 5 generations, and I created an empty first generation. Next, I have un-dummied the IMSLOGR and IEFRDER DD's by coding the new log file as follows:

```
//IMSLOGR   DD DSN=USER01.IMSLOG(+0),
//             DISP=SHR
```

---

[4] This discussion pertains to running a program in DLI mode. If you are running a program in BMP mode, you don't need these DDs because the program runs in the IMS online space which has its own transaction log.

```
//IEFRDER  DD DSN=USER01.IMSLOG(+1),
//            DISP=(NEW,CATLG,CATLG),
//            UNIT=SYSDA,
//            SPACE=(TRK,(1,1),RLSE),
//            DCB=(RECFM=VB,BLKSIZE=4096,
//            LRECL=4092,BUFNO=2)
```

Now if you specify a checkpoint value when you restart your program, IMS will scan the 0 generation of the IMS log to pick up the information from the last checkpoint. In our case, this information includes the employee id that we read before issuing the last checkpoint. You can then use that employee id key to reposition in the database.

Specifying a Checkpoint ID on Restart

You can specify the checkpoint id in the PARM value of the execute statement for your program. This is a positional parameter, so it must be placed correctly in the PARM sequence. Here is the JCL and I'm putting a sample checkpoint id at the right place in the PARM.

```
//GO       EXEC PGM=DFSRRC00,REGION=4M,
//         PARM=(DLI,&MBR,&PSB,7,0000,,0,'CHKP0003',N,0,0,,,N,N,,N,)
```

Restart Example

We need to reload the database now before we can do a restart example (remember we deleted all the records in the database earlier). You can run your COBIMS1 to do this. Although the database is empty, it is not brand new. So you can use PSB EMPPSB instead of EMPPSBL. In fact you'll get an error (AI status code) if you use the EMPPSBL, so make sure you use EMPPSB.

When finished, verify that we have nine records in the database.

```
Browse          USER01.IMS.EMPLOYEE.DATA                  Top of 9
Command ===>                                              Scroll PAGE
                        Type DATA      RBA                Format CHAR
                                       Col 1
----+----10---+----2----+----3----+----4----+----5----+----6----+----7----+----
****  Top of data   ****
......1111 VEREEN              CHARLES        12 2017-01-01 93
......1122 JENKINS             DEBORAH        05 2017-01-01 43
......3217 JOHNSON             EDWARD         04 2017-01-01 39
......4175 TURNBULL            FRED           01 2016-12-01 54
......4720 SCHULTZ             TIM            09 2017-01-01 65
......4836 SMITH               SANDRA         03 2017-01-01 02
......6288 WILLARD             JOE            06 2016-01-01 20
......7459 STEWART             BETTY          07 2016-07-31 01
......9134 FRANKLIN            BRIANNA        00 2016-10-01 93
****  End of data   ****
```

For our example, we will create a new program COBIMSE and it will delete all the records in the database as we did with COBIMSD. We will checkpoint at 5 record intervals. You can start by copying COBIMSD to create COBIMSE. There will be two differences between COBIMSD and COBIMSE. One is that COBIMSE will intentionally cause a rollback when we encounter employee 7459 (this is just to simulate an abend type error). The rollback will back out all changes made since the last checkpoint.

The other difference is that we will code restart logic in COBIMSE to reposition to the appropriate employee id in the data to continue processing on a restart. In between run 1 and run 2 of COBIMSE, the only change we will make to the program is to not do the rollback when it gets to employee id 7459. We're simulating a "problem" to cause the rollback, then we solve the cause of the rollback and restart the program.

If you copy COBIMSD to create COBIMSE, you only need to make a few changes. First, let's create some new procedures. One procedure will get the first root in the database. We've been doing that in P100-INITIALIZATION, but now on a restart we need to call the reset position procedure instead. Separating these functions into separate procedures makes the code easier to read. Let's do this:

```
P1000-GET-FIRST-ROOT.

    CALL 'CBLTDLI' USING ,
         DLI-FUNCGHN,
         PCB-MASK,
         IO-EMPLOYEE-RECORD,
         EMP-UNQUALIFIED-SSA

    IF STATUS-CODE = ' ' THEN
       NEXT SENTENCE
    ELSE
       IF STATUS-CODE = 'GB' THEN
          SET SW-END-OF-DB TO TRUE
          DISPLAY 'END OF DATABASE :'
       ELSE
          PERFORM P9000-DISPLAY-ERROR
          GOBACK
       END-IF.
```

Next let's rename P1000-RESET-POSITION to P2000-RESET-POSITION. That will keep the code more orderly.

Finally, let's add the procedure to perform the rollback.

```
P3000-ROLLBACK.

    DISPLAY 'PROCESSING IN P3000-ROLLBACK'.
```

```
        CALL 'CBLTDLI' USING ONE,
              DLI-FUNCROLL.
```

Now let's modify the initialization logic to handle either a normal start or a restart. On a normal start we'll get the first root in the database. On a restart we'll reposition at the EMP-ID saved in the checkpoint that we are using to do the restart.

```
        CALL 'CBLTDLI' USING SIX,
              DLI-FUNCXRST,
              PCB-MASK,
              IO-AREALEN,
              XRST-IOAREA,
              IMS-CHKP-AREA-LTH,
              IMS-CHKP-AREA

        IF STATUS-CODE NOT EQUAL SPACES THEN
            PERFORM P9000-DISPLAY-ERROR
            GOBACK
        END-IF

        IF XRST-ID NOT EQUAL SPACES THEN
            SET SW-IMS-RESTART TO TRUE
            MOVE CHKP-NBR-LAST TO CHKP-NBR
            DISPLAY '*** COBIMSE IMS RESTART ***'
            DISPLAY '*   LAST CHECK POINT :' XRST-ID
            DISPLAY '*   EMPLOYEE NUMBER  :' CHKP-EMP-ID
        ELSE
            DISPLAY '****** COBIMSE IMS NORMAL START ***'
            PERFORM P8000-TAKE-CHECKPOINT
        END-IF.

   *    DO INITIAL DB READ FOR FIRST EMPLOYEE RECORD
   *    OR REPOSITION IF AN IMS RESTART.

        IF SW-IMS-RESTART THEN
            MOVE CHKP-EMP-ID TO EMP-ID-VAL
            PERFORM P2000-RESET-POSITION
        ELSE
            PERFORM P1000-GET-FIRST-ROOT

        END-IF.
```

The value of `XRST-ID` will be non-blank if we are doing a restart. In that case we will turn on the `SW-IMS-RESTART` switch. Otherwise we will branch to take the initial checkpoint. Now if the `SW-IMS-RESTART` is true, it means this is a restart so we load the employee id from the checkpoint area into the qualified EMPLOYEE qualified SSA value, and then we call the procedure to reset database position to where it was at that checkpoint.

If the value of `XRST-ID` is blank, then we are **not** doing a restart. In this case, we call the procedure to get the first root.

Finally, let's add a temporary statement to the execution loop. After a successful GHN, check to see if we have employee id 7459, and if so call the rollback procedure. We will only do this on the first run of the program so as to force a rollback.

```
       DISPLAY 'SUCCESSFUL GET HOLD :'
           IO-EMPLOYEE-RECORD
       MOVE EMP-ID TO EMP-ID-VAL
       ADD +1 TO CHKP-COUNT
       IF CHKP-COUNT GREATER THAN OR EQUAL TO 5
           PERFORM P8000-TAKE-CHECKPOINT
           PERFORM P2000-RESET-POSITION
       END-IF
       IF EMP-ID = '7459'
           PERFORM P3000-ROLLBACK
           GOBACK
       END-IF
```

So here is our complete code listing. Review it carefully to be sure you understand what is happening.

```
       IDENTIFICATION DIVISION.
       PROGRAM-ID. COBIMSE.

      ***********************************************************
      *   WALK THROUGH THE EMPLOYEE (ROOT) SEGMENTS OF          *
      *   THE ENTIRE EMPLOYEE IMS DATABASE, AND ROLL BACK       *
      *   CHNGES WHEN A PARTICULAR CONDITION IS ENCOUNTERED*
      ***********************************************************

       ENVIRONMENT DIVISION.
       INPUT-OUTPUT SECTION.
       DATA DIVISION.

      ***********************************************************
```

```
      *  W O R K I N G   S T O R A G E   S E C T I O N   *
      **********************************************************

          WORKING-STORAGE SECTION.

          01  WS-FLAGS.
              05  SW-END-OF-DB-SWITCH     PIC X(1) VALUE 'N'.
                  88  SW-END-OF-DB                 VALUE 'Y'.
                  88  SW-NOT-END-OF-DB             VALUE 'N'.
              05  SW-IMS-RESTART-SW       PIC X(1) VALUE 'N'.
                  88  SW-IMS-RESTART               VALUE 'Y'.
                  88  SW-NOT-IMS-RESTART           VALUE 'N'.

          01  DLI-FUNCTIONS.
              05  DLI-FUNCISRT   PIC X(4) VALUE 'ISRT'.
              05  DLI-FUNCGU     PIC X(4) VALUE 'GU  '.
              05  DLI-FUNCGN     PIC X(4) VALUE 'GN  '.
              05  DLI-FUNCGHU    PIC X(4) VALUE 'GHU '.
              05  DLI-FUNCGHN    PIC X(4) VALUE 'GHN '.
              05  DLI-FUNCGNP    PIC X(4) VALUE 'GNP '.
              05  DLI-FUNCREPL   PIC X(4) VALUE 'REPL'.
              05  DLI-FUNCDLET   PIC X(4) VALUE 'DLET'.
              05  DLI-FUNCXRST   PIC X(4) VALUE 'XRST'.
              05  DLI-FUNCCHKP   PIC X(4) VALUE 'CHKP'.
              05  DLI-FUNCROLL   PIC X(4) VALUE 'ROLL'.

          01  IO-EMPLOYEE-RECORD.
              05  EMP-ID         PIC X(04).
              05  FILLER         PIC X(01).
              05  EMPL-LNAME     PIC X(30).
              05  FILLER         PIC X(01).
              05  EMPL-FNAME     PIC X(20).
              05  FILLER         PIC X(01).
              05  EMPL-YRS-SRV   PIC X(02).
              05  FILLER         PIC X(01).
              05  EMPL-PRM-DTE   PIC X(10).
              05  FILLER         PIC X(10).

          01  EMP-UNQUALIFIED-SSA.
              05  SEGNAME        PIC X(08) VALUE 'EMPLOYEE'.
              05  FILLER         PIC X(01) VALUE ' '.

          01  EMP-QUALIFIED-SSA.
              05  SEGNAME        PIC X(08) VALUE 'EMPLOYEE'.
              05  FILLER         PIC X(01) VALUE '('.
              05  FIELD          PIC X(08) VALUE 'EMPID'.
```

```
       05  OPER            PIC X(02) VALUE ' ='.
       05  EMP-ID-VAL      PIC X(04) VALUE '    '.
       05  FILLER          PIC X(01) VALUE ')'.

   01  SEG-IO-AREA         PIC X(80).

   01  IMS-RET-CODES.
       05  ONE             PIC S9(9) COMP VALUE +1.
       05  TWO             PIC S9(9) COMP VALUE +2.
       05  THREE           PIC S9(9) COMP VALUE +3.
       05  FOUR            PIC S9(9) COMP VALUE +4.
       05  FIVE            PIC S9(9) COMP VALUE +5.
       05  SIX             PIC S9(9) COMP VALUE +6.

   01  XRST-IOAREA.
       05  XRST-ID         PIC X(08) VALUE SPACES.
       05  FILLER          PIC X(04) VALUE SPACES.

   77  IO-AREALEN          PIC S9(9) USAGE IS BINARY VALUE 12.

   77  CHKP-ID             PIC X(08) VALUE 'IMSE-   '.

   77  CHKP-NBR            PIC 999   VALUE ZERO.
   77  CHKP-COUNT          PIC S9(9) USAGE IS BINARY VALUE ZERO.

   01  CHKP-MESSAGE.
       05  FILLER              PIC X(24) VALUE
           'COBIMSE   CHECK POINT NO:'.
       05  CHKP-MESS-NBR       PIC 999      VALUE ZERO.
       05  FILLER              PIC X(15)    VALUE '    ,AT REC#:'.
       05  FILLER              PIC X(10)    VALUE ' ,AT EMP#:'.
       05  CHKP-MESS-EMP       PIC X(04)    VALUE SPACES.

   01  IMS-CHKP-AREA-LTH.
       05  LEN             PIC S9(9) USAGE IS BINARY VALUE +7.

   01  IMS-CHKP-AREA.
       05  CHKP-EMP-ID     PIC X(04) VALUE SPACES.
       05  CHKP-NBR-LAST   PIC 999   VALUE 0.

   LINKAGE SECTION.

   01  IO-PCB.
       05  FILLER           PICTURE X(10).
       05  IO-STATUS-CODE   PICTURE XX.
       05  FILLER           PICTURE X(20).
```

```cobol
    01 PCB-MASK.
       03 DBD-NAME        PIC X(8).
       03 SEG-LEVEL       PIC XX.
       03 STATUS-CODE     PIC XX.
       03 PROC-OPT        PIC X(4).
       03 FILLER          PIC X(4).
       03 SEG-NAME        PIC X(8).
       03 KEY-FDBK        PIC S9(5) COMP.
       03 NUM-SENSEG      PIC S9(5) COMP.
       03 KEY-FDBK-AREA.
          05 EMPLOYEE-KEY  PIC X(04).
          05 EMPPAYHS-KEY  PIC X(08).

 PROCEDURE DIVISION.

     INITIALIZE IO-PCB PCB-MASK
     ENTRY 'DLITCBL' USING IO-PCB, PCB-MASK

     PERFORM P100-INITIALIZATION.
     PERFORM P200-MAINLINE.
     PERFORM P300-TERMINATION.
     GOBACK.

 P100-INITIALIZATION.

     DISPLAY '** PROGRAM COBIMSE START **'
     DISPLAY 'PROCESSING IN P100-INITIALIZATION'.

* CHECK FOR RESTART

     CALL 'CBLTDLI' USING SIX,
          DLI-FUNCXRST,
          PCB-MASK,
          IO-AREALEN,
          XRST-IOAREA,
          IMS-CHKP-AREA-LTH,
          IMS-CHKP-AREA

     IF STATUS-CODE NOT EQUAL SPACES THEN
        PERFORM P9000-DISPLAY-ERROR
        GOBACK
     END-IF

     IF XRST-ID NOT EQUAL SPACES THEN
        SET SW-IMS-RESTART TO TRUE
        MOVE CHKP-NBR-LAST TO CHKP-NBR
```

```cobol
            DISPLAY '*** COBIMSE IMS RESTART ***'
            DISPLAY '*   LAST CHECK POINT :' XRST-ID
            DISPLAY '*   EMPLOYEE NUMBER  :' CHKP-EMP-ID
        ELSE
            DISPLAY '****** COBIMSE IMS NORMAL START ***'
            PERFORM P8000-TAKE-CHECKPOINT
        END-IF.

   *    DO INITIAL DB READ FOR FIRST EMPLOYEE RECORD
   *    OR REPOSITION IF AN IMS RESTART.

        IF SW-IMS-RESTART THEN
            MOVE CHKP-EMP-ID TO EMP-ID-VAL
            PERFORM P2000-RESET-POSITION
        ELSE
            PERFORM P1000-GET-FIRST-ROOT

        END-IF.

    P200-MAINLINE.

        DISPLAY 'PROCESSING IN P200-MAINLINE'

   *    CHECK STATUS CODE AND FIRST RECORD

        IF SW-END-OF-DB THEN
            DISPLAY 'NO RECORDS TO PROCESS!!'
        ELSE

            PERFORM UNTIL SW-END-OF-DB

                CALL 'CBLTDLI' USING THREE,
                    DLI-FUNCDLET,
                    PCB-MASK,
                    IO-EMPLOYEE-RECORD

                IF STATUS-CODE NOT EQUAL SPACES THEN
                    PERFORM P9000-DISPLAY-ERROR
                    GOBACK
                ELSE
                    DISPLAY 'SUCCESSFUL DELETE OF EMPLOYEE ' EMP-ID
                    MOVE EMP-ID TO CHKP-EMP-ID
                END-IF

   *    GET THE NEXT RECORD
```

```
            CALL 'CBLTDLI' USING FOUR,
                 DLI-FUNCGHN,
                 PCB-MASK,
                 IO-EMPLOYEE-RECORD,
                 EMP-UNQUALIFIED-SSA

            IF STATUS-CODE = 'GB' THEN
               SET SW-END-OF-DB TO TRUE
               DISPLAY 'END OF DATABASE'
            ELSE
               IF STATUS-CODE NOT EQUAL SPACES THEN
                  PERFORM P9000-DISPLAY-ERROR
                  SET SW-END-OF-DB TO TRUE
                  GOBACK
               ELSE
                  DISPLAY 'SUCCESSFUL GET HOLD :'
                      IO-EMPLOYEE-RECORD
                  MOVE EMP-ID TO EMP-ID-VAL
                  ADD +1 TO CHKP-COUNT
                  IF CHKP-COUNT GREATER THAN OR EQUAL TO 5
                     PERFORM P8000-TAKE-CHECKPOINT
                     PERFORM P2000-RESET-POSITION
                  END-IF
                  IF EMP-ID = '7459'
                     PERFORM P3000-ROLLBACK
                  END-IF
               END-IF
            END-IF

       END-PERFORM.

   DISPLAY 'FINISHED PROCESSING IN P200-MAINLINE'.

P300-TERMINATION.

   DISPLAY 'PROCESSING IN P300-TERMINATION'
   ADD +1 TO CHKP-COUNT
   PERFORM P8000-TAKE-CHECKPOINT
   DISPLAY '** COBIMSE - SUCCESSFULLY ENDED **'.

P1000-GET-FIRST-ROOT.

   CALL 'CBLTDLI' USING FOUR,
        DLI-FUNCGHN,
        PCB-MASK,
        IO-EMPLOYEE-RECORD,
```

```
            EMP-UNQUALIFIED-SSA

      IF STATUS-CODE = ' ' THEN
         NEXT SENTENCE
      ELSE
         IF STATUS-CODE = 'GB' THEN
            SET SW-END-OF-DB TO TRUE
            DISPLAY 'END OF DATABASE :'
         ELSE
            PERFORM P9000-DISPLAY-ERROR
            GOBACK
         END-IF.

P2000-RESET-POSITION.

      DISPLAY 'PROCESSING IN P2000-RESET-POSITION'

      CALL 'CBLTDLI' USING ,
            DLI-FUNCGHU,
            PCB-MASK,
            IO-EMPLOYEE-RECORD,
            EMP-QUALIFIED-SSA

      IF STATUS-CODE NOT EQUAL SPACES THEN
         PERFORM P9000-DISPLAY-ERROR
         GOBACK
      ELSE
         DISPLAY 'SUCCESSFUL REPOSITION AT EMP ID ' EMP-ID.

P3000-ROLLBACK.

      DISPLAY 'PROCESSING IN P3000-ROLLBACK'.

      CALL 'CBLTDLI' USING ONE,
            DLI-FUNCROLL.

P8000-TAKE-CHECKPOINT.

    DISPLAY 'PROCESSING IN P8000-TAKE-CHECKPOINT'
    ADD +1            TO CHKP-NBR
    MOVE CHKP-NBR     TO CHKP-NBR-LAST
    MOVE CHKP-NBR-LAST TO CHKP-ID(6:3)
    DISPLAY 'CHECKPOINT ID IS ' CHKP-ID
    MOVE EMP-ID       TO CHKP-EMP-ID

    CALL 'CBLTDLI' USING SIX,
```

```
                DLI-FUNCCHKP,
                IO-PCB,
                IO-AREALEN,
                CHKP-ID,
                IMS-CHKP-AREA-LTH,
                IMS-CHKP-AREA

        IF IO-STATUS-CODE NOT EQUAL SPACES THEN
            DISPLAY 'TOOK AN ERROR DOING THE CHECKPOINT'
            DISPLAY 'IO-STATUS-CODE ' IO-STATUS-CODE
            PERFORM P9000-DISPLAY-ERROR
            GOBACK
        ELSE
            MOVE 0 TO CHKP-COUNT
            MOVE CHKP-NBR       TO CHKP-MESS-NBR
            MOVE CHKP-EMP-ID    TO CHKP-MESS-EMP
            DISPLAY CHKP-MESSAGE
        END-IF.

    P9000-DISPLAY-ERROR.

        DISPLAY 'ERROR ENCOUNTERED - DETAIL FOLLOWS'
        DISPLAY 'SEG-IO-AREA      :' SEG-IO-AREA
        DISPLAY 'DBD-NAME1:'     DBD-NAME
        DISPLAY 'SEG-LEVEL1:'    SEG-LEVEL
        DISPLAY 'STATUS-CODE:'   STATUS-CODE
        DISPLAY 'PROC-OPT1 :'    PROC-OPT
        DISPLAY 'SEG-NAME1 :'    SEG-NAME
        DISPLAY 'KEY-FDBK1 :'    KEY-FDBK
        DISPLAY 'NUM-SENSEG1:'   NUM-SENSEG
        DISPLAY 'KEY-FDBK-AREA1:' KEY-FDBK-AREA.

*       END OF SOURCE CODE
```

Compile and link, then run the program. The program will abend with IMS user code **U0778** because of the ROLL call.[5] Here is the output:

```
** PROGRAM COBIMSE START **
PROCESSING IN P100-INITIALIZATION
****** COBIMSE IMS NORMAL START ***
PROCESSING IN P8000-TAKE-CHECKPOINT
CHECKPOINT ID IS IMSE-001
COBIMSE   CHECK POINT NO:001        ,AT REC#:   ,AT EMP#:
```

---

[5] If you prefer not to take a hard abend, instead of issuing the ROLL IMS call you can issue ROLB. ROLB backs out changes the same as ROLL, but ROLB returns control to the application program instead of abending.

```
PROCESSING IN P200-MAINLINE
SUCCESSFUL DELETE OF EMPLOYEE 1111
SUCCESSFUL GET HOLD :1122 JENKINS                  DEBORAH                05
SUCCESSFUL DELETE OF EMPLOYEE 1122
SUCCESSFUL GET HOLD :3217 JOHNSON                  EDWARD                 04
SUCCESSFUL DELETE OF EMPLOYEE 3217
SUCCESSFUL GET HOLD :4175 TURNBULL                 FRED                   01
SUCCESSFUL DELETE OF EMPLOYEE 4175
SUCCESSFUL GET HOLD :4720 SCHULTZ                  TIM                    09
SUCCESSFUL DELETE OF EMPLOYEE 4720
SUCCESSFUL GET HOLD :4836 SMITH                    SANDRA                 03
PROCESSING IN P8000-TAKE-CHECKPOINT
CHECKPOINT ID IS IMSE-002
COBIMSE   CHECK POINT NO:002      ,AT REC#:   ,AT EMP#:4836
PROCESSING IN P2000-RESET-POSITION
SUCCESSFUL REPOSITION AT EMP ID 4836
SUCCESSFUL DELETE OF EMPLOYEE 4836
SUCCESSFUL GET HOLD :6288 WILLARD                  JOE                    06
SUCCESSFUL DELETE OF EMPLOYEE 6288
SUCCESSFUL GET HOLD :7459 STEWART                  BETTY                  07
PROCESSING IN P3000-ROLLBACK
```

At this point, we can verify that the first 5 records got deleted, and we can also verify that after the last checkpoint, all deleted records were backed (meaning they are still on the database).

```
Browse          USER01.IMS.EMPLOYEE.DATA               Top of 4
Command ===>                                           Scroll PAGE
                       Type DATA     RBA               Format CHAR
                                     Col 1
----+----10---+----2----+----3----+----4----+----5----+----6----+----7----+----
****  Top of data   ****
......4836 SMITH                 SANDRA            03 2017-01-01 02
......6288 WILLARD               JOE               06 2016-01-01 20
......7459 STEWART               BETTY             07 2016-07-31 01
......9134 FRANKLIN              BRIANNA           00 2016-10-01 93
****  End of data   ****
```

The next step is to remove the code in COBIMSE that forced the rollback, then restart the program. Go ahead and remove or comment out the code, recompile and then we'll set up our restart JCL.

The PARM should look like this. Note that the IMSE-002 is the last successful checkpoint in the prior run. You can verify this by looking at the output from the previous run. Here is our restart parm override:

```
//GO       EXEC PGM=DFSRRC00,REGION=4M,
//    PARM=(DLI,&MBR,&PSB,7,0000,,0,'IMSE-002',N,0,0,,,N,N,,N,)
```

Now run the program, and here is the output.

```
** PROGRAM COBIMSE START **
PROCESSING IN P100-INITIALIZATION
*** COBIMSE IMS RESTART ***
*   LAST CHECK POINT :IMSE-002
*   EMPLOYEE NUMBER  :4836
PROCESSING IN P2000-RESET-POSITION
SUCCESSFUL REPOSITION AT EMP ID 4836
PROCESSING IN P200-MAINLINE
SUCCESSFUL DELETE OF EMPLOYEE 4836
SUCCESSFUL GET HOLD :6288 WILLARD                      JOE              06
SUCCESSFUL DELETE OF EMPLOYEE 6288
SUCCESSFUL GET HOLD :7459 STEWART                      BETTY            07
SUCCESSFUL DELETE OF EMPLOYEE 7459
SUCCESSFUL GET HOLD :9134 FRANKLIN                     BRIANNA          00
SUCCESSFUL DELETE OF EMPLOYEE 9134
END OF DATABASE
FINISHED PROCESSING IN P200-MAINLINE
PROCESSING IN P300-TERMINATION
PROCESSING IN P8000-TAKE-CHECKPOINT
CHECKPOINT ID IS IMSE-003
COBIMSE   CHECK POINT NO:003      ,AT REC#:   ,AT EMP#:9134
** COBIMSE - SUCCESSFULLY ENDED **
```

We correctly restarted at employee id 4836, and then processed in GHN mode from there on. This is what should have happened. Now the database is empty, which we can confirm by trying to browse it.

```
VSAM POINT RC X"08", Error Code X"20"
VSAM GET RC X"08", Error Code X"58"
Function terminated
***
```

You now have a basic model for doing checkpoint restart. Frankly, checkpoint restart is done somewhat differently in each of the major environments I've worked in. Typically larger companies use third party products (such as BMC tools) to keep track of checkpoints and facilitate recovery. You may need to learn a bit more to use the third party products. The examples I've provided, although plain vanilla, work fine without any third party products.

Here's the PLI version of this program.

```
PLIIMSE: PROCEDURE (IO_PTR_PCB,DB_PTR_PCB) OPTIONS(MAIN);
/***************************************************************
* PROGRAM NAME: PLIIMSE - WALK THROUGH THE EMPLOYEE (ROOT)     *
*                         SEGMENTS OF THE EMPLOYEE IMS DATABASE,*
*                         AND DELETE EACH ONE. ROLL BACK CHANGES*
*                         WHEN A PARTICULAR EMP ID IS ENCOUNTERED. *
****************************************************************/

/***************************************************************
```

```
/*                    W O R K I N G    S T O R A G E                    */
/**********************************************************************/

     DCL SW_END_OF_DB              STATIC BIT(01) INIT('0'B);
     DCL SW_IMS_RESTART            STATIC BIT(01) INIT('0'B);
     DCL ONCODE                    BUILTIN;
     DCL DB_PTR_PCB                POINTER;
     DCL IO_PTR_PCB                POINTER;

     DCL PLITDLI                   EXTERNAL ENTRY;

     DCL 01 DLI_FUNCTIONS,
            05 DLI_FUNCISRT        CHAR(04) INIT ('ISRT'),
            05 DLI_FUNCGU          CHAR(04) INIT ('GU  '),
            05 DLI_FUNCGN          CHAR(04) INIT ('GN  '),
            05 DLI_FUNCGHU         CHAR(04) INIT ('GHU '),
            05 DLI_FUNCGNP         CHAR(04) INIT ('GNP '),
            05 DLI_FUNCREPL        CHAR(04) INIT ('REPL'),
            05 DLI_FUNCDLET        CHAR(04) INIT ('DLET'),
            05 DLI_FUNCXRST        CHAR(04) INIT ('XRST'),
            05 DLI_FUNCCHKP        CHAR(04) INIT ('CHKP'),
            05 DLI_FUNCROLL        CHAR(04) INIT ('ROLL');

     DCL 01 IO_EMPLOYEE_RECORD,
            05 EMPL_ID             CHAR(04),
            05 FILLER1             CHAR(01),
            05 EMPL_LNAME          CHAR(30),
            05 FILLER2             CHAR(01),
            05 EMPL_FNAME          CHAR(20),
            05 FILLER3             CHAR(01),
            05 EMPL_YRS_SRV        CHAR(02),
            05 FILLER4             CHAR(01),
            05 EMPL_PRM_DTE        CHAR(10),
            05 FILLER5             CHAR(10);

     DCL 01 EMP_UNQUALIFIED_SSA,
            05 SEGNAME             CHAR(08) INIT ('EMPLOYEE'),
            05 FILLER7             CHAR(01) INIT (' ');

     DCL 01 EMP_QUALIFIED_SSA,
            05 SEGNAME             CHAR(08) INIT('EMPLOYEE'),
            05 FILLER8             CHAR(01) INIT('('),
            05 FIELD               CHAR(08) INIT('EMPID'),
            05 OPER                CHAR(02) INIT(' ='),
            05 EMP_ID_VAL          CHAR(04) INIT('    '),
            05 FILLER9             CHAR(01) INIT(')');

     DCL ONE                       FIXED BIN (31) INIT(1);
     DCL TWO                       FIXED BIN (31) INIT(2);
     DCL THREE                     FIXED BIN (31) INIT(3);
     DCL FOUR                      FIXED BIN (31) INIT(4);
     DCL FIVE                      FIXED BIN (31) INIT(5);
     DCL SIX                       FIXED BIN (31) INIT(6);
```

```
        DCL 01 XRST_IOAREA,
               05 XRST_ID         CHAR(08) INIT('        '),
               05 FILLER10        CHAR(04) INIT('    ');

        DCL XRST_IO_AREALEN       FIXED BIN(31) INIT (12);
        DCL IO_AREALEN            FIXED BIN(31) INIT (08);
        DCL CHKP_ID               CHAR(08) INIT( 'IMSE-   ');
        DCL CHKP_NBR              PIC '999' INIT('000');
        DCL CHKP_COUNT            FIXED BIN (31) INIT(0);

        DCL 01 CHKP_MESSAGE,
               05 FILLER11        CHAR(24)   INIT(
                  'COBIMSE  CHECK POINT NO:'),
               05 CHKP_MESS_NBR   PIC '999',
               05 FILLER12        CHAR(15)   INIT( ',AT INPUT REC#:'),
               05 CHKP_MESS_REC   PIC 'ZZZZZ9',
               05 FILLER13        CHAR(10)   INIT(',AT EMP#:'),
               05 CHKP_MESS_EMP   CHAR(08)   INIT(' ');

        DCL IMS_CHKP_AREA_LTH     FIXED BIN (31) INIT(07);

        DCL 01 IMS_CHKP_AREA,
               05 CHKP_EMP_ID     CHAR(04)    INIT('0000'),
               05 CHKP_NBR_LAST   CHAR(03)    INIT('000');

        DCL 01 IO_PCB             BASED(IO_PTR_PCB),
               05 FILLER97        CHAR(10)  INIT(' '),
               05 IO_STATUS_CODE  CHAR(02)  INIT (' ');

        DCL 01 PCB_MASK           BASED(DB_PTR_PCB),
               05 DBD_NAME        CHAR(08),
               05 SEG_LEVEL       CHAR(02),
               05 STATUS_CODE     CHAR(02),
               05 PROC_OPT        CHAR(04),
               05 FILLER99        FIXED BIN (31),
               05 SEG_NAME        CHAR(08),
               05 KEY_FDBK        FIXED BIN (31),
               05 NUM_SENSEG      FIXED BIN (31),
               05 KEY_FDBK_AREA,
                  10 KFB_EMPLOYEE_ID CHAR(04);

/********************************************************************
/*              P R O G R A M   M A I N L I N E                     *
********************************************************************/

CALL P100_INITIALIZATION;
CALL P200_MAINLINE;
CALL P300_TERMINATION;

P100_INITIALIZATION: PROC;

   PUT SKIP LIST ('PLIIMSE: TRAVERSE EMPLOYEE DATABASE ROOT SEGS');
```

```
        PUT SKIP LIST ('PROCESSING IN P100_INITIALIZATION');
        IO_PCB   = '';
        PCB_MASK = '';
        IO_EMPLOYEE_RECORD  = '';

        /* CHECK FOR RESTART */

        CALL PLITDLI (SIX,
                      DLI_FUNCXRST,
                      IO_PCB,
                      XRST_IO_AREALEN,
                      XRST_IOAREA,
                      IMS_CHKP_AREA_LTH,
                      IMS_CHKP_AREA);

        IF IO_STATUS_CODE ¬= ' ' THEN
           DO;
              CALL P9000_DISPLAY_ERROR;
              RETURN;
           END;

        IF XRST_ID ¬= ' ' THEN
           DO;
              SW_IMS_RESTART = '1'B;
              CHKP_NBR = CHKP_NBR_LAST;
              PUT SKIP LIST ('*** COBIMSE IMS RESTART ***');
              PUT SKIP LIST ('*  LAST CHECK POINT :' || XRST_ID);
              PUT SKIP LIST ('*  EMPLOYEE NUMBER  :' || CHKP_EMP_ID);
           END;
        ELSE
           DO;
              PUT SKIP LIST ('****** COBIMSE IMS NORMAL START ***');
              CALL P8000_TAKE_CHECKPOINT;
           END;

        IF SW_IMS_RESTART THEN
           DO;
              EMP_ID_VAL = CHKP_EMP_ID;
              CALL P2000_RESET_POSITION;
           END;
        ELSE
           CALL P1000_GET_FIRST_ROOT;

END P100_INITIALIZATION;

P200_MAINLINE: PROC;

   /*  MAIN LOOP - CYCLE THROUGH ALL ROOT SEGMENTS IN THE DB,
                   DISPLAYING THE DATA RETRIEVED                 */

   IF SW_END_OF_DB THEN
      PUT SKIP LIST ('NO RECORDS TO PROCESS!!');
   ELSE
```

```pli
DO WHILE (¬SW_END_OF_DB);
   PUT SKIP LIST ('SUCCESSFUL GET-HOLD :'
      || EMPL_ID);

   /* DELETE THE SWGMENT */

   CALL PLITDLI (THREE,
                 DLI_FUNCDLET,
                 PCB_MASK,
                 IO_EMPLOYEE_RECORD);

   IF STATUS_CODE ¬= ' ' THEN
      DO;
         CALL P9000_DISPLAY_ERROR;
         RETURN;
      END;
   ELSE
      PUT SKIP LIST ('SUCCESSFUL DELETE OF EMP ' || EMPL_ID);

   /* NOW GET THE NEXT ROOT TO DELETE */

   CALL PLITDLI (FOUR,
                 DLI_FUNCGN,
                 PCB_MASK,
                 IO_EMPLOYEE_RECORD,
                 EMP_UNQUALIFIED_SSA);

   IF STATUS_CODE = ' ' THEN
      DO;
         PUT SKIP LIST ('SUCCESSFUL GET HOLD: ' || EMPL_ID);
         EMP_ID_VAL = EMPL_ID;
         CHKP_COUNT = CHKP_COUNT + 1;
         IF CHKP_COUNT >= 5 THEN
            DO;
               CALL P8000_TAKE_CHECKPOINT;
               CALL P2000_RESET_POSITION;
            END;
      /* IF EMPL_ID = '7459' THEN
            CALL P3000_ROLLBACK;   */
      END;
   ELSE
      IF STATUS_CODE = 'GB' THEN
         DO;
            SW_END_OF_DB = '1'B;
            PUT SKIP LIST ('** END OF DATABASE');
         END;
      ELSE
         DO;
            CALL P9000_DISPLAY_ERROR;
            RETURN;
         END;

END; /* DO WHILE */
```

```
        PUT SKIP LIST ('FINISHED PROCESSING IN P200_MAINLINE');

END P200_MAINLINE;

P300_TERMINATION: PROC;

        PUT SKIP LIST ('PROCESSING IN P300_TERMINATION');

        CHKP_COUNT = CHKP_COUNT + 1;
        CALL P8000_TAKE_CHECKPOINT;

        PUT SKIP LIST ('PLIIMSE - SUCCESSFULLY ENDED');

END P300_TERMINATION;

P1000_GET_FIRST_ROOT: PROC;

        PUT SKIP LIST ('PROCESSING IN P1000_GET_FIRST_ROOT');

    /* DO INITIAL DB READ FOR FIRST EMPLOYEE RECORD */

        CALL PLITDLI (FOUR,
                      DLI_FUNCGHN,
                      PCB_MASK,
                      IO_EMPLOYEE_RECORD,
                      EMP_UNQUALIFIED_SSA);

        IF STATUS_CODE = '  ' THEN;
        ELSE
           IF STATUS_CODE = 'GB' THEN
              DO;
                  SW_END_OF_DB = '1'B;
                  PUT SKIP LIST ('** END OF DATABASE');
              END;
           ELSE
              DO;
                  CALL P9000_DISPLAY_ERROR;
                  RETURN;
              END;

END P1000_GET_FIRST_ROOT;

P2000_RESET_POSITION: PROC;

        PUT SKIP LIST ('PROCESSING IN P2000_RESET_POSITION');

        CALL PLITDLI (FOUR,
                      DLI_FUNCGHU,
                      PCB_MASK,
                      IO_EMPLOYEE_RECORD,
                      EMP_QUALIFIED_SSA);
```

```
        IF STATUS_CODE ¬= ' ' THEN
            DO;
                CALL P9000_DISPLAY_ERROR;
                RETURN;
            END;
        ELSE
            PUT SKIP LIST ('SUCCESSFUL REPOSITION AT EMP ID ' || EMPL_ID);

END P2000_RESET_POSITION;

P3000_ROLLBACK: PROC;

    PUT SKIP LIST ('PROCESSING IN P3000_ROLLBACK');

    CALL PLITDLI (ONE,
          DLI_FUNCROLL);

    IF IO_STATUS_CODE ¬= ' ' THEN
        DO;
            CALL P9000_DISPLAY_ERROR;
            RETURN;
        END;
    ELSE
        PUT SKIP LIST ('SUCCESSFUL ROLLBACK TO CHKPID ' || CHKP_ID);

END P3000_ROLLBACK;

P8000_TAKE_CHECKPOINT: PROC;

    PUT SKIP LIST ('PROCESSING IN P8000_TAKE_CHECKPOINT');

    CHKP_NBR                = CHKP_NBR + 1;
    CHKP_NBR_LAST           = CHKP_NBR;
    SUBSTR(CHKP_ID,6,3)     = CHKP_NBR_LAST;
    CHKP_EMP_ID             = EMPL_ID;

    PUT SKIP LIST ('IO_AREALEN ' || IO_AREALEN);
    PUT SKIP LIST ('IMS_CHKP_AREA_LTH ' || IMS_CHKP_AREA_LTH);

    PUT SKIP LIST ('CHKP_ID = ' || CHKP_ID);
    PUT SKIP LIST (' ');

    CALL PLITDLI (SIX,
                  DLI_FUNCCHKP,
                  IO_PCB,
                  IO_AREALEN,
                  CHKP_ID,
                  IMS_CHKP_AREA_LTH,
                  IMS_CHKP_AREA);

    IF IO_STATUS_CODE ¬= ' ' THEN
        DO;
            PUT SKIP LIST ('TOOK AN ERROR DOING THE CHECKPOINT');
```

```
                PUT SKIP LIST ('IO_STATUS_CODE ' || IO_STATUS_CODE);
                CALL P9000_DISPLAY_ERROR;
                RETURN;
            END;
        ELSE
            DO;
                CHKP_COUNT = 0;
                CHKP_MESS_NBR = CHKP_NBR;
                CHKP_MESS_EMP = CHKP_EMP_ID;
                PUT SKIP LIST (CHKP_MESSAGE);
            END;

END P8000_TAKE_CHECKPOINT;

P9000_DISPLAY_ERROR: PROC;

    PUT SKIP LIST ('ERROR ENCOUNTERED - DETAIL FOLLOWS');
    PUT SKIP LIST ('SEG_IO_AREA    :' || SEG_IO_AREA);
    PUT SKIP LIST ('DBD_NAME1:' ||  DBD_NAME);
    PUT SKIP LIST ('SEG_LEVEL1:' || SEG_LEVEL);
    PUT SKIP LIST ('STATUS_CODE:' || STATUS_CODE);
    PUT SKIP LIST ('PROC_OPT1 :' || PROC_OPT);
    PUT SKIP LIST ('SEG_NAME1 :' || SEG_NAME);
    PUT SKIP LIST ('KEY_FDBK1 :' || KEY_FDBK);
    PUT SKIP LIST ('NUM_SENSEG1:' || NUM_SENSEG);
    PUT SKIP LIST ('KEY_FDBK_AREA1:' || KEY_FDBK_AREA);

END P9000_DISPLAY_ERROR;

END PLIIMSE;
```

That pretty well wraps up basic IMS programming. There are plenty of other features you can use, but that will depend on your work environment. Every shop and application is different. Good luck with it, and enjoy!

IMS Programming Guidelines

Consider the COBOL and PLI code examples in this text to be my own guidelines for coding IMS programs. There are more formal guidelines provided by IBM on their web site. [iv]

Chapter Two Questions

1. What is the name of the interface program you call from a COBOL program to perform IMS operations?

2. Here are some IMS return codes and . Explain briefly what each of them means: blank, GE, GB, II

3. What is an SSA?

4. Briefly explain these entities: DBD, PSB, PCB?

5. What is the use of CMPAT parameter in PSB ?

6. In IMS, what is the difference between a key field and a search field?

7. What does PROCOPT mean in a PCB?

8. What are the four basic parameters of a DLI retrieval call?

9. What are Qualified SSA and Unqualified SSA?

10. Which PSB parameter in a PSBGEN specifies the language in which the application program is written?

11. What does SENSEG stand for and how is it used in a PCB?

12. What storage mechanism/format is used for IMS index databases?

13. What are the DL/I commands to add, change and remove a segment?

14. What return code will you receive from IMS if the DL/I call was successful?

15. If you want to retrieve the last occurrence of a child segment under its parent, what command code could you use?

16. When would you use a GU call?

17. When would you use a GHU call?

18. What is the difference between running an IMS program as DLI and BMP ?

19. When would you use a GNP call?

20. Which IMS call is used to restart an abended program?

21. How do you establish parentage on a segment occurrence?

22. What is a checkpoint?

23. How do you update the primary key of an IMS segment?

24. Do you need to use a qualified SSA with REPL/DLET calls?

25. What is a root segment?

26. What are command codes?

Chapter Three: Intermediate DB2
Data Setup

The DB2 features demonstrated in this section can be understood without any kind of preliminary data setup. However, if you want to follow along and do hands-on training with the examples, you must create some DB2 objects and load some data. Follow these steps to create the DB2 objects and data.

Create the base EMPLOYEE table.

```
CREATE TABLE HRSCHEMA.EMPLOYEE(
EMP_ID INT NOT NULL,
EMP_LAST_NAME VARCHAR(30) NOT NULL,
EMP_FIRST_NAME VARCHAR(20) NOT NULL,
EMP_SERVICE_YEARS INT NOT NULL WITH DEFAULT 0,
EMP_PROMOTION_DATE DATE,
PRIMARY KEY(EMP_ID));
```

We also need to create a unique index to support the primary key:

```
CREATE UNIQUE INDEX NDX_EMPLOYEE
ON EMPLOYEE (EMP_ID);
```

Now let's insert some data.

```
INSERT INTO HRSCHEMA.EMPLOYEE
VALUES (3217,
'JOHNSON',
'EDWARD',
4,
'01/01/2017');

INSERT INTO HRSCHEMA.EMPLOYEE
VALUES (7459,
'STEWART',
'BETTY',
7,
'07/31/2016')

INSERT INTO HRSCHEMA.EMPLOYEE
VALUES (9134,
'FRANKLIN',
'BRIANNA',
DEFAULT,
NULL);

INSERT INTO HRSCHEMA.EMPLOYEE
VALUES (4720,
```

```
'SCHULTZ',
'TIM',
9,
'01/01/2017');

INSERT INTO HRSCHEMA.EMPLOYEE
VALUES (6288,
'WILLARD',
'JOE',
6,
'01/01/2016');


INSERT INTO HRSCHEMA.EMPLOYEE
VALUES
(1122,
'JENKINS',
'DEBORAH',
5,
NULL);


INSERT INTO EMPLOYEE
VALUES (3333,
'FORD',
'JAMES',
7,
 '10/01/2015');

INSERT INTO EMPLOYEE
VALUES (7777,
'HARRIS',
'ELISA',
2,
NULL);



CREATE TABLE EMP_PAY(
EMP_ID INT NOT NULL,
EMP_REGULAR_PAY DECIMAL (8,2) NOT NULL,
EMP_BONUS_PAY DECIMAL    (8,2));

INSERT INTO HRSCHEMA.EMP_PAY
VALUES (3217, 80000.00, 4000);

INSERT INTO HRSCHEMA.EMP_PAY
VALUES (7459, 80000.00, 4000);

INSERT INTO HRSCHEMA.EMP_PAY
VALUES (9134, 75000.00, 2500);

INSERT INTO HRSCHEMA.EMP_PAY
VALUES (4720, 80000.00, 2500);
```

```sql
INSERT INTO HRSCHEMA.EMP_PAY
VALUES (6288, 70000.00, 2000);


CREATE TABLE EMP_PAY_CHECK(
EMP_ID INT NOT NULL,
EMP_REGULAR_PAY  DECIMAL (8,2) NOT NULL,
EMP_SEMIMTH_PAY DECIMAL (8,2) NOT NULL)
IN TSHR;

INSERT INTO EMP_PAY_CHECK
(SELECT EMP_ID,
EMP_REGULAR_PAY,
EMP_REGULAR_PAY / 24 FROM EMP_PAY);

CREATE TABLE EMP_PAY_HIST(
EMP_ID INT NOT NULL,
EMP_PAY_DATE  DATE NOT NULL,
EMP_PAY_AMT   DECIMAL (8,2) NOT NULL)
IN TSHR;

INSERT INTO EMP_PAY_HIST
SELECT EMP_ID,
 '01/15/2017',
 EMP_SEMIMTH_PAY
 FROM EMP_PAY_CHECK;

INSERT INTO EMP_PAY_HIST
SELECT EMP_ID,
 '01/31/2017',
 EMP_SEMIMTH_PAY
    FROM EMP_PAY_CHECK;

INSERT INTO EMP_PAY_HIST
SELECT EMP_ID,
 '02/15/2017',
EMP_SEMIMTH_PAY
   FROM EMP_PAY_CHECK;

   INSERT INTO EMP_PAY_HIST
   SELECT EMP_ID,
    '02/28/2017',
    EMP_SEMIMTH_PAY
    FROM EMP_PAY_CHECK;

   INSERT INTO EMP_PAY_CHECK
   VALUES
   (7033,
   77000.00,
   77000 / 24);
```

Stored Procedures

A stored procedure is a set of compiled statements that is stored on the DB2 server. The stored procedures typically include SQL statements to access data in a DB2 table. Stored procedures are similar to sub-programs in that they can be called by other programs. Specifically, stored procedures are invoked by the CALL statement as in:

```
CALL <stored procedure name><(parameters)>
```

Stored procedures can be called from an application program such as COBOL, from a Rexx exec, from QMF or from Data Studio. Stored procedures are created using the CREATE PROCEDURE statement. The details of the stored procedure depend on whether it is external or native. We'll look at examples of each.

Types of stored procedures

There are three types of stored procedures:

- Native SQL Procedure
- External stored procedure
- External SQL Procedure

Native SQL procedures

A native SQL procedure is a procedure that consists exclusively of SQL statements, and is created entirely within the CREATE PROCEDURE statement. Native SQL procedures are not associated with an external program.

External stored procedures

An external stored procedure is one written in a programming language such as COBOL or Java.

External SQL procedures

An external SQL procedure is a procedure that is composed of SQL statements, and is created and implemented like an external stored procedure (including having an external program).

External Stored Procedure Programming Languages.

When you want to create an external stored procedure, the the following programming languages can be used:

- Assembler
- C

- C++
- COBOL
- REXX
- PL/I

Examples of Stored Procedures

Native SQL Stored Procedure

Let's start with a procedure that will return the first and last names of an employee, given an employee number. We will pass employee number as an IN parameter and receive the employee's first and last names as OUT parameters. Since we are only using SQL statements, we will specify the SQL language in the definition, and specify our intent to read data.

```
CREATE PROCEDURE GETEMP (IN EMP_NO INT,
  OUT EMP_LNAME VARCHAR(30),
  OUT EMP_FNAME VARCHAR(20))

LANGUAGE SQL
READS SQL DATA

  BEGIN
    SELECT EMP_LAST_NAME,
           EMP_FIRST_NAME
    INTO EMP_LNAME,
         EMP_FNAME
    FROM HRSCHEMA.EMPLOYEE
    WHERE EMP_ID = EMP_NO;
  END
```

Now we need a program to call the stored procedure. Here is a COBOL program to do that.

```
       IDENTIFICATION DIVISION.
       PROGRAM-ID. COBEMP6.

      **********************************************************
      *     PROGRAM USING DB2 CALL TO A NATIVE                  *
      *     STORED PROCEDURE.                                   *
      **********************************************************

       ENVIRONMENT DIVISION.
       DATA DIVISION.
       WORKING-STORAGE SECTION.
```

```
01 HV-EMP-VARIABLES.
    10  HV-ID            PIC S9(9) USAGE COMP.
    10  HV-LAST-NAME     PIC X(30).
    10  HV-FIRST-NAME    PIC X(20).

01 ERR-REC.
    05  FILLER           PIC X(10) VALUE 'SQLCODE = '.
    05  SQLCODE-VIEW     PIC -999.
    05  FILLER           PIC X(005) VALUE SPACES.
    05  ERR-TAB          PIC X(016).
    05  ERR-PARA         PIC X(015).
    05  ERR-DETAIL       PIC X(040).

77 ERR-TXT-LGTH          PIC S9(9) USAGE COMP VALUE +72.

01 ERR-MSG.
    05  ERR-MSG-LGTH     PIC S9(04) COMP VALUE +864.
    05  ERR-MSG-TXT      PIC X(072) OCCURS 12 TIMES
                                    INDEXED BY ERR-NDX.

    EXEC SQL
       INCLUDE SQLCA
    END-EXEC.

    EXEC SQL
       INCLUDE EMPLOYEE
    END-EXEC.


PROCEDURE DIVISION.

MAIN-PARA.
    DISPLAY "SAMPLE COBOL PROGRAM: CALL STORED PROCEDURE".

*   SELECT AN EMPLOYEE

    MOVE 3217 TO HV-ID

    EXEC SQL
       CALL HRSCHEMA.GETEMP(:HV-ID,
                            :HV-LAST-NAME,
                            :HV-FIRST-NAME)
    END-EXEC.

    IF SQLCODE IS NOT EQUAL TO ZERO

       MOVE SQLCODE TO SQLCODE-VIEW
       MOVE 'GETEMP2 ' TO ERR-TAB
       MOVE 'MAIN'    TO ERR-PARA
       MOVE HV-ID     TO ERR-DETAIL
       PERFORM P9999-SQL-ERROR
    ELSE
```

```
        DISPLAY   'PROC CALL SUCCESSFULL ' HV-LAST-NAME
                  HV-FIRST-NAME HV-ID
        DISPLAY SQLCODE

    END-IF


  P9999-SQL-ERROR.

    DISPLAY ERR-REC.

    CALL 'DSNTIAR' USING SQLCA,
                ERR-MSG,
                ERR-TXT-LGTH.

    IF RETURN-CODE IS EQUAL TO ZERO

        PERFORM P9999-DISP-ERR
           VARYING ERR-NDX FROM 1 BY 1
           UNTIL ERR-NDX > 12

    ELSE
        DISPLAY 'DSNTIAR ERROR CODE = ' RETURN-CODE
        STOP RUN.

  P9999-DISP-ERR.

       DISPLAY ERR-MSG-TXT(ERR-NDX).

  P9999-DISP-ERR-EXIT.
```

Now when we run the procedure we get the following results:

```
SAMPLE COBOL PROGRAM: CALL STORED PROCEDURE
PROC CALL SUCCESSFULL JOHNSON EDWARD 3217
```

The PLI version of the program is as follows:

```
PLIEMP6: PROCEDURE OPTIONS(MAIN) REORDER;
/****************************************************************
 *                                                              *
 * PROGRAM NAME :   PLIEMP6 - PROGRAM TO CALL A STORED PROCEDURE. *
 *                                                              *
 ****************************************************************/

/****************************************************************
 *              E X T E R N A L    E N T R I E S                *
 ****************************************************************/

    DCL DSNTIAR ENTRY OPTIONS(ASM INTER RETCODE);
```

```pli
/******************************************************************
*                  W O R K I N G   S T O R A G E                  *
******************************************************************/

   DCL HV_ID                FIXED BIN (31) INIT (0);
   DCL HV_LAST_NAME         CHAR(30) INIT (' ');
   DCL HV_FIRST_NAME        CHAR(20) INIT (' ');

   DCL 01 ERR_REC,
          05 FILLER1          CHAR(10) INIT ('SQLCODE = '),
          05 SQLCODE_VIEW     PIC '-999',
          05 ERR_EMPID        FIXED BIN (31) INIT (0),
          05 FILLER2          CHAR(01) INIT (' '),
          05 ERR_TAB          CHAR(08) INIT (' '),
          05 ERR_PARA         CHAR(15) INIT (' ');

   DCL 01 ERR_MSG AUTOMATIC,
          05 ERR_LGTH         FIXED BIN (31) INIT (864),
          05 ERR_TXT(10)      CHAR(72);

   DCL ERR_TXT_LGTH         FIXED BIN (15) INIT (72);
   DCL ERR_NDX              FIXED BIN (31) INIT (0);

   EXEC SQL
     INCLUDE SQLCA;

   EXEC SQL
     INCLUDE EMPLOYEE;

/******************************************************************
/*                 P R O G R A M   M A I N L I N E                 *
******************************************************************/

   PUT SKIP LIST ('SAMPLE PLI PROGRAM: CALL STORED PROCEDURE');

           DCLEMPLOYEE = '';

     /* SELECT AN EMPLOYEE */

           HV_ID = 3217;

           EXEC SQL
              CALL HRSCHEMA.GETEMP(:HV_ID,
                                   :HV_LAST_NAME,
                                   :HV_FIRST_NAME);

           IF SQLCODE ¬= 0 THEN
              DO;
                 SQLCODE_VIEW = SQLCODE;
                 ERR_TAB  = 'EMPLOYEE';
                 ERR_PARA = 'MAIN';
                 ERR_EMPID = HV_ID;
                 CALL P9999_SQL_ERROR;
```

```
                END;
            ELSE
                PUT SKIP LIST ('PROC CALL SUCCESSFUL '
                        || TRIM(HV_LAST_NAME)
                        || ' ' || TRIM(HV_FIRST_NAME)
                        || ' ' || HV_ID);


    P9999_SQL_ERROR: PROC;

        PUT SKIP LIST (ERR_REC);

        CALL DSNTIAR (SQLCA, ERR_MSG, ERR_TXT_LGTH);

        IF RETCODE = 0 THEN
            DO ERR_NDX = 1 TO 10;
                PUT SKIP DATA (ERR_TXT(ERR_NDX));
            END; /* DO */
        ELSE
            PUT SKIP LIST ('DSNTIAR ERROR CODE = ' || RETCODE);

    END P9999_SQL_ERROR;

    END PLIEMP6;
```

And here is the result of the run:

```
SAMPLE PLI PROGRAM: CALL STORED PROCEDURE
PROC CALL SUCCESSFUL JOHNSON EDWARD            3217
```

External Stored Procedure

Now let's do the same procedure but we'll make it an external procedure and we'll implement it in COBOL. First let's define the procedure and we'll call it `GETEMP2`. Note: it is important to specify the correct WLM environment for external procedures. You might need to check with your DBA or system admin for this information.

```
CREATE PROCEDURE HRSCHEMA.GETEMP2
(IN EMP_NO INT,
 OUT EMP_LNAME VARCHAR(30),
 OUT EMP_FNAME VARCHAR(20))

LANGUAGE COBOL
READS SQL DATA
EXTERNAL NAME "COBEMP7"
COLLID HRSCHEMA
ASUTIME NO LIMIT
PARAMETER STYLE GENERAL
```

```
          STAY RESIDENT NO
          WLM ENVIRONMENT DBAGENV
          PROGRAM TYPE MAIN
          SECURITY DB2
          RESULT SETS 0
          COMMIT ON RETURN NO
```

Now we need to write the COBOL program. Here is one that will perform this task. Notice that we have moved the host variables to a **Linkage section**.

```
          IDENTIFICATION DIVISION.
          PROGRAM-ID. COBEMP7.

         ******************************************************
         *       PROGRAM USED AS A STORED PROCEDURE           *
         ******************************************************

          ENVIRONMENT DIVISION.
          DATA DIVISION.
          WORKING-STORAGE SECTION.


          01 ERR-REC.
             05 FILLER              PIC X(10) VALUE 'SQLCODE = '.
             05 SQLCODE-VIEW        PIC -999.
             05 FILLER              PIC X(005) VALUE SPACES.
             05 ERR-TAB             PIC X(016).
             05 ERR-PARA            PIC X(015).
             05 ERR-DETAIL          PIC X(040).

          77 ERR-TXT-LGTH           PIC S9(9) USAGE COMP VALUE +72.

          01 ERR-MSG.
             05 ERR-MSG-LGTH        PIC S9(04) COMP VALUE +864.
             05 ERR-MSG-TXT         PIC X(072) OCCURS 12 TIMES
                                              INDEXED BY ERR-NDX.
          77 LOGONID                PIC X(8)  VALUE 'HRSCHEMA'.
          77 PWORD                  PIC X(8)  VALUE 'RWUS'.

              EXEC SQL
                INCLUDE SQLCA
              END-EXEC.




              EXEC SQL
                INCLUDE EMPLOYEE
              END-EXEC.

          LINKAGE SECTION.
```

```cobol
      ******************************************************
      *    DECLARE THE I/O PARAMETERS FOR THE PROCEDURE
      ******************************************************

       01 LK-EMP-VARIABLES.
          10  HV-ID              PIC S9(9) USAGE COMP.
          10  HV-LAST-NAME       PIC X(30).
          10  HV-FIRST-NAME      PIC X(20).

       PROCEDURE DIVISION.

       MAIN-PARA.
           DISPLAY "SAMPLE COBOL PROGRAM: STORED PROCEDURE".

      *    SELECT AN EMPLOYEE

           MOVE 3217 TO HV-ID

           EXEC SQL
              CALL HRSCHEMA.GETEMP2(:HV-ID,
                             :HV-LAST-NAME,
                             :HV-FIRST-NAME)
           END-EXEC.

           IF SQLCODE IS NOT EQUAL TO ZERO

              MOVE SQLCODE TO SQLCODE-VIEW
              MOVE 'GETEMP  ' TO ERR-TAB
              MOVE 'MAIN'     TO ERR-PARA
              MOVE HV-ID      TO ERR-DETAIL
              PERFORM P9999-SQL-ERROR

           ELSE
              DISPLAY  'PROC CALL SUCCESFULL ' HV-LAST-NAME
                       HV-FIRST-NAME
                       HV-ID
              DISPLAY SQLCODE

           END-IF

           GOBACK.


       P9999-SQL-ERROR.

           DISPLAY ERR-REC.

           CALL 'DSNTIAR' USING SQLCA,
                       ERR-MSG,
                       ERR-TXT-LGTH.

           IF RETURN-CODE IS EQUAL TO ZERO
```

```
            PERFORM P9999-DISP-ERR
               VARYING ERR-NDX FROM 1 BY 1
               UNTIL ERR-NDX > 12

         ELSE
            DISPLAY 'DSNTIAR ERROR CODE = ' RETURN-CODE
            STOP RUN.

     P9999-DISP-ERR.

         DISPLAY ERR-MSG-TXT(ERR-NDX).

     P9999-DISP-ERR-EXIT.
```

Now we need a program to call the external stored procedure. We can clone the one we used to call the native stored procedure. That was COBEMP6 and all we need to do is change the name of the procedure we are calling. The new program name is COBEMP8.

```
         IDENTIFICATION DIVISION.
         PROGRAM-ID. COBEMP8.

        *********************************************************
        *     PROGRAM USING DB2 CALL TO AN EXTERNAL             *
        *     STORED PROCEDURE.                                 *
        *********************************************************

         ENVIRONMENT DIVISION.
         DATA DIVISION.
         WORKING-STORAGE SECTION.

         01 HV-EMP-VARIABLES.
            10  HV-ID             PIC S9(9) USAGE COMP.
            10  HV-LAST-NAME      PIC X(30).
            10  HV-FIRST-NAME     PIC X(20).

         01 ERR-REC.
            05 FILLER              PIC X(10) VALUE 'SQLCODE = '.
            05 SQLCODE-VIEW        PIC -999.
            05 FILLER              PIC X(005) VALUE SPACES.
            05 ERR-TAB             PIC X(016).
            05 ERR-PARA            PIC X(015).
            05 ERR-DETAIL          PIC X(040).

         77 ERR-TXT-LGTH           PIC S9(9) USAGE COMP VALUE +72.


         01 ERR-MSG.
            05 ERR-MSG-LGTH        PIC S9(04) COMP VALUE +864.
            05 ERR-MSG-TXT         PIC X(072) OCCURS 12 TIMES
                                             INDEXED BY ERR-NDX.
         77 LOGONID                PIC X(8)  VALUE 'HRSCHEMA'.
```

```cobol
       77 PWORD                PIC X(8)   VALUE 'RWUS'.


           EXEC SQL
             INCLUDE SQLCA
           END-EXEC.

           EXEC SQL
             INCLUDE EMPLOYEE
           END-EXEC.


       PROCEDURE DIVISION.

       MAIN-PARA.
           DISPLAY "SAMPLE COBOL PROGRAM: CALL STORED PROCEDURE".


       *   SELECT AN EMPLOYEE

               MOVE 3217 TO HV-ID

               EXEC SQL
                  CALL HRSCHEMA.GETEMP2(:HV-ID,
                                   :HV-LAST-NAME,
                                   :HV-FIRST-NAME)
               END-EXEC.

               IF SQLCODE IS NOT EQUAL TO ZERO

                  MOVE SQLCODE TO SQLCODE-VIEW
                  MOVE 'GETEMP  ' TO ERR-TAB
                  MOVE 'MAIN'     TO ERR-PARA
                  MOVE HV-ID      TO ERR-DETAIL
                  PERFORM P9999-SQL-ERROR

               ELSE
                  DISPLAY  'PROC CALL SUCCESFULL ' HV-LAST-NAME
                           HV-FIRST-NAME
                           HV-ID
                  DISPLAY SQLCODE

               END-IF


       P9999-SQL-ERROR.

           DISPLAY ERR-REC.

           CALL 'DSNTIAR' USING SQLCA,
                          ERR-MSG,
                          ERR-TXT-LGTH.
```

```
            IF RETURN-CODE IS EQUAL TO ZERO

               PERFORM P9999-DISP-ERR
                  VARYING ERR-NDX FROM 1 BY 1
                  UNTIL ERR-NDX > 12

            ELSE
               DISPLAY 'DSNTIAR ERROR CODE = ' RETURN-CODE
               STOP RUN.

        P9999-DISP-ERR.

            DISPLAY ERR-MSG-TXT(ERR-NDX).

        P9999-DISP-ERR-EXIT.
```

Now when we run this program, it will call the stored procedure and display these results:

```
        SAMPLE COBOL PROGRAM: CALL STORED PROCEDURE
        PROC CALL SUCCESSFULL JOHNSON EDWARD 3217
```

Finally, if you are following the examples but prefer to use PLI, we will implement a parallel stored procedure. We have to name it something else because we've already used `GETEMP2` for the COBOL example. Let's add a P to the name and call is `GETEMP2P`. Not a very original naming convention, but it will work for our example.

Let's create the external stored procedure definition to be implemented with a PLI program. All we need to do is change the programming language.

```
        CREATE PROCEDURE HRSCHEMA.GETEMP2P
        (IN EMP_NO INT,
         OUT EMP_LNAME VARCHAR(30),
         OUT EMP_FNAME VARCHAR(20))

        LANGUAGE PLI
        READS SQL DATA
        EXTERNAL NAME "PLIEMP7"
        COLLID HRSCHEMA
        ASUTIME NO LIMIT
        PARAMETER STYLE GENERAL
        STAY RESIDENT NO
        WLM ENVIRONMENT DBAGENV1
        PROGRAM TYPE MAIN
        SECURITY DB2
        RESULT SETS 0
        COMMIT ON RETURN NO
```

Now we are ready to implement the stored procedure in the PLI language:

```pli
PLIEMP7: PROCEDURE (LK_EMP_VARIABLES);
/********************************************************************
 * PROGRAM NAME :   PLIEMP7 - PROGRAM USED AS A STORED PROCEDURE.   *
 ********************************************************************/

/********************************************************************
 *                   E X T E R N A L   E N T R I E S                *
 ********************************************************************/

    DCL DSNTIAR ENTRY OPTIONS(ASM INTER RETCODE);

/********************************************************************
 *                   W O R K I N G   S T O R A G E                  *
 ********************************************************************/

    DCL 01 LK_EMP_VARIABLES,
           05  HV_ID            FIXED BIN (31),
           05  HV_LAST_NAME     CHAR(30),
           05  HV_FIRST_NAME    CHAR(20);

    DCL 01 ERR_REC,
           05 FILLER1            CHAR(10) INIT ('SQLCODE = '),
           05 SQLCODE_VIEW       PIC '-999',
           05 ERR_EMPID          FIXED BIN (31) INIT (0),
           05 FILLER2            CHAR(01) INIT (' '),
           05 ERR_TAB            CHAR(08) INIT (' '),
           05 ERR_PARA           CHAR(15) INIT (' ');

    DCL 01 ERR_MSG AUTOMATIC,
           05 ERR_LGTH           FIXED BIN (31) INIT (864),
           05 ERR_TXT(10)        CHAR(72);

    DCL ERR_TXT_LGTH             FIXED BIN (15) INIT (72);
    DCL ERR_NDX                  FIXED BIN (31) INIT (0);


    EXEC SQL
      INCLUDE SQLCA;

    EXEC SQL
      INCLUDE EMPLOYEE;

/********************************************************************
/*                   P R O G R A M   M A I N L I N E                *
 ********************************************************************/

    PUT SKIP LIST ('SAMPLE PLI PROGRAM: CALLED STORED PROCEDURE');
```

```
            DCLEMPLOYEE = '';

     /* SELECT AN EMPLOYEE */

         EXEC SQL
            SELECT EMP_LAST_NAME,
                   EMP_FIRST_NAME
              INTO :HV_LAST_NAME,
                   :HV_FIRST_NAME
              FROM HRSCHEMA.EMPLOYEE
             WHERE EMP_ID = :HV_ID;

         IF SQLCODE ¬= 0 THEN
            DO;
               SQLCODE_VIEW = SQLCODE;
               ERR_TAB  = 'EMPLOYEE';
               ERR_PARA = 'MAIN';
               ERR_EMPID = HV_ID;
               CALL P9999_SQL_ERROR;
            END;


      P9999_SQL_ERROR: PROC;

         PUT SKIP LIST (ERR_REC);

         CALL DSNTIAR (SQLCA, ERR_MSG, ERR_TXT_LGTH);

         IF RETCODE = 0 THEN
            DO ERR_NDX = 1 TO 10;
               PUT SKIP DATA (ERR_TXT(ERR_NDX));
            END; /* DO */
         ELSE
            PUT SKIP LIST ('DSNTIAR ERROR CODE = ' || RETCODE);

         END P9999_SQL_ERROR;

      END PLIEMP7;
```

Next, here is the PLI program to call the stored procedure.

```
     PLIEMP8: PROCEDURE OPTIONS(MAIN) REORDER;
     /*******************************************************************
      * PROGRAM NAME :    PLIEMP8 - PROGRAM TO CALL A STORED PROCEDURE.  *
      *******************************************************************/

     /*******************************************************************
      *              E X T E R N A L   E N T R I E S                    *
      *******************************************************************/

        DCL DSNTIAR ENTRY OPTIONS(ASM INTER RETCODE);
```

```
/******************************************************************
*                W O R K I N G   S T O R A G E                    *
******************************************************************/

    DCL HV_ID              FIXED BIN (31) INIT (0);
    DCL HV_LAST_NAME       CHAR(30) INIT (' ');
    DCL HV_FIRST_NAME      CHAR(20) INIT (' ');

    DCL 01 ERR_REC,
           05 FILLER1          CHAR(10) INIT ('SQLCODE = '),
           05 SQLCODE_VIEW     PIC '-999',
           05 ERR_EMPID        FIXED BIN (31) INIT (0),
           05 FILLER2          CHAR(01) INIT (' '),
           05 ERR_TAB          CHAR(08) INIT (' '),
           05 ERR_PARA         CHAR(15) INIT (' ');

    DCL 01 ERR_MSG AUTOMATIC,
           05 ERR_LGTH         FIXED BIN (31) INIT (864),
           05 ERR_TXT(10)      CHAR(72);

    DCL ERR_TXT_LGTH       FIXED BIN (15) INIT (72);
    DCL ERR_NDX            FIXED BIN (31) INIT (0);

    EXEC SQL
      INCLUDE SQLCA;

    EXEC SQL
      INCLUDE EMPLOYEE;

/******************************************************************
/*             P R O G R A M   M A I N L I N E                    *
******************************************************************/

    PUT SKIP LIST ('SAMPLE PLI PROGRAM: CALL STORED PROCEDURE');

        DCLEMPLOYEE = '';

    /* SELECT AN EMPLOYEE */

        HV_ID = 3217;

        EXEC SQL
           CALL HRSCHEMA.GETEMP2P(:HV_ID,
                                  :HV_LAST_NAME,
                                  :HV_FIRST_NAME);

        IF SQLCODE ¬= 0 THEN
           DO;
               SQLCODE_VIEW = SQLCODE;
               ERR_TAB  = 'EMPLOYEE';
               ERR_PARA = 'MAIN';
               ERR_EMPID = HV_ID;
               CALL P9999_SQL_ERROR;
```

```
                END;
            ELSE
                PUT SKIP LIST ('PROC CALL SUCCESSFUL '
                        || TRIM(HV_LAST_NAME)
                        || ' ' || TRIM(HV_FIRST_NAME)
                        || ' ' || HV_ID);


    P9999_SQL_ERROR: PROC;

        PUT SKIP LIST (ERR_REC);

        CALL DSNTIAR (SQLCA, ERR_MSG, ERR_TXT_LGTH);

        IF RETCODE = 0 THEN
            DO ERR_NDX = 1 TO 10;
                PUT SKIP DATA (ERR_TXT(ERR_NDX));
            END; /* DO */
        ELSE
            PUT SKIP LIST ('DSNTIAR ERROR CODE = ' || RETCODE);

    END P9999_SQL_ERROR;

END PLIEMP8;
```

And here is the result of the run:

```
SAMPLE PLI PROGRAM: CALL STORED PROCEDURE
PROC CALL SUCCESSFUL JOHNSON EDWARD            3217
```

Stored Procedure Error Handling

So far the stored procedures we've created did not encounter error conditions. Let's refine our GETEMP stored procedure to handle unexpected SQL codes. One especially good thing about native SQL procedures is that when you call them the SQL code is reflected in the SQLCA of the calling program. So you need only interrogate the SQLCODE as you normally would to detect an error.

Let's try running our COBEMP6 (which calls GETEMP) and specify a nonexistent employee id, for example 3218. If we run this, here is the output we'll receive:

```
SAMPLE COBOL PROGRAM: CALL STORED PROCEDURE
SQLCODE = -305        GETEMP           MAIN           000003218
 DSNT408I SQLCODE = -305, ERROR:  THE NULL VALUE CANNOT BE ASSIGNED TO
          OUTPUT HOST VARIABLE NUMBER 2 BECAUSE NO INDICATOR VARIABLE IS
          SPECIFIED
 DSNT418I SQLSTATE   = 22002 SQLSTATE RETURN CODE
 DSNT415I SQLERRP    = DSNXROHB SQL PROCEDURE DETECTING ERROR
 DSNT416I SQLERRD    = -115  0  0  -1  0  0 SQL DIAGNOSTIC INFORMATION
```

```
DSNT416I SQLERRD    = X'FFFFFF8D'  X'00000000'  X'00000000'
         X'FFFFFFFF'  X'00000000'  X'00000000' SQL DIAGNOSTIC
         INFORMATION
```

This result indicates that our query in the GETEMP procedure did not return a value. The problem is that we didn't define indicator variables in our COBOL program and use them in the call to the stored procedure. Indicator variables are used to handle a situation where a NULL value was encountered in a query. This is important since a DB2 NULL value cannot be loaded into the specified COBOL host variable. Neither COBOL nor PLI knows what a DB2 NULL value is, so you must add indicator variables to your query to prevent the -305 SQL result.

Once a query completes you can check the indicator variable and if its value is -1, that means a NULL was encountered for that column and the value in the host variable is a default value (typically zero for numeric variables and space for character variables). The query does not fail and you can decide what to do with the default result value (if anything).

Let's define indicator variables in our COEMP6 program for the EMP_FIRST_NAME and EMP_LAST_NAME columns.

```
01 HV-INDICATOR-VARS.
   10  IND-HV-LAST-NAME  PIC S9(4) BINARY.
   10  IND-HV-FIRST-NAME PIC S9(4) BINARY.
```

Now these indicator variables must be used in the query. So our call to the GETEMP stored procedure becomes:

```
CALL HRSCHEMA.GETEMP(:HV-ID,
                     :HV-LAST-NAME:  IND-HV-LAST-NAME,
                     :HV-FIRST-NAME: IND-HV-FIRST-NAME)
```

Now when we call the stored procedure we will get a +100 SQLCODE which simply means the record for employee 3218 was not found.

```
SAMPLE COBOL PROGRAM: CALL STORED PROCEDURE
SQLCODE =    100      GETEMP         MAIN           000003218
 DSNT404I SQLCODE = 100, NOT FOUND:  ROW NOT FOUND FOR FETCH, UPDATE, OR
          DELETE, OR THE RESULT OF A QUERY IS AN EMPTY TABLE
 DSNT418I SQLSTATE   = 02000 SQLSTATE RETURN CODE
 DSNT415I SQLERRP    = DSNXRFF SQL PROCEDURE DETECTING ERROR
 DSNT416I SQLERRD    = -110  0  0  -1  0  0 SQL DIAGNOSTIC INFORMATION
 DSNT416I SQLERRD    = X'FFFFFF92'  X'00000000'  X'00000000'
          X'FFFFFFFF'  X'00000000'  X'00000000' SQL DIAGNOSTIC
          INFORMATION
```

Unlike native SQL procedures, when you call an external stored procedure you cannot use the calling program's `SQLCODE` value to determine the status of the procedure. However you can define additional `OUT` parameters to pass back information to the calling program. For example, in our `COBEMP7` program we have a linkage section as follows, and a reference to it with `PROCEDURE DIVISION USING LK-EMP-VARIABLES`.

```
01 LK-EMP-VARIABLES.
   10  HV-ID              PIC S9(9) USAGE COMP.
   10  HV-LAST-NAME       PIC X(30).
   10  HV-FIRST-NAME      PIC X(20).

PROCEDURE DIVISION USING LK-EMP-VARIABLES.
```

You can add some diagnostic variables to the stored procedure `OUT` parameter list, such as `SQLCODE`, `SQLSTATE` and message (the latter to send a customized message back to the calling program). Recall that program `COBEMP7` is associated with stored procedure `GETEMP2`, so let's add the new variables to `GETEMP2`:

```
CREATE PROCEDURE HRSCHEMA.GETEMP2
(IN EMP_NO INT,
 OUT EMP_LNAME VARCHAR(30),
 OUT EMP_FNAME VARCHAR(20),
 OUT PRM_SQLCODE INT,
 OUT PRM_SQLSTATE CHAR(5),
 OUT PRM_MESSAGE  CHAR(80))
```

You would also need to add these variables to the program linkage variable list.

```
01 LK-EMP-VARIABLES.
   10  HV-ID              PIC S9(9) USAGE COMP.
   10  HV-LAST-NAME       PIC X(30).
   10  HV-FIRST-NAME      PIC X(20).
   10  PRM-SQLCODE        PIC X(5).
   10  PRM-SQLSTATE       PIC X(5).
   10  PRM-MESSAGE        PIC X(80).
```

Now if an error is encountered you can assign the diagnostic values to your parameter variables:

```
MOVE SQLCODE  TO PRM-SQLCODE
MOVE SQLSTATE TO PRM-SQLSTATE
MOVE 'ERROR IN PROC GETEMP' TO PRM-MESSAGE
```

Since these variables are OUT parameters, they will be returned to the calling program and you can interrogate the values for diagnostic purposes.

More Stored Procedure Examples

Let's do a few more examples of stored procedures, and in this case we'll create some data access routines. Specifically we'll create stored procedures to retrieve information for an employee, to add or update an employee, and to delete an employee.

For retrieving employee data, we'll simply expand our GETEMP procedure to include all of the original fields we created the table with. We'll call the new procedure GET_EMP_INFO.

```
        CREATE PROCEDURE HRSCHEMA.GET_EMP_INFO
        (IN EMP_NO INT,
         OUT EMP_LNAME VARCHAR(30),
         OUT EMP_FNAME VARCHAR(20),
         OUT EMP_SRVC_YRS INT,
         OUT EMP_PROM_DATE DATE,
         OUT EMP_PROF XML,
         OUT EMP_SSN   CHAR(09))

        LANGUAGE SQL
        READS SQL DATA

        BEGIN
           SELECT EMP_LAST_NAME,
                  EMP_FIRST_NAME,
                  EMP_SERVICE_YEARS,
                  EMP_SERVICE_YEARS,
                  EMP_PROMOTION_DATE,
                  EMP_PROFILE,
                  EMP_SSN
             INTO EMP_LNAME,
                  EMP_FNAME,
                  EMP_SRVC_YRS,
                  EMP_PROM_DATE,
                  EMP_PROF,
                  EMP_SSN
             FROM HRSCHEMA.EMPLOYEE
             WHERE EMP_ID = EMP_NO;

        END #
```

Next, we'll create a procedure that merges the input data into the table, either adding it if it is a new record, or updating it if an old record.

```
CREATE PROCEDURE HRSCHEMA.MRG_EMP_INFO
(IN EMP_NO INT,
 IN EMP_LNAME VARCHAR(30),
 IN EMP_FNAME VARCHAR(20),
 IN EMP_SRVC_YRS INT,
 IN EMP_PROM_DATE DATE,
 IN EMP_PROF XML,
 IN EMP_SSN   CHAR(09))


 LANGUAGE SQL
 MODIFIES SQL DATA
BEGIN
     MERGE INTO HRSCHEMA.EMPLOYEE AS T
     USING
      (VALUES (EMP_NO,
       EMP_LNAME,
       EMP_FNAME,
       EMP_SRVC_YRS,
       EMP_PROM_DATE,
       EMP_PROF,
       EMP_SSN))
      AS S
      (EMP_ID,
       EMP_LAST_NAME,
       EMP_FIRST_NAME,
       EMP_SERVICE_YEARS,
       EMP_PROMOTION_DATE,
       EMP_PROFILE,
       EMP_SSN)
      ON S.EMP_ID = T.EMP_ID

     WHEN MATCHED
        THEN UPDATE
           SET EMP_ID             = S.EMP_ID,
               EMP_LAST_NAME      = S.EMP_LAST_NAME,
               EMP_FIRST_NAME     = S.EMP_FIRST_NAME,
               EMP_SERVICE_YEARS  = S.EMP_SERVICE_YEARS,
               EMP_PROMOTION_DATE = S.EMP_PROMOTION_DATE,
               EMP_PROFILE        = S.EMP_PROFILE,
               EMP_SSN            = S.EMP_SSN

     WHEN NOT MATCHED
        THEN INSERT
           VALUES (S.EMP_ID,
            S.EMP_LAST_NAME,
            S.EMP_FIRST_NAME,
            S.EMP_SERVICE_YEARS,
            S.EMP_PROMOTION_DATE,
            S.EMP_PROFILE,
            S.EMP_SSN) ;

   END #
```

Finally, let's take care of the delete function. This one is easy.

```
CREATE PROCEDURE HRSCHEMA.DLT_EMP_INFO
(IN EMP_NO INT)

LANGUAGE SQL
MODIFIES SQL DATA

BEGIN
   DELETE FROM HRSCHEMA.EMPLOYEE
   WHERE EMP_ID = EMP_NO;

END #
```

Before we can use these procedures we must grant access to them. In our case we will grant to PUBLIC, but normally you will grant access only to your developer and user groups.

```
GRANT EXECUTE ON PROCEDURE HRSCHEMA.GET_EMP_INFO TO PUBLIC;

GRANT EXECUTE ON PROCEDURE HRSCHEMA.MRG_EMP_INFO TO PUBLIC;

GRANT EXECUTE ON PROCEDURE HRSCHEMA.DLT_EMP_INFO TO PUBLIC;
```

Next we need a COBOL program to test each of these stored procedures. Here is one that works:

```
    IDENTIFICATION DIVISION.
    PROGRAM-ID. COBEMPH.

    *********************************************************
    *      PROGRAM USING DB2 CALL TO SEVERAL                 *
    *      STORED PROCEDURES.                                *
    *********************************************************

    ENVIRONMENT DIVISION.
    DATA DIVISION.
    WORKING-STORAGE SECTION.

    01 HV-INDICATOR-VARS.
        10  IND-HV-LAST-NAME   PIC S9(4) BINARY VALUE 0.
        10  IND-HV-FIRST-NAME  PIC S9(4) BINARY VALUE 0.
        10  IND-HV-SRVC-YEARS  PIC S9(4) BINARY VALUE 0.
        10  IND-HV-PROM-DATE   PIC S9(4) BINARY VALUE 0.
        10  IND-HV-PROFILE     PIC S9(4) BINARY VALUE 0.
        10  IND-HV-SSN         PIC S9(4) BINARY VALUE 0.

    01 ERR-REC.
        05 FILLER              PIC X(10) VALUE 'SQLCODE = '.
```

```cobol
           05 SQLCODE-VIEW      PIC -999.
           05 FILLER            PIC X(005) VALUE SPACES.
           05 ERR-TAB           PIC X(016).
           05 ERR-PARA          PIC X(015).
           05 ERR-DETAIL        PIC X(040).

       77 ERR-TXT-LGTH          PIC S9(9) USAGE COMP VALUE +72.

       01 ERR-MSG.
           05 ERR-MSG-LGTH      PIC S9(04) COMP VALUE +864.
           05 ERR-MSG-TXT       PIC X(072) OCCURS 12 TIMES
                                           INDEXED BY ERR-NDX.
           EXEC SQL
              INCLUDE SQLCA
           END-EXEC.

           EXEC SQL
              INCLUDE EMPLOYEE
           END-EXEC.


       PROCEDURE DIVISION.

       MAIN-PARA.
           DISPLAY "SAMPLE COBOL PROGRAM: CALL STORED PROCEDURES".

           DISPLAY 'MERGE EMPLOYEE INFORMATION'

           MOVE +7938       TO EMP-ID
           MOVE 'WINFIELD'  TO EMP-LAST-NAME-TEXT
           MOVE 'STANLEY'   TO EMP-FIRST-NAME-TEXT
           MOVE +3          TO EMP-SERVICE-YEARS
           MOVE SPACES      TO EMP-PROMOTION-DATE
           MOVE -1          TO IND-HV-PROM-DATE
           MOVE SPACES      TO EMP-PROFILE
           MOVE -1          TO IND-HV-PROFILE
           MOVE '382734509' TO EMP-SSN

           EXEC SQL

              CALL HRSCHEMA.MRG_EMP_INFO
                  (:EMP-ID,
                   :EMP-LAST-NAME       :IND-HV-LAST-NAME,
                   :EMP-FIRST-NAME      :IND-HV-FIRST-NAME,
                   :EMP-SERVICE-YEARS   :IND-HV-SRVC-YEARS,
                   :EMP-PROMOTION-DATE  :IND-HV-PROM-DATE,
                   :EMP-PROFILE         :IND-HV-PROFILE,
                   :EMP-SSN             :IND-HV-SSN)

           END-EXEC.

           IF SQLCODE IS NOT EQUAL TO ZERO
```

```
        DISPLAY  'MERGE CALL FAILED ' EMP-ID
        MOVE SQLCODE TO SQLCODE-VIEW
        MOVE 'EMPLOYEE' TO ERR-TAB
        MOVE 'MAIN'     TO ERR-PARA
        MOVE EMP-ID     TO ERR-DETAIL
        PERFORM P9999-SQL-ERROR

    ELSE
        DISPLAY  'MERGE CALL SUCCESSFUL ' EMP-ID
        DISPLAY  EMP-LAST-NAME
        DISPLAY  EMP-FIRST-NAME
        DISPLAY  EMP-SERVICE-YEARS
        DISPLAY  EMP-PROMOTION-DATE
        DISPLAY  EMP-SSN

END-IF

DISPLAY 'DISPLAY EMPLOYEE INFORMATION'

MOVE +7938       TO EMP-ID

EXEC SQL

    CALL HRSCHEMA.GET_EMP_INFO
       (:EMP-ID,
        :EMP-LAST-NAME        :IND-HV-LAST-NAME,
        :EMP-FIRST-NAME       :IND-HV-FIRST-NAME,
        :EMP-SERVICE-YEARS    :IND-HV-SRVC-YEARS,
        :EMP-PROMOTION-DATE   :IND-HV-PROM-DATE,
        :EMP-PROFILE          :IND-HV-PROFILE,
        :EMP-SSN              :IND-HV-SSN)

END-EXEC.

IF SQLCODE IS NOT EQUAL TO ZERO

    DISPLAY  'GET CALL FAILED ' EMP-ID
    MOVE SQLCODE TO SQLCODE-VIEW
    MOVE 'EMPLOYEE' TO ERR-TAB
    MOVE 'MAIN'     TO ERR-PARA
    MOVE EMP-ID     TO ERR-DETAIL
    PERFORM P9999-SQL-ERROR

ELSE
    DISPLAY  'GET CALL SUCCESSFUL ' EMP-ID
    DISPLAY  EMP-LAST-NAME
    DISPLAY  EMP-FIRST-NAME
    DISPLAY  EMP-SERVICE-YEARS
    DISPLAY  EMP-PROMOTION-DATE
    DISPLAY  EMP-SSN

END-IF
```

```
            DISPLAY 'UPDATE EMPLOYEE INFORMATION'

            MOVE +7938        TO EMP-ID
            MOVE 'WINFIELD'   TO EMP-LAST-NAME-TEXT
            MOVE 'SAMUEL '    TO EMP-FIRST-NAME-TEXT
            MOVE +2           TO EMP-SERVICE-YEARS
            MOVE '01/31/2017' TO EMP-PROMOTION-DATE
            MOVE 0            TO IND-HV-PROM-DATE
            MOVE SPACES       TO EMP-PROFILE
            MOVE -1           TO IND-HV-PROFILE
            MOVE '382734595'  TO EMP-SSN

            EXEC SQL

               CALL HRSCHEMA.MRG_EMP_INFO
                  (:EMP-ID,
                   :EMP-LAST-NAME        :IND-HV-LAST-NAME,
                   :EMP-FIRST-NAME       :IND-HV-FIRST-NAME,
                   :EMP-SERVICE-YEARS    :IND-HV-SRVC-YEARS,
                   :EMP-PROMOTION-DATE   :IND-HV-PROM-DATE,
                   :EMP-PROFILE          :IND-HV-PROFILE,
                   :EMP-SSN              :IND-HV-SSN)

            END-EXEC.

            IF SQLCODE IS NOT EQUAL TO ZERO

               DISPLAY  'UPDATE MERGE CALL FAILED ' EMP-ID
               MOVE SQLCODE TO SQLCODE-VIEW
               MOVE 'EMPLOYEE' TO ERR-TAB
               MOVE 'MAIN'    TO ERR-PARA
               MOVE EMP-ID    TO ERR-DETAIL
               PERFORM P9999-SQL-ERROR

            ELSE
               DISPLAY  'UPDATE MERGE CALL SUCCESSFUL ' EMP-ID
               DISPLAY  EMP-LAST-NAME
               DISPLAY  EMP-FIRST-NAME
               DISPLAY  EMP-SERVICE-YEARS
               DISPLAY  EMP-PROMOTION-DATE
               DISPLAY  EMP-SSN

            END-IF


            DISPLAY 'DISPLAY UPDATED EMPLOYEE INFORMATION'

            MOVE +7938       TO EMP-ID

            EXEC SQL

               CALL HRSCHEMA.GET_EMP_INFO
```

```
              (:EMP-ID,
               :EMP-LAST-NAME        :IND-HV-LAST-NAME,
               :EMP-FIRST-NAME       :IND-HV-FIRST-NAME,
               :EMP-SERVICE-YEARS    :IND-HV-SRVC-YEARS,
               :EMP-PROMOTION-DATE   :IND-HV-PROM-DATE,
               :EMP-PROFILE          :IND-HV-PROFILE,
               :EMP-SSN              :IND-HV-SSN)

     END-EXEC.

     IF SQLCODE IS NOT EQUAL TO ZERO

         DISPLAY 'GET CALL FAILED ' EMP-ID
         MOVE SQLCODE TO SQLCODE-VIEW
         MOVE 'EMPLOYEE' TO ERR-TAB
         MOVE 'MAIN'     TO ERR-PARA
         MOVE EMP-ID     TO ERR-DETAIL
         PERFORM P9999-SQL-ERROR

     ELSE
         DISPLAY 'GET CALL SUCCESSFUL ' EMP-ID
         DISPLAY  EMP-LAST-NAME
         DISPLAY  EMP-FIRST-NAME
         DISPLAY  EMP-SERVICE-YEARS
         DISPLAY  EMP-PROMOTION-DATE
         DISPLAY  EMP-SSN

     END-IF


     DISPLAY 'DISPLAY DELETED EMPLOYEE INFORMATION'

     MOVE +7938     TO EMP-ID

     EXEC SQL

         CALL HRSCHEMA.DLT_EMP_INFO
            (:EMP-ID)

     END-EXEC.

     IF SQLCODE IS NOT EQUAL TO ZERO

         DISPLAY  'DELETE CALL FAILED ' EMP-ID
         MOVE SQLCODE TO SQLCODE-VIEW
         MOVE 'EMPLOYEE' TO ERR-TAB
         MOVE 'MAIN'     TO ERR-PARA
         MOVE EMP-ID     TO ERR-DETAIL
         PERFORM P9999-SQL-ERROR

     ELSE
         DISPLAY  'DELETE CALL SUCCESSFUL ' EMP-ID
```

```
        END-IF

    GOBACK.

P9999-SQL-ERROR.

    DISPLAY ERR-REC.

    CALL 'DSNTIAR' USING SQLCA,
                  ERR-MSG,
                  ERR-TXT-LGTH.

    IF RETURN-CODE IS EQUAL TO ZERO

        PERFORM P9999-DISP-ERR
           VARYING ERR-NDX FROM 1 BY 1
           UNTIL ERR-NDX > 12

    ELSE
       DISPLAY 'DSNTIAR ERROR CODE = ' RETURN-CODE
       STOP RUN.

P9999-DISP-ERR.

    DISPLAY ERR-MSG-TXT(ERR-NDX).

P9999-DISP-ERR-EXIT.
```

Finally, here is the output from the program run:

```
SAMPLE COBOL PROGRAM: CALL STORED PROCEDURES
MERGE EMPLOYEE INFORMATION
MERGE CALL SUCCESSFUL 000007938
   WINFIELD
   STANLEY
000000003

382734509
DISPLAY EMPLOYEE INFORMATION
GET CALL SUCCESSFUL 000007938
   WINFIELD
   STANLEY
000000003

382734509
UPDATE EMPLOYEE INFORMATION
UPDATE MERGE CALL SUCCESSFUL 000007938
   WINFIELD
   SAMUEL
000000002
```

```
01/31/2017
382734595

DISPLAY UPDATED EMPLOYEE INFORMATION
GET CALL SUCCESSFUL 000007938
  WINFIELD
  SAMUEL
000000002
2017-01-31
382734595

DISPLAY DELETED EMPLOYEE INFORMATION
DELETE CALL SUCCESSFUL 000007938
```

Last, here is our PLI version of the program to call the data access stored procedures.

```
PLIEMPH: PROCEDURE OPTIONS(MAIN) REORDER;

/*********************************************************************
 * PROGRAM NAME :    PLIEMPH - CALL SEVERAL STORED PROCEDURES        *
 *                   FOR DATA ACCESS.                                *
 *********************************************************************/

/*********************************************************************
 *              E X T E R N A L    E N T R I E S                     *
 *********************************************************************/

   DCL DSNTIAR ENTRY OPTIONS(ASM INTER RETCODE);

/*********************************************************************
 /*            W O R K I N G    S T O R A G E                        *
 *********************************************************************/

   DCL COMMIT_CTR              FIXED BIN(31) INIT(0);
   DCL RET_SQL_CODE            FIXED BIN(31) INIT(0);
   DCL RET_SQL_CODE_PIC        PIC 'S999999999' INIT (0);

   DCL 01 ERR_REC,
          05 FILLER1           CHAR(10) INIT ('SQLCODE = '),
          05 SQLCODE_VIEW      PIC '-999',
          05 ERR_EMPID         FIXED BIN (31) INIT (0),
          05 FILLER2           CHAR(01) INIT (' '),
          05 ERR_TAB           CHAR(08) INIT (' '),
          05 ERR_PARA          CHAR(15) INIT (' ');

   DCL 01 ERR_MSG AUTOMATIC,
          05 ERR_LGTH          FIXED BIN (31) INIT (864),
          05 ERR_TXT(10)       CHAR(72);

   DCL ERR_TXT_LGTH            FIXED BIN (15) INIT (72);
   DCL ERR_NDX                 FIXED BIN (31) INIT (0);
```

```pli
       DCL 01 HV_INDICATOR_VARS,
           10  IND_HV_LAST_NAME    FIXED BIN (15) INIT(0),
           10  IND_HV_FIRST_NAME   FIXED BIN (15) INIT(0),
           10  IND_HV_SRVC_YEARS   FIXED BIN (15) INIT(0),
           10  IND_HV_PROM_DATE    FIXED BIN (15) INIT(0),
           10  IND_HV_PROFILE      FIXED BIN (15) INIT(0),
           10  IND_HV_SSN          FIXED BIN (15) INIT(0);

       EXEC SQL
         INCLUDE SQLCA;

       EXEC SQL
         INCLUDE EMPLOYEE;


/************************************************************************
/*                P R O G R A M    M A I N L I N E                      *
*************************************************************************/

       PUT SKIP LIST ('SAMPLE PLI PROGRAM: CALL SOME STORED PROCEDURE');

       PUT SKIP LIST ('DISPLAY MERGE EMPLOYEE INFORMATION');

       EMP_ID              = 7938;
       EMP_LAST_NAME       = 'WINFIELD';
       EMP_FIRST_NAME      = 'STANLEY';
       EMP_SERVICE_YEARS   = +3;
       EMP_PROMOTION_DATE  = ' ';
       IND_HV_PROM_DATE    = -1;
       EMP_PROFILE         = ' ';
       IND_HV_PROFILE      = -1;
       EMP_SSN             = '382734509';

       EXEC SQL

           CALL HRSCHEMA.MRG_EMP_INFO
             (:EMP_ID,
              :EMP_LAST_NAME        :IND_HV_LAST_NAME,
              :EMP_FIRST_NAME       :IND_HV_FIRST_NAME,
              :EMP_SERVICE_YEARS    :IND_HV_SRVC_YEARS,
              :EMP_PROMOTION_DATE   :IND_HV_PROM_DATE,
              :EMP_PROFILE          :IND_HV_PROFILE,
              :EMP_SSN              :IND_HV_SSN);

       IF SQLCODE ¬= 0 THEN
          DO;
              PUT SKIP LIST ('MERGE CALL FAILED ' || EMP_ID);
              SQLCODE_VIEW   =  SQLCODE;
              ERR_TAB        = 'EMPLOYEE';
              ERR_PARA       = 'MAIN';
              ERR_DETAIL     = EMP_ID;
```

```
                CALL P9999_SQL_ERROR;
            END;

        ELSE
           DO;
              PUT SKIP LIST ('MERGE CALL SUCCESSFUL ' || EMP_ID);
              PUT SKIP LIST (EMP_LAST_NAME);
              PUT SKIP LIST (EMP_FIRST_NAME);
              PUT SKIP LIST (EMP_SERVICE_YEARS);
              PUT SKIP LIST (EMP_PROMOTION_DATE);
              PUT SKIP LIST (EMP_SSN);
           END;

PUT SKIP LIST ('DISPLAY EMPLOYEE INFORMATION');

EMP_ID = 7938;

EXEC SQL

    CALL HRSCHEMA.GET_EMP_INFO
       (:EMP_ID,
        :EMP_LAST_NAME       :IND_HV_LAST_NAME,
        :EMP_FIRST_NAME      :IND_HV_FIRST_NAME,
        :EMP_SERVICE_YEARS   :IND_HV_SRVC_YEARS,
        :EMP_PROMOTION_DATE  :IND_HV_PROM_DATE,
        :EMP_PROFILE         :IND_HV_PROFILE,
        :EMP_SSN             :IND_HV_SSN);

    IF SQLCODE ¬= 0 THEN
       DO;
           PUT SKIP LIST ('GET CALL FAILED ' || EMP_ID);
           SQLCODE_VIEW   =  SQLCODE;
           ERR_TAB        = 'EMPLOYEE';
           ERR_PARA       = 'MAIN';
           ERR_DETAIL     = EMP_ID;
           CALL P9999_SQL_ERROR;
       END;

    ELSE
       DO;
           PUT SKIP LIST ('GET CALL SUCCESSFUL ' || EMP_ID);
           PUT SKIP LIST (EMP_LAST_NAME);
           PUT SKIP LIST (EMP_FIRST_NAME);
           PUT SKIP LIST (EMP_SERVICE_YEARS);
           PUT SKIP LIST (EMP_PROMOTION_DATE);
           PUT SKIP LIST (EMP_SSN);
       END;


PUT SKIP LIST ('UPDATE EMPLOYEE INFORMATION');

EMP_ID            = 7938;
EMP_LAST_NAME     = 'WINFIELD';
```

```
            EMP_FIRST_NAME        = 'SAMUEL';
            EMP_SERVICE_YEARS     = +2;
            EMP_PROMOTION_DATE    = ' ';
            IND_HV_PROM_DATE      = -1;
            EMP_PROFILE           = ' ';
            IND_HV_PROFILE        = -1;
            EMP_SSN               = '382734595';

            EXEC SQL

                CALL HRSCHEMA.MRG_EMP_INFO
                    (:EMP_ID,
                     :EMP_LAST_NAME       :IND_HV_LAST_NAME,
                     :EMP_FIRST_NAME      :IND_HV_FIRST_NAME,
                     :EMP_SERVICE_YEARS   :IND_HV_SRVC_YEARS,
                     :EMP_PROMOTION_DATE  :IND_HV_PROM_DATE,
                     :EMP_PROFILE         :IND_HV_PROFILE,
                     :EMP_SSN             :IND_HV_SSN);

                IF SQLCODE ¬= 0 THEN
                    DO;
                        PUT SKIP LIST ('UPDATE MERGE CALL FAILED ' || EMP_ID);
                        SQLCODE_VIEW    = SQLCODE;
                        ERR_TAB         = 'EMPLOYEE';
                        ERR_PARA        = 'MAIN';
                        ERR_DETAIL      = EMP_ID;
                        CALL P9999_SQL_ERROR;
                    END;

                ELSE
                    DO;
                        PUT SKIP LIST ('UPDATE MERGE CALL SUCCESSFUL ' ||
EMP_ID);
                        PUT SKIP LIST (EMP_LAST_NAME);
                        PUT SKIP LIST (EMP_FIRST_NAME);
                        PUT SKIP LIST (EMP_SERVICE_YEARS);
                        PUT SKIP LIST (EMP_PROMOTION_DATE);
                        PUT SKIP LIST (EMP_SSN);
                    END;


            PUT SKIP LIST ('DISPLAY UPDATED EMPLOYEE INFORMATION');

            EMP_ID = +7938;

            EXEC SQL

                CALL HRSCHEMA.GET_EMP_INFO
                    (:EMP_ID,
                     :EMP_LAST_NAME       :IND_HV_LAST_NAME,
                     :EMP_FIRST_NAME      :IND_HV_FIRST_NAME,
                     :EMP_SERVICE_YEARS   :IND_HV_SRVC_YEARS,
                     :EMP_PROMOTION_DATE  :IND_HV_PROM_DATE,
```

```
                :EMP_PROFILE           :IND_HV_PROFILE,
                :EMP_SSN               :IND_HV_SSN);

       IF SQLCODE ¬= 0 THEN
           DO;
               PUT SKIP LIST ('GET CALL FAILED ' || EMP_ID);
               SQLCODE_VIEW     =  SQLCODE;
               ERR_TAB          = 'EMPLOYEE';
               ERR_PARA         = 'MAIN';
               ERR_DETAIL       = EMP_ID;
               CALL P9999_SQL_ERROR;
           END;
       ELSE
           DO;
               PUT SKIP LIST ('GET CALL SUCCESSFUL ' || EMP_ID);
               PUT SKIP LIST (EMP_LAST_NAME);
               PUT SKIP LIST (EMP_FIRST_NAME);
               PUT SKIP LIST (EMP_SERVICE_YEARS);
               PUT SKIP LIST (EMP_PROMOTION_DATE);
               PUT SKIP LIST (EMP_SSN);
           END;

   PUT SKIP LIST ('DISPLAY DELETED EMPLOYEE INFORMATION');

   EMP_ID = 7938;

   EXEC SQL

       CALL HRSCHEMA.DLT_EMP_INFO
           (:EMP_ID);

       IF SQLCODE ¬= 0 THEN
           DO;
               PUT SKIP LIST ('DELETE CALL FAILED ' || EMP_ID);
               SQLCODE_VIEW     =  SQLCODE;
               ERR_TAB          = 'EMPLOYEE';
               ERR_PARA         = 'MAIN';
               ERR_DETAIL       = EMP_ID;
               CALL P9999_SQL_ERROR;
           END;

       ELSE
           DO;
               PUT SKIP LIST ('DELETE CALL SUCCESSFUL ' || EMP_ID);
               PUT SKIP LIST (EMP_LAST_NAME);
               PUT SKIP LIST (EMP_FIRST_NAME);
               PUT SKIP LIST (EMP_SERVICE_YEARS);
               PUT SKIP LIST (EMP_PROMOTION_DATE);
               PUT SKIP LIST (EMP_SSN);
           END;

P9999_SQL_ERROR: PROC;
```

```
        PUT SKIP LIST (ERR_REC);

        CALL DSNTIAR (SQLCA, ERR_MSG, ERR_TXT_LGTH);

        IF RETCODE = 0 THEN
           DO ERR_NDX = 1 TO 10;
              PUT SKIP DATA (ERR_TXT(ERR_NDX));
           END; /* DO */
        ELSE
           PUT SKIP LIST ('DSNTIAR ERROR CODE = ' || RETCODE);

     END P9999_SQL_ERROR;

  END PLIEMPH;
```

And here is the output:

```
        SAMPLE PLI PROGRAM: CALL SOME STORED PROCEDURE
        DISPLAY MERGE EMPLOYEE INFORMATION
        MERGE CALL SUCCESSFUL            7938
        WINFIELD
        STANLEY
                     3

        382734509


        DISPLAY EMPLOYEE INFORMATION
        GET CALL SUCCESSFUL              7938
        WINFIELD
        STANLEY
                     3

        382734509


        UPDATE EMPLOYEE INFORMATION
        UPDATE MERGE CALL SUCCESSFUL         7938
        WINFIELD
        SAMUEL
                     2

        382734595


        DISPLAY UPDATED EMPLOYEE INFORMATION
        GET CALL SUCCESSFUL              7938
        WINFIELD
        SAMUEL
                     2

        382734595


        DISPLAY DELETED EMPLOYEE INFORMATION
        DELETE CALL SUCCESSFUL           7938
```

```
        WINFIELD
        SAMUEL
                        2

        382734595
```

This concludes our discussion of stored procedures. As you can tell, stored procedures are a very powerful technology that promotes reusability and can help minimize custom coding. For more information about DB2 stored procedures, check out the IBM product documentation web site here: [v]

User Defined Functions

A user defined function (UDF) is one written by an application programmer or DBA, as opposed to those functions provided out of the box by DB2. UDFs extend DB2 functionality by allowing new functions to be created. As a function, a UDF always returns a value, and is called with the CALL statement.

```
        CALL <UDF name><parameters>
```

Types of UDF

There are five varieties of UDFs as follows:

- SQL Scalar Function
- SQL Table Function
- External Scalar Function
- External Table Function
- Sourced Function

Examples of UDFs
SQL Scalar Function

An SQL scalar function will return a single value using only SQL statements. There is no external program. You may recall earlier we established a business rule that an employee's "level" was based on their years of service. We used an SQL with a CASE statement to return a value of JUNIOR, ADVANCED or SENIOR. Here's the SQL we used earlier:

```
        SELECT EMP_ID,
        EMP_LAST_NAME,
        EMP_FIRST_NAME,
        CASE
            WHEN EMP_SERVICE_YEARS  < 1 THEN 'ENTRY'
```

```
            WHEN EMP_SERVICE_YEARS   < 5 THEN 'ADVANCED'
            ELSE 'SENIOR'
      END CASE
      FROM HRSCHEMA.EMPLOYEE
---------+---------+---------+---------+---------+---------+-----
    EMP_ID  EMP_LAST_NAME      EMP_FIRST_NAME       CASE
---------+---------+---------+---------+---------+---------+-----
      3217  JOHNSON            EDWARD               ADVANCED
      7459  STEWART            BETTY                SENIOR
      9134  FRANKLIN           BRIANNA              ENTRY
      4175  TURNBULL           FRED                 ADVANCED
      4720  SCHULTZ            TIM                  SENIOR
      6288  WILLARD            JOE                  SENIOR
DSNE610I NUMBER OF ROWS DISPLAYED IS 6
```

Now let's say we have several programs that need to generate these values. We could copy the same SQL to each program, but what if the logic changes in the future? Either the cutoff years or the named literals could change. In that case it would be convenient to only have to make the change in one place. A UDF can accomplish that objective.

We'll create a UDF that accepts an integer which is the years of service, and then it will return the literal value that represents the employee's level of service in the company. First, we must define the UDF to DB2. We need to specify at least:

- The name of the function
- Input parameter type
- Return parameter type

Now let's code the UDF:

```
      CREATE FUNCTION HRSCHEMA.EMP_LEVEL (YRS_SRVC INT)
         RETURNS VARCHAR(10)
         READS SQL DATA
         RETURN
        (SELECT
         CASE
            WHEN YRS_SRVC  < 1 THEN 'ENTRY      '
            WHEN YRS_SRVC  < 5 THEN 'ADVANCED   '
            ELSE 'SENIOR     '
         END CASE
         FROM SYSIBM.SYSDUMMY1)
```

Note that we specify SYSIBM.SYSDUMMY1 as our table. This is only to complete the SQL syntax which otherwise would fail because we don't have a source table. You can use `SYSIBM.SYSDUMMY1` any time you are executing SQL that retrieves data from a built-in or user defined function.

Finally, we can run a query against the new UDF:

```
SELECT HRSCHEMA.EMP_LEVEL(7)
AS EMP_LVL
FROM SYSIBM.SYSDUMMY1;

---------+---------+---------+---------+----
    EMP_LVL
---------+---------+---------+---------+----
    SENIOR

DSNE610I NUMBER OF ROWS DISPLAYED IS 1
```

The above is a very simple example, and the SQL in this case does not actually access a table. Let's do one more that will access a table. How about a UDF that will return the full name of an employee given the employee's id number?

```
CREATE FUNCTION HRSCHEMA.EMP_FULLNAME (EMP_NO INT)
    RETURNS VARCHAR(40)
    READS SQL DATA
    RETURN
    SELECT
    EMP_FIRST_NAME || ' ' || EMP_LAST_NAME AS FULL_NAME
    FROM HRSCHEMA.EMPLOYEE
    WHERE EMP_ID  = EMP_NO;
```

Now let's run the query to use this UDF:

```
SELECT HRSCHEMA.EMP_FULLNAME(3217) AS FULLNAME
FROM SYSIBM.SYSDUMMY1;

        ---------+---------+---------+---------+----
            FULLNAME
        ---------+---------+---------+---------+----

            EDWARD JOHNSON

        DSNE610I NUMBER OF ROWS DISPLAYED IS 1
```

SQL Table Function

An SQL table function returns a table of values. Let's again replace the common table expression we used earlier. Remember it goes like this:

```
WITH EMP_PAY_SUM (EMP_ID, EMP_PAY_TOTAL) AS
(SELECT EMP_ID,
```

```
        SUM(EMP_PAY_AMT)
        AS EMP_PAY_TOTAL
        FROM EMP_PAY_HIST
        GROUP BY EMP_ID)

        SELECT EMP_ID,
        EMP_PAY_TOTAL
        FROM EMP_PAY_SUM
        ;

---------+---------+---------+---------+----
    EMP_ID         EMP_PAY_TOTAL
---------+---------+---------+---------+----
      3217              9166.64
      7459             13333.32
      9134             13333.32
DSNE610I NUMBER OF ROWS DISPLAYED IS 3
```

Now let's define the UDF:

```
        CREATE FUNCTION HRSCHEMA.EMP_PAY_SUM ()
          RETURNS TABLE (EMP_ID   INTEGER,
                         EMP_PAY_TOTAL DECIMAL (9,2))
          READS SQL DATA
          RETURN
            SELECT EMP_ID,
            SUM(EMP_PAY_AMT)
            AS EMP_PAY_TOTAL
            FROM EMP_PAY_HIST
            GROUP BY EMP_ID;
```

And then we'll call it using SPUFI. Notice that we invoke the **TABLE** function to return the values generated by the EMP_PAY_SUM UDF.

```
        SELECT * FROM TABLE(HRSCHEMA.EMP_PAY_SUM()) AS EPS
---------+---------+---------+---------+---------+---
     EMP_ID  EMP_PAY_TOTAL
---------+---------+---------+---------+---------+---
       3217        9166.64
       7459       13333.32
       9134       13333.32
DSNE610I NUMBER OF ROWS DISPLAYED IS 3
```

External Scalar Function

An external scalar function is one that returns a single scalar value, usually based on some parameter value that is passed in. The function is implemented using a program, hence the designation as an "external" function.

You may recall earlier we created a UDF that returned a string value for an employee "level" based on the years of service. We could create a similar external UDF as follows:

```
CREATE FUNCTION HRSCHEMA.EMP_LEVEL2 (INT)
RETURNS VARCHAR(10)
EXTERNAL NAME 'EMPLEVEL'
LANGUAGE COBOL
NOSQL
FENCED
PARAMETER STYLE SQL
```

```
---------+---------+---------+---------+---------+-------
DSNE616I STATEMENT EXECUTION WAS SUCCESSFUL, SQLCODE IS 0
```

Now we need to implement this procedure by way of an external program named EMPLEVEL (the name of the external program must match what we specified above in the EXTERNAL NAME clause). Although in this case we will use COBOL, the external portion of a UDF can be written in any of these languages:

- ASSEMBLER
- C or C++
- COBOL
- JAVA
- PL/I

We'll need a linkage section in our COBOL program that accepts the integer number of years and returns the employee level literal. Here's our program:

```
           IDENTIFICATION DIVISION.
           PROGRAM-ID. EMPLEVEL.

          ******************************************************
          *      PROGRAM USED AS A USER DEFINED FUNCTION       *
          ******************************************************

           ENVIRONMENT DIVISION.
           DATA DIVISION.
           WORKING-STORAGE SECTION.

           LINKAGE SECTION.
          ******************************************************
          *    DECLARE THE I/O PARAMETERS FOR THE PROCEDURE
          ******************************************************

        01 LK-EMP-VARIABLES.
           10   LK-YEARS           PIC S9(9) USAGE COMP.
```

```
           10  LK-EMP-LEVEL      PIC X(10).
        PROCEDURE DIVISION.

        MAIN-PARA.
             DISPLAY "SAMPLE COBOL PROGRAM: USER DEFINED FUNCTION".

        *    DETERMINE AN EMPLOYEE SERVICE LEVEL BASED ON YEARS OF SERVICE

             EVALUATE LK-YEARS
                  WHEN 0           MOVE 'ENTRY    ' TO LK-EMP-LEVEL
                  WHEN 1 THRU 5    MOVE 'ADVANCED ' TO LK-EMP-LEVEL
                  WHEN OTHER       MOVE 'SENIOR   ' TO LK-EMP-LEVEL
             END-EVALUATE.

             GOBACK.
```

Now we can call this function from another program or even from SPUFI:

```
          SELECT HRSCHEMA.EMP_LEVEL2(0) AS EMP_LVL
          FROM SYSIBM.SYSDUMMY1;

          ---------+---------+---------+---------+----
          EMP_LVL
          ---------+---------+---------+---------+----

          ENTRY


          SELECT HRSCHEMA.EMP_LEVEL(2) AS EMP_LVL
          FROM SYSIBM.SYSDUMMY1;

          ---------+---------+---------+---------+----
          EMP_LVL
          ---------+---------+---------+---------+----

          ADVANCED


          SELECT HRSCHEMA.EMP_LEVEL(7) AS EMP_LVL
          FROM SYSIBM.SYSDUMMY1;
          ---------+---------+---------+---------+----
          EMP_LVL
          ---------+---------+---------+---------+----

          SENIOR
```

To create the PLI version of our function, we will create EMP_LEVEL2P.

```
       CREATE FUNCTION HRSCHEMA.EMP_LEVEL2P (INT)
       RETURNS VARCHAR(10)
```

```
      EXTERNAL NAME 'EMPLEVEP'
      LANGUAGE PLI
      NOSQL
      FENCED
      PARAMETER STYLE SQL
---------+---------+---------+---------+---------+-------
DSNE616I STATEMENT EXECUTION WAS SUCCESSFUL, SQLCODE IS 0
```

Here is the PLI program code.

```
      EMPLEVEP: PROCEDURE (LK_EMP_VARIABLES);
/********************************************************************
 * PROGRAM NAME :EMPLEVEP - PROGRAM USED AS A USER DEFINED FUNCTION.*
 ********************************************************************/

/********************************************************************
 *              E X T E R N A L    E N T R I E S                   *
 ********************************************************************/

    DCL DSNTIAR ENTRY OPTIONS(ASM INTER RETCODE);

/********************************************************************
/*             W O R K I N G    S T O R A G E                     *
 ********************************************************************/

    DCL 01 LK_EMP_VARIABLES,
           10  LK_YEARS          FIXED BIN(31),
           10  LK_EMP_LEVEL      CHAR(10);

/********************************************************************
/*             P R O G R A M    M A I N L I N E                   *
 ********************************************************************/

    PUT SKIP LIST ('SAMPLE PLI PROGRAM: USER DEFINED FUNCTION');

/* DETERMINE AN EMPLOYEE SERVICE LEVEL BASED ON YEARS OF SERVICE */

    SELECT(LK_YEARS);

       WHEN (0)           LK_EMP_LEVEL = 'ENTRY';
       WHEN (1,2,3,4)     LK_EMP_LEVEL = 'ADVANCED';
       OTHERWISE          LK_EMP_LEVEL = 'SENIOR';

    END; /* SELECT */

END EMPLEVEP;
```

External Table Function

An external table function returns a table of values. Here we could use such a function as a replacement for the common table expression we used earlier in this study guide. Let's first return to that.

```
        WITH EMP_PAY_SUM (EMP_ID, EMP_PAY_TOTAL) AS
        (SELECT EMP_ID,
        SUM(EMP_PAY_AMT)
        AS EMP_PAY_TOTAL
        FROM EMP_PAY_HIST
        GROUP BY EMP_ID)

        SELECT EMP_ID,
        EMP_PAY_TOTAL
        FROM EMP_PAY_SUM;

    ---------+---------+---------+---------+----
          EMP_ID         EMP_PAY_TOTAL
    ---------+---------+---------+---------+----
            3217              9166.64
            7459             13333.32
            9134             13333.32
    DSNE610I NUMBER OF ROWS DISPLAYED IS 3
```

Normally common table expressions are used with complex SQL to simplify things. Ours is not very complex, but we could simplify even further by using a UDF instead of the common table expression. To do this, let's define the UDF:

```
        CREATE FUNCTION HRSCHEMA.EMP_PAY_SUM2 ()
        RETURNS TABLE (EMP_ID   INTEGER,
                       EMP_PAY_TOTAL DECIMAL (8,2))
        EXTERNAL NAME 'EMPPAYTL'
        LANGUAGE COBOL
        PARAMETER STYLE DB2SQL
        READS SQL DATA
        RESULTS SETS 1
        FENCED
```

Now let's create our COBOL program that implements the UDF. This can be done by defining a cursor to return a result set to the calling program.

```
        IDENTIFICATION DIVISION.
        PROGRAM-ID. EMPPAYTL

       ******************************************************
       *     EXTERNAL TABLE FUNCTION FOR EMP_PAY TABLE      *
       ******************************************************

        ENVIRONMENT DIVISION.
        DATA DIVISION.
        WORKING-STORAGE SECTION.

            EXEC SQL
              INCLUDE SQLCA
```

```
        END-EXEC.

    EXEC SQL
       INCLUDE EMPPAYTL
    END-EXEC.

    EXEC SQL

           DECLARE EMP-PAY-CSR CURSOR WITH RETURN FOR
              SELECT EMP_ID,
              SUM(EMP_PAY_AMT)
              AS EMP_PAY_TOTAL
              FROM HRSCHEMA.EMP_PAY_HIST
              GROUP BY EMP_ID

        END-EXEC.


PROCEDURE DIVISION.

MAIN-PARA.
    DISPLAY "SAMPLE COBOL PROGRAM: EXTERNAL TABLE FUNCTION".

    EXEC SQL
         OPEN EMP-PAY-CSR
    END-EXEC.

    MOVE SQLCODE TO OUT-CODE

    DISPLAY 'OPEN CURSOR SQLCODE: ' SQLCODE.

    STOP RUN.
```

Finally, let's construct a program to call the UDF:

```
IDENTIFICATION DIVISION.
PROGRAM-ID. COBEMPA.

***********************************************************
*      PROGRAM CALLING EXTERNAL TABLE FUNCTION       *
***********************************************************

ENVIRONMENT DIVISION.
DATA DIVISION.
WORKING-STORAGE SECTION.

    EXEC SQL
       INCLUDE SQLCA
    END-EXEC.

    EXEC SQL
       INCLUDE EMPPAYTL
    END-EXEC.
```

```cobol
01  EMP-ID-PIC              PIC ZZZZZ9999.
01  EMP-PAY-TTL             PIC S9(6)V9(2) USAGE COMP-3.
01  EMP-PAY-TTL-PIC         PIC 999999.99.
01  I                       PIC S9(9) USAGE COMP.

* DEFINE CURSOR TO ITERATE THE RESULTS OF THE TABLE

    EXEC SQL
        DECLARE CRSR-EMPPAYTL CURSOR FOR
        SELECT EMP_ID, EMP_PAY_TOTAL
        FROM TABLE(HRSCHEMA.EMP_PAY_SUM2()) AS EPS
        FOR READ ONLY
    END-EXEC.

PROCEDURE DIVISION.

MAIN-PARA.
    DISPLAY "SAMPLE COBOL PROGRAM: CALL EXTERNAL TABLE FUNCTION".

* OPEN THE CURSOR

    EXEC SQL
      OPEN CRSR-EMPPAYTL
    END-EXEC.

    IF SQLCODE NOT EQUAL ZERO THEN
       DISPLAY 'BAD RC = ' SQLCODE
       STOP RUN
    END-IF.

    PERFORM RETRIEVE-DATA
       VARYING I FROM 1 BY 1
          UNTIL SQLCODE EQUAL TO +100.

RETRIEVE-DATA.

    EXEC SQL
       FETCH CRSR-EMPPAYTL INTO :EMP-ID,
                     :EMP-PAY-TTL
    END-EXEC.

    IF SQLCODE = 0
       MOVE EMP-ID      TO EMP-ID-PIC
       MOVE EMP-PAY-TTL TO EMP-PAY-TTL-PIC
       DISPLAY EMP-ID-PIC ' ' EMP-PAY-TTL-PIC
    ELSE
       DISPLAY 'SQL CODE = ' SQLCODE
       STOP RUN
    END-IF.
```

The output from the program is as follows:

SAMPLE COBOL PROGRAM: EXTERNAL TABLE FUNCTION

```
3217    9166.64
7459   13333.32
9134   13333.32
```

The PLI version of the UDF and the implementing and calling programs follows:

```
CREATE FUNCTION HRSCHEMA.EMP_PAY_SUMP ()
RETURNS TABLE (EMP_ID    INTEGER,
               EMP_PAY_TOTAL DECIMAL (9,2) )
EXTERNAL NAME EMPPAYTP
LANGUAGE PLI
PARAMETER STYLE DB2SQL
READS SQL DATA
RESULTS SETS 1
FENCED
```

The implementing program is:

```
EMPPAYTP: PROCEDURE (MAIN);
/******************************************************************
* PROGRAM NAME :   EMPPAYTP - EXTERNAL TABLEFUNCTION FOR EMP_PAY. *
******************************************************************/
/******************************************************************
*             E X T E R N A L   E N T R I E S                    *
******************************************************************/

    DCL DSNTIAR ENTRY OPTIONS(ASM INTER RETCODE);

/******************************************************************
/*              W O R K I N G   S T O R A G E                    *
******************************************************************/

    EXEC SQL
      INCLUDE SQLCA;

    EXEC SQL
      INCLUDE EMPPAYTL;

    EXEC SQL
      DECLARE EMP_PAY_CSR CURSOR WITH RETURN FOR
      SELECT EMP_ID,
      SUM(EMP_PAY_AMT)
      AS EMP_PAY_TOTAL
      FROM HRSCHEMA.EMP_PAY_HIST
      GROUP BY EMP_ID;

/******************************************************************
/*               P R O G R A M   M A I N L I N E                 *
******************************************************************/
```

```
           PUT SKIP LIST ('SAMPLE PLI PROGRAM: EXTERNAL TABLE FUNCTION');

           EXEC SQL OPEN EMP_PAY_CSR;

           PUT SKIP LIST ('OPEN CURSOR SQLCODE: ' || SQLCODE);

       END EMPPAYTP;
```

And we could call the UDF either in SPUFI or with a program such as the following.

```
       PLIEMPA: PROCEDURE OPTIONS(MAIN);

  /******************************************************************
   * PROGRAM NAME :   PLIEMPA - PROGRAM TO CALL EMP_PAY_SUM UDF.    *
   ******************************************************************/

  /******************************************************************
   *              E X T E R N A L    E N T R I E S                  *
   ******************************************************************/

           DCL DSNTIAR ENTRY OPTIONS(ASM INTER RETCODE);

  /******************************************************************
  /*              W O R K I N G    S T O R A G E                    *
   ******************************************************************/

           DCL COMMIT_CTR              FIXED BIN(31) INIT(0);
           DCL RET_SQL_CODE            FIXED BIN(31) INIT(0);
           DCL RET_SQL_CODE_PIC        PIC 'S999999999' INIT (0);

           DCL 01 ERR_REC,
                  05 FILLER1           CHAR(10) INIT ('SQLCODE = '),
                  05 SQLCODE_VIEW      PIC '-999',
                  05 ERR_EMPID         FIXED BIN (31) INIT (0),
                  05 FILLER2           CHAR(01) INIT (' '),
                  05 ERR_TAB           CHAR(08) INIT (' '),
                  05 ERR_PARA          CHAR(15) INIT (' ');

           DCL 01 ERR_MSG AUTOMATIC,
                  05 ERR_LGTH          FIXED BIN (31) INIT (864),
                  05 ERR_TXT(10)       CHAR(72);

           DCL ERR_TXT_LGTH            FIXED BIN (15) INIT (72);
           DCL ERR_NDX                 FIXED BIN (31) INIT (0);

           DCL EMP_ID_PIC              PIC 'ZZZZ9999';
           DCL EMP_PAY_TTL             FIXED DEC (8,2);
           DCL EMP_PAY_TTL_PIC         PIC '999999.99';

           EXEC SQL
             INCLUDE SQLCA;

           EXEC SQL
```

```pli
       INCLUDE EMPPAYTL;

   EXEC SQL
       DECLARE CRSR_EMPPAYTL CURSOR FOR
       SELECT EMP_ID, EMP_PAY_TOTAL
       FROM TABLE(HRSCHEMA.EMP_PAY_SUMP()) AS EPS
       FOR READ ONLY;
/*******************************************************************
/*                P R O G R A M   M A I N L I N E                  *
********************************************************************/
   PUT SKIP LIST ('SAMPLE PLI PROGRAM: CALL EXTERNAL TABLE
FUNCTION');

   EXEC SQL OPEN CRSR_EMPPAYTL;

   IF SQLCODE = 0 THEN
      DO UNTIL (SQLCODE ¬= 0);
         CALL P0100_FETCH_CURSOR;
      END;
   ELSE
      PUT SKIP LIST ('BAD SQLCODE ON CURSOR OPEN = ' || SQLCODE);

   EXEC SQL CLOSE CRSR_EMPPAYTL;

   PUT SKIP LIST ('CLOSE CURSOR SQLCODE: ' || SQLCODE);

   IF SQLCODE ¬= 0 THEN
      PUT SKIP LIST ('BAD SQLCODE ON CLOSE CURSOR ' || SQLCODE);

P0100_FETCH_CURSOR: PROC;

   EXEC SQL
       FETCH CRSR_EMPPAYTL
       INTO
       :EMP_ID,
       :EMP_PAY_TTL;

   IF SQLCODE = 0 THEN
      DO;
         EMP_ID_PIC      = EMP_ID;
         EMP_PAY_TTL_PIC = EMP_PAY_TTL;
         PUT SKIP LIST (EMP_ID_PIC || ' ' || EMP_PAY_TTL_PIC);
      END;
   ELSE
      IF SQLCODE = +100 THEN
         PUT SKIP LIST ('*** NO MORE RECORDS TO PROCESS!!');
      ELSE
         PUT SKIP LIST ('BAD SQLCODE = ' || SQLCODE);

END P0100_FETCH_CURSOR;

END PLIEMPA;
```

And here are the results

```
SAMPLE PLI PROGRAM: CALL EXTERNAL TABLE FUNCTION
      3217    9166.64
      7459   13333.32
      9134   13333.32
*** NO MORE RECORDS TO PROCESS!!
CLOSE CURSOR SQLCODE:                0
```

Sourced Function

A sourced function redefines or extends an existing DB2 function. It is typically written to enable the processing of user defined data types in a function. For example, suppose you define a Canadian dollar type as follows:

```
CREATE DISTINCT TYPE HRSCHEMA.CANADIAN_DOLLAR AS DECIMAL (9,2);
```

Now create a table using this type:

```
CREATE TABLE HRSCHEMA.CAN_PAY_TBL
  (EMP_ID INT,
   PAY_DATE DATE,
   PAY_AMT CANADIAN_DOLLAR)
  IN TSHR;
```

Now assume we've loaded 4 rows into the table, and we want to query a sum of the PAY_AMT rows. Here is our data.

```
SELECT * FROM HRSCHEMA.CAN_PAY_TBL;

---------+---------+---------+---------
    EMP_ID  PAY_DATE       PAY_AMT
---------+---------+---------+---------
      3217  2017-01-01      5500.50
      3217  2017-02-01      5500.50
      3217  2017-03-01      5500.50
      3217  2017-04-01      5500.50
DSNE610I NUMBER OF ROWS DISPLAYED IS 4
```

And here is the summarization query:

```
      SELECT SUM(PAY_AMT) FROM HRSCHEMA.CAN_PAY_TBL;
---------+---------+---------+---------+---------+---------+--------
DSNT408I SQLCODE = -440, ERROR:  NO AUTHORIZED FUNCTION NAMED SUM HAVING
COMPATIBLE ARGUMENTS WAS FOUND
DSNT418I SQLSTATE   = 42884 SQLSTATE RETURN CODE
DSNT415I SQLERRP    = DSNXORFN SQL PROCEDURE DETECTING ERROR
DSNT416I SQLERRD    = -100 0  0  -1  0  0 SQL DIAGNOSTIC INFORMATION
DSNT416I SQLERRD    = X'FFFFFF9C'  X'00000000'  X'00000000'  X'FFFFFFFF'
           X'00000000'  X'00000000' SQL DIAGNOSTIC INFORMATION
```

We received an error because the SUM function in DB2 does not know about a CANADIAN_DOLLAR type of input parameter, so the value we passed is an "incompatible argument". To fix this we must extend the SUM function to work with CANADIAN_DOLLAR input type by creating a user defined function based on the SUM function but accepting a CANADIAN_DOLLAR argument. Try this one:

```
CREATE FUNCTION SUM(CANADIAN_DOLLAR)
RETURNS DECIMAL (9,2)
SOURCE SYSIBM.SUM(DECIMAL)
---------+---------+---------+---------+---------+---------+-----
DSNE616I STATEMENT EXECUTION WAS SUCCESSFUL, SQLCODE IS 0
```

Now you have a SUM function for which CANADIAN_DOLLAR is an input parameter. When DB2 processes the query it will use the new user defined version of the SUM function because that's the one that matches your query arguments. Your SUM query will work now.

```
   SELECT SUM(PAY_AMT) FROM HRSCHEMA.CAN_PAY_TBL;
---------+---------+---------+---------+---------+---------+---

---------+---------+---------+---------+---------+---------+---
   22000.00
DSNE610I NUMBER OF ROWS DISPLAYED IS 1
```

Triggers

A trigger performs a set of actions when an INSERT, UPDATE or DELETE takes place. Triggers are stored in the database which is a significant advantage of using them instead of application logic.

The CREATE TRIGGER statement defines a trigger and builds a trigger package at the current server. Advantages of using a trigger include:

- Ability to write to other tables for audit trail.
- Ability to read other tables for validation.
- Ability to compare data before and after update operations.

Types of triggers

There are three types of triggers:

- INSERT
- UPDATE
- DELETE

A `MERGE` action also fires `INSERT` and `UPDATE` triggers (if they exist) depending on whether the `MERGE` causes an `INSERT` or `UPDATE`.

Timings of triggers

There are three timings of triggers as well:

- `BEFORE`
- `AFTER`
- `INSTEAD OF`

A `BEFORE` trigger performs its action before the SQL operation (`INSERT`, `UPDATE` or `DELETE`) that fired the trigger. An `AFTER` trigger performs its action after the SQL operation (`INSERT`, `UPDATE` or `DELETE`) that fired the trigger. An `INSTEAD OF` trigger is completely different that the other two timings – it enables `ADD`, `UPDATE` or `DELETE` operation through what would normally be a read-only view. We'll explain that more when we get to the `INSTEAD OF` example below.

The basic syntax of the `CREATE TRIGGER` statement is:

```
CREATE TRIGGER <trigger name>
<AFTER / BEFORE / INSTEAD OF>
ON <table name>
REFERENCING <see examples>
FOR EACH ROW
<action to take>
```

Examples of Triggers

Sample After Trigger

One common use of triggers is to automatically add records to a history table when there is a change to the records in a base table. In this case we will create a history table to store previous versions of pay rates in the `EMP_PAY` table. We can create the history table like this:

```
CREATE TABLE HRSCHEMA.EMP_PAY_HST LIKE HRSCHEMA.EMP_PAY;
```

And then we'll add an additional column to the history table to keep track of when the record was added:

```
ALTER TABLE HRSCHEMA.EMP_PAY_HST
ADD AUDIT_DATE TIMESTAMP DEFAULT CURRENT TIMESTAMP;
```

Now we will create a trigger so that when a change is made to an EMP_PAY record, we will write the old version of the record to the history table. The trigger knows about the old and new versions of the record we are modifying so we specify the OLD version of the record and the fields to be added to the history table.

```
CREATE TRIGGER HRSCHEMA.TRG_EMP_PAY
AFTER UPDATE ON HRSCHEMA.EMP_PAY_X
REFERENCING OLD AS oldcol NEW AS newcol
FOR EACH ROW MODE DB2SQL
INSERT INTO HRSCHEMA.EMP_PAY_HST(
EMP_ID,
EMP_REGULAR_PAY,
EMP_BONUS_PAY,
AUDIT_DATE)
VALUES
(oldcol.EMP_ID,
oldcol.EMP_REGULAR_PAY,
oldcol.EMP_BONUS_PAY,
CURRENT TIMESTAMP)
```

Now let's look at an EMP_PAY record, modify it, and then see if the old version get's added to the history table:

```
SELECT * FROM HRSCHEMA.EMP_PAY
WHERE EMP_ID = 3217;
-------+---------+---------+---------+------
   EMP_ID   EMP_REGULAR_PAY   EMP_BONUS_PAY
-------+---------+---------+---------+------
     3217        55000.00         5500.00
NE610I NUMBER OF ROWS DISPLAYED IS 1
```

Let's change the EMP_REGULAR_PAY to 57000.

```
UPDATE HRSCHEMA.EMP_PAY
SET EMP_REGULAR_PAY = 57000
WHERE EMP_ID = 3217;
```

Now if we select from the history table, we see the previous version of the record and it was added today:

```
SELECT * FROM HRSCHEMA.EMP_PAY_HST
WHERE EMP_ID = 3217;
---------+---------+---------+---------+---------+---------+-----
     EMP_ID   EMP_REGULAR_PAY   EMP_BONUS_PAY   AUDIT_DATE
---------+---------+---------+---------+---------+---------+-----
       3217         55000.00          5500.00   2017-02-24-07.08.39.
DSNE610I NUMBER OF ROWS DISPLAYED IS 1
```

Note: the temporal tables introduced in DB2 10 provides more functionality for storing record history for system time enabled tables. Keep this in mind when designing your tables. But the trigger technique described above is still a very reliable way of automating the capture of record history.

Sample BEFORE Trigger

For this example, assume two tables:

- DEPTMENT which has department codes and descriptions.
- EMP_DATA_X which has an employee id, first and last names, and a department code.

Let's say we have a business rule that the department column in EMP_DAT_X can only have values that exist in the DEPTMENT table. Of course we could create a referential constraint with a foreign key, but let's say we prefer to implement this rule as a trigger instead. The trigger should prevent invalid updates and return an error message if a user tries to update a EMP_DATA_X record using a deprtment code that is not in the DEPTMENT table. This trigger would accomplish this job:

```
CREATE TRIGGER HRSCHEMA.BLOCK_DEPT_UPDATE
   NO CASCADE BEFORE UPDATE OF
   EMP_DEPT ON HRSCHEMA.EMP_DATA_X
   REFERENCING NEW AS N
   FOR EACH ROW MODE DB2SQL
   WHEN (N.EMP_DEPT
      NOT IN (SELECT DEPT_CODE FROM DEPTMENT))
      BEGIN ATOMIC
         SIGNAL SQLSTATE '85101' ('Invalid department code');
      END
```

Currently the data in these tables looks like this:

```
     SELECT * FROM HRSCHEMA.DEPTMENT;
     ---------+---------+---------+---------+
     DEPT_CODE   DEPT_NAME
     ---------+---------+---------+---------+
     DPTA        DEPARTMENT A
     DPTB        DEPARTMENT B
     DSNE610I NUMBER OF ROWS DISPLAYED IS 2

     SELECT * FROM EMP_DATA_X
     ---------+---------+---------+---------+---------+---------+-----
         EMP_ID  EMP_LNAME             EMP_FNAME             EMP_DEPT
     ---------+---------+---------+---------+---------+---------+-----
           8888  JONES                 WILLIAM               DPTA
     DSNE610I NUMBER OF ROWS DISPLAYED IS 1
```

If we try this SQL it will fail because department code "DPTC" does not exist in the DEPTMENT table. And the result is as we expected, plus the error text is what we defined in the trigger:

```
UPDATE HRSCHEMA.EMP_DATA_X
  SET EMP_DEPT = 'DPTC'
  WHERE EMP_ID = 8888;
---------+---------+---------+---------+---------+---------+---------+--
DSNT408I SQLCODE = -438, ERROR:  APPLICATION RAISED ERROR WITH DIAGNOSTIC TEXT:
Invalid department code
DSNT418I SQLSTATE   = 85101 SQLSTATE RETURN CODE
DSNT415I SQLERRP    = DSNXRTYP SQL PROCEDURE DETECTING ERROR
DSNT416I SQLERRD    = 1 0 0 -1 0  0 SQL DIAGNOSTIC INFORMATION
DSNT416I SQLERRD    = X'00000001'  X'00000000'  X'00000000'  X'FFFFFFFF'
           X'00000000'  X'00000000' SQL DIAGNOSTIC INFORMATION
```

Sample INSTEAD OF Trigger

An INSTEAD OF trigger is different than all other types of triggers. The purpose of an INSTEAD OF trigger is to allow updates to take place from what is normally a read-only view. You may know that a view that includes more than one table is read only. Let's look at an example of creating ansd updating data using a view with an INSTEAD OF trigger.

We'll start with a query that joins certain columns in the EMPLOYEE table with the EMP_PAY table.

```
SELECT
  A.EMP_ID,
  A.EMP_LAST_NAME,
  B.EMP_REGULAR_PAY
  FROM HRSCHEMA.EMPLOYEE A, HRSCHEMA.EMP_PAY B
  WHERE A.EMP_ID = B.EMP_ID;
---------+---------+---------+---------+---------+--
    EMP_ID   EMP_LAST_NAME       EMP_REGULAR_PAY
---------+---------+---------+---------+---------+--
      3217   JOHNSON                    55000.00
      7459   STEWART                    80000.00
      9134   FRANKLIN                   80000.00
      4720   SCHULTZ                    80000.00
      6288   WILLARD                    70000.00
DSNE610I NUMBER OF ROWS DISPLAYED IS 5
```

Now let's create a view based on this query:

```
CREATE VIEW HRSCHEMA.EMP_PROFILE_PAY
AS
SELECT
A.EMP_ID,
```

```
            A.EMP_LAST_NAME,
            B.EMP_REGULAR_PAY
        FROM HRSCHEMA.EMPLOYEE A, HRSCHEMA.EMP_PAY B
        WHERE A.EMP_ID = B.EMP_ID;
---------+---------+---------+---------+---------+--------
DSNE616I STATEMENT EXECUTION WAS SUCCESSFUL, SQLCODE IS 0
---------+---------+---------+---------+---------+--------
```

And now we can query the data using the view:

```
        SELECT * FROM HRSCHEMA.EMP_PROFILE_PAY

---------+---------+---------+---------+---------+-
      EMP_ID  EMP_LAST_NAME       EMP_REGULAR_PAY
---------+---------+---------+---------+---------+-
        3217  JOHNSON                    55000.00
        7459  STEWART                    80000.00
        9134  FRANKLIN                   80000.00
        4720  SCHULTZ                    80000.00
        6288  WILLARD                    70000.00
DSNE610I NUMBER OF ROWS DISPLAYED IS 5
```

Now suppose we want to use this view to update the EMP_REGULAR_PAY column. Let's try and see what happens:

```
        UPDATE HRSCHEMA.EMP_PROFILE_PAY
        SET EMP_REGULAR_PAY = 65000
        WHERE EMP_ID = 3217;

---------+---------+---------+---------+---------+---------+---------+------
DSNT408I SQLCODE = -151, ERROR:  THE UPDATE OPERATION IS INVALID BECAUSE THE
CATALOG DESCRIPTION OF COLUMN RSCHEMA.EMP_PROFILE_PAY.EMP_REGULAR_PAY
INDICATES THAT IT CANNOT BE UPDATED
DSNT418I SQLSTATE   = 42808 SQLSTATE RETURN CODE
DSNT415I SQLERRP    = DSNXOST SQL PROCEDURE DETECTING ERROR
DSNT416I SQLERRD    = -400 0  0  -1  0  0 SQL DIAGNOSTIC INFORMATION
DSNT416I SQLERRD    = X'FFFFFE70'  X'00000000'  X'00000000'  X'FFFFFFFF'
           X'00000000'  X'00000000' SQL DIAGNOSTIC INFORMATION
```

As you can see, we are not allowed to perform updates using this view. However, we can perform the updates through this view if we create an INSTEAD OF trigger on the view. The DDL looks like this:

```
        CREATE TRIGGER HRSCHEMA.EMP_PROF_PAY_UPDATE
        INSTEAD OF UPDATE ON HRSCHEMA.EMP_PROFILE_PAY
            REFERENCING NEW AS NEWEMP OLD AS OLDEMP
              FOR EACH ROW
              MODE DB2SQL
                BEGIN ATOMIC
                    UPDATE HRSCHEMA.EMP_PAY AS E
                      SET (EMP_REGULAR_PAY)
```

```
                    = (NEWEMP.EMP_REGULAR_PAY)
          WHERE NEWEMP.EMP_ID = E.EMP_ID ;
    END
```

The trigger is intercepting the UPDATE request from the EMP_PROFILE_PAY view and performing a direct update to the EMP_PAY table.

Now let's try our update:

```
UPDATE HRSCHEMA.EMP_PROFILE_PAY
SET EMP_REGULAR_PAY = 65000
WHERE EMP_ID = 3217;
```

Finally let's select the row we just changed using the view:

```
SELECT * FROM HRSCHEMA.EMP_PROFILE_PAY
WHERE EMP_ID = 3217;

EMP_ID      EMP_LAST_NAME        EMP_REGULAR_PAY
------      -------------        ---------------
  3217      JOHNSON                     65000.00
```

And as we can see, the EMP_REGULAR_PAY did get changed.

Of course when all is said and done, you could simply have updated the base table to begin with. However, views can give you more control over what users and/or programmers are allowed to see and change in a table. The point of the INSTEAD OF triggers is to allow you to use a view as the interface for all adds, changes and deletes.

Important to Remember Trigger Information

- A trigger is fired by an INSERT, UPDATE or DELETE of a record in a table.

- By default, the LOAD operation does not fire triggers. However, if the SHRLEVEL CHANGE option is included on the LOAD statement, triggers will be fired.

- You cannot use a FOR EACH STATEMENT with BEFORE or INSTEAD OF timing. FOR EACH STATEMENT means your trigger logic is to be applied only once after the triggering statement finishes processing the affected rows.

- If you do not specify a list of column names in the trigger, an update operation on any column of the subject table will fire the trigger.

- A trigger can call a local stored procedure.

- A trigger cascade occurs when the SQL statements executed by one trigger fires one or more other triggers (for example, a trigger action on one table might write a row to another table which in turn has an INSERT trigger on it that performs some other action).

- If a column is included on a table for which a trigger is defined, the column cannot be dropped from the table unless the trigger is first dropped.

- If you alter a column definition for a table in which a trigger is defined on that column, the trigger packages are invalidated.

- If you drop a table for which a trigger has been defined, the trigger is also dropped automatically.

Additional information about triggers is available in the IBM product documentation: [vi]

Referential Integrity

Referential Constraints Overview
A referential constraint is the rule that the non-NULL values of a foreign key are valid only if they also appear as values of a parent key. The table that contains the parent key is called the parent table of the referential constraint, and the table that contains the foreign key is a dependent of that table. Referential integrity ensures data integrity by using primary and foreign key relationships between tables.

In DB2 you define a referential constraint by specifying in the child table a column which references a column in a parent table. For example, in a company you could have a DEPARTMENT with column DEPT_CODE, and an EMPLOYEE table that includes a column DEPT that represents the department code an employee is assigned to. The rule would be that you cannot have a value in the EMPLOYEE table DEPT column that does not have a corresponding DEPT_CODE value in the DEPARTMENT table. You can think of this as a parent and child relationship between the DEPARTMENT table and the EMPLOYEE table.

Adding a Foreign Key Relationship

You add a foreign key relationship by performing an ALTER on the child table.

```
ALTER TABLE EMPLOYEE
    FOREIGN KEY FK_DEPT_EMP (DEPT)
        REFERENCES DEPARTMENT(DEPT_CODE) ;
```

```
---------+---------+---------+---------+---------+---------+--------
DSNT404I SQLCODE = 162, WARNING:   TABLE  SPACE  DBHR.TSHR  HAS  BEEN
PLACED IN CHECK PENDING
```

The constraint was built, but before you can use it you must do a CHECK DATA on your tablespace which has been put into CHECK PENDING status. The DB2 command for this is CHECK DATA and our case the command will be:

```
CHECK DATA TABLESPACE DBHR.TSHR
```

Once the CHECK DATA finishes, your tablespace is taken out of CHECK PENDING and you can continue, provided there were no errors.

Now if you try to update an EMPLOYEE record with a DEPT value that does not have a DEPT_CODE with the same value as the DEPT value you are using, you'll get an SQL error -530 which means a violation of a foreign key.

```
UPDATE HRSCHEMA.EMP_DATA
SET DEPT = 'DPTB'
```

```
---------+---------+---------+---------+---------+---------+--------
DSNT408I SQLCODE = -530, ERROR:   THE  INSERT  OR  UPDATE  VALUE  OF
FOREIGN KEY FK_DEPT_EMP IS INVALID
```

And this is the full explanation of the error.

```
-530
THE INSERT OR UPDATE VALUE OF FOREIGN KEY constraint-name IS INVALID
```
Explanation
```
An  insert  or  update  operation  attempted  to  place  a  value  in  a
foreign  key  of  the  object  table;  however,  this  value  was  not  equal
to some value of the parent key of the parent table.
When  a  row  is  inserted  into  a  dependent  table,  the  insert  value  of  a
foreign  key  must  be  equal  to  the  value  of  the  parent  key  of  some  row
of the parent table in the associated relationship.
When  the  value  of  the  foreign  key  is  updated,  the  update  value  of  a
foreign  key  must  be  equal  to  the  value  of  the  parent  key  of  some  row
of the parent table of the associated relationship.
```

We know now that the parent table DEPARTMENT does not have DEPT_CODE DPTB in it, and it must be added before the EMPLOYEE record can be updated.

Deleting a Record from the Parent Table

Now let's talk about what happens if you want to delete a record from the parent table. Assuming no EMPLOYEE records are linked to that DEPARTMENT record, deleting that record may be fine. But what if you are trying to delete a DEPARTMENT record whose DEPT_CODE is referenced by one or more records in the EMPLOYEE table?

Let's look at a record in the table:

```
SELECT EMP_ID, DEPT
 FROM HRSCHEMA.EMPLOYEE
WHERE EMP_ID = 1788;
--------+---------+------
  EMP_ID  DEPT
--------+---------+------
    1788  DPTA
```

Ok, we know that the DEPT_CODE in use is DPTA. Now let's try to delete DPTA from the DEPARTMENT table.

```
DELETE FROM DEPARTMENT
WHERE DEPT_CODE = 'DPTA';
--------+---------+---------+---------+---------+---------+--------
DSNT408I  SQLCODE  =  -532,  ERROR:    THE  RELATIONSHIP  FK_DEPT_EMP
RESTRICTS THE DELETION OF ROW WITH RID X'0000002201'
```

If we try to remove the DEPT_CODE from the DEPARTMENT table, we will get a -532 SQL error telling us our SQL is in violation of the referential constraint. That's probably what we want, but there are some other options for how to handle the situation.

You can specify the action that will take place upon deleting a parent record by including an ON DELETE clause in the foreign key definition. If no action is specified, or if RESTRICT is specified with the ON DELETE clause, then the parent record cannot be deleted unless all child records which reference that record are first deleted. RESTRICT is the most commonly used ON DELETE value (or just omitting the ON DELETE clause which has the same effect). This is the case above. Here are the two other options:

If **ON DELETE CASCADE** is specified, then any rows in the child table that correspond to the parent record will also be deleted. Wow, that is probably not what we want, but there may be cases where this function is useful. Possibly if a certain product is discontinued you might want to delete all pending SHIPPING table entries for it. I can't think of many other needs for this, but be aware that this option is available.

If **ON DELETE SET NULL** is specified, then the foreign key field will be set to NULL for corresponding rows that reference the parent record that is being deleted.

Let's redefine our constraint to use this last:

```
    ALTER TABLE HRSCHEMA.EMPLOYEE
    DROP CONSTRAINT FK_DEPT_EMP;

    ALTER TABLE HRSCHEMA.EMPLOYEE
        FOREIGN KEY FK_DEPT_EMP (DEPT)
           REFERENCES HRSCHEMA.DEPARTMENT (DEPT_CODE)
             ON DELETE SET NULL;
---------+---------+---------+---------+---------+---------+--------
DSNT404I SQLCODE = 162, WARNING:  TABLE SPACE DBHR.TSHR HAS BEEN
PLACED IN CHECK PENDING
```

Go ahead and run the CHECK DATA to clear the CHECK PENDING condition.

Now try deleting the DPTA record from the DEPARTMENT table:

```
    DELETE FROM DEPARTMENT
    WHERE DEPT_CODE = 'DPTA';
---------+---------+---------+--------
DSNE615I NUMBER OF ROWS AFFECTED IS 1
```

We see that the delete was successful. So now let's check and see if the DEPT value for the child record has been set to NULL.

```
    SELECT EMP_ID, DEPT
    FROM HRSCHEMA.EMP_DATA
    WHERE EMP_ID = 1788;
---------+---------+---------+--------
       EMP_ID   DEPT
---------+---------+---------+--------
         1788   ----
DSNE610I NUMBER OF ROWS DISPLAYED IS 1
```

And in fact the DEPT column has been set to NULL.

This closes our discussion of referential integrity. For designing and maintaining your systems, make sure you understand what a referential constraint is, the syntax for creating a foreign key relationship, and the various options/outcomes for the ON DELETE clause.

Special Tables
Temporal and Archive Tables

Temporal Tables
Temporal tables were introduced to DB2 in version 10. Briefly, a temporal table is one that keeps track of "versions" of data over time and allows you to query data according to the time frame. It is important to understand what problems you can solve with the technologies, such as automatically preventing overlapping rows for business time. We'll get to that in the examples.

Some benefits of DB2's built in support for managing temporal data include:

- Reduces application logic
- Can automatically maintain a history of table changes
- Ensures consistent handling of time related events

Now let's look at the two varieties of time travel in DB2, which are business time (sometimes referred to as application time) and system time.

Business Time
An employee's pay typically changes over time. Besides wanting to know the current salary, there may be many scenarios under which an HR department or supervisor might need to know what pay rate was in effect for an employee at some time in the past. We might also need to allow for cases where the employee terminated for some period of time and then returned. Or maybe they took a non-paid leave of absence. This is the concept of business time and it can be fairly complex depending on the business rules required by the application. It basically means a period of time in which the data is accurate. You could think of it as a data value an effective date and discontinue date.

A table can only have one business time period. When a BUSINESS_TIME period is defined for a table, DB2 generates a check constraint in which the end column value must be greater than the begin column value. Once a table is version enabled, the following clauses allow you to pull data for a particular bsuiness time period:

```
FOR BUSINESS_TIME FROM ... TO ...
FOR BUSINESS_TIME BETWEEN... AND...
```

For example:

```
SELECT * FROM HRSCHEMA.EMP_PAY
FOR BUSINESS_TIME BEWTWEEN '2017-01-01' AND '2017-02-01'
ORDER BY EMP_ID;
```

System Time

System time simply means the time during which a piece of data is in the database, i.e., when the data was added, changed or deleted. Sometimes it is important to know this. For example a user might enter an employee's salary change on a certain date but the effective date of the salary change might be earlier or later than the date it was actually entered into the system. An audit trail table often has a timestamp that can be considered system time at which a transaction occurred.

Like with business time, once a table is version-enabled for system time, the following clauses allow you to pull data for a particular system period:

```
FOR SYSTEM_TIME FROM ... TO ...
FOR SYSTEM_TIME BETWEEN... AND...
```

For example, maybe we want to know see several series of EMPLOYEE table records that were changed over a period of a month. Assuming a system version enabled table, this would work:

```
SELECT * FROM HRSCHEMA.EMPLOYEE
FOR SYSTEM_TIME BEWTWEEN '2017-01-01' AND '2017-02-01'
ORDER BY EMP_ID;
```

Bitemporal Support

In some cases you may need to support both business and system time in the same table. DB2 supports this and it is called bitemporal support. Now let's move on to some examples of all three types of temporal tables!

Business Time Example

You create a temporal table by adding columns for the start and ending period for which the data is valid. Let's do an example. We could modify our existing EMP_PAY table and we'll do that, but first let's look at how we would have defined it if we originally made it a temporal table.

Our original DDL for creating EMP_PAY looks like this:

```
CREATE TABLE HRSCHEMA.EMP_PAY(
```

```
EMP_ID INT NOT NULL,
EMP_REGULAR_PAY DECIMAL (8,2) NOT NULL,
EMP_BONUS_PAY DECIMAL    (8,2))
PRIMARY KEY (EMP_ID))
IN TSHR;
```

To create this table as a temporal table, we could have used this DDL instead and our new table name is `EMP_PAYX`:

```
CREATE TABLE HRSCHEMA.EMP_PAYX(
EMP_ID INT NOT NULL,
EMP_REGULAR_PAY DECIMAL (8,2) NOT NULL,
EMP_BONUS_PAY DECIMAL    (8,2)),
BUS_START    DATE   NOT NULL,
BUS_END      DATE   NOT NULL,

PERIOD BUSINESS_TIME(BUS_START, BUS_END),

PRIMARY KEY (EMP_ID, BUSINESS_TIME WITHOUT OVERLAPS))
IN TSHR;
```

Now let's insert a few rows into the table. Keep in mind that we now have a start and end date for which the information is valid. That could pose a problem if our end date is really "until further notice". Some applications solve that problem by establishing a date in the distant future as the standard end date for current data. We'll use 12/31/2099 for this example. For convenience we can use the existing `EMP_PAY` table to load `EMP_PAYX` using a query:

```
INSERT INTO HRSCHEMA.EMP_PAYX
SELECT EMP_ID,
EMP_REGULAR_PAY,
EMP_BONUS_PAY,
'2017-01-01',
'2099-12-31'
FROM HRSCHEMA.EMP_PAY;
```

Here's our resulting data:

```
SELECT * FROM HRSCHEMA.EMP_PAYX;

EMP_ID    EMP_REGULAR_PAY    EMP_BONUS_PAY  BUS_START   BUS_END
------    ---------------    -------------  ----------  ----------
  3217           55000.00          5500.00  2017-01-01  2099-12-31
  7481           80000.00          4500.00  2017-01-01  2099-12-31
  9134           80000.00          2500.00  2017-01-01  2099-12-31
```

Now let's suppose employee 3217 has been given a raise to 60K per year effective 2/1/2017. First we need to set the end business date on the existing record.

```
UPDATE HRSCHEMA.EMP_PAYX
SET BUS_END     = '2017-02-01'
WHERE EMP_ID = 3217;
```

IMPORTANT: both system and business time are inclusive of start date and exclusive of end date. That means when you set an end date, you'll usually want to add a day to the true end date and use that as the end date. For example, to set an employee salary effective January 1, 2017 and ending at midnight on January 31, 2017 you would use start date 2017-01-01. But you would use end date 2017-02-01. Otherwise January 31 will not be included when you do your query for business time through 1/31/2017.

If the above is a little confusing, it is because generally date related evaluations do not work this way (if you say BETWEEN two dates, it means inclusive at both ends), but this one does work this way. So be sure that you get this! For setting business and system time, the **start date is inclusive** but the **end date is exclusive**. Now let's add the new row:

```
INSERT INTO HRSCHEMA.EMP_PAYX
VALUES (3217,
60000.00,
5500.00,
'2017-02-01',
'2099-12-31');
```

Here's the result when you query all rows:

```
SELECT * FROM HRSCHEMA.EMP_PAYX ORDER BY EMP_ID;

EMP_ID EMP_REGULAR_PAY  EMP_BONUS_PAY BUS_START   BUS_END
------ ---------------  ------------- ----------  ----------
  3217         55000.00       5500.00 2017-01-01  2017-02-01
  3217         60000.00       5500.00 2017-02-01  2099-12-31
  7459         80000.00       4500.00 2017-01-01  2099-12-31
  9134         80000.00       2500.00 2017-01-01  2099-12-31
```

Note that there are now two records for employee 3217. However, if you query this data as of 2/1/2017, you would get a different result than if you queried it for business time 1/15/2017. Recall that querying data in temporal tables is supported by specific temporal clauses, including:

```
AS OF
```

```
        FROM
        BETWEEN


SELECT * FROM HRSCHEMA.EMP_PAYX
FOR BUSINESS_TIME AS OF '2017-02-01'
ORDER BY EMP_ID;

  EMP_ID      EMP_REGULAR_PAY    EMP_BONUS_PAY  BUS_START   BUS_END
  ------      ---------------    -------------  ----------  ----------
    3217             60000.00          5500.00  2017-02-01  2099-12-31
    7459             80000.00          4500.00  2017-01-01  2099-12-31
    9134             80000.00          2500.00  2017-01-01  2099-12-31

SELECT * FROM HRSCHEMA.EMP_PAYX
FOR BUSINESS_TIME AS OF '2017-01-15'
ORDER BY EMP_ID;

  EMP_ID      EMP_REGULAR_PAY    EMP_BONUS_PAY  BUS_START   BUS_END
  ------      ---------------    -------------  ----------  ----------
    3217             55000.00          5500.00  2017-01-01  2017-02-01
    7459             80000.00          4500.00  2017-01-01  2099-12-31
    9134             80000.00          2500.00  2017-01-01  2099-12-31
```

Since you defined the primary key with non-overlapping business times, DB2 will not allow you to enter any overlapping start and end dates. That saves some coding and solves one of the most pervasive and time-consuming application design errors I've observed over the years.

System Time Example

When you want to capture actions taken on a table at a particular time, use system time. Suppose you want to keep a snapshot of every record BEFORE it is changed. DB2's temporal table functionality also includes automated copying of a "before" image of each record to a history table. This feature can be used in lieu of using triggers which are also often used to store a history of each version of a record.

Let's take the example of our EMPLOYEE table. For business audit purposes, we want to capture all changes made to it. To do this is pretty easy. Follow these steps:

- Add system time fields to the base table
- Create a history table
- Version-enable the base table

Adding system time to the table is as simple as adding the time fields needed to track system time.

```
ALTER TABLE HRSCHEMA.EMPLOYEE
ADD COLUMN SYS_START TIMESTAMP(12)
GENERATED ALWAYS AS ROW BEGIN NOT NULL;

ALTER TABLE HRSCHEMA.EMPLOYEE
ADD COLUMN SYS_END TIMESTAMP(12)
GENERATED ALWAYS AS ROW END NOT NULL;

ALTER TABLE HRSCHEMA.EMPLOYEE
ADD COLUMN TRANS_ID TIMESTAMP(12) NOT NULL GENERATED
ALWAYS AS TRANSACTION START ID;

ALTER TABLE HRSCHEMA.EMPLOYEE
ADD PERIOD SYSTEM_TIME (SYS_START, SYS_END);
```

Now let's explore one more temporal table feature – the history table. There may be cases in which you want to maintain a record of all changes made to table. You can do this automatically by defining a history table and enabling your base table for versioning. Let's create a history table EMPLOYEE_HISTORY and we'll make it identical to EMPLOYEE.

```
CREATE TABLE EMPLOYEE_HISTORY LIKE EMPLOYEE;
```

Now we can enable versioning in the EMPLOYEE table like this:

```
ALTER TABLE EMPLOYEE
ADD VERSIONING
USE HISTORY TABLE EMPLOYEE_HISTORY
```

At this point we can make a change to one of the EMPLOYEE records and we expect to see the old version of the record in the history table.

```
UPDATE HRSCHEMA.EMPLOYEE
SET EMP_FIRST_NAME = 'FREDERICK'
WHERE EMP_ID = 4175;
```

Assume that today is January 30, 2017 so that's when we changed our data. When you query with a specified system time, DB2 implicitly joins the base table and the history table. For example, let's pull data for employee 4175 as of 1/15/2017:

```
SELECT EMP_ID, EMP_FIRST_NAME, SYS_START, SYS_END
FROM HRSCHEMA.EMPLOYEE
FOR SYSTEM_TIME AS OF '2017-01-15'
```

```
WHERE EMP_ID = 4175;

EMP_ID  EMP_FIRST_NAME        SYS_START                   SYS_END
------  --------------        ---------------------       -------------------------
  4175  FRED                  0001-01-01 00:00:00.0       2017-01-30 17:29:38.608073
```

Notice that the previous version of the record is pulled up (FRED instead of FREDERICK) because we specified system time 1/15/2017, so that means we want the record that was present in the table on 1/15/2017.

Now let's perform the same query for system time as of February 1, 2017.

```
SELECT EMP_ID, EMP_FIRST_NAME, SYS_START, SYS_END
FROM HRSCHEMA.EMPLOYEE
FOR SYSTEM_TIME AS OF '2017-02-01'
WHERE EMP_ID = 4175;

EMP_ID          EMP_FIRST_NAME  SYS_START                   SYS_END
------          --------------  -------------------------   -------------------
  4175          FREDERICK       2017-01-30 17:29:38.608073  9999-12-30 00:00:00.0
```

Now you've got the most current record with the modified name FREDERICK. That is pretty cool feature and most if it happens automatically once you set it up. It can really help save time when researching particular values that were in the table sometime in the past.

NOTE: You can only use a history table with a system time enabled table.

Bi-Temporal Example

Finally, let's do an example where you need both business time and system time enabled for the same table. Let's go back go our EMP_PAY table and create yet another version called EMP_PAYY:

```
CREATE TABLE HRSCHEMA.EMP_PAYY(
EMP_ID INT NOT NULL,
EMP_REGULAR_PAY DECIMAL (8,2) NOT NULL,
EMP_BONUS_PAY DECIMAL    (8,2)),
BUS_START    DATE    NOT NULL,
BUS_END      DATE    NOT NULL,
SYS_START    TIMESTAMP(12)
GENERATED ALWAYS AS ROW BEGIN NOT NULL,
SYS_END      TIMESTAMP(12)
GENERATED ALWAYS AS ROW END NOT NULL,
 TRANS_ID TIMESTAMP(12) NOT NULL GENERATED
                          ALWAYS AS TRANSACTION START ID;

PERIOD BUSINESS_TIME(BUS_START, BUS_END),
PERIOD SYSTEM_TIME (SYS_START, SYS_END);
```

```
        PRIMARY KEY (EMP_ID, BUSINESS_TIME WITHOUT OVERLAPS))
    IN TSHR;
```

You'll still need to create the history table and version enable `EMP_PAYY`.

```
    CREATE TABLE EMP_PAYY_HISTORY LIKE EMP_PAYY;
```

Now we can enable versioning in the `EMP_PAYY` table like this:

```
    ALTER TABLE EMP_PAYY
    ADD VERSIONING
    USE HISTORY TABLE EMP_PAYY_HISTORY;
```

This concludes our discussion of DB2's support for temporal tables and time travel queries. This is a very powerful technology and I encourage you to learn it not just to pass the exam, but to take advantage of it's features that improve your client's access to actionable business information. It can also ease the application development and production support efforts!

Archive Tables

Archive tables are similar to history tables, but are unrelated to temporal tables. An **archive table** is a table that stores data that was deleted from another table which is called an **archive-enabled table**. When a row is deleted from the archive-enabled table, DB2 automatically adds the row to the archive table. When you query the archive-enabled table, you can specify whether or not to include archived records or not. We'll look at these features in an example.

Assume we want to delete some records from our `EMPLOYEE` table and we want to automatically archive the deleted records to a new table `EMPLOYEE_ARCHIVE`. Assume that the new table is already set up and defined correctly, i.e., with the same column definitions as `EMPLOYEE`.

To enable archiving of deleted records from table `EMPLOYEE` you would execute the following:

```
        ALTER TABLE EMPLOYEE ENABLE ARCHIVE USE EMPLOYEE_ARCHIVE;
```

To automatically archive records, set the global variable `SYSIBMADM.MOVE_TO_ARCHIVE` to Y or E. `MOVE_TO_ARCHIVE` indicates whether deleting a record from an archive-enabled table should store a copy of the deleted record in the archive table. The values are:

- Y - store a copy of the deleted record, and also make any attempted insert/update operation against the archive table an error.
- E - store a copy of the deleted record.
- N - do not store a copy of the deleted record.

In the future when you query the EMPLOYEE you can choose to include or exclude the archived records in a given session. To do this, your package must first be bound with the ARCHIVESENSITIVE(YES) bind option. Then the package/program should set the GET_ARCHIVE global variable to Y (the default is N). At this point, any query against the archive-enabled table during this session will automatically include data from both the archive-enabled table and its corresponding archive table.

In our EMPLOYEE example, suppose we have a package EMP001 that is bound with ARCHIVESENSITIVE(YES). Suppose further that the program issues this SQL:

```
SET SYSIBMADM.GET_ARCHIVE = 'Y';
```

At this point any query we issue during this session against EMPLOYEE will automatically return any qualifying rows from both EMPLOYEE and EMPLOYEE_ARCHIVE. For example:

```
SELECT EMP_ID, EMP_LAST_NAME, EMPL_FIRST_NAME
FROM EMPLOYEE
ORDER BY EMP_ID;
```

If the package needs to revert to only picking up data from the EMPLOYEE table, it can simply issue the SQL:

```
SET SYSIBMADM.GET_ARCHIVE = 'N';
```

Some design advantages of an archive table are:

1. Your historical data is managed automatically. You don't need to manually move older data to a separate table.

2. The scope of your query is controlled using a global variable. Consequently you can modify your query results to include or exclude the archive table data and you don't have to change the SQL statement (only the global variable value).

3. Older rows that are less often retrieved can be stored in a separate table which could potentially be located on a cheaper device.

Materialized Query Tables

A materialized query table (MQT) basically stores the result set of a query. It is used to store aggregate results from one or more other tables. MQTs are often used to improve performance for certain aggregation queries by providing pre-computed results. Consequently, MQTs are most often used in analytic or data warehousing environments.

MQTs are either system-maintained or user maintained. For a system maintained table, the data can be updated using the REFRESH TABLE statement. A user-maintained MQT can be updated using the LOAD utility, and also the UPDATE, INSERT, and DELETE SQL statements.

Let's do an example of an MQT that summarizes monthly payroll. Assume we have a source table named EMP_PAY_HIST which will be a history of each employee's salary for each paycheck. The table is defined as follows:

Column Name	Definition
EMP_ID	Numeric
EMP_PAY_DATE	Date
EMP_PAY_AMT	Decimal(8,2)

The DDL for the table is as follows:

```
CREATE TABLE HRSCHEMA.EMP_PAY_HIST(
EMP_ID              INT NOT NULL,
EMP_PAY_DATE        DATE NOT NULL,
EMP_PAY_AMT         DECIMAL (8,2) NOT NULL)
IN TSHR;
```

Now let's assume the data in the table is the twice-monthly pay amount for each employee for the first two months of 2017. Perhaps you have a payroll program that loads the table each pay period, possibly using a query like this where the date changes with the payroll period:

```
INSERT INTO HRSCHEMA.EMP_PAY_HIST
SELECT EMP_ID,
'01/15/2017',
EMP_SEMIMTH_PAY
FROM HRSCHEMA.EMP_PAY_CHECK;
```

Assume that the data is as follows:

```
SELECT * FROM EMP_PAY_HIST ORDER BY EMP_PAY_DATE, EMP_ID;
---------+---------+---------+---------+---------+---------
    EMP_ID  EMP_PAY_DATE  EMP_PAY_AMT
---------+---------+---------+---------+---------+---------
      3217  2017-01-15       2291.66
      7459  2017-01-15       3333.33
      9134  2017-01-15       3333.33
      3217  2017-01-31       2291.66
      7459  2017-01-31       3333.33
      9134  2017-01-31       3333.33
      3217  2017-02-15       2291.66
      7459  2017-02-15       3333.33
      9134  2017-02-15       3333.33
      3217  2017-02-28       2291.66
      7459  2017-02-28       3333.33
      9134  2017-02-28       3333.33
DSNE610I NUMBER OF ROWS DISPLAYED IS 12
```

Finally, let's assume we regularly need an aggregated total of each employee's year to date pay. We could do this with a materialized query table. Let's build the query that will summarize the employee pay from the beginning of the year to current date:

```
SELECT EMP_ID, SUM(EMP_PAY_AMT) AS EMP_PAY_YTD
FROM HRSCHEMA.EMP_PAY_HIST
GROUP BY EMP_ID
ORDER BY EMP_ID;
---------+---------+---------+---------+---------
    EMP_ID          EMP_PAY_YTD
---------+---------+---------+---------+---------
      3217              9166.64
      7459             13333.32
      9134             13333.32
DSNE610I NUMBER OF ROWS DISPLAYED IS 3
```

Now let's create the MQT using this query and we'll make it a system managed table:

```
CREATE TABLE EMP_PAY_TOT (EMP_ID, EMP_PAY_YTD) AS
(SELECT EMP_ID, SUM(EMP_PAY_AMT) AS EMP_PAY_YTD
FROM HRSCHEMA.EMP_PAY_HIST
GROUP BY EMP_ID)
DATA INITIALLY DEFERRED
REFRESH DEFERRED
MAINTAINED BY SYSTEM
ENABLE QUERY OPTIMIZATION;
```

We can now populate the table by issuing the REFRESH TABLE statement as follows:

```
REFRESH TABLE HRSCHEMA.EMP_PAY_TOT;
```

Finally we can query the MQT as follows:

```
SELECT * FROM HRSCHEMA.EMP_PAY_TOT;

---------+---------+---------+---------+---------+--------
     EMP_ID              EMP_PAY_YTD
---------+---------+---------+---------+---------+--------
       3217                  9166.64
       7459                 13333.32
       9134                 13333.32
DSNE610I NUMBER OF ROWS DISPLAYED IS 3
```

Temporary Tables

Sometimes you may need to create a DB2 table for the duration of a session but no longer than that. For example you may have a programming situation where it is convenient to have a temporary table which you can load for these operations:

- To join the data in the temporary table with another table
- To store intermediate results that you can query later in the program
- To load data from a flat file into a relational format

Let's assume that you only need the temporary table for the duration of a session or iteration of a program because temporary tables are dropped automatically as soon as the session ends.

Temporary tables are created using either the CREATE statement or the DECLARE statement. The differences will be explored in the Application Design section of this book. For now we will just look at an example of creating a table called EMP_INFO using both methods:

```
CREATE GLOBAL TEMPORARY TABLE
EMP_INFO(
EMP_ID     INT,
EMP_LNAME  VARCHAR(30),
EMP_FNAME  VARCHAR(30));

DECLARE GLOBAL TEMPORARY TABLE
EMP_INFO(
EMP_ID     INT,
EMP_LNAME  VARCHAR(30),
EMP_FNAME  VARCHAR(30));
```

When using the LIKE clause to create a temporary table, the implicit table definition includes only the column name, data type and NULLability characteristic of each of the columns of the source table, and any column defaults. The temporary table does NOT have any unique constraints, foreign key constraints, triggers, indexes, table partitioning keys, or distribution keys.

CREATED Temporary Tables
Created temporary tables:

- Have an entry in the system catalog (SYSIBM.SYSTABLES)
- Cannot have indexes
- Their columns cannot use default values (except NULL)
- Cannot have constraints
- Cannot be used with DB2 utilities
- Cannot be used with the UPDATE statement
- If DELETE is used at all, it will delete all rows from the table
- Do not provide for locking or logging

DECLARED Temporary Tables
A declared temporary table offers some advantages over created temporary tables.

- Can have indexes and check constraints
- Can use the UPDATE statement
- Can do positioned deletes

So declared temporary tables offer more flexibility than created temporary tables. However, when a session ends, DB2 will automatically delete both the rows in the table and the table definition. So if you want a table definition that persists in the DB2 catalog for future use, you would need to use a created temporary table.

Things to remember about temporary tables:

- Use temporary tables when you need the data only for the duration of the session.

- Created temporary tables can provide excellent performance because they do not use locking or logging.

- Declared temporary tables can also be very efficient because you can choose not to log, and they only allow limited locking.

- The schema for a temporary table is always SESSION.
- If you create a temporary table and you wish to replace any existing temporary table that has the same name, use the `WITH REPLACE` clause.
- If you create a temporary table from another table using the `LIKE` clause, the temporary table will NOT have any unique constraints, foreign key constraints, triggers, indexes, table partitioning keys, or distribution keys from the original table.

More information about temporary tables is available on the IBM product documentation site: [vii]

Auxiliary Tables

An auxiliary table is used to store Large Object (LOB) data that is linked to another table. To fully understand auxiliary tables, it is necessary to know how DB2 handles large object data. Let's review LOB basics and then we'll do a programming example.

Basic LOB Concepts

A large object (LOB) is a data type for large, unstructured data such as photographs, audio or video files, large character data files, etc. There are three types of LOB:

CLOB is a character large object. CLOBs are used to store single byte character type files up to 2 GB in size. This includes large documents and other text files.

BLOB is a binary large object. BLOBs are used to store binary unstructured data, often multimedia files such as photos, music or video files up to 2 GB in size.

DBCLOB is a double byte character large object. It is used for storing up to 1 GB of double byte character data. It is often used for storing text files in languages that require two bytes per character.

LOB Example

To store and retrieve LOB data, you follow these steps:

- Add an LOB column to a table.
- Create an auxiliary LOB tablespace (if one doesn't already exist for your purpose).

- Create an auxiliary table to store the actual LOB value and to tie it to the column from the base table.
- Create an index on the LOB table.

For an example, let's add an employee photo column to the EMPLOYEE table. Since photo data is large binary data, we will define our employee photo column as a BLOB column of up to 5 MB. We also need to define a ROWID column which will be used to locate the actual BLOB value in the auxiliary table:

```
ALTER TABLE EMPLOYEE
ADD ROW_ID ROWID NOT NULL GENERATED ALWAYS;
```

Now let's add the LOB photo column.

```
ALTER TABLE EMPLOYEE
ADD EMP_PHOTO BLOB(5M);
```

Next, if we do not already have an LOB table space, we can create one as follows:

```
CREATE LOB TABLESPACE
EMP_PHOTO_TS
IN HRDB
LOG NO;
```

While not mandatory, it is good practice to **NOT** log the LOB data, as this can slow performance considerably when dealing with large amounts of LOB data. Of course if the data is mission or time critical you may need to log it for recovery purposes.

Now we need to create the auxiliary table. We have to specify that the table be created in the new LOB tablespace, and that it will store column EMP_PHOTO from table EMPLOYEE. And we need a unique index on the auxiliary table. Here's the DDL for these operations.

```
CREATE AUX TABLE EMP_PHOTOS_TAB
IN EMP_PHOTO_TS
STORES EMPLOYEE
COLUMN (EMP_PHOTO);

CREATE UNIQUE INDEX XEMP_PHOTO
ON EMP_PHOTOS_TAB;
```

Now we would need to rerun the DCLGEN on the EMPLOYEE table. You'll notice that the DCLGEN now specifies the EMP_PHOTO as a BLOB type.

```
SQL TYPE is BLOB (5M) EMP_PHOTO;
```

Our update program can now load the photo data by defining a host variable into which you load the binary photo data. The host variable PHOTO-DATA must be defined as usage SQL and type as BLOB(5M). This is the COBOL declaration for the SQL host variable:

```
01 EMP-PHOTO USAGE IS SQL TYPE IS BLOB(5M).
```

Here it gets a little different from how we use other host variables. DB2 will generate an appropriate host language variable for you based on the SQL variable. When referring to the host variable in SQL you must use the name you declared (EMP-PHOTO). However, when you refer to that host variable in the host language (in this case COBOL), you'll need to use the variable name that DB2 generates (EMP-PHOTO-DATA).

```
 01   EMP-PHOTO.
    49 EMP-PHOTO-LENGTH              PIC S9(9) COMP-5.
    49 EMP-PHOTO-DATA                PIC X(5242880).
*01 EMP-PHOTO USAGE IS SQL TYPE IS BLOB(5M).
```

You can now retrieve an LOB value into your host variable just like any other variable:

```
SELECT EMP_PHOTO
INTO   :PHOTO-DATA
WHERE  EMP_ID = :EMP-ID;
```

If your program modifies the PHOTO-DATA, you can then update the stored BLOB value by updating the length and data portions of the DB2-generated variable, and then issuing an UPDATE using the SQL host variable. Assuming you have read a binary photo file into EMP-PHOTO-DATA and then set the EMP-PHOTO-LENGTH to the actual length of the file, you can now do the update.

```
MOVE <length of the file> to EMP-PHOTO-LENGTH

EXEC SQL
   UPDATE EMPLOYEE SET EMP_PHOTO = :PHOTO-DATA
   WHERE EMP_ID = :EMP-ID;
END-EXEC.
```

The above is a fairly inefficient way of retrieving or updating photo data if the data is acquired from an external file system. Materializing an LOB value inside a program space is usually not the best way to go because it takes a lot of overhead in the program space, and there are other alternatives. First let's mention LOB locator variables, and then we'll look at file reference variables. Finally we'll consider inline LOBs where a portion of the LOB value is actually stored in the base table.

LOB Locators

In the previous example, we materialized the LOB data when we read it into the host variable PHOTO-DATA. By materialized, we mean the data was copied from the LOB record to the host variable in the program. In many cases you may wish to work with LOBs where you simply locate the value without actually materializing it. In that case, you can use locator host variables.

A locator variable is a locator to the actual LOB data in the auxiliary table. So if you execute a query in which you read an LOB column into a locator host variable, only the locator information is contained in the host variable. That saves a lot of space.

We could define a locator host variable for the example as follows:

```
77 PHOTO-DATA-LOC USAGE IS SQL TYPE IS BLOB LOCATOR.
```

Now if you issue a query against this, only the locator value will be returned in the query.

```
SELECT EMP_PHOTO
INTO   :PHOTO-DATA-LOC
WHERE EMP_ID = :EMP-ID;
```

Then if your program logic determines that it really needs to materialize the BLOB, you could do so by reading the BLOB column into the BLOB host variable rather than into the locator variable. That's what we did in the first example a few pages back.

File Reference Variables

Sometimes you need to load a value into a LOB column using the content of an external file. In other cases you may need to unload an LOB value from DB2 into an external file. In these cases, you can avoid having to allocate program storage for the LOB value by using file reference variables.

With file reference variables you define a file as the source of an LOB value, and you can then perform an insert or update to the DB2 table without materializing the LOB inside the program. In this way the I/O takes place strictly between DB2 and the file system. This saves a lot of overhead because the program does not need to materialize the `LOB` value.

Here's an example of defining a file reference and using it to load a photo to the `EMP_PHOTO` table for employee 3217. Assume we have a binary file named `EMP3217.PHOTO` that is sized 1.786835 MB.

```
       IDENTIFICATION DIVISION.
       PROGRAM-ID. COBEMPB.

      ******************************************************
      *    PROGRAM USING DB2 FOR LOB FILE VARIABLE DEC.    *
      ******************************************************

       ENVIRONMENT DIVISION.
       DATA DIVISION.
       WORKING-STORAGE SECTION.


       01  ERR-REC.
           05  FILLER              PIC X(10) VALUE 'SQLCODE = '.
           05  SQLCODE-VIEW        PIC -999.
           05  FILLER              PIC X(005) VALUE SPACES.
           05  ERR-TAB             PIC X(016).
           05  ERR-PARA            PIC X(015).
           05  ERR-DETAIL          PIC X(040).

       77  ERR-TXT-LGTH            PIC S9(9) USAGE COMP VALUE +72.

       01  ERR-MSG.
           05  ERR-MSG-LGTH        PIC S9(04) COMP VALUE +864.
           05  ERR-MSG-TXT         PIC X(072) OCCURS 12 TIMES
                                         INDEXED BY ERR-NDX.

       01 EMP-PHOTO-FILE USAGE IS SQL TYPE IS BLOB-FILE.

           EXEC SQL
              INCLUDE SQLCA
           END-EXEC.



       PROCEDURE DIVISION.

       MAIN-PARA.
           DISPLAY "SAMPLE COBOL PROGRAM: LOB WITH FILE REF VAR".

           MOVE 13 TO EMP-PHOTO-FILE-NAME-LENGTH
           MOVE 1786835 TO EMP-PHOTO-FILE-DATA-LENGTH
           MOVE 1 TO EMP-PHOTO-FILE-FILE-OPTION
```

```
        MOVE 'EMP3217.PHOTO' TO EMP-PHOTO-FILE-NAME


        EXEC SQL
           UPDATE HRSCHEMA.EMPLOYEE
           SET EMP_PHOTO = :EMP-PHOTO-FILE
           WHERE EMP_ID = 3217
        END-EXEC.

        IF SQLCODE IS NOT EQUAL TO ZERO

           MOVE SQLCODE TO SQLCODE-VIEW
           MOVE 'EMPLOYEE' TO ERR-TAB
           MOVE 'MAIN'     TO ERR-PARA
           MOVE 3217       TO ERR-DETAIL
           PERFORM P9999-SQL-ERROR

        ELSE
           DISPLAY 'UPDATE CALL SUCCESFULL ' HV-ID

        END-IF

        STOP RUN.

   P9999-SQL-ERROR.

        DISPLAY ERR-REC.

        CALL 'DSNTIAR' USING SQLCA,
                     ERR-MSG,
                     ERR-TXT-LGTH.

        IF RETURN-CODE IS EQUAL TO ZERO

           PERFORM P9999-DISP-ERR
              VARYING ERR-NDX FROM 1 BY 1
              UNTIL ERR-NDX > 12

        ELSE
           DISPLAY 'DSNTIAR ERROR CODE = ' RETURN-CODE
           STOP RUN.

   P9999-DISP-ERR.

        DISPLAY ERR-MSG-TXT(ERR-NDX).

   P9999-DISP-ERR-EXIT.
```

The above is a very simple example of working with LOBs and file locator variables. If you had more file names and file sizes, you could set up a loop to process the photo files. You'd need a way of passing the multiple file names and file sizes to the program, perhaps by storing these in a text file. There are a lot of possibilities, but I think you know the basics now.

Here is the PLI version of the program.

```
PLIEMPB: PROCEDURE OPTIONS(MAIN) REORDER;
/********************************************************************
* PROGRAM NAME :    PLIEMPB - LOB FILE VARIABLE DECLARATION/USAGE   *
********************************************************************/

/********************************************************************
*              E X T E R N A L    E N T R I E S                     *
********************************************************************/
   DCL DSNTIAR ENTRY OPTIONS(ASM INTER RETCODE);

/********************************************************************
/*             W O R K I N G    S T O R A G E                       *
********************************************************************/

   DCL 01  HV_ID              FIXED BIN(31);

   DCL EMP_PHOTO_FILE USAGE IS SQL TYPE IS BLOB_FILE;

   DCL RET_SQL_CODE            FIXED BIN(31) INIT(0);
   DCL RET_SQL_CODE_PIC        PIC 'S999999999' INIT (0);

   DCL 01 ERR_REC,
          05 FILLER1           CHAR(10) INIT ('SQLCODE = '),
          05 SQLCODE_VIEW      PIC '-999',
          05 ERR_EMPID         FIXED BIN (31) INIT (0),
          05 FILLER2           CHAR(01) INIT (' '),
          05 ERR_TAB           CHAR(08) INIT (' '),
          05 ERR_PARA          CHAR(15) INIT (' ');

   DCL 01 ERR_MSG AUTOMATIC,
          05 ERR_LGTH          FIXED BIN (31) INIT (864),
          05 ERR_TXT(10)       CHAR(72);

   DCL ERR_TXT_LGTH            FIXED BIN (15) INIT (72);
   DCL ERR_NDX                 FIXED BIN (31) INIT (0);

   EXEC SQL
     INCLUDE SQLCA;


/********************************************************************
/*             P R O G R A M    M A I N L I N E                     *
********************************************************************/
   PUT SKIP LIST ('SAMPLE PLI PROGRAM: LOB WITH FILE REF VAR');

      EMP_PHOTO_FILE_NAME_LENGTH = 12;
```

```
            EMP_PHOTO_FILE_DATA_LENGTH = 1786835;
            EMP_PHOTO_FILE_FILE_OPTION = 1;
            EMP_PHOTO_FILE_NAME        = 'HRSCHEMA.PHOTO';

            EXEC SQL

               UPDATE HRSCHEMA.EMP_PHOTO
               SET EMP_PHOTO = :EMP_PHOTO_FILE
               WHERE EMP_ID = 3217;

            IF SQLCODE ¬= 0 THEN
               DO;
                  SQLCODE_VIEW = SQLCODE;
                  ERR_TAB = 'EMPLOYEE';
                  ERR_PARA = 'MAIN';
                  ERR_EMPID = HV_ID;
                  CALL P9999_SQL_ERROR;
               END;
            ELSE
               PUT SKIP LIST ('UPDATE CALL SUCCESFULL ' || HV_ID);


      P9999_SQL_ERROR: PROC;

         PUT SKIP LIST (ERR_REC);

         CALL DSNTIAR (SQLCA, ERR_MSG, ERR_TXT_LGTH);

         IF RETCODE = 0 THEN
            DO ERR_NDX = 1 TO 10;
               PUT SKIP DATA (ERR_TXT(ERR_NDX));
            END; /* DO */
         ELSE
            PUT SKIP LIST ('DSNTIAR ERROR CODE = ' || RETCODE);

      END P9999_SQL_ERROR;

      END PLIEMPB;
```

LOB Inline

You can store part or all of a LOB inline which means that part or all of the LOB value can be stored in the base table. That way some part of the data is available without materializing the entire LOB. This has some advantages, especially when you are using CLOBs where a given query may only need to reference data at the beginning of the CLOB record.

You define how much of the LOB will be stored in the base table using the INLINE LENGTH clause. So in the case of a CLOB named EMP_RECOG_TEXT you might define it as follows:

```
CREATE TABLE HRSCHEMA.EMP_RECOG_HIST
(EMP_ID INT NOT NULL,
EMP_RECOG_TEXT CLOB(1M) INLINE LENGTH 5000)
IN TSHR;
```

Now any value in the EMP_RECOG_TEXT field up to 5000 bytes will be stored in the base table. You still need to define the auxiliary table for the LOB, just as we did in the earlier examples. However, defining your LOB with an inline length means you avoid the additional I/O of bringing in the CLOB from the LOB tablespace any time the data you need is within the first 5000 bytes of the CLOB. That can be quite an advantage.

Additional information about large object table spaces can be found on the IBM product documentation web site: [viii]

Additional information about large objects can be found on the IBM product documentation web site here: [ix]

XML DATA

Introduction to XML

XML is a highly used standard for exchanging self-describing data files or documents. Even if you work in a shop that does not use the DB2 XML data type or XML functions, it is good to know how to use these. You will not be expected to have mastered advanced XML concepts for the exam, but you will need to know the basics of how to use XML in DB2 in order to answer the XML-related DB2 questions.

A complete tutorial on XML is well beyond the scope of this book, but we'll review some XML basics. If you have little or no experience with XML, I strongly suggest that you purchase some books to acquire this knowledge. The following are a few that can help fill in the basics:

> XML in a Nutshell, Third Edition 3rd Edition by Elliotte Rusty Harold (ISBN 978-0596007645)
>
> XSLT 2.0 and XPath 2.0 Programmer's Reference by Michael Kay (ISBN: 978-0470192740)
>
> XQuery: Search Across a Variety of XML Data by Priscilla Walmsley (ISBN: 978-1491915103)

Basic XML Concepts

You may know that XML stands for Extensible Markup Language. XML technology is cross-platform and independent of machine and software. It provides a structure that consists of both data and data element tags, and so it describes the data in both human readable and machine readable format. The tag names for the elements are defined by the developer/user of the data.

XML Structure

XML has a tree type structure that is required to begin with a root element and then it expands to the branches. To continue our discussion of the EMPLOYEE domain, let's take a simple XML example with an employee profile as the root. We'll include the employee id, the address and birth date. The XML document might look like this:

```xml
<?xml version="1.0" encoding="UTF-8"?>
<EMP_PROFILE>
    <EMP_ID>4175</EMP_ID>
    <EMP_ADDRESS>
       <STREET>6161 MARGARET LANE</STREET>
       <CITY>ERINDALE</CITY>
```

```
            <STATE>AR</STATE>
            <ZIP_CODE>72653</ZIP_CODE>
         </EMP_ADDRESS>
         <BIRTH_DATE>07/14/1991</BIRTH_DATE>
      </EMP_PROFILE>
```

XML documents frequently begin with a declaration which includes the XML version and the encoding scheme of the document. In our example, we are using XML version 1.0 which is still very common. This declaration is optional but it's a best practice to include it.

Notice after the version specification that we continue with the tag name `EMP_PROFILE` enclosed by the <> symbols. The employee profile element ends with `/EMP_PROFILE` enclosed by the <> symbols. Similarly each sub-element is tagged and enclosed and the value (if any) appears between the opening and closing of the element.

XML documents must have a single root element, i.e., one element that is the root of all other elements. If you want more than one `EMP_PROFILE` in a document, then you would need a higher level element to contain the profiles. For example you could have a `DEPARTMENT` element that contains employee profiles, and a `COMPANY` element that contains `DEPARTMENTS`.

All elements must have a closing tag. Elements that are not populated can be represented by an opening and closing with nothing in between. For example, if an employee's birthday is not know, it can be represented by `<BIRTH_DATE></BIRTH_DATE>` or you can use the short hand form `<BIRTH_DATE/>`.

The example document includes elements such as the employee id, address and birth date. The address is broken down into a street name, city, state and zip code. Comments can be included in an XML document by following the following format:

```
      <!-- This is a sample comment -->
```

By default, white space is preserved in XML documents.

Ok, so we've given you a drive-thru version of XML. We'll provide more information later in the Application Design section, but for now we have almost enough to move on to how to manipulate XML data in DB2. Before we get to that, let's first look at two XML-related technologies that we will need.

XML Related Technologies

XPath
The extensible path language (XPath) is used to locate and extract information from an XML document using "path" expressions through the XML nodes. For example, in the case of the employee XML document we created earlier, you could locate and return a zip code value by specifying the path.

Recall this structure:

```
<EMP_PROFILE>
    <EMP_ID>4175</EMP_ID>
    <EMP_ADDRESS>
<STREET>6161 MARGARET LANE</STREET>
<CITY>ERINDALE</CITY>
<STATE>AR</STATE>
<ZIP_CODE>72653</ZIP_CODE>
</EMP_ADDRESS>
<BIRTH_DATE>07/14/1991</BIRTH_DATE>
</EMP_PROFILE>
```

In this example, the employee profile nodes with zip code 72653 can be identified using the following path:

```
/EMP_PROFILE/ADDRESS[ZIP_CODE=72653]
```

The XPath expression for all employees who live in Texas as follows:

```
/EMP_PROFILE/ADDRESS[STATE="TX"]
```

For more on the XPath syntax, check out this W3SCHOOLS reference: [x]

XQuery
XQuery enables us to query XML data using XPath expressions. It is similar to how we query relational data using SQL, but of course the syntax is different. Here's an example of pulling the employee id of every employee who lives at a zip code greater than 90000 from an XML document named **employees.xml**.

```
for                          $x                            in
doc("employees.xml")employee/profile/address/zipcode
where                                       $x/zipcode>90000
```

```
              order                  by              $x/zipcode
              return $x/empid
```

In DB2 you run an XQuery using the built-in function **XMLQUERY**. We'll show you some examples using XMLQUERY shortly. For now, if you are not very familiar with XQuery, I suggest browsing the IBM redbook for XQuery: [xi] You can also take a look at these IBM references for XPath [xii] and Xquery. [xiii]

DB2 Support for XML

The pureXML technology provides support for XML under DB2 for z/OS. DB2 includes an XML data type and many built-in DB2 functions to validate, traverse and manipulate XML data. The DB2 XML data type can store well-formed XML documents in their hierarchical form and retrieve entire documents or portions of documents.

You can execute DML operations such as inserting, updating and deleting XML documents. You can index and create triggers on XML columns. Finally, you can extract data items from an XML document and then store those values in columns of relational tables using the SQL XMLTABLE built-in function.

XML Example Operations

XML for the EMPLOYEE table

Suppose we need to implement a new interface with our employee benefits providers who use XML as the data exchange format. This could be a reason to store our detailed employee information in an XML structure within the DB2 table. For our purposes, we will add a column named EMP_PROFILE XML to the EMPLOYEE table. Here's the DDL to add the XML column:

```
ALTER TABLE HRSCHEMA.EMPLOYEE
ADD COLUMN EMP_PROFILE XML;
```

We could establish an XML schema to validate our data structure, for the moment we'll just deal with some basic SQL operations. As long as the XML is well formed, DB2 will accept it without a schema to validate against. We'll talk more about validation in the Non-Relational Data sub-section of the Application Design chapter later in this book.

Let's assume we are going to add a record to the EMPLOYEE table for employee Fred Turnbull who has employee id 4175, has 1 year if service and was promoted on 12/1/2016.

Here's the XML document structure we want for storing the employee profile:

```
<EMP_PROFILE>
    <EMP_ID>4175</EMP_ID>
    <EMP_ADDRESS>
       <STREET>6161 MARGARET LANE</STREET>
       <CITY>ERINDALE</CITY>
       <STATE>AR</STATE>
       <ZIP_CODE>72653</ZIP_CODE>
    </EMP_ADDRESS>
    <BIRTH_DATE>07/14/1991</BIRTH_DATE>
</EMP_PROFILE>
```

INSERT With XML

Now we can insert the new record as follows:

```
INSERT INTO HRSCHEMA.EMPLOYEE
(EMP_ID,
 EMP_LAST_NAME,
 EMP_FIRST_NAME,
 EMP_SERVICE_YEARS,
 EMP_PROMOTION_DATE,
 EMP_PROFILE)
VALUES (4175,
'TURNBULL',
'FRED',
1,
'12/01/2016',
'
<EMP_PROFILE>
    <EMP_ID>4175</EMP_ID>
    <EMP_ADDRESS>
<STREET>6161 MARGARET LANE</STREET>
<CITY>ERINDALE</CITY>
<STATE>AR</STATE>
<ZIP_CODE>72653</ZIP_CODE>
</EMP_ADDRESS>
<BIRTH_DATE>07/14/1991</BIRTH_DATE>
</EMP_PROFILE>
');
```

SELECT With XML

You can do a SELECT on an XML column and depending on what query tool you are using, you can display the content of the record in fairly readable form. Since the XML data is stored as one long string, it may be difficult to read without reformatting. We'll look at some options for that later.

```
SELECT EMP_ID, EMP_PROFILE FROM HRSCHEMA.EMPLOYEE
WHERE EMP_ID = 4175;
-------+---------+---------+---------+---------+---------+---------+---------+
   EMP_ID   EMP_PROFILE
-------+---------+---------+---------+---------+---------+---------+---------+
    4175                                  <?xml                  version="1.0"
encoding="IBM037"?><EMP_PROFILE><EMP_ID>4175</E
```

UPDATE With XML

To update an XML column you can use standard SQL if you want to update the entire content of the column. This SQL will do it:

```
UPDATE HRSCHEMA.EMPLOYEE
SET EMP_PROFILE
 = '<EMP_PROFILE>
              <EMP_ID>3217</EMP_ID>
              <EMP_ADDRESS>
              <STREET>2913 PATE DR</STREET>
              <CITY>FORT WORTH</CITY>
              <STATE>TX</STATE>
              <ZIP_CODE>76105</ZIP_CODE>
          </EMP_ADDRESS>
          <BIRTH_DATE>03/15/1952</BIRTH_DATE>
       </EMP_PROFILE>
    '
WHERE EMP_ID = 3217;

SELECT EMP_ID, EMP_PROFILE FROM HRSCHEMA.EMPLOYEE
WHERE EMP_ID = 3217;
-------+---------+---------+---------+---------+---------+---------+---------+
   EMP_ID   EMP_PROFILE
-------+---------+---------+---------+---------+---------+---------+---------+
    3217   <?xml version="1.0" encoding="IBM037"?><EMP_PROFILE><EMP_ID>3217</E
```

DELETE With XML

If you wish to delete the entire EMP_PROFILE, you can set it to NULL as follows:

```
UPDATE HRSCHEMA.EMPLOYEE
SET EMP_PROFILE = NULL
WHERE EMP_ID = 3217;

SELECT EMP_ID, EMP_PROFILE FROM HRSCHEMA.EMPLOYEE
WHERE EMP_ID = 3217;
-------+---------+---------+---------+---------+---------+---------+---------+
   EMP_ID   EMP_PROFILE
-------+---------+---------+---------+---------+---------+---------+---------+
    3217   ----------------------------------------------------------------
```

As you can see, the EMP_PROFILE column has been set to NULL. At this point, only one row in the EMPLOYEE table has the EMP_PROFILE populated.

```
SELECT EMP_ID, EMP_PROFILE FROM HRSCHEMA.EMPLOYEE;

-------+---------+---------+---------+---------+---------+---------+-------
  EMP_ID  EMP_PROFILE
-------+---------+---------+---------+---------+---------+---------+-------
    3217  ------------------------------------------------------------
    7459  ------------------------------------------------------------
    9134  ------------------------------------------------------------
    4175  <?xml version="1.0" encoding="IBM037"?><EMP_PROFILE><EMP_ID>4175<
```

Schema Validation for XML

DB2 does a basic check to ensure that the data you use to populate an XML column is well formed. We saw an example of this check back in section 1. As long as the XML is well formed, DB2 will apply it to the XML column.

In addition to ensuring well formed XML, you can also validate the XML against an XML schema. XML schema help you ensure that the XML content meets the rules you define. Again, if you are not very familiar with these concepts, I encourage you to read the recommended XML books. Let's create an example to go with the EMP_PROFILE column of the EMPLOYEE table.

First, let's review the XML column and some sample content.

```
<?xml version="1.0" encoding="UTF-8"?>
<EMP_PROFILE>
   <EMP_ID>4175</EMP_ID>
   <EMP_ADDRESS>
      <STREET>6161 MARGARET LANE</STREET>
      <CITY>ERINDALE</CITY>
      <STATE>AR</STATE>
      <ZIP_CODE>72653</ZIP_CODE>
   </EMP_ADDRESS>
   <BIRTH_DATE>1991-07-14</BIRTH_DATE>
</EMP_PROFILE>
```

Now let's establish some rules for the content of the EMP_PROFILE structure:

- EMP_ID is required and must be an integer greater than zero.
- STREET, CITY and STATE are required and must be string values.
- ZIP_CODE must be an integer greater than zero.
- BIRTH_DATE is optional, but if entered must be a valid date.

An XML schema for this structure might look like this:

```xml
<?xml version="1.0" encoding="UTF-8" ?>
<xs:schema xmlns:xs="http://www.w3.org/2001/XMLSchema">
<xs:element name="EMP_PROFILE">
   <xs:complexType>
     <xs:sequence>
        <xs:element name="EMP_ID" type="xs:positiveInteger" />
        <xs:element name="EMP_ADDRESS">
        <xs:complexType>
        <xs:sequence>
           <xs:element name="STREET" type="xs:string" />
           <xs:element name="CITY" type="xs:string" />
           <xs:element name="STATE" type="xs:string" />
            <xs:element name="ZIP_CODE" type="xs:positiveInteger"/>
        </xs:sequence>
        </xs:complexType>
        </xs:element>
         <xs:element name="BIRTH_DATE" minOccurs="0"
           type="xs:date" />
     </xs:sequence>
   </xs:complexType>
</xs:element>
</xs:schema>
```

Now we need to know how to define the XML schema to DB2. The schema must be added to the XML Schema Repository (XSR) before it can be used to validate XML docs. The XSR is a repository for all XML schemas that are required to validate and process the XML documents that are stored in XML columns. DB2 creates the XSR tables during installation or migration.

You can register an XML schema by calling these DB2-supplied stored procedures:

SYSPROC.XSR_REGISTER - Begins registration of an XML schema. You call this stored procedure when you add the first XML schema document to an XML schema.

SYSPROC.XSR_ADDSCHEMADOC - Adds additional XML schema documents to an XML schema that you are in the process of registering. You can call SYSPROC.XSR_ADDSCHEMADOC only for an existing XML schema that is not yet complete.

SYSPROC.XSR_COMPLETE - Completes the registration of an XML schema.

The stored procedures must be called either from an application program (such as a COBOL program), from Rexx or from Data Studio. Once registers, we can validate against the specified schema. Let try inserting an XML column with an invalid birth date:

```
UPDATE HRSCHEMA.EMPLOYEE
SET EMP_PROFILE
 = DSN_XMLVALIDATE (
 XMLPARSE(
 DOCUMENT(
 '<EMP_PROFILE>
  <EMP_ID>3217</EMP_ID>
  <EMP_ADDRESS>
     <STREET>2913 PATE DR</STREET>
     <CITY>FORT WORTH</CITY>
     <STATE>TX</STATE>
     <ZIP_CODE>76105</ZIP_CODE>
  </EMP_ADDRESS>
     <BIRTH_DATE>1952-02-30</BIRTH_DATE>
     </EMP_PROFILE>'))   ACCORDING    TO    XMLSCHEMA    ID
HRSCHEMA.EMP_PROFILE )
WHERE EMP_ID = 3217;


SQLCODE=-16105, SQLSTATE=2200M

Incorrect XML data. Expected data of type "dateTime" and found value
"1952-02-30" which is not a valid value for that type..
```

Now let's correct the birth date. We'll change it from February 30 to February 28, and we'll see that it now executes correctly:

```
UPDATE HRSCHEMA.EMPLOYEE
SET EMP_PROFILE
 = DSN_XMLVALIDATE (
 XMLPARSE(
 DOCUMENT(
 '<EMP_PROFILE>
  <EMP_ID>3217</EMP_ID>
  <EMP_ADDRESS>
     <STREET>2913 PATE DR</STREET>
     <CITY>FORT WORTH</CITY>
     <STATE>TX</STATE>
     <ZIP_CODE>76105</ZIP_CODE>
  </EMP_ADDRESS>
     <BIRTH_DATE>1952-02-28</BIRTH_DATE>
     </EMP_PROFILE>'))   ACCORDING    TO    XMLSCHEMA    ID
HRSCHEMA.EMP_PROFILE )
WHERE EMP_ID = 3217;


Updated 1 rows.
```

Finally, let's look at how we could change the `EMP_PROFILE` column in the `EMPLOYEE` table to automatically do the XML validation instead of us having to code it using the `DSN_XMLVALIDATE` routine. Assume we have created the XML schema named `EMP_PROFILE`. We can tie it to our `EMP_PROFILE` column as follows:

```
ALTER TABLE HRSCHEMA.EMPLOYEE
ALTER EMP_PROFILE
SET DATA TYPE XML(XMLSCHEMA ID HRSCHEMA.EMP_PROFILE)
```

Now when we try to add a value to an XML column that violates these rules, we will get an error. For example, let's try to add this structure using the same value we tried earlier, with an invalid birth date:

```
UPDATE HRSCHEMA.EMPLOYEE
SET EMP_PROFILE
 = XMLPARSE(
 DOCUMENT(
 '<EMP_PROFILE>
  <EMP_ID>3217</EMP_ID>
  <EMP_ADDRESS>
     <STREET>2913 PATE DR</STREET>
     <CITY>FORT WORTH</CITY>
     <STATE>TX</STATE>
     <ZIP_CODE>76105</ZIP_CODE>
     </EMP_ADDRESS>
     <BIRTH_DATE>1952-02-30</BIRTH_DATE>
     </EMP_PROFILE>'))
WHERE EMP_ID = 3217;


SQLCODE=-16105, SQLSTATE=2200M

Incorrect XML data. Expected data of type "dateTime" and found value
"1952-02-30" which is not a valid value for that type.
```

Again, we get an error because the birth date value is not a valid date and the XML schema requires it to be. From now on, any record we try to add to the `EMPLOYEE` table will fail if it includes an `EMP_PROFILE` value that does not conform to the schema we set up.

NOTE: To use the XSR, you must first set it up. This is an installation task and is beyond the scope of study for this text book. The procedure is available in the DB2 product documentation: [xiv]

XML Built-In Functions

XMLQUERY

XMLQUERY is the DB2 builtin function that enables you to run XQuery. Here is an example of using XMLQUERY with the XQuery xmlcolumn function to retrieve an XML element from the EMP_PROFILE element.

```
SELECT XMLQUERY
('for $info
in db2-fn:xmlcolumn("HRSCHEMA.EMPLOYEE.EMP_PROFILE")/EMP_PROFILE
return $info/EMP_ADDRESS/ZIP_CODE') AS ZIPCODE
from HRSCHEMA.EMPLOYEE
where EMP_ID = 4175

ZIPCODE
---------------------------
<ZIP_CODE>72653</ZIP_CODE>
```

Notice that the data is returned in XML format. If you don't want the XML structure to be returned, then add the XQuery text() function at the end of the return string, as below:

```
SELECT XMLQUERY
('for $info
in db2-fn:xmlcolumn("HRSCHEMA.EMPLOYEE.EMP_PROFILE")/EMP_PROFILE
return $info/EMP_ADDRESS/ZIP_CODE/text()') AS ZIPCODE
from HRSCHEMA.EMPLOYEE
where EMP_ID = 4175
```

The result of this query is not in XML format.

```
ZIPCODE
-------
  72653
```

For more information on XQuery for DB2, consult the IBM Redbook. [xv]

XMLEXISTS

The XMLEXISTS predicate specifies an XQuery expression. If the XQuery expression returns an empty sequence, the value of the XMLEXISTS predicate is false. Otherwise, XMLEXISTS returns true and those rows matching the XMLEXISTS value of true are returned.

The XMLEXISTS function enables us to specify rows based on the XML content which is often what you want to do. Suppose you want to return the first and last names of all employees who live in the state of Texas? This query with XMLEXISTS would accomplish it:

```
SELECT EMP_LAST_NAME, EMP_FIRST_NAME
FROM HRSCHEMA.EMPLOYEE
WHERE
XMLEXISTS('$info/EMP_PROFILE[EMP_ADDRESS/STATE/text()="TX"]'
PASSING EMP_PROFILE AS "info");

---------+---------+---------+---------+---------+---------+---
EMP_LAST_NAME                        EMP_FIRST_NAME
---------+---------+---------+---------+---------+---------+---
JOHNSON                              EDWARD
STEWART                              BETTY
```

You can also use XMLEXISTS with update and delete functions.

XMLSERIALIZE

The XMLSERIALIZE function returns a serialized XML value of the specified data type that is generated from the first argument.

```
SELECT E.EMP_ID,
XMLSERIALIZE(XMLELEMENT ( NAME "EMP_FULL_NAME",
   E.EMP_FIRST_NAME || ' ' || E.EMP_LAST_NAME)
             AS CLOB(100)) AS "RESULT"
   FROM HRSCHEMA.EMPLOYEE E;
-------+---------+---------+---------+---------+---------+--
   EMP_ID  RESULT
-------+---------+---------+---------+---------+---------+--
    3217   <EMP_FULL_NAME>EDWARD JOHNSON</EMP_FULL_NAME>
    7459   <EMP_FULL_NAME>BETTY STEWART</EMP_FULL_NAME>
    9134   <EMP_FULL_NAME>BRIANNA FRANKLIN</EMP_FULL_NAME>
    4175   <EMP_FULL_NAME>FRED TURNBULL</EMP_FULL_NAME>
    4720   <EMP_FULL_NAME>TIM SCHULTZ</EMP_FULL_NAME>
    6288   <EMP_FULL_NAME>JOE WILLARD</EMP_FULL_NAME>
NE610I NUMBER OF ROWS DISPLAYED IS 6
```

XMLTABLE

This function can be used to convert XML data to relational data. You can then use it for traditional SQL such as in joins. To use XMLTABLE you must specify the relational column names you want to use. Then you point these column names to the XML content using path expressions. For this example we'll pull address information from the profile:

```
SELECT X.*
FROM HRSCHEMA.EMPLOYEE,
XMLTABLE ('$x/EMP_PROFILE'
         PASSING EMP_PROFILE as "x"

   COLUMNS
      STREET   VARCHAR(20) PATH 'EMP_ADDRESS/STREET',
      CITY     VARCHAR(20) PATH 'EMP_ADDRESS/CITY',
      STATE    VARCHAR(02) PATH 'EMP_ADDRESS/STATE',
      ZIP      VARCHAR(10) PATH 'EMP_ADDRESS/ZIP_CODE')
   AS X;
---------+---------+---------+---------+---------+-------
STREET                CITY                STATE   ZIP
---------+---------+---------+---------+---------+-------
2913 PATE DR          FORT WORTH          TX      76105
6742 OAK ST           DALLAS              TX      75277
6161 MARGARET LANE    ERINDALE            AR      72653
```

XMLMODIFY

XMLMODIFY allows you to make changes within the XML document. There are three expressions available for XMLMODIFY: insert, delete and replace. Here is a sample of using the replace expression to change the ZIP_CODE element of the EMP_ADDRESS for employee 4175:

```
UPDATE HRSCHEMA.EMPLOYEE
SET EMP_PROFILE
= XMLMODIFY('replace value of node
HRSCHEMA.EMPLOYEE/EMP_PROFILE/EMP_ADDRESS/ZIP_CODE
with "72652" ')
WHERE EMP_ID = 4175;
```

Important: to use XMLMODIFY, you must have created the table in a universal table space (UTS). Otherwise you will receive this SQLCODE error when you try to use the XMLMODIFY function:

```
DSNT408I SQLCODE = -4730, ERROR:  INVALID SPECIFICATION OF XML
COLUMN EMPLOYEE.EMP_PROFILE IS NOT DEFINED IN THE XML VERSIONING
FORMAT, REASON 1
```

Performance

It's vital to design your DB2 applications with optimal performance in mind. Resolving existing performance issues can also be part of your job when enhanced functionality or larger data volumes begin to cause performance problems. This chapter looks at several areas you should be familiar with to develop and tune your applications.

Creating and Using Explain Data

The `EXPLAIN` statement helps you to gather information about the access paths DB2 uses when retrieving or updating data. This in turn can help you to diagnose performance related issues, such as excessively long running queries.

Creating Plan Tables

If you bind a plan using the `EXPLAIN(YES)` option, then appropriate explain tables will be created for you automatically using your login id as the schema (provided you have access to the appropriate tablespace). At a minimum the `PLAN_TABLE` will be created and this is usually what you will query to get information about the access paths DB2 has chosen.

If you simply want to determine the access path for a query, and explain tables do not already exist, you must create them. To create the `PLAN_TABLE` you can modify the sample `CREATE TABLE` statements in the `DSNTESC` member of the `SDSNSAMP` library. You may need to ask your system admin which library these samples are stored on your local system. On my system the file name for the `SDSNSAMP` PDS is `DSNxxxx.SDSNSAMP` where the `xxxx` is the DB2 instance name.

You only need the `PLAN_TABLE` to enable the basic `EXPLAIN` function. If you need the other tables (enumerated below), you can create those as well.

Here is the query I used to create my `PLAN_TABLE` in my tablespace `TSHR` (naturally you must use whatever tablespace name is appropriate for your system).

```
CREATE TABLE PLAN_TABLE
 (QUERYNO           INTEGER     NOT NULL,
  QBLOCKNO          SMALLINT    NOT NULL,
  APPLNAME          CHAR(8)     NOT NULL,
  PROGNAME          CHAR(8)     NOT NULL,
  PLANNO            SMALLINT    NOT NULL,
  METHOD            SMALLINT    NOT NULL,
  CREATOR           CHAR(8)     NOT NULL,
  TNAME             CHAR(18)    NOT NULL,
  TABNO             SMALLINT    NOT NULL,
  ACCESSTYPE        CHAR(2)     NOT NULL,
```

```
    MATCHCOLS          SMALLINT       NOT NULL,
    ACCESSCREATOR      CHAR(8)        NOT NULL,
    ACCESSNAME         CHAR(18)       NOT NULL,
    INDEXONLY          CHAR(1)        NOT NULL,
    SORTN_UNIQ         CHAR(1)        NOT NULL,
    SORTN_JOIN         CHAR(1)        NOT NULL,
    SORTN_ORDERBY      CHAR(1)        NOT NULL,
    SORTN_GROUPBY      CHAR(1)        NOT NULL,
    SORTC_UNIQ         CHAR(1)        NOT NULL,
    SORTC_JOIN         CHAR(1)        NOT NULL,
    SORTC_ORDERBY      CHAR(1)        NOT NULL,
    SORTC_GROUPBY      CHAR(1)        NOT NULL,
    TSLOCKMODE         CHAR(3)        NOT NULL,
    TIMESTAMP          CHAR(16)       NOT NULL,
    REMARKS            VARCHAR(254)   NOT NULL,
    PREFETCH           CHAR(1)        NOT NULL,
    COLUMN_FN_EVAL     CHAR(1)        NOT NULL,
    MIXOPSEQ           SMALLINT       NOT NULL,
    VERSION            VARCHAR(64)    NOT NULL,
    COLLID             CHAR(18)       NOT NULL,
    ACCESS_DEGREE      SMALLINT,
    ACCESS_PGROUP_ID   SMALLINT,
    JOIN_DEGREE        SMALLINT,
    JOIN_PGROUP_ID     SMALLINT,
    SORTC_PGROUP_ID    SMALLINT,
    SORTN_PGROUP_ID    SMALLINT,
    PARALLELISM_MODE   CHAR(1),
    MERGE_JOIN_COLS    SMALLINT,
    CORRELATION_NAME   CHAR(18),
    PAGE_RANGE         CHAR(1)        NOT NULL WITH DEFAULT,
    JOIN_TYPE          CHAR(1)        NOT NULL WITH DEFAULT,
    GROUP_MEMBER       CHAR(8)        NOT NULL WITH DEFAULT,
    IBM_SERVICE_DATA   VARCHAR(254)   NOT NULL WITH DEFAULT,
    WHEN_OPTIMIZE      CHAR(1)        NOT NULL WITH DEFAULT, -- V5
    QBLOCK_TYPE        CHAR(6)        NOT NULL WITH DEFAULT, -- V5
    BIND_TIME          TIMESTAMP      NOT NULL WITH DEFAULT, -- V5
    OPTHINT            CHAR(8)        NOT NULL WITH DEFAULT, -- V6
    HINT_USED          CHAR(8)        NOT NULL WITH DEFAULT, -- V6
    PRIMARY_ACCESSTYPE CHAR(1)        NOT NULL WITH DEFAULT, -- V6
    PARENT_QBLOCKNO    SMALLINT       NOT NULL WITH DEFAULT, -- V7
    TABLE_TYPE         CHAR(1)                             , -- V7
    TABLE_ENCODE       CHAR(1)        NOT NULL WITH DEFAULT, -- V8
    TABLE_SCCSID       SMALLINT       NOT NULL WITH DEFAULT, -- V8
    TABLE_MCCSID       SMALLINT       NOT NULL WITH DEFAULT, -- V8
    TABLE_DCCSID       SMALLINT       NOT NULL WITH DEFAULT, -- V8
    ROUTINE_ID         INTEGER        NOT NULL WITH DEFAULT, -- V8
    CTEREF             SMALLINT       NOT NULL WITH DEFAULT, -- V8
    STMTTOKEN          VARCHAR(240))                         -- V8
    IN TSHR;
```

For an understanding of what all these columns mean, check here: [xvi]

The EXPLAIN Statement

The EXPLAIN statement generates explain data that can be analyzed to determine access paths the DB2 Optimizer has chosen for a query or plan. We'll look first at the EXPLAIN syntax, generate some data into the PLAN_TABLE and then query it. Later we'll look at the EXPLAIN bind option and how it adds data to the PLAN_TABLE. Finally we'll look at using the Visual Explain component of IBM's Data Studio to see a visual representation of the access path associated with a query.

EXPLAIN Data with Queries

With the explain statement you can get information about packages, plans and queries. Let's start with a very simple example. This is just to get us somewhat familiar with the PLAN_TABLE.

Here is the query:

```
EXPLAIN PLAN SET QUERYNO = 1
   FOR SELECT EMP_ID, EMP_LAST_NAME
      FROM HRSCHEMA.EMPLOYEE
         WHERE EMP_ID IN (3217, 9134)
         ORDER BY EMP_ID;
```

The above generates explain data into the PLAN_TABLE. Now we can select some of the fields from the table to determine what access path the query is taking. Here's our first query:

```
SELECT TNAME,
       ACCESSTYPE,
       MATCHCOLS,
       ACCESSNAME
   FROM HRSCHEMA.PLAN_TABLE
   WHERE QUERYNO = 1;
```

TNAME	ACCESSTYPE	MATCHCOLS	ACCESSNAME
EMPLOYEE	N	1	NDX_EMPLOYEE

The result from the PLAN_TABLE indicates that the dynamic query we explained will use an index -- specifically the NDX_EMPLOYEE index -- to access the data. We'll be looking at all the access types in a few minutes, but for now just be aware that access type N means an index call based on an "IN" predicate in the SQL.

Now recall that earlier we defined NDX_EMPLOYEE as follows:

```
CREATE UNIQUE INDEX NDX_EMPLOYEE
ON EMPLOYEE (EMP_ID);
```

This is good because our EXPLAIN data tells us an index exists and is being used to locate the data rows needed by the query. That typically means we can expect pretty good performance.

Now let's take a different scenario where we are trying to solve a performance issue. Let's assume we are pulling data from the EMP_PAY_CHECK table and the query is running very slow. Here is the query:

```
SELECT EMP_ID, EMP_REGULAR_PAY
FROM HRSCHEMA.EMP_PAY_CHECK
WHERE (EMP_ID = 3217 OR EMP_ID = 9134);
```

Let's create an EXPLAIN statement for this as follows:

```
EXPLAIN PLAN SET QUERYNO = 2
   FOR SELECT EMP_ID, EMP_REGULAR_PAY
      FROM HRSCHEMA.EMP_PAY_CHECK
      WHERE (EMP_ID = 3217 OR EMP_ID = 9134);
```

Now we can run this query to determine what access path is being used.

```
SELECT TNAME,ACCESSTYPE,
      PREFETCH,MATCHCOLS,
      ACCESSNAME
      FROM HRSCHEMA.PLAN_TABLE
      WHERE QUERYNO = 2;
```

TNAME	ACCESSTYPE	PREFETCH	MATCHCOLS	ACCESSNAME
EMP_PAY_CHECK	R	S	0	

A brief look at the result tells us what our problem is. DB2 is using access type R which means a table scan. We are walking through the entire table record-by-record to find the qualifying rows. For a very small table this may be ok, but for tables that have any significant amount of data, this is the slowest way to access the data.

Let's try to solve this problem by creating an index on EMP_ID and then see the result.

```
CREATE UNIQUE INDEX HRSCHEMA.EMP_PC_NDX
    ON HRSCHEMA.EMP_PAY_CHECK (EMP_ID);
```

Now we can rerun the explain statement:

```
EXPLAIN PLAN SET QUERYNO = 2
    FOR SELECT EMP_ID, EMP_REGULAR_PAY
        FROM HRSCHEMA.EMP_PAY_CHECK
            WHERE (EMP_ID = 3217 OR EMP_ID = 9134);
```

Finally let's requery the `PLAN_TABLE` and see the results.

```
SELECT TNAME,
       ACCESSTYPE,
       MATCHCOLS,
       ACCESSNAME
    FROM HRSCHEMA.PLAN_TABLE
    WHERE QUERYNO = 2;
---------+---------+---------+---------+---------+---------+-----
TNAME                   ACCESSTYPE  MATCHCOLS  ACCESSNAME
---------+---------+---------+---------+---------+---------+-----
EMP_PAY_CHECK           N                    1  EMP_PC_NDX
```

Ok, we're in business now. Our access type is N which means an index. Specifically ACCESSNAME column tells us DB2 will use the index EMP_PC_NDX that we just created. We are matching on one column, the EMP_ID. This is good. Again, using an index should mean fairly good performance.

Now let's do a third example. Suppose we have a new requirement to order the results of our previous query by regular pay in descending order. And this time we want all the employees (not a specific one). What effect will that have? Let's run the EXPLAIN statement again, changing the SQL and also the QUERYNO so that it is unique.

```
EXPLAIN PLAN SET QUERYNO = 3
    FOR SELECT EMP_ID, EMP_REGULAR_PAY
        FROM HRSCHEMA.EMP_PAY_CHECK
            ORDER BY EMP_REGULAR_PAY DESC;
```

Now let's run our query against PLAN_TABLE and see what we have.

```
SELECT TNAME,
       ACCESSTYPE,
       MATCHCOLS,
       ACCESSNAME,
       SORTC_ORDERBY
    FROM HRSCHEMA.PLAN_TABLE
    WHERE QUERYNO = 3;
---------+---------+---------+---------+---------+---------+--------
TNAME                ACCESSTYPE  MATCHCOLS  ACCESSNAME          SORTC_ORDERBY
```

```
---------+---------+---------+---------+---------+---------+---------+--------
EMP_PAY_CHECK         R            0                          N
                                   0                          Y
```

Now we see there are two entries in the table, which means there are two steps to satisfy the query. We are first doing a table scan (since we are reading all the records we don't need the `EMP_ID` index). Second we are doing a sort on the data. The sort is not necessarily so good. Once again, if the table contents is fairly small then the SORT step is not likely to be a problem. But if there are many rows in the table we may take a performance hit for having to do the sort to satisfy the ORDER BY clause.

One way to resolve the issue could be to create another index that includes both the employee id and the regular pay column. We'll do that momentarily. First I want to pause to state that adding new indexes is not always the best approach to resolving a performance issue. There are tradeoffs between the overhead cost of additional indexes versus the cost of a long running query. Moreover there are other things to look into besides indexing, such as how the SQL statement is structured to begin with and whether it is using stage 1 or stage 2 predicates.

Having issued the above caveat, let's assume that we decide to create the new index and then run the EXPLAIN statement again. Here is the DDL for the new index which will be organized by EMP_REGULAR_PAY.

```
CREATE INDEX HRSCHEMA.EMP_PC_RP_NDX
ON HRSCHEMA.EMP_PAY_CHECK
(EMP_REGULAR_PAY DESC, EMP_ID ASC);
```

Here's the EXPLAIN statement for our query:

```
EXPLAIN PLAN SET QUERYNO = 4
    FOR SELECT EMP_REGULAR_PAY, EMP_ID
        FROM HRSCHEMA.EMP_PAY_CHECK
            ORDER BY EMP_REGULAR_PAY DESC;
```

And let's retrieve the information from the PLAN_TABLE:

```
SELECT TNAME,
       ACCESSTYPE,
       ACCESSNAME,
       INDEXONLY,
       SORTC_ORDERBY
    FROM HRSCHEMA.PLAN_TABLE
    WHERE QUERYNO = 4;
---------+---------+---------+---------+---------+---------+---------+---------+
TNAME                ACCESSTYPE ACCESSNAME              INDEXONLY SORTC_ORDERBY
---------+---------+---------+---------+---------+---------+---------+---------+
EMP_PAY_CHECK         I         EMP_PC_RP_NDX            Y         N
```

This access path looks a lot better. We've eliminated the sort step because we have an index that is available to order the results. Notice also that we are doing an **index-only** scan (`ACCESSTYPE IS I`) with the new index `EMP_PC_RP_NDX`. Since all the columns we are requesting are available in the index itself, we don't even need to touch the base table. This should be a very efficient scan!

Ok, that fairly well wraps up `EXPLAIN` statement basics. The above examples, while trivial, should give us a basic understanding of how to use the `PLAN_TABLE` with the `EXPLAIN` statement. To conclude, here is a table of all the various access types you might encounter in the `EXPLAIN` table and what they mean.

Access Types
The various access types and their meaning is as follows:

Value	Meaning
'A'	The query is sent to an accelerator server.
'DI'	By an intersection of multiple DOCID lists to return the final DOCID list
'DU'	By a union of multiple DOCID lists to return the final DOCID list
'DX'	By an XML index scan on the index that is named in ACCESSNAME to return a DOCID list
'E'	By direct row access using a row change timestamp column.
'H'	By hash access. IF an overflow condition occurs, the hash overflow index that is identified by ACCESSCREATOR and ACCESSNAME is used.
'HN'	By hash access using an IN predicate, or an IN predicate that DB2 generates. If a hash overflow condition occurs, the hash overflow index that is identified in ACCESSCREATOR and ACCESSNAME is used.
'I' ACCESSNAME)	By an index (identified in ACCESSCREATOR and

'IN'	By an index scan when the matching predicate contains an IN predicate and the IN-list is accessed through an in-memory table.
'I1'	By a one-fetch index scan
'M'	By a multiple index scan. A row that contains this value might be followed by a row that contains one of the following values: 'DI' 'DU' 'MH' 'MI' 'MU' 'MX'
'MH'	By the hash overflow index named in ACCESSNAME. A row that contains this value always follows a row that contains M.
'MI'	By an intersection of multiple indexes. A row that contains this value always follows a row that contains M.
'MU'	By a union of multiple indexes. A row that contains this value always follows a row that contains M.
'MX'	By an index scan on the index named in ACCESSNAME. When the access method MX follows the access method DX, DI, or DU, the table is accessed by the DOCID index by using the DOCID list that is returned by DX, DI, or DU. A row that contains this value always follows a row that contains M.
'N'	One of the following types: 1. By an index scan when the matching predicate contains the IN keyword 2. By an index scan when DB2 rewrites a query using the IN keyword
'O'	By a work file scan, as a result of a correlated subquery.

'NR'	Range list access.
'P'	By a dynamic pair-wise index scan
'R'	By a table space scan
'RW'	By a work file scan of the result of a materialized user-defined table function
'V'	By buffers for an INSERT statement within a SELECT
Blank	Not applicable to the current row

EXPLAIN Bind Option

If you bind your application plan with EXPLAIN(YES) then the bind process automatically adds info to the PLAN_TABLE. For example let's go back to program COBEMP2 which was our update program. We'll rebind it with EXPLAIN(YES). Now let's look at the explain table results.

```
SELECT
TNAME,
QBLOCK_TYPE,
ACCESSTYPE,
MATCHCOLS,
ACCESSNAME,
SORTC_ORDERBY
FROM HRSCHEMA.PLAN_TABLE
WHERE PROGNAME = 'COBEMP2'

---------+---------+---------+---------+---------+---------+---------+---------+
TNAME              QBLOCK_TYPE  ACCESSTYPE  MATCHCOLS  ACCESSNAME
---------+---------+---------+---------+---------+---------+---------+---------+
EMPLOYEE           SELUPD       R                      0
EMPLOYEE           UPDCUR                              0
```

We can see that there are two queries in the program. One is a cursor to SELECT for UPDATE, and the second is to perform the update (again via the cursor). The access type for the retrieval is R which means a table scan. If we look at the query, this makes sense because there is no index on EMP_LAST_NAME.

```
EXEC SQL
    DECLARE EMP-CURSOR CURSOR FOR
    SELECT EMP_ID, EMP_LAST_NAME
    FROM HRSCHEMA.EMPLOYEE
    WHERE EMP_LAST_NAME <> UPPER(EMP_LAST_NAME)
    FOR UPDATE OF EMP_LAST_NAME
END-EXEC.
```

The second query (UPDCUR) does not have an accesstype because it is based on a positional update. So the record is already acquired.

So besides explaining individual queries, you can use the EXPLAIN statement to generate and review access paths for an entire program. It is worthwhile to do this before you implement a program, and also periodically afterwards, especially if data volumes increase.

Visual Explain Using Data Studio

You can also use Data Studio to evaluate the EXPLAIN statement results and it will give you a visual result. Let's run through a couple of queries just to see how we would do it.

Suppose again we run this SQL and that we discover it is a very long running query:

```
SELECT * FROM HRSCHEMA.EMP_PAY_CHECK
WHERE EMP_ID = 3217;
```

To check why we might be having a performance issue, we can use visual explain with Data Studio to check the access path chosen by the DB2 Optimizer. Simply open Data Studio, select the RUN SQL perspective, type the query in and select it, right click and select Open Visual Explain. You can accept the defaults on the configuration panels and then click Finish. You will see this screen:

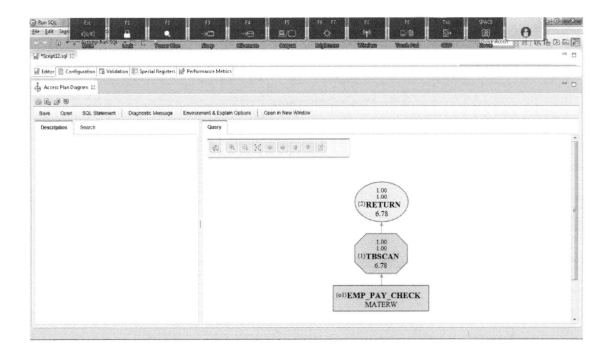

Note the TBSCAN in the middle of the diagram. This indicates you are doing a table scan, which means you are not using an index. Unless your table is very small, doing a table scan can definitely create a performance problem.

Now let's go back and try to solve our performance problem by creating an index.

```
CREATE UNIQUE INDEX HRSCHEMA.EMP_PC_NDX
ON HRSCHEMA.EMP_PAY_CHECK (EMP_ID);
```

And now retry the explain table with our query and check the result.

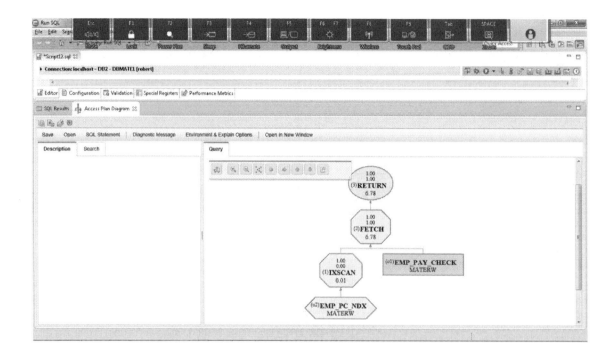

And now we can see the optimizer chose our new index – note the path is to use an index scan (IXSCAN) using index EMP_PC_NDX. This should increase the performance considerably. You could use Visual Explain for all the queries we looked at earlier. Some people prefer the raw data from the PLAN_TABLE and some like the visualization of the results you get with Visual Explain.

As we wrap up this troublshooting topic, here is a list of all the EXPLAIN table types and what they contain. This should give you an idea of how the information in them can help you. I would suggest becoming familiar with these tables and expect that a question or two could come up on the example.

All Explain Tables and Their Contents
The following is a list of all the EXPLAIN tables and what they are for. For comprehensive information about these EXPLAIN tables, see the IBM product documentation. [xvii]

PLAN_TABLE   Contains information about access paths
                              that is collected from the results of
                              EXPLAIN statements.

DSN_COLDIST_TABLE	Contains non-uniform column group statistics that are obtained dynamically by DB2 from non-index leaf pages.
DSN_DETCOST_TABLE	Contains information about detailed cost estimation of the mini-plans in a query.
DSN_FILTER_TABLE	Contains information about how predicates are used during query processing.
DSN_FUNCTION_TABLE	Contains descriptions of functions that are used in specified SQL statements.
DSN_KEYTGTDIST_TABLE	Contains non-uniform index expression statistic that are obtained dynamically by the DB2 optimizer.
DSN_PGRANGE_TABLE	Contains information about qualified partitions for all page range scans in a query.
DSN_PGROUP_TABLE	Contains information about the parallel groups in a query.
DSN_PREDICAT_TABLE	Contains information about all of the predicates in a query.
DSN_PTASK_TABLE	Contains information about all of the parallel tasks in a query.
DSN_QUERYINFO_TABLE	Contains information about the eligibility of query blocks for automatic query rewrite, information about the materialized query tables that are considered for eligible query blocks, reasons why ineligible query blocks are not eligible, and information about acceleration of query blocks.
DSN_QUERY_TABLE	Contains information about a SQL statement, and displays the statement before and after query transformation.
DSN_SORTKEY_TABLE	Contains information about sort keys for all of the sorts required by a query.

`DSN_SORT_TABLE`	Contains information about the sort operations required by a query.
`DSN_STATEMENT_CACHE_TABLE`	Contains information about the SQL statements in the statement cache, information captured as the results of an EXPLAIN STATEMENT CACHE ALL statement.
`DSN_STATEMNT_TABLE`	Contains information about the estimated cost of specified SQL statements.
`DSN_STRUCT_TABLE`	Contains information about all of the query blocks in a query.
`DSN_VIEWREF_TABLE`	Contains information about all of the views and materialized query tables that are used to process a query.

Stage 1 versus Stage 2 Predicates

In terms of both development standards and resolving performance issues, focus upon preferring stage 1 predicates over stage 2 predicates. By predicates I am referring to the WHERE clause as well as HAVING and ON clauses of the SELECT statement. When you retrieve rows from a table it is done through two stages. Some predicates can be applied during the first stage, and other predicates must wait until the second. You can improve performance by employing stage 1 predicates instead of stage 2 predicates.

The following is the order in which predicates are evaluated and applied:

1. Indexable predicates are applied when DB2 accesses the index to match on key columns. This is a first level of selection.

2. Stage 1 predicates are applied to determine the data rows to be returned.

3. Stage 2 predicates are applied to the rows returned by stage 1.

Stage 1 and Stage 2 predicates are enumerated below and on the IBM product documentation web site: [xviii]

Indexable and Stage 1 Predicates
COL = value
COL = noncol expr
COL IS NULL
COL op value
COL op noncol expr
value BETWEEN COL1 AND COL2
COL BETWEEN value1 AND value2
COL BETWEEN noncol expr 1 AND noncol expr
COL BETWEEN expr-1 AND expr-2
COL LIKE 'pattern'
COL IN (list)
COL IS NOT NULL
COL LIKE host variable
COL LIKE UPPER ('pattern')
COL LIKE UPPER (host-variable)
COL LIKE UPPER (SQL-variable)
COL LIKE UPPER (global-variable)
COL LIKE UPPER (CAST ('pattern' AS data-type))
COL LIKE UPPER (CAST (host-variable AS data-type))
COL LIKE UPPER (CAST (SQL-variable AS data-type))
COL LIKE UPPER (CAST (global-variable AS data-type))
T1.COL = T2.COL
T1.COL op T2.COL
T1.COL = T2 col expr
T1.COL op T2 col expr
COL = (noncor subq)
COL op (noncor subq)
COL = ANY (noncor subq)
(COL1,...COLn) IN (noncor subq)
COL = ANY (cor subq)
COL IS NOT DISTINCT FROM value
COL IS NOT DISTINCT FROM noncol expr
T1.COL1 IS NOT DISTINCT FROM T2.COL2
T1.COL1 IS NOT DISTINCT FROM T2 col expr
COL IS NOT DISTINCT FROM (noncor subq)
SUBSTR(COL,1,n) = value
SUBSTR(COL,1,n) op value
DATE(COL) = value
DATE(COL) op value
YEAR(COL) = value
YEAR(COL) op value
Stage 1 not indexable predicates - these might be evaluated during stage 1 processing, during index

screening, or after data page access.
COL <> value
COL <> noncol expr
COL NOT BETWEEN value1 AND value2
COL NOT IN (list)
COL NOT LIKE ' char'
COL LIKE '%char'
COL LIKE '_char'
T1.COL <> T2 col expr
COL op ANY (noncor subq)
COL op ALL (noncor subq)
COL IS DISTINCT FROM value
COL IS DISTINCT FROM (noncor subq)
STAGE 2 Predicates — these must be processed during stage 2, after the data is returned.
COL BETWEEN COL1 AND COL2
value NOT BETWEEN COL1 AND COL2
value BETWEEN col expr and col expr
T1.COL <> T2.COL
T1.COL1 = T1.COL2
T1.COL1 op T1.COL2
T1.COL1 <> T1.COL2
COL = ALL (noncor subq)
COL <> (noncor subq)
COL <> ALL (noncor subq)
COL NOT IN (noncor subq)
COL = (cor subq)
COL = ALL (cor subq)
COL op (cor subq)
COL op ANY (cor subq)
COL op ALL (cor subq)
COL <> (cor subq)
COL <> ANY (cor subq)
(COL1,...COLn) IN (cor subq)
COL NOT IN (cor subq)
(COL1,...COLn) NOT IN (cor subq)
T1.COL1 IS DISTINCT FROM T2.COL2
T1.COL1 IS DISTINCT FROM T2 col expr
COL IS NOT DISTINCT FROM (cor subq)
EXISTS (subq)
expression = value
expression <> value
expression op value

expression op (subq)
NOT XMLEXISTS
CASE expression WHEN expression ELSE expression END = value

Indexable but not stage 1 predicates can be processed during index access, but cannot be processed during stage 1.

XMLEXISTS

Basic Query Optimization:

- Always prefer stage 1 predicates over stage 2 if you have a choice. Stage 1 are more efficient because they eliminate rows earlier and thereby reduce the processing to be done at stage 2.

- Write your queries such that the most restrictive predicates are evaluated first. For example if you have a nation-wide company and you run a query to return all male employees who live in the state of Texas, the query is more efficient if written as:

    WHERE EMP_ADDRESS_STATE = 'TX' AND EMP_SEX = 'M'

    instead of:

    WHERE EMP_SEX = 'M' AND EMP_ADDRESS_STATE = 'TX'

    It likely that there are many more employees who are male than the number of employees who live in Texas. By specifying the state of residence as the first predicate you automatically eliminate all the employees living anywhere else, hence you restrict the initial selection to a smaller number of rows than if you specified all male employees first.

Best Practices
The following are some best practices to observe when developing and maintaining applications.

1. When coding queries, prefer stage 1 predicates over stage 2 predicates.

2. Make sure that your table statistics are current. This is required to support your queries' access paths. Perform RUNSTATS periodically to refresh the statistics, and then rebind packages to take advantage of changes.

3. Create appropriate indexes that support efficient access paths for queries. This is especially helpful to prevent unnecessary sort operations.

If you have designed your queries efficiently and still encounter issues, you can also perform the following actions to resolve specific problems.

- Enable queries to be re-optimized at run time (the REOPT bind option).

- Specify optimization parameters at the statement level.

- Specify an access path at the statement level.

- Specify an access path in a PLAN_TABLE instance.

DB2 Trace

When you are trying to solve a problem it helps a lot to have accurate information about what DB2 is doing. One way of obtaining useful information is to use the DB2 trace feature. There are several trace types to investigate different kinds of problems.

Trace Types

The following table summarizes the valid DB2 trace types and what they are used for. The only one you will be tested on is the accounting trace, but it is good to know the full trace capabilities of DB2.

Trace Type	Description
Accounting trace	The accounting trace records transaction-level data that is written when the processing for a transaction is completed. It provides data that enables you to conduct DB2 capacity planning and to tune application programs.
Audit trace	The audit trace collects information about DB2 security controls and can be used to ensure that data access is allowed only for authorized purposes.
Monitor trace	The monitor trace enables attached monitor programs to access DB2 trace data through calls to the instrumentation facility interface (IFI). Monitor programs can access the

	trace data asynchronously through an OPx buffer by issuing READA requests, or synchronously in the monitor return area by issuing READS requests.
Performance trace	The performance trace is intended for performance analysis and tuning. This trace includes records of specific events in the system, including events related to distributed data processing. The data can be used for program, resource, user, and subsystem-related tuning.
Statistics trace	The statistics trace captures information about DB2 system and database services. You would use this when you want to do capacity planning.

Accounting Trace Basics

The accounting trace collects processing data that is written when a transaction completes. The monitor trace permits attached monitor programs to access DB2 trace data via calls to the instrumentation facility interface (IFI). A statistics trace provides data about how much the DB2 system and database services are used.

DB2 Trace Commands

START TRACE
To initiate a DB2 accounting trace, you would issue this abbreviated command:

```
STA TRA (ACCTG)
```

You could also issue `START TRACE(ACCTG)` which has the same meaning.

If you want to limit the trace to a particular DB2 plan, you can specify it. For example:

```
STA TRACE(ACCTG) PLAN(COBEMP4)
```

In fact you can get even more specific with your trace. Here's an example of capturing only class xyz for package COBEMP4 and userid HRUSER07:

```
STA TRACE(ACCTG) CLASS(1,2,3) PKGPROG(COBEMP4)   USERID(HRUSER07)
```

DISPLAY TRACE
The `DISPLAY TRACE` command displays a list of active traces.

```
DISPLAY TRACE (*)
```

You can also limit the display to a particular plan, user or class.

```
DISPLAY TRACE(ACCTG) PLAN(COBEMP6) USERID(HRUSER02)
```

MODIFY TRACE

You can change an active trace by issuing a `MODIFY TRACE` command. Typically you will need to know the trace number to modify a specific trace. For example, suppose we have issued an accounting trace for plan COBEMP4 and the trace number (the TNO) is 5. Now we decide to change the trace to only report class 1 or 2 events. We could change it as follows:

```
MOD TRA(ACCTG)   PLAN (COBEMP4) TNO(5)   CLASS(1,2)
```

STOP TRACE

The `STOP TRACE` command terminates an active trace. To stop all trace activity, issue:

```
STO TRA(*)
```

To stop an accounting trace, issue:

```
STO TRA (ACCTG)
```
To stop the accounting trace on plan COBEMP4, issue:

```
STO TRA (ACCTG) PLAN (COBEMP4)
```

The DB2 accounting trace provides the following types of information:
- Start and stop times
- Number of commits and aborts
- The number of times certain SQL statements are issued
- Number of buffer pool requests
- Counts of certain locking events
- Processor resources consumed
- Thread wait times for various events
- RID pool processing
- Distributed processing
- Resource limit facility statistics

DB2 trace begins collecting these items when a thread is successfully allocated to DB2. DB2 trace writes a completed record when the thread terminates or when the authorization ID changes.

Full information about DB2 traces can be found on the IBM web site. [xix]

Special Project

I want to finish out the text book with a project that applies some of the skills and knowledge we've learned, but in a different problem domain. Let's switch from the HR domain to a simple frequent buyer domain (also known these days as loyalty systems). We'll provide a skeleton set of requirements, work through creating tables, indexes, stored procedures and so forth.

Project Requirements

At its most basic a frequent buyer system includes members, deposits and rewards. Let's use FB as an acronym for our frequent buyer program. Besides creating a new FB database and tablespace, we will also be creating a Members table, a Deposit table, and a Rewards table to track the various transactions in our Frequent Buyer system – let's call it FB for an acronym. In addition, we should be thinking about referential integrity. So let's plan on creating a Deposits Type table and a Rewards Type table.

Here are the requirements for the aforementioned tables:

Member Table

Field	Type	Constraints
Member Number	Integer	NOT NULL, autogenerated
Last Name	Character up to 20	NOT NULL
First Name	Character up to 15	NOT NULL
Street	Character up to 30	NOT NULL
City	Character up to 20	NOT NULL
State	Character 2	NOT NULL
Zip Code	Big Integer	NOT NULL
Telephone	Big Integer	
Points Balance	Integer	NOT NULL

Deposits Table

Field	Type	Constraints
Member Number	Integer	NOT NULL, must exist on MEMBER table
Activity Date	Date	NOT NULL
Deposit Type	Character 3	NOT NULL, must exist in Deposit Type table
Deposit Amount	Integer	NOT NULL
Deposit Posted Date	Date	NOT NULL

Rewards Table

Field	Type	Constraints
Member Number	Integer	NOT NULL, must exist on MEMBER table
Reward Date	Date	NOT NULL
Reward Type	Char 3	NOT NULL, must exist in REWARD TYPE table
Reward Amount	Integer	NOT NULL

Deposit Type Table

Field	Type	Constraints
Deposit Type Code	Char 3	NOT NULL
Deposit Type Description	Char up to 20	NOT NULL
Maintenance Date	Date	NOT NULL

Reward Type Table

Field	Type	Constraints
Reward Type Code	Char 3	NOT NULL
Reward Type Description	Char up to 20	NOT NULL
Maintenance Date	Date	NOT NULL

We've made a few assumptions to keep things simple, such as that the credited points are always whole numbers (so we defined them as integers). Similarly the choice of DATE versus TIMESTAMP is somewhat arbitrary, and in a real production situation you could have reasons for choosing one over the other. TIMESTAMP of course is more precise but we'll stick with DATE.

Project DDL

Create the Tables
Now let's start to work on our DB2 system. Let's build the DDL to create the database, tablespace and a schema. Also since the member number is to be generated, we will create a sequence. Here's our DDL:

```
CREATE DATABASE DBFB
STOGROUP SGFB
BUFFERPOOL BPFB
INDEXBP IBPFB
CCSID UNICODE;


CREATE TABLESPACE TSFB
    IN DBFB
    USING STOGROUP SGHR
      PRIQTY 50
      SECQTY 20
    LOCKSIZE PAGE
    BUFFERPOOL BPFB;


CREATE SCHEMA FBSCHEMA
AUTHORIZATION DBA001;     ←  This should be your DB2 id, whatever it is.
```

Now let's create the sequence object. We specified it should be auto-numbered beginning with 100100. Here is our sequence DDL:

```
CREATE SEQUENCE FBSCHEMA.MBRSEQ
START WITH 100100
INCREMENT BY 1
NO CYCLE;
```

Finally, let's create the DDL for our tables.

```
CREATE TABLE FBSCHEMA.MEMBER(
MBR_NBR          INT NOT NULL,
MBR_LAST_NAME    VARCHAR(20) NOT NULL,
MBR_FIRST_NAME   VARCHAR(15) NOT NULL,
MBR_ADDRESS      VARCHAR(30) NOT NULL,
MBR_CITY         VARCHAR(20) NOT NULL,
MBR_STATE        CHAR(02)    NOT NULL,
MBR_ZIP          BIGINT      NOT NULL,
MBR_PHONE        BIGINT      NOT NULL,
MBR_BALANCE      INTEGER     NOT NULL,
   PRIMARY KEY(MBR_NBR))
      IN TSFB;

CREATE UNIQUE INDEX FBSCHEMA.NDX_MEMBER
    ON FBSCHEMA.MEMBER (MBR_NBR);

CREATE TABLE FBSCHEMA.DEPOSITS(
```

```
DEP_MBR_NBR      INT          NOT NULL,
DEP_ACT_DATE     DATE         NOT NULL,
DEP_TYPE         CHAR(03)     NOT NULL,
DEP_AMOUNT       INTEGER      NOT NULL,
DEP_POST_DATE    DATE         NOT NULL)
    IN TSFB;

CREATE TABLE FBSCHEMA.REWARDS(
RWD_MBR_NBR      INT          NOT NULL,
RWD_ACT_DATE     DATE         NOT NULL,
RWD_TYPE         CHAR(03)     NOT NULL,
RWD_AMOUNT       INTEGER      NOT NULL)
    IN TSFB;


CREATE TABLE FBSCHEMA.DEPOSIT_TYPE(
DEP_TYPE         CHAR(03)     NOT NULL,
DEP_DESC         VARCHAR(20)  NOT NULL,
DEP_MAINT_DATE DATE           NOT NULL,
    PRIMARY KEY(DEP_TYPE))
    IN TSFB;


CREATE UNIQUE INDEX FBSCHEMA.NDX_DEP_TYPE
    ON FBSCHEMA.DEPOSIT_TYPE (DEP_TYPE);


CREATE TABLE FBSCHEMA.REWARD_TYPE(
REW_TYPE         CHAR(03)     NOT NULL,
REW_DESC         VARCHAR(20)  NOT NULL,
REW_MAINT_DATE DATE           NOT NULL,
    PRIMARY KEY(REW_TYPE))
    IN TSFB;

CREATE UNIQUE INDEX FBSCHEMA.NDX_REW_TYPE
    ON FBSCHEMA.REWARD_TYPE (REW_TYPE);
```

Ok, now that we've created the tables and indexes, let's do the referential constraints. We'll need several. First, we need to make sure that no record can be added to the DEPOSITS or REWARDS tables if the type on the record does not have an entry in the DEPOSIT_TYPE or REWARD_TYPE table respectively. So here is the DDL for that:

```
ALTER TABLE FBSCHEMA.DEPOSITS
    FOREIGN KEY FK_DEP_TYPE (DEP_TYPE)
        REFERENCES FBSCHEMA.DEPOSIT_TYPE (DEP_TYPE)
            ON DELETE RESTRICT;
```

```
ALTER TABLE FBSCHEMA.REWARDS
    FOREIGN KEY FK_REW_TYPE (RWD_TYPE)
        REFERENCES FBSCHEMA.REWARD_TYPE (REW_TYPE)
            ON DELETE RESTRICT;
```

Next, we need to ensure that any member number entered on the `DEPOSITS` and `REWARDS` table actually exists in the `MEMBER` table. Here's the DDL for that.

```
ALTER TABLE FBSCHEMA.DEPOSITS
    FOREIGN KEY FK_DEP_MBR (DEP_MBR_NBR)
        REFERENCES FBSCHEMA.MEMBER (MBR_NBR)
            ON DELETE RESTRICT;

ALTER TABLE FBSCHEMA.REWARDS
    FOREIGN KEY FK_REW_MBR (RWD_MBR_NBR)
        REFERENCES FBSCHEMA.MEMBER (MBR_NBR)
            ON DELETE RESTRICT;
```

Ok that takes care of referential constraints. You could also add some check constraints if you wanted to restrict the value or format of certain fields. I'll leave that to your imagination and business requirements, and we'll just use what we have.

Initial Testing

We'll do some testing to ensure our tables, indexes and so forth have been set up and function correctly. Due to our referential constraints, let's first populate the `DEPOSIT_TYPE` and `REWARD_TYPE` tables. Let us say we have these entries, and we'll always use the current date as the maintenance date when we add or change a value.

Deposit Type Entries

DEP_TYPE	DEP_DESC
PUR	MEMBER PURCHASE
BON	BONUS POINTS
MGR	MANAGER DISCRETION

Reward Type Entries

REW_TYPE	REW_DESC
DEB	DEBITED DOLLAR AMOUNT REWARD
PRM	FREE PROMOTIONAL REWARD

Let's go ahead and add these entries and then verify them. First the `DEPOSIT_TYPE` entries:

```
INSERT INTO FBSCHEMA.DEPOSIT_TYPE
VALUES('PUR',
'MEMBER PURCHASE',
CURRENT DATE);

INSERT INTO FBSCHEMA.DEPOSIT_TYPE
VALUES('BON',
'BONUS POINTS',
CURRENT DATE);

INSERT INTO FBSCHEMA.DEPOSIT_TYPE
VALUES('MGR',
'MANAGER DISCRETION',
CURRENT DATE);

SELECT *
FROM FBSCHEMA.DEPOSIT_TYPE;
---------+---------+---------+---------+---------+
DEP_TYPE  DEP_DESC             DEP_MAINT_DATE
---------+---------+---------+---------+---------+
PUR       MEMBER PURCHASE      2017-09-28
BON       BONUS POINTS         2017-09-28
MGR       MANAGER DISCRETION   2017-09-28
DSNE610I NUMBER OF ROWS DISPLAYED IS 3
```

And now the `REWARD_TYPE` entries:

```
INSERT INTO FBSCHEMA.REWARD_TYPE
VALUES('DEB',
'DOLLAR AMT REWARD',
CURRENT DATE);

INSERT INTO FBSCHEMA.REWARD_TYPE
VALUES('PRM',
'FREE PROMOTIONAL REW',
CURRENT DATE);

  SELECT *
  FROM FBSCHEMA.REWARD_TYPE;
---------+---------+---------+---------+---------+-
REW_TYPE  REW_DESC             REW_MAINT_DATE
---------+---------+---------+---------+---------+-
DEB       DOLLAR AMT REWARD    2017-09-28
PRM       FREE PROMOTIONAL REW 2017-09-28
DSNE610I NUMBER OF ROWS DISPLAYED IS 2
```

Ok, we have our control tables populated. Now let's add a member to the table, and then add the first deposit and withdrawal. Here's the DDL to add the first member:

```
INSERT INTO FBSCHEMA.MEMBER
(MBR_NBR,
 MBR_LAST_NAME,
 MBR_FIRST_NAME,
 MBR_ADDRESS,
 MBR_CITY,
 MBR_STATE,
 MBR_ZIP,
 MBR_PHONE,
 MBR_BALANCE)
VALUES
(NEXT VALUE FOR FBSCHEMA.MBRSEQ,
 'JEFFERSON',
 'RICHARD',
 '2497 MYRTLE LANE',
 'HOUSTON',
 'TX',
 77099,
 '2815683572',
 0);
---------+---------+---------+---------+---------+------
DSNE615I NUMBER OF ROWS AFFECTED IS 1
```

```
SELECT * FROM FBSCHEMA.MEMBER;
---------+---------+---------+---------+---------+---------+---------+--------
   MBR_NBR  MBR_LAST_NAME          MBR_FIRST_NAME  MBR_ADDRESS              MBR_CI
---------+---------+---------+---------+---------+---------+---------+--------
    100100  JEFFERSON              RICHARD         2497 MYRTLE LANE         HOUSTO
DSNE610I NUMBER OF ROWS DISPLAYED IS 1
```

Ok now let's test our referential constraints on the deposits and awards table. We'll try adding a deposit for which the member number does not exist and for which the deposit type does not exist. We should get SQL errors indicating violation of the constraints.

```
INSERT INTO FBSCHEMA.DEPOSITS
(DEP_MBR_NBR,
 DEP_ACT_DATE,
 DEP_TYPE,
 DEP_AMOUNT,
 DEP_POST_DATE)
VALUES
(100222,
 '08/01/2017',
 'ZZZ',
 15,
 CURRENT DATE);
---------+---------+---------+---------+---------+---------+---------+--------
DSNT408I SQLCODE = -530, ERROR:  THE INSERT OR UPDATE VALUE OF FOREIGN KEY
```

```
        FK_DEP_MBR IS INVALID
DSNT418I SQLSTATE     = 23503 SQLSTATE RETURN CODE
DSNT415I SQLERRP      = DSNXRINS SQL PROCEDURE DETECTING ERROR
DSNT416I SQLERRD      = -110 13172774  0  -1  0  0 SQL DIAGNOSTIC INFORMATION
DSNT416I SQLERRD      = X'FFFFFF92'  X'00C90026'  X'00000000'  X'FFFFFFFF'
           X'00000000'  X'00000000' SQL DIAGNOSTIC INFORMATION
```

And as you can see there is a violation of the FK_DEP_MBR constraint because there is no member 100222 in the table. Let's fix this by specifying a real member such as 100100 and then try an invalid deposit type.

```
        INSERT INTO FBSCHEMA.DEPOSITS
        (DEP_MBR_NBR,
         DEP_ACT_DATE,
         DEP_TYPE,
         DEP_AMOUNT,
         DEP_POST_DATE)
         VALUES
         (100100,
          '08/01/2017',
          'ZZZ',
          15,
          CURRENT DATE);
---------+---------+---------+---------+---------+---------+---------+--------
DSNT408I SQLCODE = -530, ERROR:  THE INSERT OR UPDATE VALUE OF FOREIGN KEY
           FK_DEP_TYPE IS INVALID
DSNT418I SQLSTATE     = 23503 SQLSTATE RETURN CODE
DSNT415I SQLERRP      = DSNXRINS SQL PROCEDURE DETECTING ERROR
DSNT416I SQLERRD      = -110 13172774  0  -1  0  0 SQL DIAGNOSTIC INFORMATION
DSNT416I SQLERRD      = X'FFFFFF92'  X'00C90026'  X'00000000'  X'FFFFFFFF'
           X'00000000'  X'00000000' SQL DIAGNOSTIC INFORMATION
```

Ok good, this is what we were expecting. Out insert failed with invalid foreign key in the deposit type field. Let's clean that up and do a good insert.

```
        INSERT INTO FBSCHEMA.DEPOSITS
        (DEP_MBR_NBR,
         DEP_ACT_DATE,
         DEP_TYPE,
         DEP_AMOUNT,
         DEP_POST_DATE)
         VALUES
         (100100,
          '08/01/2017',
          'PUR',
          15,
          CURRENT DATE);
---------+---------+---------+---------+---------+---------+---------+--------
DSNE615I NUMBER OF ROWS AFFECTED IS 1
```

And we can verify our result by querying the DEPOSITS table.

```
          SELECT * FROM FBSCHEMA.DEPOSITS;
---------+---------+---------+---------+---------+---------+-----
DEP_MBR_NBR  DEP_ACT_DATE  DEP_TYPE  DEP_AMOUNT  DEP_POST_DATE
---------+---------+---------+---------+---------+---------+-----
     100100    2017-08-01      PUR              15    2017-09-28
DSNE610I NUMBER OF ROWS DISPLAYED IS 1
```

Now let's check the REWARDS table for referential constraints.

```
          INSERT INTO FBSCHEMA.REWARDS
          (RWD_MBR_NBR,
           RWD_ACT_DATE,
           RWD_TYPE,
           RWD_AMOUNT)
          VALUES
          (100199,
           '09/01/2017',
           'XXX',
           10);
---------+---------+---------+---------+---------+---------+---------+--------
DSNT408I SQLCODE = -530, ERROR:  THE INSERT OR UPDATE VALUE OF FOREIGN KEY
         FK_REW_MBR IS INVALID
DSNT418I SQLSTATE   = 23503 SQLSTATE RETURN CODE
DSNT415I SQLERRP    = DSNXRINS SQL PROCEDURE DETECTING ERROR
DSNT416I SQLERRD    = -110 13172774  0  -1  0  0 SQL DIAGNOSTIC INFORMATION
DSNT416I SQLERRD    = X'FFFFFF92'  X'00C90026'  X'00000000'  X'FFFFFFFF'
             X'00000000'  X'00000000' SQL DIAGNOSTIC INFORMATION
```

Let's fix the member and try again.

```
          INSERT INTO FBSCHEMA.REWARDS
          (RWD_MBR_NBR,
           RWD_ACT_DATE,
           RWD_TYPE,
           RWD_AMOUNT)
          VALUES
          (100100,
           '09/01/2017',
           'XXX',
           10);
---------+---------+---------+---------+---------+---------+---------+--------
DSNT408I SQLCODE = -530, ERROR:  THE INSERT OR UPDATE VALUE OF FOREIGN KEY
         FK_REW_TYPE IS INVALID
DSNT418I SQLSTATE   = 23503 SQLSTATE RETURN CODE
DSNT415I SQLERRP    = DSNXRINS SQL PROCEDURE DETECTING ERROR
DSNT416I SQLERRD    = -110 13172774  0  -1  0  0 SQL DIAGNOSTIC INFORMATION
DSNT416I SQLERRD    = X'FFFFFF92'  X'00C90026'  X'00000000'  X'FFFFFFFF'
```

Finally, let's go ahead and do a good insert, and we see it works fine.

```
          INSERT INTO FBSCHEMA.REWARDS
          (RWD_MBR_NBR,
           RWD_ACT_DATE,
           RWD_TYPE,
```

```
            RWD_AMOUNT)
       VALUES
       (100100,
        '09/01/2017',
        'DEB',
        10);
---------+---------+---------+---------+--------
DSNE615I NUMBER OF ROWS AFFECTED IS 1


       SELECT * FROM FBSCHEMA.REWARDS;
---------+---------+---------+---------+---------+----
RWD_MBR_NBR  RWD_ACT_DATE  RWD_TYPE   RWD_AMOUNT
---------+---------+---------+---------+---------+----
     100100  2017-09-01    DEB              10
DSNE610I NUMBER OF ROWS DISPLAYED IS 1
```

We should do additional testing, of course. Such as with 5-digit zip codes versus 9-digit. Also we should test incoming data to see what happens if someone sends a phone number with non-numeric values, such as punctuation. I'll leave these tasks to you to complete as an exercise, and we'll move on to loading and accessing data.

Stored Procedures and Programs for Data Access

Here we are going to create four stored procedures, all of which pertain to the MEMBER table. One procedure will be to retrieve data from the table. The second will be to add data to the table. The third will be to update data on the table. The fourth will be to delete data from the table. In all four cases we will use native SQL procedures, and I recommend that you do so whenever possible.

Stored Procedure to Select

Let's begin by defining the retrieval procedure which we will name GETMEM. Here is the DDL.

```
       CREATE PROCEDURE FBSCHEMA.GETMEM
       (IN   M_NBR         INTEGER,
        OUT  M_LAST_NAME   VARCHAR(20),
        OUT  M_FIRST_NAME  VARCHAR(15),
        OUT  M_ADDRESS     VARCHAR(30),
        OUT  M_CITY        VARCHAR(20),
        OUT  M_STATE       CHAR(02),
        OUT  M_ZIP         INTEGER,
        OUT  M_PHONE       BIGINT,
        OUT  M_BALANCE     BIGINT)

       LANGUAGE SQL
       READS SQL DATA
```

```
         BEGIN
             SELECT MBR_LAST_NAME,
                    MBR_FIRST_NAME,
                    MBR_ADDRESS,
                    MBR_CITY,
                    MBR_STATE,
                    MBR_ZIP,
                    MBR_PHONE,
                    MBR_BALANCE
               INTO M_LAST_NAME,
                    M_FIRST_NAME,
                    M_ADDRESS,
                    M_CITY,
                    M_STATE,
                    M_ZIP,
                    M_PHONE,
                    M_BALANCE
             FROM FBSCHEMA.MEMBER
             WHERE M_NBR  = MBR_NBR ;

         END
```

You'll also need to grant security on your stored procedure as follows (grant it to your id, to whichever group you belong to, or in this case I am granting to PUBLIC).

```
         GRANT EXECUTE ON PROCEDURE FBSCHEMA.GETMEM TO PUBLIC;
```

Now let's test our stored procedure. We'll create a COBOL program for this. The code should look very similar to the previous programs earlier in the text book. Notice we are including indicator variables for all columns to allow for the possibility the record does not exist.

```
         IDENTIFICATION DIVISION.
         PROGRAM-ID. COBMEM1.

        *******************************************************
        *      PROGRAM USING DB2 CALL TO SEVERAL FREQUENT      *
        *      BUYER STORED PROCEDURES.                        *
        *******************************************************

         ENVIRONMENT DIVISION.
         DATA DIVISION.
         WORKING-STORAGE SECTION.

         01 INDICATOR-VARS.
            10 IND-MBR-LAST-NAME      PIC S9(4) BINARY VALUE 0.
            10 IND-MBR-FIRST-NAME     PIC S9(4) BINARY VALUE 0.
            10 IND-MBR-ADDRESS        PIC S9(4) BINARY VALUE 0.
            10 IND-MBR-CITY           PIC S9(4) BINARY VALUE 0.
            10 IND-MBR-STATE          PIC S9(4) BINARY VALUE 0.
```

```
            10 IND-MBR-ZIP           PIC S9(4) BINARY VALUE 0.
            10 IND-MBR-PHONE         PIC S9(4) BINARY VALUE 0.
            10 IND-MBR-BALANCE       PIC S9(4) BINARY VALUE 0.

        01 ERR-REC.
            05 FILLER                PIC X(10) VALUE 'SQLCODE = '.
            05 SQLCODE-VIEW          PIC -999.
            05 FILLER                PIC X(005) VALUE SPACES.
            05 ERR-TAB               PIC X(016).
            05 ERR-PARA              PIC X(015).
            05 ERR-DETAIL            PIC X(040).

        77 ERR-TXT-LGTH              PIC S9(9) USAGE COMP VALUE +72.

        01 ERR-MSG.
            05 ERR-MSG-LGTH          PIC S9(04) COMP VALUE +864.
            05 ERR-MSG-TXT           PIC X(072) OCCURS 12 TIMES
                                               INDEXED BY ERR-NDX.
            EXEC SQL
              INCLUDE SQLCA
            END-EXEC.

            EXEC SQL
              INCLUDE MEMBER
            END-EXEC.


    PROCEDURE DIVISION.

    MAIN-PARA.
        DISPLAY "SAMPLE COBOL PROGRAM: CALL STORED PROCEDURES".

        DISPLAY 'DISPLAY MEMBER INFORMATION'

        MOVE +100100    TO MBR-NBR

        EXEC SQL

            CALL FBSCHEMA.GETMEM
               (:MBR-NBR,
                :MBR-LAST-NAME   :IND-MBR-LAST-NAME,
                :MBR-FIRST-NAME  :IND-MBR-FIRST-NAME,
                :MBR-ADDRESS     :IND-MBR-ADDRESS,
                :MBR-CITY        :IND-MBR-CITY,
                :MBR-STATE       :IND-MBR-STATE,
                :MBR-ZIP         :IND-MBR-ZIP,
                :MBR-PHONE       :IND-MBR-PHONE,
                :MBR-BALANCE     :IND-MBR-BALANCE)

        END-EXEC.

        IF SQLCODE IS NOT EQUAL TO ZERO
```

```
            DISPLAY 'GET CALL FAILED ' MBR-NBR
            MOVE SQLCODE TO SQLCODE-VIEW
            MOVE 'MEMBER'   TO ERR-TAB
            MOVE 'MAIN'     TO ERR-PARA
            MOVE MBR-NBR    TO ERR-DETAIL
            PERFORM P9999-SQL-ERROR

       ELSE
            DISPLAY 'GET CALL SUCCESSFUL ' MBR-NBR
            DISPLAY 'MBR-NBR         = ' MBR-NBR
            DISPLAY 'MBR-LAST-NAME   = ' MBR-LAST-NAME
            DISPLAY 'MBR-FIRST-NAME  = ' MBR-FIRST-NAME
            DISPLAY 'MBR-ADDRESS     = ' MBR-ADDRESS
            DISPLAY 'MBR-CITY        = ' MBR-CITY
            DISPLAY 'MBR-ZIP         = ' MBR-ZIP
            DISPLAY 'MBR-PHONE       = ' MBR-PHONE
            DISPLAY 'MBR-BALANCE     = ' MBR-BALANCE

       END-IF

       GOBACK.

   P9999-SQL-ERROR.

       DISPLAY ERR-REC.

       CALL 'DSNTIAR' USING SQLCA,
                            ERR-MSG,
                            ERR-TXT-LGTH.

       IF RETURN-CODE IS EQUAL TO ZERO

           PERFORM P9999-DISP-ERR
              VARYING ERR-NDX FROM 1 BY 1
              UNTIL ERR-NDX > 12

       ELSE
           DISPLAY 'DSNTIAR ERROR CODE = ' RETURN-CODE
           STOP RUN.

   P9999-DISP-ERR.

       DISPLAY ERR-MSG-TXT(ERR-NDX).

   P9999-DISP-ERR-EXIT.
```

And here is the output from our program run:

```
SAMPLE COBOL PROGRAM: CALL STORED PROCEDURES
DISPLAY MEMBER INFORMATION
GET CALL SUCCESSFUL 000100100
MBR-NBR         = 000100100
```

```
MBR-LAST-NAME    =   JEFFERSON
MBR-FIRST-NAME   =   RICHARD
MBR-ADDRESS      =   2497 MYRTLE LANE
MBR-CITY         =   HOUSTON
MBR-ZIP          =   000000000000077099
MBR-PHONE        =   000000002815683572
MBR-BALANCE      =   000000000
```

Finally, let's change the searched member number to 100101 which we know does not yet exist in the table, and then rerun. Here is the result, and of course we get an SQLCODE +100 meaning the record is not found.

```
SAMPLE COBOL PROGRAM: CALL STORED PROCEDURES
DISPLAY MEMBER INFORMATION
GET CALL FAILED 000100101
SQLCODE =  100       MEMBER          MAIN           000100101
 DSNT404I SQLCODE = 100, NOT FOUND:  ROW NOT FOUND FOR FETCH, UPDATE,
OR DELETE, OR THE RESULT OF A QUERY IS AN EMPTY TABLE
 DSNT418I SQLSTATE    = 02000 SQLSTATE RETURN CODE
 DSNT415I SQLERRP     = DSNXRFF SQL PROCEDURE DETECTING ERROR
 DSNT416I SQLERRD     = -110  0  0  -1  0  0 SQL DIAGNOSTIC
INFORMATION
 DSNT416I SQLERRD     = X'FFFFFF92'  X'00000000'  X'00000000'
           X'FFFFFFFF'  X'00000000'  X'00000000'  SQL DIAGNOSTIC
           INFORMATION
```

Ok, let's take a short break and then come back and add the calls for add, update and delete.

Stored Procedure to INSERT

Alright, I'm back – hope you are too. Let's create and test an INSERT stored procedure. You can use any earlier example in the HR system as a model. Give it a try on your own and then you can compare your DDL to mine.

Alright, here is my DDL. Notice there is a single OUT parameter which will be used to return the value of the generated MBR_NBR. Your calling program will likely need that number – otherwise it won't know what account number was generated for the new member.

```
CREATE PROCEDURE FBSCHEMA.ADD_MEM_INFO
(OUT M_NBR           INTEGER,
 IN M_LAST_NAME      VARCHAR(20),
 IN M_FIRST_NAME     VARCHAR(15),
 IN M_ADDRESS        VARCHAR(30),
 IN M_CITY           VARCHAR(20),
 IN M_STATE          CHAR(02),
 IN M_ZIP            INTEGER,
```

```
            IN M_PHONE       BIGINT,
            IN M_BALANCE     BIGINT)

         LANGUAGE SQL
         MODIFIES SQL DATA

         BEGIN
            INSERT INTO FBSCHEMA.MEMBER
             (MBR_NBR,
              MBR_LAST_NAME,
              MBR_FIRST_NAME,
              MBR_FIRST_NAME,
              MBR_ADDRESS,
              MBR_CITY,
              MBR_STATE,
              MBR_ZIP,
              MBR_PHONE,
              MBR_BALANCE)
             VALUES
             (NEXT VALUE FOR FBSCHEMA.MBRSEQ,
              M_LAST_NAME,
              M_FIRST_NAME,
              M_ADDRESS,
              M_CITY,
              M_STATE,
              M_ZIP,
              M_PHONE,
              M_BALANCE);

          SET M_NBR = PREVIOUS VALUE FOR FBSCHEMA.MBRSEQ;

         END #
```

Now we must grant security on the stored procedure.

```
         GRANT EXECUTE ON PROCEDURE FBSCHEMA.ADD_MEM_INFO TO PUBLIC;
```

And finally let's look at our COBOL program to call the stored procedure.

```
         IDENTIFICATION DIVISION.
         PROGRAM-ID. COBMEM2.

        *******************************************************
        *      PROGRAM USING DB2 CALL TO STORED PROCEDURE      *
        *      TO ADD NEW MEMBERS                              *
        *******************************************************

         ENVIRONMENT DIVISION.
         DATA DIVISION.
         WORKING-STORAGE SECTION.
```

```
       01 ERR-REC.
          05 FILLER              PIC X(10) VALUE 'SQLCODE = '.
          05 SQLCODE-VIEW        PIC -999.
          05 FILLER              PIC X(005) VALUE SPACES.
          05 ERR-TAB             PIC X(016).
          05 ERR-PARA            PIC X(015).
          05 ERR-DETAIL          PIC X(040).

       77 ERR-TXT-LGTH           PIC S9(9) USAGE COMP VALUE +72.

       01 ERR-MSG.
          05 ERR-MSG-LGTH        PIC S9(04) COMP VALUE +864.
          05 ERR-MSG-TXT         PIC X(072) OCCURS 12 TIMES
                                            INDEXED BY ERR-NDX.
           EXEC SQL
             INCLUDE SQLCA
           END-EXEC.

           EXEC SQL
             INCLUDE MEMBER
           END-EXEC.

       PROCEDURE DIVISION.

       MAIN-PARA.
           DISPLAY "SAMPLE COBOL PROGRAM: CALL STORED PROCEDURES".


           DISPLAY 'ADD NEW MEMBER INFORMATION'

           MOVE ZERO             TO MBR-NBR
           MOVE 'BROWN'           TO MBR-LAST-NAME-TEXT
           MOVE 'OSCAR'           TO MBR-FIRST-NAME-TEXT
           MOVE '5162 HUNTINGTON RD'
                                 TO MBR-ADDRESS-TEXT
           MOVE 'FRIENDSWOOD'    TO MBR-CITY-TEXT

           MOVE LENGTH OF MBR-LAST-NAME-TEXT   TO MBR-LAST-NAME-LEN
           MOVE LENGTH OF MBR-FIRST-NAME-TEXT  TO MBR-FIRST-NAME-LEN
           MOVE LENGTH OF MBR-ADDRESS-TEXT     TO MBR-ADDRESS-LEN
           MOVE LENGTH OF MBR-CITY-TEXT        TO MBR-CITY-LEN

           MOVE 'TX'             TO MBR-STATE
           MOVE 770822154        TO MBR-ZIP
           MOVE 7139873472       TO MBR-PHONE
           MOVE ZERO             TO MBR-BALANCE

           EXEC SQL

              CALL FBSCHEMA.ADD_MEM_INFO
                 (:MBR-NBR,
                  :MBR-LAST-NAME,
```

```
            :MBR-FIRST-NAME,
            :MBR-ADDRESS,
            :MBR-CITY,
            :MBR-STATE,
            :MBR-ZIP,
            :MBR-PHONE,
            :MBR-BALANCE)

    END-EXEC.

    IF SQLCODE IS NOT EQUAL TO ZERO

        DISPLAY 'ADD CALL FAILED ' MBR-NBR
        MOVE SQLCODE TO SQLCODE-VIEW
        MOVE 'MEMBER'   TO ERR-TAB
        MOVE 'MAIN'     TO ERR-PARA
        MOVE MBR-NBR    TO ERR-DETAIL
        PERFORM P9999-SQL-ERROR
        DISPLAY 'MBR-NBR         = ' MBR-NBR
        DISPLAY 'MBR-LAST-NAME   = ' MBR-LAST-NAME
        DISPLAY 'MBR-FIRST-NAME  = ' MBR-FIRST-NAME
        DISPLAY 'MBR-ADDRESS     = ' MBR-ADDRESS
        DISPLAY 'MBR-CITY        = ' MBR-CITY
        DISPLAY 'MBR-ZIP         = ' MBR-ZIP
        DISPLAY 'MBR-PHONE       = ' MBR-PHONE
        DISPLAY 'MBR-BALANCE     = ' MBR-BALANCE

    ELSE
        DISPLAY  'ADD CALL SUCCESSFUL ' MBR-NBR
        DISPLAY 'MBR-NBR         = ' MBR-NBR
        DISPLAY 'MBR-LAST-NAME   = ' MBR-LAST-NAME
        DISPLAY 'MBR-FIRST-NAME  = ' MBR-FIRST-NAME
        DISPLAY 'MBR-ADDRESS     = ' MBR-ADDRESS
        DISPLAY 'MBR-CITY        = ' MBR-CITY
        DISPLAY 'MBR-ZIP         = ' MBR-ZIP
        DISPLAY 'MBR-PHONE       = ' MBR-PHONE
        DISPLAY 'MBR-BALANCE     = ' MBR-BALANCE

    END-IF

    GOBACK.

P9999-SQL-ERROR.

    DISPLAY ERR-REC.

    CALL 'DSNTIAR' USING SQLCA,
                 ERR-MSG,
                 ERR-TXT-LGTH.

    IF RETURN-CODE IS EQUAL TO ZERO

        PERFORM P9999-DISP-ERR
```

```
              VARYING ERR-NDX FROM 1 BY 1
              UNTIL ERR-NDX > 12

       ELSE
          DISPLAY 'DSNTIAR ERROR CODE = ' RETURN-CODE
          STOP RUN.

   P9999-DISP-ERR.

       DISPLAY ERR-MSG-TXT(ERR-NDX).

   P9999-DISP-ERR-EXIT.
```

And here is the result of our run:

```
SAMPLE COBOL PROGRAM: CALL STORED PROCEDURES
ADD NEW MEMBER INFORMATION
ADD CALL SUCCESSFUL 000100101
MBR-NBR          = 000100101
MBR-LAST-NAME    =   BROWN
MBR-FIRST-NAME   =   OSCAR
MBR-ADDRESS      =   5162 HUNTINGTON RD
MBR-CITY         =   FRIENDSWOOD
MBR-ZIP          = 000000000770822154
MBR-PHONE        = 000000007139873472
MBR-BALANCE      = 000000000
```

The UPDATE and DELETE stored procedures follow the examples given earlier in the text. It is best if you work on these yourself first, and then compare to the code examples. Take some time to do that now.

Stored Procedure to UPDATE

Here is the DDL to create the stored procedure to update the MEMBER table.

```
CREATE PROCEDURE FBSCHEMA.UPD_MEM_INFO
(IN M_NBR          INTEGER,
 IN M_LAST_NAME    VARCHAR(20),
 IN M_FIRST_NAME   VARCHAR(15),
 IN M_ADDRESS      VARCHAR(30),
 IN M_CITY         VARCHAR(20),
 IN M_STATE        CHAR(02),
 IN M_ZIP          INTEGER,
 IN M_PHONE        BIGINT,
 IN M_BALANCE      BIGINT)

LANGUAGE SQL
MODIFIES SQL DATA

BEGIN
   UPDATE FBSCHEMA.MEMBER
```

```
            SET MBR_NBR          = M_NBR,
                MBR_LAST_NAME    = M_LAST_NAME,
                MBR_FIRST_NAME   = M_FIRST_NAME,
                MBR_ADDRESS      = M_ADDRESS,
                MBR_ADDRESS      = M_ADDRESS,
                MBR_CITY         = M_CITY,
                MBR_STATE        = M_STATE,
                MBR_ZIP          = M_ZIP,
                MBR_PHONE        = M_PHONE,
                MBR_BALANCE      = M_BALANCE
            WHERE MBR_NBR = M_NBR;

      END #
```

Don't forget to grant security on the procedure:

```
      GRANT EXECUTE ON PROCEDURE FBSCHEMA.UPD_MEM_INFO TO PUBLIC;
```

Now here's a program to run the stored procedure. We'll just change the first name on the second record (100101) from Oscar to Osborne. You can change more fields if you like. Also, we could have read the record into the host variables first and then not had to reassign all the values for the call. That is more typical, but you can do it either way.

```
      IDENTIFICATION DIVISION.
       PROGRAM-ID. COBMEM3.

      **********************************************************
      *      PROGRAM USING DB2 CALL TO STORED PROCEDURE        *
      *      TO MODIFY MEMBER DATA                             *
      **********************************************************

       ENVIRONMENT DIVISION.
       DATA DIVISION.
       WORKING-STORAGE SECTION.

       01 INDICATOR-VARS.
           10 IND-MBR-NBR            PIC S9(4) BINARY VALUE 0.
           10 IND-MBR-LAST-NAME      PIC S9(4) BINARY VALUE 0.
           10 IND-MBR-FIRST-NAME     PIC S9(4) BINARY VALUE 0.
           10 IND-MBR-ADDRESS        PIC S9(4) BINARY VALUE 0.
           10 IND-MBR-CITY           PIC S9(4) BINARY VALUE 0.
           10 IND-MBR-STATE          PIC S9(4) BINARY VALUE 0.
           10 IND-MBR-ZIP            PIC S9(4) BINARY VALUE 0.
           10 IND-MBR-PHONE          PIC S9(4) BINARY VALUE 0.
           10 IND-MBR-BALANCE        PIC S9(4) BINARY VALUE 0.

       01 ERR-REC.
           05 FILLER                 PIC X(10) VALUE 'SQLCODE = '.
           05 SQLCODE-VIEW           PIC -999.
           05 FILLER                 PIC X(005) VALUE SPACES.
```

```
           05  ERR-TAB            PIC X(016).
           05  ERR-PARA           PIC X(015).
           05  ERR-DETAIL         PIC X(040).

       77  ERR-TXT-LGTH           PIC S9(9) USAGE COMP VALUE +72.

       01  ERR-MSG.
           05  ERR-MSG-LGTH       PIC S9(04) COMP VALUE +864.
           05  ERR-MSG-TXT        PIC X(072) OCCURS 12 TIMES
                                             INDEXED BY ERR-NDX.
           EXEC SQL
              INCLUDE SQLCA
           END-EXEC.

           EXEC SQL
              INCLUDE MEMBER
           END-EXEC.


       PROCEDURE DIVISION.

       MAIN-PARA.
           DISPLAY "SAMPLE COBOL PROGRAM: CALL STORED PROCEDURES".

           DISPLAY 'UPDATE NEW MEMBER INFORMATION'

           MOVE 100101          TO MBR-NBR
           MOVE 'BROWN'         TO MBR-LAST-NAME-TEXT
           MOVE 'OSBORNE'       TO MBR-FIRST-NAME-TEXT
           MOVE '5162 HUNTINGTON RD'
                                TO MBR-ADDRESS-TEXT
           MOVE 'FRIENDSWOOD'   TO MBR-CITY-TEXT

           MOVE LENGTH OF MBR-LAST-NAME-TEXT  TO MBR-LAST-NAME-LEN
           MOVE LENGTH OF MBR-FIRST-NAME-TEXT TO MBR-FIRST-NAME-LEN
           MOVE LENGTH OF MBR-ADDRESS-TEXT    TO MBR-ADDRESS-LEN
           MOVE LENGTH OF MBR-CITY-TEXT       TO MBR-CITY-LEN

           MOVE 'TX'            TO MBR-STATE
           MOVE 770822154       TO MBR-ZIP
           MOVE 7139873472      TO MBR-PHONE
           MOVE ZERO            TO MBR-BALANCE

           EXEC SQL

              CALL FBSCHEMA.UPD_MEM_INFO
                 (:MBR-NBR,
                  :MBR-LAST-NAME,
                  :MBR-FIRST-NAME,
                  :MBR-ADDRESS,
                  :MBR-CITY,
                  :MBR-STATE,
```

```cobol
                :MBR-ZIP,
                :MBR-PHONE,
                :MBR-BALANCE)

        END-EXEC.

        IF SQLCODE IS NOT EQUAL TO ZERO

            DISPLAY  'UPD CALL FAILED ' MBR-NBR
            MOVE SQLCODE TO SQLCODE-VIEW
            MOVE 'MEMBER'   TO ERR-TAB
            MOVE 'MAIN'     TO ERR-PARA
            MOVE MBR-NBR    TO ERR-DETAIL
            PERFORM P9999-SQL-ERROR
            DISPLAY 'MBR-NBR          = ' MBR-NBR
            DISPLAY 'MBR-LAST-NAME    = ' MBR-LAST-NAME
            DISPLAY 'MBR-FIRST-NAME   = ' MBR-FIRST-NAME
            DISPLAY 'MBR-ADDRESS      = ' MBR-ADDRESS
            DISPLAY 'MBR-CITY         = ' MBR-CITY
            DISPLAY 'MBR-ZIP          = ' MBR-ZIP
            DISPLAY 'MBR-PHONE        = ' MBR-PHONE
            DISPLAY 'MBR-BALANCE      = ' MBR-BALANCE

        ELSE
            DISPLAY  'ADD CALL SUCCESSFUL ' MBR-NBR
            DISPLAY 'MBR-NBR          = ' MBR-NBR
            DISPLAY 'MBR-LAST-NAME    = ' MBR-LAST-NAME
            DISPLAY 'MBR-FIRST-NAME   = ' MBR-FIRST-NAME
            DISPLAY 'MBR-ADDRESS      = ' MBR-ADDRESS
            DISPLAY 'MBR-CITY         = ' MBR-CITY
            DISPLAY 'MBR-ZIP          = ' MBR-ZIP
            DISPLAY 'MBR-PHONE        = ' MBR-PHONE
            DISPLAY 'MBR-BALANCE      = ' MBR-BALANCE

        END-IF

        GOBACK.

    P9999-SQL-ERROR.

        DISPLAY ERR-REC.

        CALL 'DSNTIAR' USING SQLCA,
                    ERR-MSG,
                    ERR-TXT-LGTH.

        IF RETURN-CODE IS EQUAL TO ZERO

            PERFORM P9999-DISP-ERR
                VARYING ERR-NDX FROM 1 BY 1
                UNTIL ERR-NDX > 12

        ELSE
```

```
             DISPLAY 'DSNTIAR ERROR CODE = ' RETURN-CODE
             STOP RUN.

     P9999-DISP-ERR.

         DISPLAY ERR-MSG-TXT(ERR-NDX).

     P9999-DISP-ERR-EXIT.
```

And here are the results.

```
     SAMPLE COBOL PROGRAM: CALL STORED PROCEDURES
     UPDATE NEW MEMBER INFORMATION
     ADD CALL SUCCESSFUL 000100101
     MBR-NBR         = 000100101
     MBR-LAST-NAME   =   BROWN
     MBR-FIRST-NAME  =   OSBORNE
     MBR-ADDRESS     =   5162 HUNTINGTON RD
     MBR-CITY        =   FRIENDSWOOD
     MBR-ZIP         = 000000000770822154
     MBR-PHONE       = 000000007139873472
     MBR-BALANCE     = 000000000
```

Stored Procedure to DELETE

Finally, let's create the delete stored procedure and program. The stored procedure is easy:

```
CREATE PROCEDURE FBSCHEMA.DLT_MEM_INFO
(IN M_NBR INT)

 LANGUAGE SQL
 MODIFIES SQL DATA

 BEGIN
    DELETE FROM FBSCHEMA.MEMBER
    WHERE MBR_NBR = M_NBR;

 END #
```

And again we will grant access to use the procedure:

```
GRANT EXECUTE ON PROCEDURE FBSCHEMA.DLT_MEM_INFO TO PUBLIC;
```

Now for variety, instead of writing another COBOL program, let's test the delete using a Rexx script. Here is mine:

```
/* REXX */
SUBSYS = "DB2X"
address TSO
/*  set steplib    */
  "FREE  FI(STEPLIBX) DA('DSNA10.SDSNLOAD')"
  "ALLOC FI(STEPLIBX) DA('DSNA10.SDSNLOAD') SHR REUSE"
  if rc <> 0
  then do
       say "DB2 SDSNLOAD library for SSID="ssid" is not available!"
       say "Check z/OS LINKLIST or allocate to STEPLIB in advance!"
       signal error
  end
ADDRESS TSO "SUBCOM DSNREXX" /* HOST CMD ENV AVAILABLE ? */
IF RC <> 0 THEN S_RC = RXSUBCOM('ADD','DSNREXX','DSNREXX')
say 'About to connect...'
ADDRESS DSNREXX "CONNECT" SUBSYS
IF SQLCODE =  0 THEN say 'Connected...'
IF SQLCODE <> 0 THEN CALL SQLCA
say 'About to call SP...'
/* Identify Stored procedure, define host variables */
STOPRO = 'FBSCHEMA.DLT_MEM_INFO'
MBR_NBR = +100101
/* call the stored procedure   */
ADDRESS DSNREXX
"EXECSQL CALL :STOPRO(:MBR_NBR)"
IF SQLCODE <> 0 THEN CALL SQLCA
say SQLCODE
IF SQLCODE = 0 THEN
SAY "Stored Procedure: " DLT_MEM_INFO " was successful"
SAY "MBR_NBR       = " MBR_NBR
```

And here is the result:

```
About to call SP...
0
Stored Procedure:  DLT_MEM_INFO  was successful
MBR_NBR       = 100101
***
```

And we can verify that the record 100101 was deleted by listing the content of the MEMBER table:

```
SELECT MBR_NBR,
MBR_LAST_NAME,
MBR_FIRST_NAME
FROM FBSCHEMA.MEMBER;
---------+---------+---------+---------+---------+-------
    MBR_NBR  MBR_LAST_NAME      MBR_FIRST_NAME
---------+---------+---------+---------+---------+-------
     100100  JEFFERSON          RICHARD
DSNE610I NUMBER OF ROWS DISPLAYED IS 1
```

Special Project Wrap-up

There are many other things you could do with this project. Lacking a real world project, I encourage you to use your imagination. For example you might need a UDF to extract all member activity (deposits and rewards) for an online display on a web page.

Here are just a few more ideas you can consider. How about setting up archive tables for the DEPOSIT_TYPE and REWARD_TYPE tables – the archive records will come in handy when someone asked when these tables changed and what the previous entries were. Similarly you could set up an archive table for the MEMBER table. This way whenever a MEMBER record changes you will always have a copy of the previous version. Set up DEPOSITS and REWARDS as temporal tables to enable time travel queries to show activity such as BALANCE as of a certain period of time. The possibilities are endless but the necessities will depend on your actual project requirements.

We've come to the end of this text book, so let me close with a sincere "best of luck". It's been a pleasure walking you through VSAM, IMS and intermediate level DB2 concepts. I truly hope you do exceptionally well as an IBM z/OS application developer, and that you have every success!

Robert Wingate

Chapter Three Questions

1. Consider the following stored procedure:

   ```
   CREATE PROCEDURE GET_PATIENTS
   (IN intHosp INTEGER)
   DYNAMIC RESULT SETS 1
   LANGUAGE SQL
   P1: BEGIN

   DECLARE cursor1 CURSOR
   WITH RETURN FOR
   SELECT PATIENT_ID,
   LNAME,
   FNAME
   FROM PATIENT
   WHERE PATIENT_HOSP = intHosp
   ORDER BY PATIENT_ID ASC;

   OPEN cursor1;
   END P1
   ```

   Answer this question: How many parameters are used in this stored procedure?

   a. 0
   b. 1
   c. 2
   d. 3

2. When you want to create an external stored procedure, which of the following programming languages can NOT be used?

   a. COBOL
   b. REXX
   c. Fortran
   d. C++

3. In order to invoke a stored procedure, which keyword would you use?

    a. RUN
    b. CALL
    c. OPEN
    d. TRIGGER

4. Which of the following is NOT a valid return type for a User Defined Function?

    a. Scalar
    b. Aggregate
    c. Column
    d. Row

5. Which of the following is NOT a valid type of user-defined function (UDF)?

    a. External sourced
    b. SQL sourced
    c. External table
    d. SQL table

6. Assume the following trigger DDL:

    ```
    CREATE TRIGGER SAVE_EMPL
    AFTER UPDATE ON EMPL
    FOR EACH ROW
    INSERT INTO EMPLOYEE_HISTORY
    VALUES (EMPLOYEE_NUMBER,
    EMPLOYEE_STATUS,
    CURRENT TIMESTAMP)
    ```

    What will the result of this DDL be, provided the tables and field names are correctly defined?

    a. The DDL will create the trigger successfully and it will work as intended.
    b. The DDL will fail because you cannot use an INSERT with a trigger.
    c. The DDL will fail because the syntax of this statement is incorrect.
    d. The DDL will create the trigger successfully but it will fail when executed.

7. Which ONE of the following actions will NOT cause a trigger to fire?

    a. INSERT
    b. LOAD
    c. DELETE
    d. MERGE

8. If you use the "FOR EACH STATEMENT" granularity clause in a trigger, what type of timing can you use?

    a. BEFORE
    b. AFTER
    c. INSTEAD OF
    d. All of the above.

9. Assume you have a column FLD1 with a referential constraint that specifies that the FLD1 value must exist in another table. What type of field is FLD1?

    a. FOREIGN KEY
    b. PRIMARY KEY
    c. UNIQUE KEY
    d. INDEX KEY

10. Review the following and then answer the question.

    ```
    CREATE TABLE "DBO"."HOSPITAL"  (
    "HOSP_ID" INTEGER NOT NULL ,
    "HOSP_NAME" CHAR(25) )
    IN "USERSPACE1" ;

    ALTER TABLE "DBO"."HOSPITAL"
    ADD CONSTRAINT "PKeyHosp" PRIMARY KEY
    ("HOSP_ID");

    CREATE TABLE "DBO"."PATIENT"  (
    "PATIENT_ID" INTEGER NOT NULL ,
    "PATIENT_NAME" CHAR(30) ,
    "PATIENT_HOSP" INTEGER )
    IN "USERSPACE1" ;
    ```

```
ALTER TABLE "DBO"."PATIENT"
ADD CONSTRAINT "PKeyPat" PRIMARY KEY
("PATIENT_ID");

ALTER TABLE "DBO"."PATIENT"
ADD CONSTRAINT "FKPatHosp" FOREIGN KEY
("PATIENT_HOSP")
REFERENCES "DBO"."HOSPITAL"
("HOSP_ID")
ON DELETE SET NULL;
```

If a row is deleted from the HOSPITAL table, what will happen to the PATIENT_HOSP rows that used the HOSP_ID value?

    a. The PATIENT_HOSP field will be set to NULLS.
    b. The PATIENT rows will be deleted from the PATIENT table.
    c. Nothing will be changed on the PATIENT records.
    d. The delete of the HOSPITAL record will fail.

11. Review the following DDL and then answer the question.

```
CREATE TABLE "DBO"."HOSPITAL"  (
"HOSP_ID" INTEGER NOT NULL ,
"HOSP_NAME" CHAR(25) )
IN "USERSPACE1" ;

ALTER TABLE "DBO"."HOSPITAL"
ADD CONSTRAINT "PKeyHosp" PRIMARY KEY
("HOSP_ID");

CREATE TABLE "DBO"."PATIENT"  (
"PATIENT_ID" INTEGER NOT NULL ,
"PATIENT_NAME" CHAR(30) ,
"PATIENT_HOSP" INTEGER )
IN "USERSPACE1" ;

ALTER TABLE "DBO"."PATIENT"
ADD CONSTRAINT "PKeyPat" PRIMARY KEY
("PATIENT_ID");

ALTER TABLE "DBO"."PATIENT"
ADD CONSTRAINT "FKPatHosp" FOREIGN KEY
("PATIENT_HOSP")
REFERENCES "DBO"."HOSPITAL"
```

```
                ("HOSP_ID")
                ON DELETE CASCADE;
```

If a row is deleted from the HOSPITAL table, what will happen to the PATIENT_HOSP rows that used the HOSP_ID value?

    a. The PATIENT_HOSP field will be set to NULLS.
    b. The PATIENT rows will be deleted from the PATIENT table.
    c. Nothing will be changed on the PATIENT records.
    d. The delete of the HOSPITAL record will fail.

12. Review the following DDL, and then answer the question:

```
                CREATE TABLE "DBO"."HOSPITAL"
                ("HOSP_ID" INTEGER NOT NULL,
                "HOSP_NAME" CHAR(25) )   IN "USERSPACE1";

                ALTER TABLE "DBO"."HOSPITAL"
                ADD CONSTRAINT "PKeyHosp"
                PRIMARY KEY ("HOSP_ID");

                CREATE TABLE "DBO"."PATIENT"
                ("PATIENT_ID" INTEGER NOT NULL,
                "PATIENT_NAME" CHAR(30) ,
                "PATIENT_HOSP" INTEGER )   IN "USERSPACE1" ;

                ALTER TABLE "DBO"."PATIENT"
                ADD CONSTRAINT "PKeyPat"
                PRIMARY KEY    ("PATIENT_ID");

                ALTER TABLE "DBO"."PATIENT"
                ADD CONSTRAINT "FKPatHosp"
                FOREIGN KEY ("PATIENT_HOSP")
                REFERENCES "DBO"."HOSPITAL" ("HOSP_ID")
                ON DELETE RESTRICT;
```

If a row is deleted from the HOSPITAL table, what will happen to the PATIENT_HOSP rows that used the HOSP_ID value?

    a. The PATIENT_HOSP field will be set to NULLS.
    b. The PATIENT rows will be deleted from the PATIENT table.
    c. Nothing will be changed on the PATIENT records.
    d. The delete of the HOSPITAL record will fail.

13. What is the schema for a declared GLOBAL TEMPORARY table?

    a. SESSION
    b. DB2ADMIN
    c. TEMP1
    d. USERTEMP

14. If you create a temporary table and you wish to replace any existing temporary table that has the same name, what clause would you use?

    a. WITH REPLACE
    b. OVERLAY DATA ROWS
    c. REPLACE EXISTING
    d. None of the above.

15. What happens to the rows of a temporary table when the session that created it ends?

    a. The rows are deleted when the session ends.
    b. The rows are preserved in memory until the instance is restarted.
    c. The rows are held in the temp table space.
    d. None of the above.

16. Which is true of temporary tables declared within a SAVEPOINT after a ROLLBACK TO SAVEPOINT command has been issued?

    a. Temporary tables declared within the savepoint are still in the system catalog.
    b. Temporary tables declared within the savepoint are dropped and no longer accessible.
    c. Temporary tables declared within the savepoint are still accessible.
    d. None of the above.

17. Which of the following clauses DOES NOT allow you to pull data for a particular period from a version enabled table?

   a. FOR BUSINESS_TIME UP UNTIL
   b. FOR BUSINESS_TIME FROM ... TO ...
   c. FOR BUSINESS_TIME BETWEEN... AND...
   d. All of the above enable you to pull data for a particular period.

18. Assume you have an application that needs to aggregate and summarize data from several tables multiple times per day. One way to improve performance of that application would be to use a:

   a. Materialized query table
   b. View
   c. Temporary table
   d. Range clustered table

19. Assume you want to track employees in your company over time. Review the following DDL:

    ```
    CREATE TABLE HRSCHEMA.EMPLOYZZ(
    EMP_ID INT NOT NULL,
    EMP_LAST_NAME VARCHAR(30) NOT NULL,
    EMP_FIRST_NAME VARCHAR(20) NOT NULL,
    EMP_SERVICE_YEARS INT
    NOT NULL WITH DEFAULT 0,
    EMP_PROMOTION_DATE DATE,
    BUS_START    DATE   NOT NULL,
    BUS_END      DATE   NOT NULL,

    PERIOD BUSINESS_TIME(BUS_START, BUS_END),

    PRIMARY KEY (EMP_ID, BUSINESS_TIME WITHOUT OVERLAPS));
    ```

    What will happen when you execute this DDL?

   a. It will fail because you cannot specify WITHOUT OVERLAPS in the primary key – the WITHOUT OVERLAPS clause belongs in the BUSINESS_TIME definition.

b. It will fail because you must specify SYSTEM_TIME instead of BUSINESS_TIME.
   c. It will fail because the BUS_START has a syntax error.
   d. It will execute successfully.

20. Given the previous question, assume there is a table named EMPLOYEE_HIST defined just like EMPLOYEE. What will happen when you execute the following DDL?

    ```
    ALTER TABLE EMPLOYEE
    ADD VERSIONING
    USE HISTORY TABLE EMPLOYEE_HIST
    ```

   a. The DDL will execute successfully and updates to EMPLOYEE will generate records in the EMPLOYEE_HIST table.
   b. The DDL will succeed but you must still enable the history table.
   c. The DDL will generate an error – only SYSTEM time enabled tables can use a history table.
   d. The DDL will generate an error – only BUSINESS time enabled tables can use a history table.

21. For a system managed Materialized Query Table (MQT) named EMPMQT, how does the data get updated so that it becomes current?

   a. Issuing INSERT, UPDATE and DELETE commands against EMPMQT.
   b. Issuing the statement REFRESH TABLE EMPMQT.
   c. Issuing the statement MATERIALIZE TABLE EMPMQT.
   d. None of the above.

22. Which of the following is TRUE about SQLJ applications that need to handle XML data?

   a. You cannot select or update XML data as textual XML data.
   b. For update of data in XML columns, xmlFormat does the appropriate formatting.
   c. You can store an entire XML document into an XML column using a single UPDATE, INSERT or MERGE statement.
   d. External encoding for Java applications cannot use Unicode encoding.

23. Which of the following is NOT true about XML validation using an XML type modifier?

    a. An XML type modifier associates the type with an XML schema.
    b. The XML type modifier can identify a single XML schema only.
    c. An XML type modifier is defined in a CREATE TABLE or ALTER TABLE statement as part of an XML column definition.
    d. You can use an ALTER TABLE statement to remove an XML schema from the column XML type definition.

24. An XML index can be created on what column types?

    a. VARCHAR and XML.
    b. CLOB AND XML.
    c. XML only.
    d. Any of the above.

25. Which of the following can be used to validate an XML value according to a schema?

    a. Defining a column as type XML.
    b. Manually running the DSN_XMLVALIDATE.
    c. Both of the above.
    d. Neither of the above.

26. To determine whether an XML document has been validated, which function could you use?

    a. XMLXSROBJECTID.
    b. XMLDOCUMENT.
    c. XMLPARSE.
    d. None of the above.

27. Which bind option would you use to enable parallel processing to improve performance of a query?

    a. DEGREE(1)
    b. DEGREE(2)
    c. DEGREE(ANY)
    d. DEGREE(PARALLEL)

28. To improve performance for read-only queries against remote sites, which DBPROTOCOL value should be used when binding applications?

    a. DRDACBF
    b. DRDA
    c. PRIVATE
    d. DRDABCF

29. Which of the following is a Stage 2 predicate?

    a. COL IS NULL
    b. SUBSTR(COL,1,n) = value
    c. EXISTS(subquery)
    d. COL LIKE pattern

30. Which of the following would probably NOT improve query performance?

    a. Use indexable predicates in your queries.
    b. Execute the RUNSTATS utility and rebind application programs.
    c. Use the EXISTS clause instead of COL IN (value list).
    d. All of the above could improve application performance.

31. Which of the following trace types could be used to collect information about which users tried to access DB2 objects and were denied due to inadequate authorization?

    a. ACCTG
    b. MONITOR
    c. AUDIT
    d. STATISTICS

32. Which of the following is NOT a valid value for the SMFACCT subsystem parameter?

    a. YES
    b. NO
    c. $
    d. *

33. Which of the following EXPLAIN tables includes information about the access path that will be used to return data?

    a. PLAN_TABLE
    b. DSN_QUERY_TABLE
    c. DSN_STATEMENT_TABLE
    d. None of the above.

34. If you find out that your application query is doing a table space scan, what changes could you make to improve the scan efficiency?

    a. Create one or more indexes on the query search columns.
    b. Load the data to a temporary table and query that table instead of the base table.
    c. If the table is partitioned, change it to a non-partitioned table.
    d. All of the above could improve the scan efficiency.

APPENDICES
Chapter Questions and Answers
Chapter One: VSAM

1. What are the three types of VSAM datasets?

    Entry-sequenced datasets (ESDS), key-sequenced datasets (KSDS) and relative record dataset (RRDS).

2. How are records stored in an ESDS (entry sequenced) dataset?

    They are stored in the order in which they are inserted into the file.

3. What VSAM feature enables you to access the records in a KSDS dataset based on a key that is different than the file's primary key?

    VSAM allows creation of an alternate index which enables you to access the records in a KSDS dataset based on that alternate index rather than the primary key.

4. What is the general purpose utility program that provides services for VSAM files?

    Access Method Services is the utility program that provides services for VSAM files. Often it is referred to as IDCAMS which is the executable program in batch.

5. Which AMS function lists information about datasets?

    The LISTCAT function lists information about datasets. An example is:

```
//STEP1    EXEC PGM=IDCAMS
//SYSPRINT DD SYSOUT=X
//SYSIN    DD *
 LISTCAT GDG ENT('DSNAME.GDGFILE.TEST1') ALL
```

6. If you are mostly going to use a KSDS file for sequential access, should you define a larger or smaller control interval when creating the file?

   For sequential access a larger control interval is desirable for performance because you maximize the data brought in with each I/O.

7. What is the basic AMS command to create a VSAM file?

   DEFINE CLUSTER is the basic command to create a VSAM file.

8. To use the REWRITE command in COBOL, the VSAM file must be opened in what mode?

   To use the REWRITE command in COBOL, the VSAM file must be opened for I-O.

9. When you define an alternate index, what is the function of the RELATE parameter?

   The RELATE parameter associates your alternate index with the base cluster that you are creating the alternate index for.

10. When you define a path using DEFINE PATH, what does the PATHENTRY parameter do?

    The PATHENTRY parameter includes the name of the alternate index that you are creating the path for.

11. After you've defined an alternate index and path, what AMS command must you issue to actually populate the alternate index?

    Issue the BLXINDEX command to populate an alternate index.

12. After you've created a VSAM file, if you need to add additional DASD volumes that can be used with that file, what command would you use?

    Use an ALTER command and specify the keyword ADDVOLUMES(XXX001 YYY002) where XXX001 and YYY002 are DASD volume names.

13. If you want to set a VSAM file to read only status, what command would you use?

    Use the ALTER command with the INHIBIT keyword. For example:

    ```
    //STEP1 EXEC PGM=IDCAMS
    //SYSPRINT DD SYSOUT=*
    //SYSIN DD *
    ALTER -
    PROD.EMPL.DATA -
    INHIBIT
    ALTER -
    PROD.EMPL.INDEX -
    INHIBIT
    /*
    ```

    To return the file to read/update, use ALTER with the UNINHIBIT keyword.

14. What are some ways you can improve the performance of a KSDS file?

    - **Ensure that the control interval is optimally sized (smaller for random access and larger for sequential access).**

    - **Allocate additional index buffers to reduce data I/Os by keeping needed records in virtual storage.**

    - **Ensure sufficient free space in control intervals to avoid control interval splits.**

15. Do primary key values in a KSDS have to be unique?

   Yes the primary key has to be unique. However, alternate index values need not be unique. For example if an EMPLOYEE file uses employee number as the primary key, then the employee number must be unique. However the EMPLOYEE file could be alternately indexed on department. In this case, the department need not be unique.

16. In the COBOL SELECT statement what organization should be specified for a KSDS file?

   In a COBOL SELECT statement, the organization for a KSDS file is INDEXED.

17. In the COBOL SELECT statement for a KSDS what are the three possibilities for ACCESS?

   In the COBOL SELECT statement for a KSDS, ACCESS can be SEQUENTIAL, RANDOM or DYNAMIC.

18. Is there a performance penalty for using an alternate index compared to using the primary key?

   Yes because if you access a record through an ALTERNATE INDEX, the alternate key must first be located and then it points to the primary key entry which is finally used to locate the actual record.

19. What file status code will you receive if an operation succeeded?

   If an operation succeeded without any problem you will receive a 00 file status code.

Chapter Two: IMS DB

1. What is the name of the interface program you call from a COBOL program to perform IMS operations?

    CBLTDLI is the normal interface program for a COBOL program to access IMS.

2. Here are some IMS return codes and . Explain briefly what each of them means: blank, GE, GB, II

    Blank – successful operation
    GE – segment not found
    GB – end of database
    II – duplicate key, insert failed

3. What is an SSA?

    Segment Search Argument – it is used to select segments by name and to specify search criteria for specific segments.

4. Briefly explain these entities: DBD, PSB, PCB?

    A Database Description (DBD) specifies characteristics of a database. The name, parent, and length of each segment type in the database.

    A Program Specification Block (PSB) is the program view of one or more IMS databases. The PSB includes one or more program communication blocks (PCB) for each IMS database that the program needs access to.

    A Program Communication Block (PCB) specifies the database to be accessed, the processing options such as read-only or various updating options, and the database segments that can be accessed.

5. What is the use of CMPAT parameter in PSB ?

    It is required if you are going to run your program in Batch Mode Processing (BMP), that is - in the online region. If you always run the program in DL/I

mode, you do not need the CMPAT. If you are going to run BMP, you need the CMPAT=YES specified in the PSB.

6. In IMS, what is the difference between a key field and a search field?

   A key field is used to make the record unique and to order the database. A search field is a field that is needed to search the database on but does not have to be unique and does not order the database. For example, an EMPLOYEE database might be keyed on unique EMP-NUMBER. A search field might be needed on PHONE-NUMBER or ZIP-CODE. Even though the database is not ordered by these fields, they can be made search fields to query the database.

7. What does PROCOPT mean in a PCB?

   The PROCOPT parameter specifies *processing options* that are allowed for this PCB when operating on a segment.

   The different PROCOPTs and their meaning are:

       G - Get segment from DB
       I - Insert segment into DB
       R - Replace segment
       D - Delete segment
       A - All the above operations

8. What are the four basic parameters of a DLI retrieval call?

   - **Function**
   - **PCB mask**
   - **SSAs**
   - **IO Area**

9. What are Qualified SSA and Unqualified SSA?

   A qualified SSA specifies the segment type and the specific instance (key) of the segment to be returned. An unqualified SSA simply supplies the name of the segment type that you want to operate upon. You could use the latter if you don't care which specific segment you retrieve.

10. Which PSB parameter in a PSBGEN specifies the language in which the application program is written?

    The LANG parameter specifies the language in which the application program is written. Examples:

    ```
    LANG=COBOL
    LANG=PLI
    LANG=ASSEM
    ```

11. What does SENSEG stand for and how is it used in a PCB?

    SENSEG is known as Segment Level Sensitivity. It defines the program's access to parts of the database and it is identified at the segment level. For example, PROCOPT=G on a SENSEG means the segment is read-only by this PCB.

12. What storage mechanism/format is used for IMS index databases?

    IMS index databases must use VSAM KSDS.

13. What are the DL/I commands to add, change and remove a segment?

    The following are the DL/I commands for adding, changing and removing a segment:

    - ISRT
    - REPL
    - DLET

14. What return code will you receive from IMS if the DL/I call was successful?

    IMS returns blanks/spaces in the PCB STATUS-CODE field when the call was successful.

15. If you want to retrieve the last occurrence of a child segment under its parent, what command code could you use?

    Use the L command code to retrieve the last child segment under its parent. Incidentally, IMS ignores the L command code at the root level.

16. When would you use a GU call?

    GU is used to retrieve a segment occurrence based on SSA supplied arguments.

17. When would you use a GHU call?

    GHU (Get Hold Unique) retrieves and locks the record that you intend to update or delete.

18. What is the difference between running an IMS program as DLI and BMP ?

    DLI runs within its own address space. BMP runs under the IMS online control region. The practical difference concerns programs that update the database. If performing updates, DLI requires exclusive use of the database. Running BMP does not require exclusive use because it runs under control of the online region.

19. When would you use a GNP call?

    The GNP call is used for Get Next within Parent. This function is used to retrieve segment occurrences in sequence subordinate to an established parent segment.

20. Which IMS call is used to restart an abended program?

   The XRST IMS call is made to restart an abended IMS program. Assuming the program has taken checkpoints during the abended program execution, the XRST call is used to restart from the last checkpoint taken instead of starting the processing all over.

21. How do you establish parentage on a segment occurrence?

   By issuing a successful GU or GN (or GHU or GHN) call that retrieves the segment on which the parentage is to be established. IMS normally sets parentage at the lowest level segment retrieved in a call. If you want to establish parentage at a level other than the normal level, use the P command code.

22. What is a checkpoint?

   A checkpoint is a stage where the modifications done to a database by an application program are considered complete and are committed to the database with the CKPT IMS call.

23. How do you update the primary key of an IMS segment?

   You cannot update the primary key of a segment. If the key on a record must be changed, you can DLET the existing segment and then ISRT a new segment with the new key.

24. Do you need to use a qualified SSA with REPL/DLET calls?

   No, you don't need to include an SSA with REPL/DLET calls. This is because the target segment has already been retrieved and held by a get hold call (that is the only way you can update or delete a segment).

25. What is a root segment?

   A segment that lies at the top of the hierarchy is called the root segment. It is the only segment through which all dependent segments are accessed.

26. What are command codes?

   Command codes are used along with SSAs to perform additional operations.

   Common command codes used are:

   'P' - used to set parentage on a particular segment.
   'D' - used for path calls, to retrieve the entire hierarchical path.

Chapter Three: Intermediate DB2

1. Consider the following stored procedure:

    ```
    CREATE PROCEDURE GET_PATIENTS
    (IN intHosp INTEGER)
    DYNAMIC RESULT SETS 1
    LANGUAGE SQL
    P1: BEGIN

    DECLARE cursor1 CURSOR
    WITH RETURN FOR
    SELECT PATIENT_ID,
    LNAME,
    FNAME
    FROM PATIENT
    WHERE PATIENT_HOSP = intHosp
    ORDER BY PATIENT_ID ASC;

    OPEN cursor1;
    END P1
    ```

    Answer this question: How many parameters are used in this stored procedure?

    a. 0
    b. 1
    c. 2
    d. 3

    The correct answer is B (1). intHosp is accepted as an IN parameter that is used in the query. Parameters can be IN (they pass a value to the stored procedure), OUT (they return a value from a stored procedure), or INOUT (they pass a value to and return a value from a stored procedure). The answers 0, 2, and 3 are incorrect because exactly 1 parameter is used in this stored procedure.

2. When you want to create an external stored procedure, which of the following programming languages can NOT be used?

    a. COBOL
    b. REXX
    c. Fortran
    d. C++

The correct answer is C. You cannot use Fortran to create an external stored procedure. The valid programming languages for creating an external stored procedure are:

- Assembler
- C
- C++
- COBOL
- REXX
- PL/I

3. In order to invoke a stored procedure, which keyword would you use?

   a. RUN
   b. CALL
   c. OPEN
   d. TRIGGER

The correct answer is B. CALL is the correct statement to invoke a stored procedure. The syntax is CALL <procedure-name>. RUN is not a valid DB2 statement or command unless you are issuing the command to RUN(DSN). The OPEN statement opens a cursor in an embedded SQL program. A TRIGGER is an object that performs some predefined action when it is activated by an INSERT, UPDATE or DELETE of a record in a particular table.

4. Which of the following is NOT a valid return type for a User Defined Function?

    a. Scalar
    b. Aggregate
    c. Column
    d. Row

    The correct answer is C. There is no "column" return type for a UDF. A user-defined function can be any of the following which returns the specific data type:

    - **A scalar function, which returns a single value each time it is called.**
    - **An aggregate function, which is passed a set of like values and returns a single value for the set.**
    - **A row function, which returns one row.**
    - **A table function, which returns a table.**

5. Which of the following is NOT a valid type of user-defined function (UDF)?

    a. External sourced
    b. SQL sourced
    c. External table
    d. SQL table

    The correct answer is B. There is no SQL sourced user-defined function type. Valid types of user defined functions include:

    - **External scalar**
    - **External table**
    - **External sourced**
    - **SQL scalar**
    - **SQL table**

    An external scalar function is written in a programming language and returns a scalar value. An external table function is written in a programming language and returns a table to the subselect from which it was started. A sourced function is implemented by starting another function that exists at the server. An SQL scalar function is written exclusively in SQL statements and returns a scalar value. An SQL table function is written exclusively as an SQL RETURN statement and returns a set of rows.

6. Assume the following trigger DDL:

```
CREATE TRIGGER SAVE_EMPL
AFTER UPDATE ON EMPL
FOR EACH ROW
INSERT INTO EMPLOYEE_HISTORY
VALUES (EMPLOYEE_NUMBER,
EMPLOYEE_STATUS,
CURRENT TIMESTAMP)
```

What will the result of this DDL be, provided the tables and field names are correctly defined?

    a. The DDL will create the trigger successfully and it will work as intended.
    b. The DDL will fail because you cannot use an INSERT with a trigger.
    c. The DDL will fail because the syntax of this statement is incorrect.
    d. The DDL will create the trigger successfully but it will fail when executed.

The correct answer is A. The DDL is syntactically correct and will sucessfully create a trigger that will work as intended.

7. Which ONE of the following actions will NOT cause a trigger to fire?

    a. INSERT
    b. LOAD
    c. DELETE
    d. MERGE

The correct answer is B. The LOAD action does not (by default) causes triggers to fire. The INSERT, DELETE and MERGE do cause INSERT, UPDATE and DELETE triggers to fire.

8. If you use the "FOR EACH STATEMENT" granularity clause in a trigger, what type of timing can you use?

    a. BEFORE
    b. AFTER
    c. INSTEAD OF
    d. All of the above.

   The correct answer is B. You cannot use a FOR EACH STATEMENT with BEFORE or INSTEAD OF timing. FOR EACH STATEMENT means your trigger logic is to be applied only once after the triggering statement finishes processing the affected rows.

9. Assume you have a column FLD1 with a referential constraint that specifies that the FLD1 value must exist in another table. What type of field is FLD1?

    a. FOREIGN KEY
    b. PRIMARY KEY
    c. UNIQUE KEY
    d. INDEX KEY

   The correct answer is A. A foreign key relationship is a constraint that says a column must only contain values that exist in another (parent) table. A PRIMARY KEY ensures that all values in a table are unique and non-NULL. A UNIQUE key ensures that no two rows have the same value in the column defined as being UNIQUE. INDEX KEY is incorrect because no information in the question suggested that an index was involved.

10. Review the following and then answer the question.

```
CREATE TABLE "DBO"."HOSPITAL"  (
"HOSP_ID" INTEGER NOT NULL ,
"HOSP_NAME" CHAR(25) )
IN "USERSPACE1" ;

ALTER TABLE "DBO"."HOSPITAL"
ADD CONSTRAINT "PKeyHosp" PRIMARY KEY
("HOSP_ID");

CREATE TABLE "DBO"."PATIENT"   (
```

```
"PATIENT_ID" INTEGER NOT NULL ,
"PATIENT_NAME" CHAR(30) ,
"PATIENT_HOSP" INTEGER )
IN "USERSPACE1" ;

ALTER TABLE "DBO"."PATIENT"
ADD CONSTRAINT "PKeyPat" PRIMARY KEY
("PATIENT_ID");

ALTER TABLE "DBO"."PATIENT"
ADD CONSTRAINT "FKPatHosp" FOREIGN KEY
("PATIENT_HOSP")
REFERENCES "DBO"."HOSPITAL"
("HOSP_ID")
ON DELETE SET NULL;
```

If a row is deleted from the HOSPITAL table, what will happen to the PATIENT_HOSP rows that used the HOSP_ID value?

    a. The PATIENT_HOSP field will be set to NULLS.
    b. The PATIENT rows will be deleted from the PATIENT table.
    c. Nothing will be changed on the PATIENT records.
    d. The delete of the HOSPITAL record will fail.

The correct answer is A - the PATIENT_HOSP field will be set to NULL because of the ON DELETE SET NULL clause in the foreign key definition. You can specify the action to take in the foreign key definition by including the ON DELETE clause. Besides SET NULL, there are other possibilities for the ON DELETE clause. If ON DELETE CASCADE is specified, then references in the child table to the parent record being deleted will cause the child records to also be deleted. If no action is specified, or if RESTRICT is specified in the ON DELETE clause, then the parent record cannot be deleted unless all child records which reference that record are first deleted.

11. Review the following DDL and then answer the question.

```
CREATE TABLE "DBO"."HOSPITAL"  (
"HOSP_ID" INTEGER NOT NULL ,
"HOSP_NAME" CHAR(25) )
IN "USERSPACE1" ;

ALTER TABLE "DBO"."HOSPITAL"
ADD CONSTRAINT "PKeyHosp" PRIMARY KEY
```

```
("HOSP_ID");

CREATE TABLE "DBO"."PATIENT"  (
"PATIENT_ID" INTEGER NOT NULL ,
"PATIENT_NAME" CHAR(30) ,
"PATIENT_HOSP" INTEGER )
IN "USERSPACE1" ;

ALTER TABLE "DBO"."PATIENT"
ADD CONSTRAINT "PKeyPat" PRIMARY KEY
("PATIENT_ID");

ALTER TABLE "DBO"."PATIENT"
ADD CONSTRAINT "FKPatHosp" FOREIGN KEY
("PATIENT_HOSP")
REFERENCES "DBO"."HOSPITAL"
("HOSP_ID")
ON DELETE CASCADE;
```

If a row is deleted from the HOSPITAL table, what will happen to the PATIENT_HOSP rows that used the HOSP_ID value?

    a. The PATIENT_HOSP field will be set to NULLS.
    b. The PATIENT rows will be deleted from the PATIENT table.
    c. Nothing will be changed on the PATIENT records.
    d. The delete of the HOSPITAL record will fail.

The correct answer is B - when ON DELETE CASCADE is specified, then references in the child table to the parent record being deleted will cause the child records to also be deleted. You can specify the action to take in the foreign key definition by including the ON DELETE clause. If no action is specified, or if RESTRICT is specified in the ON DELETE clause, then the parent record cannot be deleted unless all child records which reference that record are first deleted. If the clause ON DELETE SET NULL was present in the foreign key definition, the PATIENT_HOSP field will be set to NULL.

12. Review the following DDL, and then answer the question:

    ```
    CREATE TABLE "DBO"."HOSPITAL"
    ("HOSP_ID" INTEGER NOT NULL,
    "HOSP_NAME" CHAR(25) )  IN "USERSPACE1";

    ALTER TABLE "DBO"."HOSPITAL"
    ADD CONSTRAINT "PKeyHosp"
    PRIMARY KEY ("HOSP_ID");

    CREATE TABLE "DBO"."PATIENT"
    ("PATIENT_ID" INTEGER NOT NULL,
    "PATIENT_NAME" CHAR(30) ,
    "PATIENT_HOSP" INTEGER )   IN "USERSPACE1" ;

    ALTER TABLE "DBO"."PATIENT"
    ADD CONSTRAINT "PKeyPat"
    PRIMARY KEY    ("PATIENT_ID");

    ALTER TABLE "DBO"."PATIENT"
    ADD CONSTRAINT "FKPatHosp"
    FOREIGN KEY ("PATIENT_HOSP")
    REFERENCES "DBO"."HOSPITAL" ("HOSP_ID")
    ON DELETE RESTRICT;
    ```

    If a row is deleted from the HOSPITAL table, what will happen to the PATIENT_HOSP rows that used the HOSP_ID value?

    a. The PATIENT_HOSP field will be set to NULLS.
    b. The PATIENT rows will be deleted from the PATIENT table.
    c. Nothing will be changed on the PATIENT records.
    d. The delete of the HOSPITAL record will fail.

The correct answer is D - the delete of the HOSPITAL record will fail because ON DELETE RESTRICT has been specified. You can specify the action to take in the foreign key definition by including the ON DELETE clause. If no action is specified, or if RESTRICT is specified in the ON DELETE clause, then the parent record cannot be deleted unless all child records which reference that record are first deleted. If ON DELETE CASCADE is specified, then references in the child table to the parent record being deleted will cause the child records to also be deleted.   If ON DELETE SET NULL is specified, then the foreign key field will be set to NULL for corresponding rows that reference the parent record to be deleted.

13. What is the schema for a declared GLOBAL TEMPORARY table?

    a. SESSION
    b. DB2ADMIN
    c. TEMP1
    d. USERTEMP

The correct answer is A. The schema for a GLOBAL TEMPORARY table is always SESSION. The schema for a GLOBAL TEMPORARY table cannot be DB2ADMIN, TEMP1, or USERTEMP.

14. If you create a temporary table and you wish to replace any existing temporary table that has the same name, what clause would you use?

    a. WITH REPLACE
    b. OVERLAY DATA ROWS
    c. REPLACE EXISTING
    d. None of the above.

The correct answer is A. If you create a temporary table and you wish to replace any existing temporary table that has the same name, use the WITH REPLACE clause. OVERLAY DATA ROWS and REPLACE EXISTING are fictitious clauses that would result in an error.

15. What happens to the rows of a temporary table when the session that created it ends?

    a. The rows are deleted when the session ends.
    b. The rows are preserved in memory until the instance is restarted.
    c. The rows are held in the temp table space.
    d. None of the above.

The correct answer is A. When the session that created a temporary table ends, any rows in the table are deleted, along with the table and table definition.

16. Which is true of temporary tables declared within a SAVEPOINT after a ROLLBACK TO SAVEPOINT command has been issued?

    a. Temporary tables declared within the savepoint are still in the system catalog.
    b. Temporary tables declared within the savepoint are dropped and no longer accessible.
    c. Temporary tables declared within the savepoint are still accessible.
    d. None of the above.

The correct answer is B, temporary tables declared within the savepoint are dropped and no longer accessible after a ROLLBACK TO SAVEPOINT. Issuing a SAVEPOINT enables you to execute several SQL statements as a single executable block. You can then undo changes back out to that savepoint by issuing a ROLLBACK TO SAVEPOINT statement. The DECLARE GLOBAL TEMPORARY TABLE statement defines a temporary table for the current session. The declared temporary table description does not appear in the system catalog.

17. Which of the following clauses DOES NOT allow you to pull data for a particular period from a version enabled table?

    a. FOR BUSINESS_TIME UP UNTIL
    b. FOR BUSINESS_TIME FROM ... TO ...
    c. FOR BUSINESS_TIME BETWEEN... AND...
    d. All of the above enable you to pull data for a particular period.

The correct answer is A. There is no UP UNTIL clause in DB2 temporal data management. The other two clauses may be used to specify the time period on a query against a version enabled table.

18. Assume you have an application that needs to aggregate and summarize data from several tables multiple times per day. One way to improve performance of that application would be to use a:

    a. Materialized query table
    b. View
    c. Temporary table
    d. Range clustered table

    The correct answer is A, a materialized query table (MQT) is a table whose definition is based upon the result of a query, similar to a view. The difference is that the query on which a view is based must generate the resultset each time the view is referenced. In contrast, an MQT stores the query results as table data, and you can work with the data that is in the MQT instead of incurring the overhead of running a query to generate the data each time you run it. An MQT can thereby significantly improve performance for applications that need summarized, aggregated data.

19. Assume you want to track employees in your company over time. Review the following DDL:

    ```
    CREATE TABLE HRSCHEMA.EMPLOYZZ(
    EMP_ID INT NOT NULL,
    EMP_LAST_NAME VARCHAR(30) NOT NULL,
    EMP_FIRST_NAME VARCHAR(20) NOT NULL,
    EMP_SERVICE_YEARS INT
    NOT NULL WITH DEFAULT 0,
    EMP_PROMOTION_DATE DATE,
    BUS_START    DATE  NOT NULL,
    BUS_END      DATE  NOT NULL,

    PERIOD BUSINESS_TIME(BUS_START, BUS_END),

    PRIMARY KEY (EMP_ID, BUSINESS_TIME WITHOUT OVERLAPS));
    ```

    What will happen when you execute this DDL?

a. It will fail because you cannot specify WITHOUT OVERLAPS in the primary key – the WITHOUT OVERLAPS clause belongs in the `BUSINESS_TIME` definition.
   b. It will fail because you must specify SYSTEM_TIME instead of BUSINESS_TIME.
   c. It will fail because the BUS_START has a syntax error.
   d. It will execute successfully.

The correct answer is D. It will execute successfully.

20. Given the previous question, assume there is a table named `EMPLOYEE_HIST` defined just like `EMPLOYEE`. What will happen when you execute the following DDL?

    ```
    ALTER TABLE EMPLOYEE
    ADD VERSIONING
    USE HISTORY TABLE EMPLOYEE_HIST
    ```

    a. The DDL will execute successfully and updates to `EMPLOYEE` will generate records in the `EMPLOYEE_HIST` table.
    b. The DDL will succeed but you must still enable the history table.
    c. The DDL will generate an error – only SYSTEM time enabled tables can use a history table.
    d. The DDL will generate an error – only BUSINESS time enabled tables can use a history table.

The correct answer is C. Only SYSTEM time enabled tables can use a history table.

21. For a system managed Materialized Query Table (MQT) named EMPMQT, how does the data get updated so that it becomes current?

    a. Issuing INSERT, UPDATE and DELETE commands against EMPMQT.
    b. Issuing the statement REFRESH TABLE EMPMQT.
    c. Issuing the statement MATERIALIZE TABLE EMPMQT.
    d. None of the above.

The correct answer is B. The REFRESH TABLE statement refreshes the data in a materialized query table. This is the only way to refresh a system-managed MQT. For example:

```
REFRESH TABLE EMPMQT;
```

For a user defined MQT you can use INSERT, UPDATE, DELETE, TRUNCATE, MERGE or LOAD to make the data current. There is no MATERIALIZE TABLE statement.

22. Which of the following is TRUE about SQLJ applications that need to handle XML data?

    a. You cannot select or update XML data as textual XML data.
    b. For update of data in XML columns, xmlFormat does the appropriate formatting.
    c. You can store an entire XML document into an XML column using a single UPDATE, INSERT or MERGE statement.
    d. External encoding for Java applications cannot use Unicode encoding.

The correct answer is C. You can store an entire XML document into an XML column using a single UPDATE, INSERT or MERGE statement. The other statements are false. You can select or update XML data as textual XML data (or as binary XML data). For update of data in XML columns, xmlFormat has no effect. External encoding for Java applications is always Unicode encoding.

23. Which of the following is NOT true about XML validation using an XML type modifier?

    a. An XML type modifier associates the type with an XML schema.
    b. The XML type modifier can identify a single XML schema only.
    c. An XML type modifier is defined in a CREATE TABLE or ALTER TABLE statement as part of an XML column definition.
    d. You can use an ALTER TABLE statement to remove an XML schema from the column XML type definition.

The correct answer is B. It is not true that you can only specify one schema in the XML type modifier. In fact, the XML type modifier can identify more than one XML schema. For example:

```
CREATE TABLE EMPLOYEE(
ID INT NOT NULL,
CONTENT XML(XMLSCHEMA ID SYSXSR.ID01,
ID SYSXSR.ID02))
```

The other statements are true. An XML type modifier associates the type with an XML schema. An XML type modifier is defined in a CREATE TABLE or ALTER TABLE statement as part of an XML column definition. You can use an ALTER TABLE statement to remove an XML schema from the column XML type definition. An example of removing any XML schema modifiers could be:

```
ALTER TABLE EMPLOYEE
ALTER CONTENT
SET DATA TYPE XML
```

24. An XML index can be created on what column types?

    a. VARCHAR and XML.
    b. CLOB AND XML.
    c. XML only.
    d. Any of the above.

The correct answer is C. An XML index can be created only on an XML type column.

25. Which of the following can be used to validate an XML value according to a schema?

    a. Defining a column as type XML.
    b. Manually running the DSN_XMLVALIDATE.
    c. Both of the above.
    d. Neither of the above.

The correct answer is C. There are two ways to validate an XML value. Defining a column with the XML type modifier ensures that all XML documents stored in an XML column are validated according to a specified XML schema. You can also manually do the validation using the DSN_XMLVALIDATE function. DSN_XMLVALIDATE returns an XML value that is the result of applying XML schema validation to the first argument of the function.

26. To determine whether an XML document has been validated, which function could you use?

    a. XMLXSROBJECTID.
    b. XMLDOCUMENT.
    c. XMLPARSE.
    d. None of the above.

The correct answer is A. The XMLXSROBJECTID function returns the XSR object identifier of the XML schema that was used to validate the specified XML document. If the value returned is zero, then the document was not validated.

The XMLDOCUMENT function returns an XML value with a single document node and its children nodes (if any). The XMLPARSE function parses an argument as an XML document and returns an XML value.

27. Which bind option would you use to enable parallel processing to improve performance of a query?

    a. DEGREE(1)
    b. DEGREE(2)
    c. DEGREE(ANY)
    d. DEGREE(PARALLEL)

The correct answer is C. The DEGREE option determines whether to attempt to run a query using parallel processing to maximize performance. Specifying DEGREE(1) prohibits parallel processing, while DEGREE(ANY) enables parallel processing. The values 2 and PARALLEL are invalid.

28. To improve performance for read-only queries against remote sites, which DBPROTOCOL value should be used when binding applications?

    a. DRDACBF
    b. DRDA
    c. PRIVATE
    d. DRDABCF

The correct answer is A. Binding applications with the new DBPROTOCOL (DRDACBF) option results in package-based continuous block fetch. Package-based continuous block fetch provides a performance advantage for an application that generates large read-only result sets for remote sites.

DRDA protocol is the default and is a standard architecture for accessing distributed databases. PRIVATE is no longer supported as a DBPROTOCOL value in DB2 10 and later. DRDABCF is an invalid value for DBPROTOCOL.

29. Which of the following is a Stage 2 predicate?

    a. COL IS NULL
    b. SUBSTR(COL,1,n) = value
    c. EXISTS(subquery)
    d. COL LIKE pattern

The correct answer is C. EXISTS(subquery) is a stage two predicate. The other choices are stage 1.

30. Which of the following would probably NOT improve query performance?

    a. Use indexable predicates in your queries.
    b. Execute the RUNSTATS utility and rebind application programs.
    c. Use the EXISTS clause instead of COL IN (value list).
    d. All of the above could improve application performance.

The correct answer is C. EXISTS is a stage 2 predicate, whereas COL IN (value list) is stage 1. Stage 2 predicates are always processed after Stage 1, thereby slowing performance. The other choices could all potentially improve performance in an application. All indexable predicates are stage one and refer to table indexes (both of which could improve performance). Executing RUNSTATS and rebinding application programs uses the latest information on the tables and could improve the access path chosen in the DB2 plan.

31. Which of the following trace types could be used to collect information about which users tried to access DB2 objects and were denied due to inadequate authorization?

    a. ACCTG
    b. MONITOR
    c. AUDIT
    d. STATISTICS

The correct answer is C. An audit trace gathers information about DB2 security controls. Class 1 for this trace gathers information about which users tried to access DB2 objects and were denied due to inadequate authorization.

The accounting trace collects processing data that is written when a transaction completes. The monitor trace permits attached monitor programs to access DB2 trace data via calls to the instrumentation facility interface (IFI). A statistics trace provides data about how much the DB2 system and database services are used.

32. Which of the following is NOT a valid value for the SMFACCT subsystem parameter?

    a. YES
    b. NO
    c. $
    d. *

The correct answer is C. $ is not a valid value for SMFACCT. The SMFACCT subsystem parameter indicates whether DB2 will send accounting data to SMF automatically when DB2 is started. The four valid values are:

- YES
- NO
- A list of classes separated by commas
- * (starts all classes)

33. Which of the following EXPLAIN tables includes information about the access path that will be used to return data?

    a. PLAN_TABLE
    b. DSN_QUERY_TABLE
    c. DSN_STATEMENT_TABLE
    d. None of the above.

The correct answer is A. The PLAN_TABLE includes information about access paths that is derived from the explain statements.

The DSN_QUERY_TABLE includes information about a SQL statement both before and after transformation. The DSN_STATEMENT_TABLE contains information about the estimated cost of specified SQL statements.

34. If you find out that your application query is doing a table space scan, what changes could you make to improve the scan efficiency?

    a. Create one or more indexes on the query search columns.
    b. Load the data to a temporary table and query that table instead of the base table.
    c. If the table is partitioned, change it to a non-partitioned table.
    d. All of the above could improve the scan efficiency.

The correct answer is A. You could create one or more indexes on the search columns so that an index scan would occur instead of the tablespace scan. The other choices would not improve scan efficiency. Temporary tables do not allow for indexes and so a full table scan would still occur. It would not make sense to change partitioned tables to non-partitioned if you were trying to improve scan efficiency. Partitioned tables have some advantage over non-partitioned if the table is partitioned by one of the fields being searched on. In that case the search could be automatically limited to only certain

partitions instead of the entire table. Also, partitioned tables enable other performance improving techniques such as parallel processing.

Additional Resources

DB2 11 for z/OS Application Programming and SQL Guide

DB2 11 for z/OS SQL Reference

Index

DB2 Support for XML, 323
EXPLAIN Statement
    Access Types, 339
    Creating Plan Tables, 333
    EXPLAIN BIND Option, 341
    Explain Data with Queries, 335
    EXPLAIN with Data Studio, 342
    Other Explain Tables, 344
IMS
    CBLTDLI, 75
    CHKP Call, 199
    Command Codes, 184, 194
    Committing and Rolling Back Changes, 196
    Database Descriptor (DBD), 70
    Deleting a Segment (GHU/DLET), 113
    IMS calls, 76
    IMS Programming Guidelines, 234
    IMS Status Codes, 78
    Inserting Child Segments, 119
    Loading an IMS Database, 80
    Performing Checkpoint Restart, 214
    Program Status Block (PSB), 74
    Reading a Database Sequentially (GN), 98
    Reading a Segment (GU), 92
    Reading Child Segments Sequentially (GNP), 130
    Retrieve Segments Using Boolean SSAs, 175
    Retrieve Segments Using Searchable Fields, 167
    Updating a Segment (GHU/REPL), 106
    XRST Call, 197
Information Management System (IMS), 67
LARGE OBJECTS (LOB)
    Basic Concepts, 311
    Inline LOBs, 318
    LOB Example, 311
    LOB File Reference Variables, 314
    LOB Locator Variables, 314
STORED PROCEDURES
    Types of Stored Procedures, 242
TEMPORAL TABLES
    Bi-Temporal Example, 304
    Bitemporal Support, 299
    Business Time, 298
    Business Time Example, 299
    System Time, 299
    System time Example, 302
TEMPORARY Tables
    CREATED Temporary Table, 310
    DECLARED Temporary Table, 310
TRIGGERS
    Examples of Triggers, 288
    Timings of Triggers, 288
    Types of Triggers, 287
USER DEFINED FUNCTIONS (UDF)
    External Scalar Function, 276
    External Table Function, 279
    Sourced Function, 286
    SQL Scalar Function, 273
    SQL Table Function, 275
    Types of UDF, 273
VSAM, 15
    Application Programming with VSAM, 27
    Creating and Accessing Alternate Indexes, 49
    Creating VSAM Files, 16
    Entry Sequence Data Set, 16
    File Status Codes, 62
    Key Sequence Data Set, 16
    Linear Data Set, 16
    Loading and Unloading VSAM Files, 18
    Relative Record Data Set, 16
XML Builtin Functions
    XMLEXISTS, 330
    XMLMODIFY, 332
    XMLPARSE, 331
    XMLQUERY, 330
    XMLTABLE, 331
XML OPERATIONS
    DELETE With XML, 325
    INSERT With XML, 324
    SELECT With XML, 324
    UPDATE With XML, 325
XML Related Technologies, 322
XML Structure, 320
XQuery, 322

Sources

IBM (2018) www.ibm.com. Retrieved from z/OS Concepts documentation. https://www.ibm.com/support/knowledgecenter/zosbasics/com.ibm.zos.zconcepts/zconcepts_169.htm

IBM (2018) www.ibm.com. Retrieved from Application Programming for IMS DB. https://www.ibm.com/support/knowledgecenter/en/SSEPH2_12.1.0/com.ibm.ims12.doc.apg/ims_appdb.htm

IBM. (2018). *www.ibm.com*. Retrieved from DB2 11 for z/OS Documentation: https://www.ibm.com/support/knowledgecenter/en/SSEPEK_11.0.0/home/src/tpc/db2z_11_prodhome.html

Other Titles by Robert Wingate

Quick Start Training for IBM z/OS Application Developers, Volume 1

ISBN-13: 978-1986039840
This book will teach you the basic information and skills you need to develop applications on IBM mainframes running z/OS. The instruction, examples and sample programs in this book are a fast track to becoming productive as quickly as possible in JCL, MVS Utilities, COBOL, PLI and DB2. The content is easy to read and digest, well organized and focused on honing real job skills. IBM z/OS Quick Start Training for Application Developers is a key step in the direction of mastering IBM application development so you'll be ready to join a technical team.

Additional titles are on the following pages.

DB2 Exam C2090-313 Preparation Guide

ISBN 13: 978-1548463052

This book will help you pass IBM Exam C2090-313 and become an IBM Certified Application Developer - DB2 11 for z/OS. The instruction, examples and questions/answers in the book offer you a significant advantage by helping you to gauge your readiness for the exam, to better understand the objectives being tested, and to get a broad exposure to the DB2 11 knowledge you'll be tested on.

DB2 Exam C2090-320 Preparation Guide

ISBN 13: 978-1544852096

This book will help you pass IBM Exam C2090-320 and become an IBM Certified Database Associate - DB2 11 Fundamentals for z/OS. The instruction, examples and questions/answers in the book offer you a significant advantage by helping you to gauge your readiness for the exam, to better understand the objectives being tested, and to get a broad exposure to the DB2 11 knowledge you'll be tested on. The book is also a fine introduction to DB2 for z/OS!

DB2 Exam C2090-313 Practice Questions

ISBN 13: 978-1534992467

This book will help you pass IBM Exam C2090-313 and become an IBM Certified Application Developer - DB2 11 for z/OS. The 180 questions and answers in the book (three full practice exams) offer you a significant advantage by helping you to gauge your readiness for the exam, to better understand the objectives being tested, and to get a broad exposure to the DB2 11 knowledge you'll be tested on.

DB2 Exam C2090-615 Practice Questions

ISBN 13: 978-1535028349

This book will help you pass IBM Exam C2090-615 and become an IBM Certified Database Associate (DB2 10.5 for Linux, Unix and Windows). The questions and answers in the book offer you a significant advantage by helping you to gauge your readiness for the exam, to better understand the objectives being tested, and to get a broad exposure to the knowledge you'll be tested on.

DB2 10.1 Exam 610 Practice Questions

ISBN 13: 978-1-300-07991-0

This book will help you pass IBM Exam 610 and become an IBM Certified Database Associate. The questions and answers in the book offer you a significant advantage by helping you to gauge your readiness for the exam, to better understand the objectives being tested, and to get a broad exposure to the knowledge you'll be tested on.

DB2 10.1 Exam 611 Practice Questions

ISBN 13: 978-1-300-08321-4

This book will help you pass IBM Exam 611 and become an IBM Certified Database Administrator. The questions and answers in the book offer you a significant advantage by helping you to gauge your readiness for the exam, better understand the objectives being tested, and get a broad exposure to the knowledge you'll be tested on.

DB2 9 Exam 730 Practice Questions: Second Edition

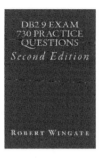

ISBN-13: 978-1463798833

This book will help you pass IBM Exam 730 and become an IBM Certified Database Associate. The questions and answers in the book offer you a significant advantage by helping you to gauge your readiness for the exam, to better understand the objectives being tested, and to get a broad exposure to the knowledge you'll be tested on.

DB2 9 Certification Questions for Exams 730 and 731: Second Edition

ISBN-13: 978-1466219755

This book is targeted for IBM Certified Database Administrator candidates for DB2 9 for Windows, Linux and UNIX. It includes approximately 400 practice questions and answers for IBM Exams 730 and 731 (6 complete practice exams).

About the Author

Robert Wingate is a computer services professional with over 30 years of IBM mainframe programming experience. He holds several IBM certifications, including IBM Certified Application Developer - DB2 11 for z/OS, and IBM Certified Database Administrator for LUW. He lives in Fort Worth, Texas.

End Notes

[i] https://www.ibm.com/support/knowledgecenter/en/SSEPH2_13.1.0/com.ibm.ims13.doc.dag/ims_hisamdb.htm

[ii] https://www.ibm.com/support/knowledgecenter/en/SSEPH2_13.1.0/com.ibm.ims13.doc.msgs/compcodes/ims_dlistatuscodestables.htm#ims_dlistatuscodestables__catdlistatuscodes

[iii] https://www.ibm.com/support/knowledgecenter/en/SSEPH2_13.1.0/com.ibm.ims13.doc.apr/ims_cmdcodref.htm

[iv] https://www.ibm.com/support/knowledgecenter/SSEPH2_12.1.0/com.ibm.ims12.doc.apg/ims_programguidelines.htm

[v] https://www.ibm.com/support/knowledgecenter/en/SSEPEK_11.0.0/apsg/src/tpc/db2z_storedprocedure.html

[vi] http://www.ibm.com/support/knowledgecenter/en/SSEPEK_12.0.0/sqlref/src/tpc/db2z_sql_createtrigger.html

[vii] http://www.ibm.com/support/knowledgecenter/en/SSEPEK_11.0.0/intro/src/tpc/db2z_creationoftemporarytables.html

[viii] https://www.ibm.com/support/knowledgecenter/SSEPEK_11.0.0/intro/src/tpc/db2z_largeobjecttablespaces.html

[ix] https://www.ibm.com/support/knowledgecenter/SSEPEK_11.0.0/intro/src/tpc/db2z_creationoflargeobjects.html

[x] http://www.w3schools.com/xml/xpath_syntax.asp

[xi] http://www.redbooks.ibm.com/technotes/tips0896.pdf.

[xii] http://www.ibm.com/support/knowledgecenter/en/SSEPEK_11.0.0/xml/src/tpc/db2z_xpxqoverview.html

[xiii] http://www.ibm.com/support/knowledgecenter/en/SSEPEK_11.0.0/xml/src/tpc/db2z_xmlbestuseofxqueryorxpath.html

[xiv] https://www.ibm.com/support/knowledgecenter/SSEPEK_11.0.0/xml/src/tpc/db2z_xsrsetup.html

[xv] http://www.redbooks.ibm.com/technotes/tips0896.pdf

[xvi] https://www.ibm.com/support/knowledgecenter/SSEPEK_10.0.0/usrtab/src/tpc/db2z_plantable.html

[xvii] https://www.ibm.com/support/knowledgecenter/en/SSEPEK_11.0.0/usrtab/src/tpc/db2z_explaintables.html

[xviii] https://www.ibm.com/support/knowledgecenter/en/SSEPEK_11.0.0/perf/src/tpc/db2z_summarypredicateprocessing.html

[xix] https://www.ibm.com/support/knowledgecenter/SSEPEK_11.0.0/perf/src/tpc/db2z_tracetypes.html

CREATE VSAM - IDCAMS